OUTDOOR AND ENVIRONMENTAL EDUCATION

DIVERSE PURPOSES AND PRACTICES

OUTDOOR AND ENVIRONMENTAL EDUCATION

DIVERSE PURPOSES AND PRACTICES

EDITED BY KEITH McRAE

Senior Lecturer in Outdoor Education
Canberra College of Advanced Education

First published 1990 by
THE MACMILLAN COMPANY OF AUSTRALIA PTY LTD
107 Moray Street, South Melbourne 3205
6 Clarke Street, Crows Nest 2065

Associated companies and representatives
throughout the world

National Library of Australia
cataloguing in publication data

Outdoor and environmental education.

   ISBN 0 7329 0115 4.
   ISBN 0 7329 0114 6 (pbk.).

   1. Outdoor education. 2. Environmental education. I.
   McRae, Keith, 1941–

371.38

Set in 10/11pt Plantin
by Times Graphics, Singapore
Printed in Hong Kong

Contents

A Rationale for Adventure Education
Planning for Adventure
Case Study: Camp Knox
Conclusion

Notes on Contributors

Editor

Keith McRae is currently completing a PhD in outdoor education. He is a senior Lecturer in Outdoor Education, University of Canberra. He has taught in primary schools and in a teachers' college in Papua New Guinea, and in secondary schools in Australia. He was brought up in a part of Sydney where 'native' trees and plants were regarded as nuisances and when people held the bush in fear. He has since walked extensively in may parts of the world, but feels most at home in the mountains around Canberra, and has become progressively 'greener' as threats to natural environments have increased.

Contributors

Colin Abbot directs a wilderness programme for young people experiencing drug-related problems. Born in Melbourne, he was introduced to bushwalking at eleven, his university years were spent dividing time between study and participation in a wide variety of outdoor pursuits, including walking, canoeing, skiing and climbing. He lived for many years in New Zealand, where he was involved in the early development of the Outdoor Pursuit Centre and was an Outdoor recreation adviser to the NZ Council for Sport and Recreation for ten years. He is keenly interested in the use of the outdoors for youth-at-risk and management training.

Keith Cook taught in primary and secondary schools in Western Australia and Canada. He was Co-ordinator of Outdoor Education in the Western Australian Department of Education for eleven years before moving to the position as Consultant in Vocational and Youth Education in 1988. He is currently president of the Camping and Outdoor Education Association in WA.

Graeme Cooksey as Principal Education Officer for the Tasmanian Education Department, has the opportunity to promote outdoor education which he sees as a most effective means of enhancing the personal skills and attitudes important in today's educational environment. He is working towards giving all Tasmanian students opportunities to participate in integrated outdoor experiences, and aims to have outdoor education included in the formal record of achievement of students.

Oswald Goering developed an interest in the outdoors as a child on a Kansas farm. He was a church camp director, then joined the Outdoor Teacher Education faculty at Northern Illinois University in 1958, becoming chairperson in 1977. He is co-author of three books, numerous articles and a popular film entitled *Just beyond the Chalkboard*. He was chairman of the US Council on Outdoor Education in 1970–71, receiving the Julian W. Smith award in 'recognition of meritorious service and major contributions to outdoor education' from that organisation in 1979, on his retirement. He is currently an Emeritus Professor at NIU and involved in special projects at Bethal College, Kansas.

Annette Greenall Gough has taught science and geography in high schools in Victoria. She was Environmental Education co-ordinator in the Australian Curriculum Development Centre from 1974–81. She has been a consultant to the United Nations Environment Programme and represented Australia at several international conferences on environmental education, including the 1987 UNESCO-UNEP congress in Moscow. She has been Director of Environmental Education in the Australian Department of Arts, Sports, the Environment, Tourism and Territories since 1983. She is currently on leave to continue doctoral studies in environmental education. A past president of the Australian Association for Environmental Education, she currently co-edits the association newsletter, *ozEEnews*.

Bruce Hayllar is Senior Lecturer in the Department of Leisure Studies at the University of Technology, Sydney. He was introduced to teaching in the outdoors when he began a bushcraft club at his first school. Attracted by the 'glamour' of outdoor education, he got a job at the Broken Bay National Fitness (now Sport and Recreation) Centre, the 'home' of outdoor education in New South Wales. His time there confirmed his views that teaching and learning in and through outdoor experiences was more enjoyable and meaningful than the classroom variety. Except for intermittent periods of study, he has been involved in outdoor education ever since. Along with his teaching commitments, he has worked in programmes for young offenders and youth-at-risk, and has conducted adventure camps for both able-bodied and disabled people.

Rob Hogan is Lecturer in Outdoor Education at the Salisbury Campus of the South Australian College of Advanced Education. A background in residential camping with the YMCA, and in expeditioning with the Duke of Edinburgh's Award Scheme, complemented his studies in physical education and led to a career in outdoor education. He taught PE and outdoor recreation activities in a large Adelaide high school before being appointed as Camping Advisor with the Education Department in 1975. He became Co-ordinator of the Outdoor Education Unit in 1980 and moved to his present position in 1985. He teaches courses in outdoor teaching methods, outdoor skills and outdoor leadership. Personal outdoor interests include bushwalking, Nordic skiing and sailing.

Chuck Hopkins was the first principal of Boyne River Natural Science School and the Toronto Urban Studies Centre. He is the national chairman of the Canada/Man and the Biosphere Working Group on Environmental Information and Teaching, and is currently a School Superintendent for the Toronto Board of Education

Cliff Knapp is Full Professor of Education and past chairperson and Director of Outdoor Teacher Education Faculty at the Lorado Taft Field Campus of Northern Illinois University. Previously a science teacher, camp counsellor and Director of Outdoor Education in a New Jersey school district, and Assistant Co-ordinator of Outdoor Education at Southern Illinois University, he is the author or co-author of seven books or monographs and over 100 articles in the fields of outdoor/environmental/science education. He has taught many different courses in outdoor education, but has a particular interest in environmental ethics and human relations skills.

Liz Liebing is currently a teacher at the Arbury Park Outdoor School in South Australia. She earlier taught as a junior primary school teacher at Port Pirie, where she became the school's Outdoor Education Co-ordinator. She worked as an Outdoor Education Consultant in the State Outdoor Education Unit for seven years from 1979, and before that specialised in outdoor education in her Advanced Diploma studies. An adviser with the Bush and Mountain Walking Leadership Training Board, Elizabeth enjoys bushwalking, sailing and skiing.

Chris Loynes is an active mountaineer, sailor and kayaker, with an interest in youth expeditions and marine wildlife. He started work as a geology teacher and co-ordinated and directed outdoor education programmes which included outdoor pursuit activities, field studies and residential experiences. He developed and managed a residential and Outreach Development Training Programme for young people and their leaders at the Brathay Hall Trust. He is currently working as a self-employed consultant on staff and programme development with several outdoor and experiential education initiatives in the UK and overseas. He publishes and edits the journal *Adventure Education and Outdoor Leadership*, which has an international circulation.

Norm McIntyre read geology at university and indulged passions for bushwalking and geology by travelling and working in many parts of the world. He is currently a lecturer at the Brisbane College of Advanced Education where he co-ordinates the Graduate Diploma in Outdoor Education he helped establish in 1976. He teaches courses in nature interpretation, evaluation, and the leadership and organisation of expeditions. He has conducted numerous evaluation studies and is currently examining the relationship between previous outdoor experiences and the responses of participants to extended field trips in remote areas.

Lesley Pearse taught PE in a number of independent schools before joining the Western Australian Education Department to develop an outdoor education programme. He initiated the Expedition Skills Course of Western Australia for teachers, tertiary students and members of the community and was appointed to the Expedition Leadership Advisory Board in 1986. He has made a major contribution to the development of outdoor education in Western Australia, and was recently made a Life Member of the Outdoor Education Association of Western Australia and a Fellow of the Australian Council of Health, Physical Education and Recreation.

Vanessa Reynolds came to Australia from England as a child and fell in love with the 'great Australian outdoors'. She taught at a boys' technical school in Geelong for nine years and fought successfully to get outdoor education accepted into the curriculum. She worked in the outdoor education section of the Victorian Curriculum Branch for a year before moving to a regional office as a consultant for outdoor education programmes and other curriculum areas. She has been secretary of the Victorian Outdoor Education Association for three years and is actively involved in a number of leadership training courses. She still finds time for bushwalking, ski-touring, cycle-touring, canoeing, snorkelling and hockey.

Ian Street, an Australian, is past Director of the New Zealand Outdoor Pursuits Centre, who currently teaches in a high school in Auckland.

Joan Thompson has been involved in outdoor education as a classroom teacher and as a teacher at the Sheldon Centre for Outdoor Education, in the countryside near Toronto, Canada, for over fifteen years. She is presently Outdoor Education Consultant for the East York Board of Education in Toronto.

Joan Webb taught secondary school science for twenty-two years before moving into teacher education. An early interest in environmental education became focused on education in field studies centres. She has published two books in this area. She has also regularly conducted courses in Thailand. Apart from lecturing, she is Director of the Ku-ring-gai Community Environmental Centre, an out-reach to the adult community aimed at increasing awareness of, and interest in, the environment. She is working on a PhD on the work of an early New South Wales botanical collector. She has 'trekked' in Africa, Nepal, the Falkland Islands and Australia.

Malcolm Wells is Assistant Director with the Tasmania Department of Sport and Recreation, responsible for outdoor programmes including leadership training programmes for bushwalkers, teachers and others, a variety of water safety and aquatic programmes, and outdoor challenge programmes for different target groups, including disadvantaged youth. He is a keen scuba diver and nature photographer and is the author of several publications on these subjects.

Acknowledgements

Photographs: Chapter 2, Northern Illinois University; Chapter 4, Bushwalking, Colin Abbott, Rafting, Leon Kibka; Chapter 11, Touching, E. Liebing; Chapter 14, Canoeing, Kevin McGennan, Bushwalking, Paul Thomas; Chapter 15, New Zealand Cycling and Tramping, Colin Abbott.

Preface

Australia is a big country with a small population. In spite of the popularity of images such as 'the outback' and 'the bush', it remains highly urbanised. Most Australians live, work and spend their free time in the constructed environments of cities and towns. Most have little knowledge about, or even contact with, natural environments. Indeed, there has always been a degree of unfamiliarity with, contempt for, and hostility towards, the 'outdoors', notwithstanding the myths (Crocodile Dundee and the sun-bronzed Anzac, for example) and the occasional outdoor picnic or barbecue. We have gained vicarious satisfaction from the exploits of such people as Aborigines, explorers, drovers and others who were prepared to live, or work in an environment regarded by most people as uninviting, unattractive, threatening and of little value except for economic exploitation. We remain closeted in our homes and schools, offices and factories, theatres and sporting grounds, protected from and ignorant of, 'the great outdoors'.

In recent years, there have been some changes to this scenario. Increasing numbers of Australians have come to appreciate the beauty and value of the Australian landscape, the bush and the birds and animals which live on this vast island continent. White Australians used to prefer planting 'exotic' trees and shrubs in suburban gardens because they were neat and tidy and reminded them of a European 'home'. They are now more inclined to seek out eucalypts, acacias, grevilleas, leptospermum and other native flora and to be thrilled at the return of birds. Australians are beginning to feel at home in this 'wide brown land' and to be proud of it. They are becoming more interested in using outdoor settings for leisure purposes, including adventurous ones. They are even learning to feel at ease in the bush. A growing environmental movement and the questioning of unrestrained development provides an indication that Australians are beginning to realise that there is a need to protect our remaining natural environments for human reasons, rather than with the amassing of wealth. Some Australians even believe that trees, plants, animals, birds, snakes and other natural entities have a right to exist as part of the Australian community.

This general picture of the attitudes of Australians to their environment has a strong parallel with the attitudes and behaviour of teachers. The process of education has often been undertaken principally within the safe walls of classrooms. There has been little recognition that worthwhile learning experiences are possible in the bush or even in the more immediate outdoor environment. Teachers have neglected opportunities offered by outdoor settings to enhance learning in general, to promote leisure knowledge and skills, to foster environmental concepts and values or to enhance the personal and social development of their students. But lost opportunities can be reclaimed.

This book has been written for teachers and others who use or want to use the outdoors for educational purposes — in Australia or in other countries. The purposes and practices of outdoor education are diverse and these are explored throughout the book. The major forms of this kind of education are explored in the first four chapters. The fifth chapter presents a model for outdoor education which integrates these forms. Chapters 7 to 10 discuss different approaches to, and settings for, outdoor education. Ways of fostering an environmental ethic are outlined in Chapter 11 and outdoor education programmes for some specific populations are described in Chapter 12. Chapter 13 spells out the reasons for evaluating outdoor education programmes and describes methods which could be used by the busy outdoor educator. In the final two chapters, reports from the Australian states and from other countries demonstrate the diversity of outdoor education and identify the major common elements.

Outdoor education programmes can have a single focus. They can be directed towards enhancing teaching and learning in any curriculum area. They can be designed to foster leisure knowledge, skills and attitudes. They can aim to foster environmental concepts and a commitment to environmental protection. The major emphasis of other kinds of programme can be to enhance the personal and social development of participants through adventurous activities. Others still will attempt to integrate some or all of these broad aims into a cohesive whole.

There is a place for diversity in outdoor education. There was never any intention in preparing this book to present a manual, a handbook, a step-by-step guide on 'how to do outdoor education'. Teachers and outdoor educators will find many ideas in this book, but they will have to make decisions, select and plan. Encouragement is given to developing programmes which are appropriate to students, teachers and the local community. The book should provide assistance in choosing objectives which are relevant and in designing programmes and learning experiences which will help achieve selected intentions. It is hoped it will also provide inspiration and ideas for those who want to develop a broader or integrated programme in outdoor education.

But the book is really only a beginning: it is seen as being far from comprehensive or complete. It is designed for all those who are currently involved, or are likely to be involved, in planning, implementing and evaluating outdoor education programmes. These present or future outdoor educators are encouraged to go beyond the confines of this book for additional material. Other books relating to the development of outdoor skills and of environmental and leisure concepts and values are freely available and should also be used.

There is no other Australian book which attempts what this one does. There is a need for material which is home-grown. It is hoped that the ideas given here will help in the growth of outdoor education in Australia, in making programmes more effective. Maybe, the book will also inspire other Australian outdoor educators to publish further material. Although much of the content is Australian-based and Australian-biased, the book is not designed for Australians alone. The purposes and practices of outdoor education are common to many countries, as the contributions from the United States, Canada, Britain, Germany and New Zealand demonstrate. The sharing of ideas with outdoor educators in other countries is an important purpose of the book.

The Australian and overseas contributors to this book are all experienced, practising outdoor educators. They have been tolerant of an editor who was inclined to think that the only priority in their busy lives should be to complete their writing for the book. Although the editorial pen has been wielded with some severity on occasion, the general intention has been to allow contributors to write about outdoor education in their own styles and from their own perspectives. The contributions demonstrate the diversity of outdoor educators. They also demonstrate that such educators have many common bonds, shared purposes and practices. Above all, they all share an interest in helping their students improve the quality of their lives and of the environment in which they live.

Keith McRae 1989

1
Introduction to the Purposes and Practices of Outdoor Education

Keith McRae

The Movement of Education Indoors

In a sense, outdoor education has been present and has evolved in all societies throughout history: education from the earliest times has involved some learning in the outdoors. Some human groups even today have no formal education system or specially-designed schools or classrooms. Education is a process involving the total environment. Socialising young people into the culture of a group in order that they may have the knowledge, patterns of behaviour and the specific skills, attitudes and values which are considered to be necessary for the maintenance of a particular cultural entity is part of all human societies. Until comparatively recently, the socialisation process involved the outdoors because much essential human activity took place there.

The Ancient Egyptians were concerned to ensure that the education of their aristocratic young was broadly-based in terms of both goals and settings. Greek teachers supplemented their instruction by using direct and first-hand experiences which were not restricted to indoors. As Cliff Knapp describes, later in this book, early European thinkers argued for the use of observation of phenomena in natural settings and for the development of inquiry approaches to learning.

The widespread adoption of formalised schools as the medium for socialising large numbers of young people has been a recent historical development. During the past two centuries, increasing numbers of people previously available to 'educate' children became involved in working for employers in work places outside their homes. As work became increasingly specialised, adults no longer had the time, let alone the physical or emotional energy which were required to fully prepare children for an increasingly complex world. As schools were built, and teachers were employed, education moved indoors. Much of the teaching and learning that has recently taken place in Western industrialised countries has been centred on classrooms.

The Diversity of Outdoor Education: Some Selected Practices

In Australia and elsewhere, teachers have used outdoor settings for many reasons. Programmes and practices to which the label 'outdoor education' have been applied include:

—the use of a school site to enhance the learning of mathematical concepts
—a field trip to a farm to introduce city children to farm animals
—an excursion to an historical town
—a day visit by a class to an environmental field study centre
—a three-day programme at a residential centre in which the students undertake a variety of activities designed to enhance learning in a number of curriculum areas
—a four-day camp in a bush setting as part of a Social Studies unit with the theme of 'Life on the Goldfields'
—a weekend bushwalking trip as an extra-curricular activity;
—a term programme of nature study involving observation sessions in appropriate outdoor settings
—a term programme of outdoor pursuits such as skiing, rock-climbing and canoeing
—a semester programme of outdoor pursuits and environmental studies

Enjoying

Communicating

Checking

Different Approaches to Outdoor Education

These few examples make it is obvious that a number of different approaches to outdoor education are taken in Australia. It is seen by many teachers as the use of the outdoors to enhance teaching and learning in all curriculum areas. There have always been some imaginative teachers who have supplemented classroom learning with field trips to a variety of outdoor settings including botanical gardens, forests, farms, vacant blocks, city footpaths, zoos, parks, nature and wildlife reserves, quarries, mountains, lakes, rivers, ponds, snowfields, shopping centres and factories. Over recent years, more and more teachers have become aware that a significant effect of the changes that have occurred in Australian society is that many people have become passive participants, spectators, recipients of second-hand knowledge, attitudes and values, increasingly removed from real first-hand experiences. Many teachers are realising that inclusion in the curriculum of such experiences as a history excursion, a geology field trip, a ramble in the bush to observe natural phenomena or a visit to the school grounds by the art class for a drawing lesson can all have educational advantages. However, the opportunities to enhance learning through the use of appropriate outdoor settings have been neglected by many other teachers.

The assumption that learning can be more effective if first-hand experiences are included is particularly relevant to those areas of the curriculum which deal with environmental concepts and issues. Outdoor education, as perceived by some in Australia, is concerned with the experiences involved in teaching and learning about the natural environment and the need to protect it and about the constructed environment and the need to improve it. Although there is no evidence that the laudable aims of environmental education have achieved any marked penetration of school curricula, three main practices for implementing environmental education exist:

(1) The most common approach is to teach environmental concepts wherever they may be appropriate in existing subjects such as Science, Geography, Social Studies or Social Science. The use of the outdoors for field trips, when such settings are used, is seen simply as being the implementation of an appropriate teaching-learning experience. The term 'outdoor education' is rarely used to describe this process of teaching outdoors.

(2) Becoming more common is the introduction of programmes under the heading environmental education which are designed to cover, in a cohesive way, concepts and issues which were previously taught in separate subjects. Again, the term 'outdoor education' is rarely used to describe the subject, the process of going outdoors or the teaching methods which are employed outdoors.

(3) Much less common is the practice of labelling both the content involved in teaching about the natural and constructed environment and the process of teaching and learning in the outdoors as outdoor education. While this is not the approach adopted by the majority of teachers and other educators, it does have support from those who

argue that it demonstrates clearly that it is concerned with the study of the outdoors and that it emphasises its use as a learning laboratory.

Another approach to outdoor education involves the use of outdoor settings for satisfying leisure pursuits. Some programmes have concentrated on challenging and physically-demanding outdoor pursuits such as bushwalking, canoeing, rock-climbing, abseiling and cross-country skiing. Other programmes include physical activities which involve less risk or injury, such as horse-riding, sailing and cycling. Still others have included less physical outdoor activities such as photography, bird-watching, plant identification and the collection and study of fossils, butterflies or geological specimens. All the activities take place in the outdoors and have the potential to become life-long leisure activities which provide satisfaction and a degree of fulfilment.

Another important approach to outdoor education is the use of day and residential outdoor education and field centres run by government departments in the various states, private organisations or by individual schools. A typical residential centre is the Birrigai Outdoor School near Canberra in the Australian Capital Territory. This centre is used by school groups during the week and by community groups during weekends and in vacation periods. Established in 1979, the centre staff offer schools a range of short-term experiences, but teachers are also encouraged to develop their own outdoor education programmes to be implemented in the Birrigai setting. Birrigai staff give assistance with planning and teachers are encouraged to integrate the Birrigai experience into on-going educational programmes.

Common Assumptions about Outdoor Education

There is great diversity of purpose, content and approach in outdoor education in Australia. Without discounting the differences, it is possible to identify assumptions which are common to many outdoor education programmes. In 1986, a survey of outdoor education practices and programmes in ACT schools was undertaken and a number of generalisations emerged from this which illustrate the broad scope of the field. Outdoor education proponents consider that:

—first-hand experiences in the outdoors can enhance learning in all areas of the curriculum
—the use of outdoor settings for educational purposes is necessary in order to compensate for the limited opportunities young people have for direct learning experiences and the tendency of teachers to restrict teaching and learning to classrooms
—the development of skills, attitudes and values is at least as important as the acquisition of knowledge
—it has become increasingly necessary to develop understanding of natural environments and a commitment to protecting natural com-

munities and entities
—there is a need to develop awareness about the total human environment through programmes designed to foster positive attitudes to
environmental improvement
—there is a need for schools to place increased emphasis on educating
students for life-long leisure
—individual and social benefits can be achieved as a result of participation in satisfying leisure activities in the outdoors
—students should be introduced to outdoor leisure activities which range
from those which are relaxed and contemplative to those which are
vigorous and challenging
—participation in outdoor education experiences can help in the
personal development of students, i.e., in increasing constructs such as
self-reliance, confidence and self-esteem
—outdoor education experiences can help in the process of socialising
young people and in fostering social interaction

Defining Outdoor Education

Many writers have attempted to develop a definition of outdoor education
which would encompass all its purposes, practices and assumptions.
Knapp, in Chapter 2 of this book, defines outdoor education as 'the use of
resources outside the formal school classroom to meet educational goals
and objectives'. Similar general definitions abound in the literature
(Donaldson and Donaldson 1958: 17, Hammerman, Hammerman and
Hammerman 1985: 5, Priest 1985–86: 19), but they give little indication of
the objectives, content or learning experiences involved in it.

Ford (1981: 2–7) reviewed definitions of outdoor education and
concluded that it involves the use of outdoor settings to enhance teaching
and learning in 'existing curricula', to develop the knowledge, skills and
attitudes required for 'the wise use' of 'leisure pursuits', or to develop
understanding about 'the outdoors'.

Hammerman *et al.* (1985: 2–5) define outdoor education as any
educational experience which takes place in the outdoors and then
proceed to identify different emphases which are found in various
practices. They describe outdoor education as an approach to helping
students to learn concepts 'by means of first-hand observation and
experience outside the classroom'; or to 'develop greater insight and
understanding of ecological relationships and appreciation of humankind's responsibility for the quality of the environment'; or to use their
leisure wisely through participation in 'outdoor recreational pursuits'.

Knapp (1981: 14–15) accepts that different educators emphasise 'certain
objectives over others, even in cases where there is an attempt to provide a
balanced curriculum'. In this book, he notes that some outdoor education
programmes have been designed to enhance the teaching and learning of
'traditional academic subjects', while others emphasise the 'development
of environmental and ecological awareness'. Other programmes, according to Knapp, involve the use of outdoor settings to foster 'outdoor living
skills' such as backpacking, canoeing and mountain-climbing.

Identification of Outdoor Education Forms

Three broad categories or forms of outdoor education can be identified from the practices and definitions which have been outlined.

Outdoor education as *outdoor teaching and learning* denotes any teaching and learning of traditional subjects which takes place in the outdoors, and may include the use of a school site to enhance the learning of mathematical concepts, a geology field trip or an overnight history excursion.

Outdoor education as *outdoor environmental education* involves teaching and learning about natural environments and the need to protect them and about constructed environments and the need to improve them. Primary school programmes in nature study, secondary school programmes in environmental or conservation education and units of work in a variety of subjects areas such as social science, science and geography fall into this category if they are intended to foster environmental knowledge, attitudes and values.

Outdoor education as *outdoor leisure education* incorporates any teaching and learning which focuses on outdoors pursuits which could be under-taken during leisure. This form is exemplified by a day trip to the snow-fields to practise cross-country skiing skills, a weekend bushwalking trip as an extra-curricular activity, or a semester programme of outdoor pursuits such as rock-climbing, abseiling and canoeing.

There is no universal acceptance of these forms, and there is much overlapping of practices. For example, an outdoor education programme which places emphasis on the development of leisure knowledge, skills and attitudes could also include activities designed to foster environmental awareness. A teacher may take students on a day-trip to an appropriate out-door setting to sketch a variety of landscape features or to observe colour tones in an Art class or to listen to and reproduce natural sounds in Music. In the process, the students may learn camping skills and become aware of the need to protect natural environments. A third teacher could imple-ment a four-day camping experience in a bush setting as part of a social studies unit with the theme of 'Life on the Goldfields'. The programme could be designed to develop outdoor leisure skills, to enhance learning in a variety of curriculum areas including social studies and to promote an awareness of the impact of human activity on natural environments.

Outdoor education practices, it can be seen, are essentially idiosyncratic. The characteristics of a particular programme will depend on factors such as the background, interests and values of the teachers and other curriculum decision-makers. A particular programme might fit neatly into one of the identified forms of outdoor education or it might be impossible to categorise. The three identified forms of outdoor education do, however, represent practices which are different in terms of the specific objectives being sought and are perceived as being different by many teachers and outdoor educators. The three forms also correspond to the different emphases seen as applying in outdoor education programmes by writers who have grappled with the problem of definition.

Outdoor Education as Outdoor Teaching and Learning

This form involves any educational experience which takes place in the outdoors with the intention of enhancing teaching and learning in any area of the curriculum, at any level. The guiding principle is that of L. B. Sharp (1947: ii) who argued that any part of the curriculum 'which can best be learned in the out-of-doors through direct experience, dealing with native materials and life situations, should there be learned'.

Other writers have followed the direction given by Sharp. Mand (1967: 27–28) argued that outdoor education involved all areas of the curriculum. Smith (1970: 1) insisted that it was 'not a separate discipline with prescribed objectives like science and mathematics'. Garrison (1966: 16) and Nolan (1967: 17) reinforced Sharp's view that outdoor education was intended to complement rather than replace classroom learning. Fitzpatrick (1968: 8) wrote that by 'extending the learning environment beyond the classroom, theoretical knowledge is enriched through first-hand experiences with people, places and things'.

This form of outdoor education is seen as placing emphasis on the learning of concepts (Hammerman, Hammerman and Hammerman 1985: 10); the clarification of attitudes and values (Thompson 1955: 13–15); the active participation of students in the whole learning process (Sharp 1947: ii); the use of all senses by students to assist their learning (Lewis 1975: 9); students learning to work co-operatively (Donaldson 1945: 65–66); both students and teachers gaining some benefit from mutual learning experiences (Masters 1951: 15); and the identification and clarification of 'real-life problems' (Smith 1970: 2).

Why Teach in the Outdoors?

Apart from these emphases, Australian teachers have found that outdoor experiences (a) provide a 'break in routine', (b) are often more enjoyable than classroom experiences, and (c) can help develop 'closer and more meaningful relationships' between the students, and between students and teachers.

There has been a considerable amount of research, principally in the United States, into the effectiveness of learning experiences undertaken in the outdoors. For example, Brady (1972) shows that field trips are more effective than the use of audio-visual aids in the teaching of environmental concepts and awareness. Hoeksma (1964) concludes that outdoor teaching methods help develop arithmetic reasoning and computation skills. Acuff (1976) finds that outdoor education experiences help reduce anxiety levels in students from different cultures. A complete review of research design, methods and findings is not feasible here, but generally it has been shown that outdoor education can be effective in:

—improving the learning of concepts in virtually all subject areas
—fostering higher-order learning skills such as the ability to apply knowledge, to analyse real-life situations, to develop solutions to

problems, and to make decisions
—helping students to clarify attitudes and values
—improving understanding and relationships between students and between teachers and students
—fostering such personal and social traits as self-esteem, co-operation and leadership
—developing positive attitudes to learning generally

The Status of Outdoor Teaching and Learning in Australia

In spite of the weight of evidence which supports the use of the outdoors as a teaching-learning laboratory, many teachers decline to take up the opportunities available to them. School sites remain underdeveloped. Field trips and excursions to such outdoor settings as the nearby city park, the shopping centre, the factory, the old people's home, the botanical gardens, the pond, the river (even a polluted river offers opportunities for learning) remain underused. A number of factors seem to be involved in this situation. In the period 1981–85, case studies were undertaken in twenty-five ACT schools to investigate the nature, scope and status of outdoor, leisure and environmental education. In interviews, teachers indicated that they avoided outdoor experiences because of factors such as increasing costs, logistical difficulties, the time and effort required to arrange trips, questions of liability and perceived difficulties in controlling the behaviour of students outside the four walls of classrooms. The interviews also revealed that the major reason why teachers do not use the outdoors is that, in the courses undertaken to prepare them to become teachers, they were *not* helped to:

—identify the community resources available for educational use
—explore ways of enhancing the teaching of the different curriculum areas by using outdoor settings
—gain skills in planning outdoor experiences
—become familiar with a range of outdoor education curriculum materials and ways of implementing these, or
—gain insights into methods of developing school sites for educational purposes

Although many teachers do take students on field trips, excursions and camps, there is much neglect of opportunities:

—for using the resources of the local and wider community
—to demonstrate in a practical way the opportunities and benefits of learning any subject away from classrooms
—to improve understanding of the abilities, interests, needs and problems of the students; and
—to allow students to get to know staff members better as people, warts and all

While there is no guarantee that improved communication, understanding and relationships will be the result of trips away, there is evidence that there is the potential for this to happen. At least participation in such experiences can help teachers know their students better as individuals; allows them to be able to use more appropriate teaching-learning strategies, and to assess more accurately the extent to which students are learning, as well as being more aware of factors which inhibit learning; and to be in a better position to implement action designed to maximise learning. Participation in outdoor experiences is not, of course, the only approach which can be used to develop understanding of students as individuals, but it can help. It is certainly claimed here that learning could be more effective if teachers organised field trips, excursions or other outdoor education experience as an integral part of the learning activities they plan.

The importance and appropriateness of outdoor education experiences can obviously be more readily demonstrated in some curriculum areas than in others. Teaching programmes in areas such as history, social science, geography, science and environmental education should include outdoor experiences as essential components, but learning in all other curriculum areas, including English, language, drama, physical education, music, art and mathematics can be enhanced by trips which involve visits to relevant places, institutions and people in towns and in the countryside. The benefits may lie more in improved communication, understanding and rapport than in improved knowledge and skills, although there is also evidence that improvements can be made in the latter as well.

The settings for, and length of, outdoor education experiences can vary from a vigorous bushwalk spread over several days and involving camping in tents, to a gentle one-hour stroll around a neighbourhood park or shopping centre. It can be argued that the longer the experience and the more removed the setting is from the usual environments of the participants, the greater the potential for learning and for the development of self and group awareness. But not all teachers are prepared to endure physical hardship or discomfort. Not everyone would want to sit around a camp-fire on a cold, frosty night or to sleep in a tent or to go without a warm shower or a flushing toilet. For those who are prepared to undertake overnight trips, cheap but comfortable accommodation is available at resident outdoor education centres, field study or conference centres and at Youth Hostels.

While it is, perhaps, unfortunate that some teachers are not prepared, under any circumstances, to spend a night or more away with a group of students, there are still real benefits to be achieved from trips and visits which do not involve overnight stays. Day-trips to places reasonably close to campuses and homes can be worthwhile and enjoyable experiences.

It is, of course, recognised that outdoor education experiences which involve physically demanding, adventurous and potentially dangerous outdoor pursuits such as bushwalking in wilderness areas, canoeing or cross-country skiing should remain the province of educators who have the necessary knowledge and skills to lead such activities safely. Indeed, teachers at all levels who do not have the required skills are urged to refrain from activities in natural environments which might involve any significant risk of injury to their students. However, while keeping in mind the recommendation to avoid undue risk, it is clear that all teachers can, and should, be outdoor educators. It is imperative that teacher educators ensure that student teachers are given experience in using settings outside classrooms and associated discovery/inquiry approaches to learning. It is also important that education authorities ensure that teachers are made aware, through in-service courses, of the potential benefits to be achieved from learning experiences out-of-doors, and that they have the skills necessary to implement such experiences.

Outdoor Education as Outdoor Environmental Education

This form of outdoor education is seen by some writers and practitioners as involving teaching and learning about natural environments and the need to protect them, and about altered or constructed environments and the need to improve them. The assumption that teaching and learning can be more effective if first-hand experiences are included is particularly relevant to those areas of the curriculum which deal with environmental concepts, issues and values.

Kirk (1968: 3) saw outdoor education as a 'method which utilises the out-of-doors to cultivate a reverence of life through an ecological exploration of the interdependence of all living things, one on the other, and to form a land ethic illustrating man's temporary stewardship for the land'. Garrison (1966: 4) and Heffernan (1967: 17) adopted similar stances, as did Link (1981: 3), who wrote that outdoor education's challenge was 'to provide inspiration, to encourage observation, to develop ethical values, and to gain a perspective on the human role in the mechanism called Earth'.

Although the specific objectives of this form of outdoor education vary from one programme to another, the competencies required by high school teachers of science, social studies and agriculture and by early childhood and primary teachers in Wisconsin in the United States, provide an indication of the objectives of this form of outdoor education and of the importance placed on outdoor teaching. Swan (1984: 1) reported that Wisconsin student teachers were required to 'have adequate instruction in the conservation of natural resources'. The seven competencies required by the Environmental Education Rule of 1983 were:

(1) Knowledge of the wide variety of natural resources and methods of conserving these . . . resources
(2) Knowledge of interactions between living and non-living elements of the natural environment
(3) Knowledge of the concept of energy and its transformations in physical and biological systems
(4) Knowledge of local, national and global interactions among people and the natural and built environments
(5) Ability to use affective education methods to examine attitudes and values inherent in environmental problems
(6) Ability to incorporate the study of environmental problems in whatever subjects or grade level programmes (the teacher) is permitted to teach through the use of the following methodologies:

(a) outdoor teaching strategies; (b) simulation; (c) case studies; (d) community resource use; (e) environmental issue investigation, evaluation and action planning
(7) Knowledge of ways in which citizens can actively participate in the resolution of environmental problems.

The high status given to environmental objectives by Wisconsin authorities has never been matched in Australia, although programmes which aimed to teach students about nature have long been included in Australian school curricula. Prior to the 1970s, however, the study of nature was not a significant part of secondary school curricula in Australia. Concepts from biology, botany and geology were included in junior high school science courses, but objectives relating to ecological and environmental concepts, issues and values were neglected.

Why Teach about the Environment?

According to Greenall (1980a: 64), Link noted that the development of an awareness of the inter-relationships between human beings and their environment, concern for the quality of life, and commitment to the principles of environmental conservation, did not suddenly emerge in the late 1960s. Greenall (1980a: 64) contends that 'the threat of environmental degradation and global repercussions' was brought to the public's attention in the 1970s. This awareness was developed as a result of the attention given by the media and by publications such as Rachel Carson's *Silent Spring* (1963) and Paul Ehrlich's works on the dangers inherent in uncontrolled population growth, the depletion of finite resources and environmental pollution and degradation; and by calamities such as the sinking of oil-tankers, and potential disasters such as the near melt-down of the Three Mile Island nuclear plant. Australian examples of ecological concerns and problems relating to human settlements were also brought to the attention of the public: the smog in Sydney ranked among the world's worst; saltation in the Murray irrigation area was beginning to ruin agricultural land; our flora and fauna were threatened by human activity; much of Australia was threatened by erosion and desertification; and many of our historical buildings were threatened by new developments.

The development of environmental education curriculum guidelines in the late 1970s was an attempt to promote this awareness. Following the establishment of the Curriculum Development Centres Environmental Education Committee in 1975, Australian groups participated in the UNESCO Seminar on Education and the Human Environment in May 1975, the UNESCO-UNEP International Environmental Education Programme workshop held at Belgrade, Yugoslavia in October 1975, and the UNESCO-UNEP Intergovernmental Conference on Environmental Education held in Tbilisi, USSR, in October 1977. Greenall (1980a: 83) notes that an attempt was made at the Tbilisi conference to establish guidelines for the implementation of environment education which, it was hoped, would be practical and written in language that teachers in schools could understand.

The aims of environmental education, as finally published in the

Curriculum Development Centre's document *Environmental Education for Schools* (Greenall: 1980b), were:

(a) to help students acquire an awareness of and sensitivity to the total environment
(b) to help students develop a basic understanding of the total environment and the inter-relationships of man and the environment
(c) to help students develop the skills necessary for investigating the total environment and for identifying and solving environmental problems
(d) to help students acquire social values and strong feelings of concern for the environment
(e) to help students acquire the motivation for actively participating in environmental improvement and protection
(f) to help students identify alternative approaches and make informed decisions about the environment based on ecological, political, economic, social and aesthetic factors
(g) to provide students with the opportunities to be actively involved at all levels in working towards the resolution of environmental problems

The Status of Outdoor Environmental Education in Australia

As laudable as these aims might have been, case studies undertaken in Canberra schools suggest that they have made little marked impact on educational practice, for a number of reasons. First, they tend to be lacking in specificity and, therefore, give inadequate direction to teachers. Second, they are perceived by many teachers as being unrealistic. Third, inadequate pre-service and in-service education has been provided for student teachers and teachers. Fourth, inadequate teaching-learning materials have been available. Fifth, the expectation that all teachers would integrate the aims of environmental education into their teaching programmes was misguided and unrealistic. Sixth, and perhaps most important, the major responsibility for environmental education was seen as falling to secondary schools. Informants thought that primary schools should also have been involved in the process.

Proponents of environmental education have argued that activities designed to achieve the aims should be integrated into all areas of the curriculum. The Canberra case studies found that many teachers were confused about the nature of environmental education and of approaches which could be used. Many teachers consequently neglected opportunities for introducing environmental education activities. On the other hand, there was substantial interest among teachers, parents and students about the notion of education about the environment and a recognition that 'it's about time something was done'.

This form of outdoor education is rarely known by that term in Australia. More commonly, the term 'environmental education' is used. Alternatively, the aims of environmental education, where they are included as curriculum intentions, are included in subjects areas such as natural and social science in primary schools, or in science in secondary schools.

Environmental Objectives in Outdoor Leisure Education

A survey of secondary school outdoor leisure education programmes in Australia has shown that there is an increasing tendency for teachers responsible for these programmes to include activities designed to achieve the major environmental objectives. Objectives identified in this survey are listed below and, although the emphasis is placed on natural rather than built environments, similarities with the aims of environmental education in Australia and with the competencies required by teachers in Wisconsin, will be obvious. Many outdoor leisure education programmes are designed to help students:

—develop a sense of respect for natural environments and entities
—understand key ecological concepts
—recognise the capacity of human beings to alter or damage fragile natural environments and entities
—appreciate the need to take individual responsibility for the protection of natural environments and entities
—avoid or minimise damage to natural environments and entities during outdoor experiences
—develop a commitment to supporting policies and practices designed to protect and improve natural environments
—develop the knowledge and skills necessary to identify and resolve potential threats to natural environments

It is a truism, of course, that the mere listing of objectives in curriculum documents does not necessarily mean that they will be implemented in practice. No rigorous research has been undertaken to determine whether or not the environmental objectives of outdoor leisure education are being translated into teaching-learning experiences in programmes. Leading outdoor educators in Australia have suggested that many teachers who are responsible for outdoor leisure education programmes do not have the knowledge to implement learning experiences related to these environmental objectives, even when they are stated in curriculum documents. It has also been suggested that outdoor leisure education teachers and leaders, even when they have the required knowledge, tend to avoid or neglect environmental objectives. Simpson (1984) contends that these objectives are avoided because of inadequate training, and discarded whenever experiences designed to achieve other objectives are perceived as having higher priority at a given time.

There are, nevertheless, some hopeful signs. At the Sixth National Outdoor Education Conference held in Sydney in January 1989, considerable interest was expressed by participants in including environmental objectives in programmes, and there were indications that appropriate curriculum materials may soon be developed.

Outdoor Education as Outdoor Leisure Education

This form of outdoor education involves outdoor leisure activities in which there is adventure, challenge and even a degree of risk for participants. As well as outdoor education, this form has been given a variety of labels, with the most common being *outdoor pursuits* or *adventure education*. The central focus is on helping students acquire the knowledge, skills and attitudes required to participate in outdoor leisure pursuits such as bushwalking, skiing, rock-climbing and canoeing. The objectives sought in these programmes vary considerably depending on the personal preferences of the responsible teachers and the accessibility of natural settings appropriate to the preferred outdoor leisure pursuits.

Many outdoor educators have urged schools and teachers to give attention to fostering outdoor leisure interests. Carlson (1972: 2), writing from the perspective of a recreation educator, urges that it 'should be remembered that one of the objectives of education is worthy use of leisure. The outdoors provides some of the most satisfying and worthy uses of leisure; and outdoor education, therefore, has a responsibility in the development of leisure interests.' Smith (1973: 20) reminds teachers and youth leaders that they can 'find outdoor resources which they can use . . . to provide opportunities for acquiring knowledge and skills for wholesome outdoor pursuits'. Other writers such as Gabrielsen and Holtzer (1965: 22), Darst and Armstrong (1980: 8), Ford (1981: 13) and Loynes (1988: 1) have also stressed the role outdoor education can play in helping students acquire the knowledge, skills and attitudes needed to participate in outdoor leisure pursuits. These exhortations, however, lack specificity and concepts such as 'worthy uses of leisure' and 'wholesome outdoor pursuits' have subsequently been subject to rigorous analysis by Mundy and Odum (1979) to clarify their meaning and provide direction for teachers. The meaning has, however, been clear enough to practitioners, who recognise that students can gain enjoyment and a sense of satisfaction from participation in outdoor leisure pursuits and that these pursuits could become life-long leisure interests.

What is Leisure Education?

The Leisure Education Advancement Project's Kangaroo Kit (1977) describes leisure education as a process which helps individuals to:

—recognise that leisure is an avenue for personal satisfaction and enrichment
—be aware of the many valuable leisure opportunities available
—understand the significance of leisure to society
—appreciate natural resources and their relationship to leisure and life quality
—develop the attitudes, knowledge and skills that will assist in making leisure satisfying
—be able to make responsible decisions regarding their own leisure
—be able to act on their leisure interests and needs

The process of educating for leisure is not, of course, restricted to activities that take place outdoors. Leisure is a broad concept encompassing many different types of activity including, importantly, those which do take place outdoors. The remarks made in this section apply equally to indoor and outdoor leisure activities.

Why Educate for Outdoor Leisure?

The aim of all leisure education is to teach people to enhance or enrich their lives far beyond the bounds of the limited contact teachers have with them. Ultimate success will be achieved when people can function independently in pursuing rich, meaningful, fulfilling leisure experiences.

It is frequently said that we are living in a constantly and rapidly changing world. Indeed, the industrial and technological base of our society has been expanding at an accelerating rate ever since the Industrial Revolution. There is no doubting the immense benefits which have flowed from technological change, but there remain attendant serious social problems. Although the use of machines and automation can displace people from work, technology also creates new kinds of work, requiring new kinds of skills. Unfortunately, indications are that more jobs will be lost than created. It appears likely that more and more people will become chronically unemployed. More young people will never find work. More older people will be made redundant. More people will have to face the prospect of early, unexpected and unwanted retirement. Attempts to respond to this situation by implementing different patterns of work and leisure such as flexi-time, permanent part-time work and job-sharing, even if important and necessary, are unlikely to change the overall trend: towards increasing numbers of people having more leisure time at their disposal.

Technological changes have had another disturbing effect. As the industrial process has become more complex, its human factor has been significantly reduced. Opportunities for workers to gain the satisfaction flowing from involvement in an entire process have been almost eliminated. The advent of technological processing and specialisation has increasingly obliged the human worker to focus on a particular function or task, to be a mere 'part' of the process. This depersonalisation of the work role appears to be a major factor in the increased dissatisfaction and frustration found in work.

Industrialisation has also been accompanied by the growth of urbanisation. Industrial growth is dependent upon the availability of investment capital and access to raw materials, but another essential ingredient has been large concentrations of workers who would also be consumers of goods and services. Many urban areas have become crowded and polluted environments. Morris (1979) has argued that such environments are alien to human beings and that the fear, neuroses and aggression they exhibit can be equated with the behaviour of captive animals. Even if this analogy is hard to accept, there is no doubt that such conditions have an impact on leisure behaviour and attitudes. Urbanisation, the degradation of human and natural environments and the general conditions of life limit the choices available to many people for satisfying and fulfilling leisure pursuits in pleasant and stimulating settings. Other consequences are the tendency of urban dwellers to opt for passive and non-creative leisure activities; an increasing incidence of illnesses and diseases associated with the frenzied pace of urban life-styles; the tendency of people to be spectators, passive recipients of second-hand and mass-produced attitudes and values relating to leisure; and the poor fitness levels of the many modern people who have grown sedentary and soft.

There are obviously a whole range of reforms which could be made in Western society in order for it to become more just and equitable. At present, many people are not leading satisfying, enjoyable, stimulating or enriching lives. Much imaginative thinking and effort is needed to devise strategies for making work available for all who want it; for improving working conditions and the satisfaction that can be derived from work; for improving constructed and protecting natural environments; and for improving leisure opportunities. The human search for satisfaction, fulfilment and quality of life is unending. Leisure education is no panacea; nor should it be seen as a substitute for essential social reforms. But it can play a significant role, because it seeks the achievement of four main goals. The purpose of leisure education is to help individuals:

—enhance the quality of their lives through and in leisure and to recognise that status and self-esteem can be obtained in leisure as well as work
—understand the opportunities, potentials and challenges of leisure
—understand the impact of leisure on the quality of their lives as individuals and on the fabric of society
—have the knowledge, skills and appreciation that enable broad leisure choices

The Status of Leisure Education in Australia

Unfortunately, it would appear that leisure education, like environmental education, is making little headway in schools. The Canberra case studies reveal that:

(1) few schools place emphasis on the development of leisure concepts or skills in general statements of philosophy or in particular curriculum documents
(2) there is a tendency on the part of teachers of subjects such as Art, Music and Physical Education to emphasise the importance of 'high standards of achievement' rather than enjoyment. The effect is to lead many students to perceive of themselves as under-achievers in the many leisure activities associated with these and other similar subjects and to discard the activities from their list of possible leisure choices, at least in the short term
(3) students are deficient in terms of their grasp of leisure concepts and skills
(4) teachers are confused about the nature of leisure education and tend to equate the process with recreation programmes which emphasise the development of skills rather than concepts
(5) teachers are also uncertain about approaches which can be adopted to integrate or infuse leisure education concepts and skills into their

programmes
(6) many opportunities are missed to promote the objectives of leisure
education and to enhance teaching effectiveness and enjoyment in
learning by the use of leisure activities which have direct or indirect
educational worth
(7) in spite of the fact that teachers feel and are ill-equipped to educate
for leisure, there is considerable interest among teachers (and
students and parents) in the process

Outdoor leisure education is seen as an ideal vehicle for the promotion of
leisure concepts, skills and attitudes. What is required is a determined and
systematic attempt by those responsible for outdoor leisure education
programmes to, at least:

—understand the past, present and possible future relationships between
work and leisure
—clarify their own attitudes and values relating to leisure
—identify the range of outdoor leisure activities
—understand the needs and desires of people of all ages in relation to
leisure in the outdoors
—determine the knowledge, skills and attitudes required by different
people in order that they may lead satisfying outdoor leisure lives
—become aware of the factors which constrain people from utilising
leisure time to their best advantage
—discover the leisure resources and facilities available for outdoor leisure
activities

Other Key Emphases in Outdoor Leisure Education

In the past decade, many outdoor leisure education programmes have been
designed to promote learning outcomes other than those involving leisure.
Priest (1985–86: 19) writes that:

> The adventure education or outdoor pursuits approach to outdoor education is a
> vehicle for facilitating the individual's discovery of interpersonal and intra-
> personal relationships. The 'interpersonal' refers to the individual's socialised
> involvement with others: either person to person or person to group. The
> 'intrapersonal' refers to the individual's concern with their inner Self.

The archetypal programmes of this type are those provided by Outward
Bound. The objectives listed in the Canadian Outward Bound Instructors'
Handbook (undated) can be summarised as:

> —personal development by helping individuals gain an increased sense of self-
> worth, compassion for others and enthusiasm for living
> —group development, i.e., the development of trust, respect and co-operation
> —interpersonal effectiveness, i.e., the capacity to communicate effectively, to
> resolve conflicts and to participate in meaningful relationships
> —the capacity of participants to learn experientially and to respond to challenge
> —the testing and refining of personal values

In research involving twenty-five ACT primary and secondary schools, McRae (1987: 39–45) found that only two schools had written philosophies which emphasised the essential aims and objectives of leisure education. Passing reference to the role of schools in educating for leisure was noted in eight other philosophical statements. However, all these school philosophies gave prominence to the role of the schools in developing the personal and social qualities and capacities of students. Objectives relating to leisure and the personal and social development of students are not the sole preserve of outdoor education, but such objectives are central intentions of an increasing number of outdoor leisure education programmes.

Outdoor leisure education programmes can vary in terms of the age level of the students, the emphasis given to different objectives, the settings used and the activities included, the degree of adventure or risk involved, and the length of the experience or programme. Three examples will provide some indication of the variety of purposes and practices. A primary teacher might take a group of Year 4 students to a bush setting close to a farmhouse for an overnight camping experience. The students might be expected to enjoy a new leisure experience, to develop some basic bushcraft and camping skills, to overcome apprehension felt about the outdoors, and to learn to co-operate with other students when undertaking group tasks. A secondary teacher might take a group of Year 10 students on a physically-demanding five-day bushwalk designed to introduce skills in the planning of bushwalks, bushcraft and campcraft, map-reading, navigation and first aid, and to develop an awareness of the importance of physical fitness. A third teacher might implement a year-long programme seeking to give students a sense of achievement; to enhance their self-concepts; to improve their ability to develop relationships and to communicate with other students, and to see value in teamwork; to refine their skills in a number of outdoor pursuits including bushwalking, rock-climbing, abseiling, canoeing and cross-country skiing; and to help them develop positive attitudes towards participation in outdoor leisure activities.

In recent years, teachers of outdoor leisure education have also begun to incorporate environmental objectives in their programmes. A policy statement on outdoor education issued by the Cumbria Local Education Authority (*Adventure Education* 1984: 8), for example, includes a definition indicating a trend towards a more integrated form of outdoor education:

> Outdoor Education is widely accepted as the term to describe all learning, social development and the skill associated with living and journeying in the outdoors. . . Apart from opportunities for personal fulfilment and development of leisure interests, outdoor education stimulates the development of self-reliance, judgement, responsibility, relationships and the capacity for sustained physical endeavour. . . In addition to physical endeavour, it embraces environmental and ecological understanding.

The Cumbria statement sees outdoor education as embracing 'three interlinked areas' of learning. The following model shows the objectives of each of the major elements of outdoor education identified by the Cumbria Education Authority and outlined in *Adventure Education* (1984: 8):

Figure 1.1   The Cumbria Model of Outdoor Education

(1) Outdoor Pursuits
    Physical skill   SAFETY
    Person and social   ACHIEVEMENT
    development   SATISFACTION
    Leisure preparation   SENSITIVITY
    Adventure   ENJOYMENT
    Safety awareness

(2) Outdoor Studies
    Enjoyment of living things
    Sensitivity
    Aesthetic awareness
    Academic development
    Environmental awareness
    Respect and concern
    Conservation

(3) The Residential Experience
    Personal and social development
    Self-awareness/Awareness of others
    Independence and self-confidence
    Develop relationships with others
    Work closely with others
    Learn to co-operate with others
    Develop a sense of responsibility

Writers such as Darst and Armstrong (1980: 10–11), Mortlock (1984: 17), Gibbison (1984: 13) and Donnan (1985: 26–28) agree that the 'outdoor pursuits' component of the Cumbria Model and the outcomes shown at its centre are central to outdoor leisure education programmes. The findings of an Australian survey to be presented later in this chapter show that most of the objectives listed as 'outdoor studies' in the Cumbria Model are also being incorporated into programmes of outdoor leisure education. The residential experience is not an essential element of this form of outdoor education in Australia, and the objectives listed under this component are sought in programmes which do not use resident centres.

Crowther (1984: 12–15), Priest (1985–86: 19) and other writers have also encouraged a more holistic approach to outdoor education similar to the Cumbria Model, a development apparent in outdoor education programmes implemented in Australian schools in recent years.

Historical Development of Outdoor Leisure Education in Australia

Educational programmes which aim to promote skills in adventurous leisure pursuits are a comparatively recent development in Australia although there were some links with the Rural School Camps of the early twentieth century and the National Fitness Camps which began throughout Australia in the early 1940s.

Rural School Camps were introduced as an experiment in New South Wales in 1906, but were discontinued with the onset of World War I in 1914. The aim was to provide 'city school children with opportunities for observing country life' (Department of Education 1922). Although 'desultory efforts' had been made by a few teachers previously, the first large-scale experiment occurred in 1906, when 146 boys were grouped in sections of twelve under the supervision of fourteen teachers and spent a week at a farm in the Hunter Valley. Tents and camping equipment were borrowed from the Defence Department, a hospital tent was established;

and a medical officer and cook were employed. The departmental report noted that:

> The experiment proved eminently successful. Before the end of the year 1906, a total of 576 boys and 48 masters had participated. The local farmers rendered every assistance to the teachers and boys. To many of the boys the camp school was the means of their obtaining their first glimpse of country life. Wherever possible the lads took a hand in the various operations of the neighbouring farms. Strict discipline was maintained and this, together with instruction . . . constituted influences favourable to the cadet and citizen soldier movement and to the development of the broad national sentiment that should underlie it.

In 1909, the Chief Inspector's report for that year provides an insight into the nature of the rural school camps:

> It is now over three years since this movement was inaugurated, and it is not too much to say that it has proved most successful in regard to the objects for which it was intended. Continuous instruction is the keynote of these camp schools. The venue is simply changed from the public schools to the tented field, and instead of the prescribed text-books being in use the book of Nature is studied, and the lads are brought in an interesting way into contact with every form of agricultural labour.

Rural Camps involved teaching and learning in the outdoors. 'Instruction' and observation took place about 'nature' even if the emphasis was on agricultural pursuits. The students learnt skills in camping, a common activity in outdoor leisure education today. Activities designed to foster the personal and social development of students, in ways considered appropriate to the historical period, were considered important. The Camps, which were 'run on military lines', sought to develop personal attributes such as 'independence', 'co-operativeness', 'discipline' and a sense of 'nationalism' (NSW Department of Education *Report* 1921).

The National Fitness camping policy was formulated by the Director of Physical Education in New South Wales, with the advice of camping authorities and with the recommendation of the National Fitness Council. The first resident camp was established at Broken Bay in 1941 (Webb 1981) and others followed soon afterwards. Although the promotion of physical fitness was seen as being central to the camps, an original intention was for the camps to be based on the American and English models and to use an 'outdoor camping environment' to provide appropriate learning experiences in all subject areas. However, the programmes of the National Fitness Camps or the Sport and Recreation Centres, as they became known, always had a major emphasis on physical leisure activities. This was not surprising given that control of the camps was vested in the physical education section of the Department of Education and that most of the staff members were physical education teachers.

This situation applied also in other states of Australia where National Fitness Camps were established. In Western Australia, for example, the first camp was established at Cape Peron in 1946. In the early years 'ordinary school work plus special work in physical education, health and swimming was given' (Cook 1988). In practice, however, camp programmes concentrated on physical recreational activities. In 1967, Adventure Camps were introduced in the summer vacations, and these programs, according to Cook, 'were intended to provide situations calling for initiative and a spirit of adventure'. These early adventure-oriented programmes led to the introduction of the 'outdoor education courses now offered in high school Years 9–12' (Cook 1988).

A key factor influencing the development of outdoor education programmes which aimed to develop skills in adventurous leisure pursuits was the increased interest in outdoor leisure activities amongst people in the community generally. Apart from private, individual or group activity, educational institutions, including schools, commercial organisations such as Wilderness Expeditions and non-profit-making groups such as Outward Bound provided programmes which were designed to meet a growing demand.

Darst and Armstrong (1980: 10–11) contend that a 'variety of educational and recreational benefits can be derived from outdoor adventure activities' and outlined a number of reasons for the growth in popularity of these activities. They thought that individuals participated for personal reasons, e.g., to try a new experience 'filled with adventure, fun, and challenge'; to experience 'stressful activities that border on the physically dangerous' to help them 'overcome fear, gain self-confidence, obtain emotional stability, and successfully cope with additional responsibility'; to 'escape from the complexities of modern life' by undertaking activities which help them to 'relax, change their usual pace, slow down, and experience freedom'; to achieve 'a highly personal sense of achievement' even if they do have 'limited physical ability'; to 'learn more about the earth's environment'; and to 'promote cardio-vascular-respiratory fitness'. Darst and Armstrong also say that people were attracted to outdoor adventure activities because of the social opportunities presented to 'meet others who have similar reasons' for participation; to engage in activities which 'promote cohesiveness among peoples and groups'; and because 'of the development of co-operation, trust and appreciation of other people' which can occur during the activities.

Australian teachers may have taken part in these activities for any or all of these reasons. However, the outdoor educators interviewed in my study agreed that most of the outdoor education programmes which began to appear in the 1970s had the narrow focus of providing enjoyable, satisfying and adventurous activities for students; of developing the skills required to pursue the activities in their own leisure time; and of promoting physical fitness. The inclusion of other objectives in outdoor leisure education programmes is, however, becoming more common, as shown in the findings of the national survey of outdoor education objectives to be outlined later in this chapter.

The informants (outdoor educators and teachers) interviewed considered that outdoor leisure education is implemented principally in secondary schools by physical education teachers. However, they believe that increasing numbers of secondary teachers of other subject areas and also primary teachers are implementing programmes, which vary from single experiences of one or two hours, to more comprehensive and longer-term programmes which vary in length from several weeks to one or more years. Most extended programmes are found in secondary schools.

Most programmes are known by the term Outdoor Education although some use is made of the alternative labels, Adventure Education or Outdoor Pursuits. The survey informants agree that programmes of this type are more commonly recognised as outdoor education by teachers and by people in the Australian community than any other form.

Australian Survey of Objectives in Outdoor Leisure Education

As part of a review of current Australian practices, a survey was undertaken of objectives being sought in junior secondary school outdoor leisure education courses. Letters were sent to the teachers in which they were asked to forward outdoor education curriculum documents listing 'the aims, objectives and content' of their programmes.

The letters were distributed to schools in each state and 43 responses were received, a return rate of 84.3 per cent; 7 of the curriculum documents received contained no list of aims and objectives. Only 10 documents contained comprehensive lists of aims and objectives. The stated aims and objectives of the submitted documents were examined in order to develop an initial list of outdoor education objectives. In examining each document, multi-barrelled objectives were split up into single objectives. After finalising the list, objectives which appeared to have similar meanings or intentions were amalgamated.

The content of all courses was also examined and objectives reflecting the key concepts and skills of outdoor education not already included in the survey list of aims and objectives, were formulated. In an attempt to avoid the amalgamated list becoming too cumbersome, a number of aims or objectives were eliminated, either because they were obscure in meaning or intention, or because they were mentioned in fewer than three curriculum documents.

The list which resulted from this process contained 12 broad and 69 more specific objectives, with the latter contributing to the achievement of the former. The list was validated with 5 outdoor education teachers in the ACT in order to determine if meanings were clear; minor amendments were made.

Broad Objectives of Outdoor Leisure Education

Table 1.1. ranks the broad objectives identified in the survey. The rank order was based on the percentage of objectives which were stated or implied in curriculum documents. The broad objectives were categorised into five groups, viz., Outdoor Skills, Personal Development, Social Development, Environmental Concern and School Learning. The table ranks the broad objectives in terms of the frequency with which they were included in curriculum documents and indicates the category in which they belong:

Before discussing Table 1.1, it is necessary to reinforce an earlier comment that only a small proportion of the examined documents contained comprehensive lists of objectives. As with other curriculum areas, outdoor education statements of curriculum intent are often incomplete. Survey informants suggested that objectives which are regarded as important are

Table 1.1   Categories and Rankings of Broad Objectives

	Category	%	Rank
Develop the basic skills required to participate in selected outdoor experiences	O/Skills	100.0	1
Develop basic skills in bushcraft	O/Skills	86.0	2
Develop positive attitudes to physical fitness	Personal	65.1	3
Enhance personal qualities and abilities	Personal	62.8	4
Enhance relations with others	Social	55.8	5
Develop positive attitudes to leisure	Personal	53.5	6
Become environmentally concerned	E/Concern	51.2	7
Become proficient in the basic skills of map-reading and navigation	O/Skills	46.5	8
Enhance their abilities to plan outdoor experiences	O/Skills	44.6	9
Develop basic skills in first aid	O/Skills	39.5	10
Cope with emergencies in the outdoors	O/Skills	37.2	11
Enhance learning in a range of curriculum areas	Learning	18.6	12

often not included in course documents and that many teachers include only sufficient objectives 'to make it look respectable enough' to meet the basic requirements of school authorities. In addition, it is important to emphasise that a mere statement of curriculum intent is no guarantee that teaching-learning activities designed to achieve the objective will be implemented. Nevertheless, the survey does provide the best available information about the relative importance of objectives sought in outdoor leisure education programmes in Australia.

The table shows strong emphasis is still given to the development of the basic outdoor skills involved in particular outdoor pursuits and in camping. One survey informant remarked that outdoor education 'was about helping students to play and live in the bush'. Outdoor skills relating to map-reading and navigation, the planning of outdoor experiences, first aid and coping with emergencies were, however, stated in fewer than half of the programmes. Subsequent interviews with survey informants identified three possible reasons for this situation. The short duration of many programmes was thought to prevent many outdoor educators from giving attention to skills which 'were advanced and sophisticated'. It was also suggested that some teachers did not regard junior secondary students 'as capable of handling these difficult skills'; and that the major emphasis of many programmes was placed on providing the students 'with an enjoyable and challenging experience' rather than on developing skills which 'would enable them to take off on their own'.

The high ranking for the development of positive attitudes to physical fitness is explained partly by the involvement of many physical education teachers in outdoor leisure education programmes. It is also a result of the high value placed on physical fitness by outdoor education teachers drawn from curriculum areas other than physical education. It is, perhaps, surprising that this objective was not stated in even more curriculum documents. Responses to the more specific objectives of the survey suggest that teachers see outdoor education more as a vehicle for developing positive attitudes to physical fitness than for developing higher sustained levels of physical fitness.

Just over a half the curriculum documents listed the development of positive attitudes to leisure as a broad objective. The relative lack of awareness and understanding of ACT teachers of leisure concepts is not matched by outdoor educators. At least, it would appear that the teachers of outdoor leisure education may be more aware of leisure concepts than teachers generally.

Objectives relating to the enhancement of personal qualities and capacities and of relations with other persons were stated in three out of every five documents. Survey informants suggested that these objectives were intended even when they were not stated in curriculum documents. It was thought that many outdoor education teachers considered that 'it was not necessary to state the obvious'.

The development of knowledge, skills and attitudes towards natural environments was stated in about half the documents. Although no comparative data is available, survey informants agreed that this figure is considerably higher that it would have been a decade ago. Apart from the teaching of environment concepts, it is apparent that few secondary school outdoor education teachers currently place emphasis on enhancing learning in other curriculum areas.

Conclusion

The review of purposes and practices of outdoor education undertaken in this chapter is incomplete. The range of outdoor settings which could be used has not been explored fully. The contributions that field study centres and resident outdoor education centres of various kinds, and organisations such as Outward Bound make to the various forms of outdoor education, if mentioned, have been largely ignored. The trend towards a more holistic form of outdoor education which integrates elements from the different forms has also been mentioned only in passing. Some of these matters, including an approach to incorporating all forms of outdoor education into an integrated model, are addressed in subsequent chapters. It is clear, however, that outdoor education is a very diverse field with programmes varying considerably in terms of their purposes and practices. It is clear, also, that all teachers and students can benefit from using outdoor settings. It is hoped that the following chapters will provide readers with some inspiration and ideas for maximizing these potential benefits.

References

Acuff, D.S. (1976) 'The Effect of an Outdoor Education Experience on the General and Intercultural Anxiety of Anglo and Black Sixth Graders', Unpublished doctoral dissertation, University of Southern California, USA.

Brady, E.R. (1972) 'The Effectiveness of Field Trips compared to Media in

Teaching Selected Environmental Concepts', Unpublished doctoral dissertation, Iowa State University, USA.

Canadian Bound Outward Bound School (undated) *Instructor's Handbook*.

Cook, K. (1988) Early draft of 'Outdoor Education in Western Australia' which appears as part of Chapter 14 of this book.

Crowther, N. (1984) 'The Role of Outdoor Education Teachers in providing for the Needs of Tomorrow's Society', *Adventure Education* 1 (6).

Darst, P.W. and Armstrong, G.P. (1980) *Outdoor Adventure Activities for Schools and Recreation Programs*, Burgess, Minneapolis.

Donaldson, G.W. (1945) 'Living and Learning Outdoors', *The School Executive*, February.

— and Donaldson, L.E. (1958) 'Outdoor Education: A Definition, *Journal of the American Association for Health, Physical Education and Recreation*, May–June.

Donnan, G.E. (1985) 'Trouble with Ice and Scorpions', *Adventure Education* 2 (4/5).

Fitzpatrick, C.N. (1968) 'Philosophy and Goals for Outdoor Education', Unpublished doctoral dissertation, Colorado State College, USA.

Ford, P.M. (1981) *Principles and Practices of Outdoor/Environmental Education*, John Wiley, New York.

Gabrielsen, M.A. and Holtzer, C. (1965) *Outdoor Education*, Center for Applied Research in Education, New York, USA.

Garrison, C. (1966) *Outdoor Education*, Charles Thomas, Springfield, Ill., USA.

Gibbison, J. (1984) 'Outdoor Education in the Secondary School Curriculum', *Adventure Education* 1 (5).

Greenall, A.E. (1980a) *Environmental Education in Australia: Phenomenon of the Seventies*, Occasional Paper No. 7, Curriculum Development Centre, Canberra.

—(1980b), *Environmental Education for Schools*, Curriculum Development Centre, Canberra.

Hammerman, D.R., W.M. and E.L. (1985) *Teaching in the Outdoors*, Interstate, Danville, Ill., USA.

Heffernan, H. (1967) 'They Grow Ten Feet High', *Childhood Education*, October.

Hoeksma, H. (1964) 'An Experiment Dealing with the Effects of Outdoor Education on the Achievement of 6th Graders in Arithmetic, Unpublished Masters' thesis, University of Northern Illinois, USA.

Kirk, J. (1968) 'Outdoor Education—Its Origin and Purpose', Paper presented at the Outdoor Education Conference, Toronto, Canada.

Lewis, C.A. (1975) *The Administration of Outdoor Education Programs*, Kendall–Hunt, Dubuque, Iowa, USA.

Link, M. (1981) *Outdoor Education: A Manual for Teaching in Nature's Classroom*, Prentice-Hall, Englewood Cliffs, NJ, USA.

Mand, C. (1967) *Outdoor Education*, J. Lowell-Pratt, New York, USA.

Masters, H.B. (1951) 'Values of School Camping', *Journal of Health, Physical Education and Recreation* 22 (1).

McRae, K. (1987) 'Leisure Education: Case Study Findings and Implications for Practice', *Curriculum Perspectives* 7 (1).

Morris, D. (1979) *The Human Zoo*, Jonathan Cape, London.

Mortlock, C. (1984) 'Outdoor Education in the Community', *Adventure Education* 1 (5).

Mundy, J. and Odum, L. (1979) *Leisure Education: Theory and Practice*, John Wiley and Sons, New York, USA.

Nolan, H.B. (1967) 'Outdoor Education, Frederick Country School System, Maryland', *Actions Models*, The Pinchot Institute, USA.

Priest, S. (1985–86) 'Functional Outdoor Education', *Adventure Education* 2 (6).

Sharp, L.B. (1947) 'Basic Considerations in Outdoor and Camping Education', *The Bulletin of the National Association of Secondary School Principals*, May.

Simpson, S. (1985) 'Short-term Wilderness Expeditions and Environmental Ethics', *Journal of Experiential Education* 8 (3).

Smith, J. (1970) *Outdoor Education*, American Association for Health, Physical Education and Recreation, Washington, DC, USA.

—Carlson, R., Donaldson, G. and Masters, H. (1973) *Outdoor Education*, Prentice-Hall, Englewood Cliffs, NJ, USA.

Swan, M. (1984) 'Wisconsin sets New Standards', *Illinois Environmental Education Update* IX (6).

Thompson, H. (1955) 'Basic Guides for the Establishment and Development of School Outdoor Education', Unpublished doctoral dissertation, Columbia University, USA.

Webb, J. (1981) *Environmental Field Study Centres in Australia*, Australian Parks and Wildlife Service, 1981.

2
Outdoor Education In the United States: Yesterday, Today and Tomorrow

Cliff Knapp

Defining Terms

Outdoor education is commonly defined as the use of resources outside the formal school classroom to meet educational goals and objectives. These resources are primarily studied directly through experience rather than vicariously through books, films, television, computers, or other technological means. Outdoor education is usually considered within the context of public and private educational systems, although non-school agencies and organisations such as scouting, YMCA or YWCA groups also conduct outdoor programmes. Outdoor education, as a field of study, involves more than selecting a setting outside a school building. Practitioners espouse particular educational philosophies which incorporate first-hand experience with resources in context. Outdoor educators also strive to achieve certain goals and objectives through the application of specific principles and teaching techniques.

This chapter briefly traces the historical evolution of the movement from the early nineteenth century to the present, through the use of examples involving people and types of programmes. It describes the underlying rationale for using outdoor settings for learning and elaborates upon the philosophical and pedagogical implications. Based upon this description and analysis, some trends and future projections will be described.

Programme Scope

Outdoor education in the United States has been implemented most successfully in the elementary (or primary) and middle grades (Kindergarten to Grade 8), due largely to self-contained classrooms and more flexibility in scheduling. Some high schools (Grades 9–12) conduct lessons away from schools, but most of the learning at this level takes place inside the school building. In the broad sense, any activity which involves leaving the school building for a field trip qualifies as outdoor education. Some examples are: kindergartens taking temperatures to discover the warmest and coldest places in the school yard; first graders planting beans in the school garden; third graders writing a poem about ducks observed in the park; fourth graders doing a traffic survey downtown; fifth graders visiting a fish hatchery; sixth graders staying overnight at a resident outdoor school (camp) for two nights and two days; seventh graders visiting a nuclear plant to learn about energy; or eighth graders testing for dissolved oxygen in a local body of water. Outdoor education can involve a multi-disciplinary approach to the curriculum in which a variety of subject matter is applied to investigating various topics. Mathematics, science, music, language arts, art, social studies, and physical education all possess some objectives that are judged to be achieved effectively outdoors. This outdoor curriculum is usually selected on the basis of how well students learn and retain concepts, skills, and attitudes. Environments for learning include the cultural (built) resources of cities, as well as natural areas such as forests, fields, deserts, lakes, streams, caves or mountains.

Programme Goals and Objectives

The goals of outdoor programmes vary somewhat, depending upon the sponsoring institution, agency, or organisation. However, some commonalities can be identified. Fitzpatrick (1968: 49–50) developed a set of goal statements by searching the professional literature and submitting the derived list to selected outdoor educators and other professionals for their rankings of importance. The 'highly significant' goals were to:

—realise the individual's full potential of mind, body, and spirit
—utilise resources beyond the classroom as stimuli for learning and curriculum enrichment
—develop awareness, appreciation, and understanding of humankind's relationship to the natural environment
—develop knowledge, skills and attitudes towards wise use of leisure time
—promote democratic human relations and procedures
—encourage the use of resources within the community, state, nation and the world
—permit an atmosphere conducive to aesthetic development

Upon examination of this list, it becomes evident that the goals of outdoor education correspond to many of the wider goals of educational institutions. The specific objectives of outdoor education vary somewhat with the grade levels, geographic areas, socio-economic conditions and levels of teacher and administrator expertise and commitment. Usually, outdoor programmes emphasise certain objectives over others, even in cases where there are attempts to provide a balanced curriculum (Knapp 1981: 14–15). Most commonly, elementary (primary) schools use traditional academic subjects to guide the selection of outdoor activities. The majority of the outdoor programmes centre around science, mathematics, social studies and language arts, even though evidence of art, music, physical education and recreation can be found. Sometimes the outdoor programme is structured around problem-solving and inquiry skills development. Exploring local environments such as water, forests, or fields, serve to focus outdoor lessons. Older students in junior and senior high schools sometimes focus their outdoor activities on monitoring environmental quality by detecting evidence of pollution. The science or social studies classes usually become involved in this way and sometimes extend the data-gathering phase by initiating action projects to improve the environment in their community.

Other outdoor education programmes emphasise outdoor living skills such as backpacking, orienteering, canoeing, mountain-climbing and rappelling, fire-building, cooking, skiing or archery. This type of programme is largely determined by daily needs for food, shelter, rest and outdoor adventure. Usually little attempt is made to teach school subjects directly when students go to natural areas.

Another type of programme focus is the development of environmental and ecological awareness. Such an approach uses senses to interact with nature: for instance, hugging a tree, or exploring objects while blindfolded. In addition, ecological concepts such as adaptation, habitat and diversity are taught through structured outdoor lessons. Van Matre has made contributions in this area with his writings dealing with acclimatisation (1972) and Sunship Earth (1979), and Cornell has contributed books on sharing nature (1979) and listening to nature (1987).

Some programmes centre upon the identification of plants, animals, rocks, constellations, clouds and other natural phenomena. Students become knowledgeable in identifying and understanding the roles of these components in various ecosystems.

Another programme objective is using the outdoors to build a sense of community and self-awareness. Socialisation and the learning of human relations skills becomes the central focus by using nature metaphors, symbols and group living situations. More emphasis is given to affective development than to cognitive objectives.

These different curricular objectives rarely appear in pure form. They are often combined in unique ways to meet the goals of the school and needs of the students. Diversity is the hallmark when outdoor educators plan activities beyond the four walls of the classroom to meet educational objectives.

One example of an adventure-based programme which combines several objectives is the PROVE Adventure Education Programme, headquartered in Maywood, Illinois (Proviso Area for Exceptional Children, 1000 Van Buren Street, Maywood, Illinois 60153). Based on the philosophy of Kurt Hahn, the founder of the Outward Bound Schools, this PAEC programme is designed for behaviour-disordered high school youth. This special student population usually exhibits defiance of authority, anti-social behaviour, physical and verbal aggression and negative self-image. Specific goals include:

—The development of responsible control of individual inappropriate behaviour
—a co-operative attitude in peer group associations
—the ability to deal more effectively and comfortably with stress situations and conflict
—a sense of accomplishment and confidence developed through success-oriented activities
—the ability to accept fair and consistent limits on behaviour and acceptance of the consequences of their actions
—the development of social skills
—an acceptance of the expectations of the school year programme

The programme focuses upon achieving positive social change and improved confidence and self-image through outdoor challenges in wilderness settings. Students usually participate in classroom units containing approximately ten students and two to four specially trained instructors. Developing group cohesiveness through positive peer regard, sharing feelings, honest communication and mutual support are given top priority. Typical problem-solving activities include backpacking, canoeing, camping, caving and rock-climbing. Solving these outdoor problems requires the use of emotional, cognitive and physical resources. The outdoor adventure component of the students' education is not isolated from the ongoing school classroom curriculum. Pre-trip classroom preparation provides the input to help them deal with the stress created by the outdoor setting and activities. Classroom follow-ups, upon returning to school, complete the instructional package. The adventure instructors work closely with classroom teachers in addressing individual education plans for students. An offshoot of the PROVE programme is the PAEC Trainably Mentally Handicapped (TMH) Camping and Adventure Programme. This programme has been adapted from the PROVE programme, but differs in the degree of difficulty and the population it serves. The students are all mentally retarded and range in age from 14–21, with IQs in the mid-30 to high-60 range.

Appreciating

This programme consists of six excursions each year: a Fall tent camping trip for beginners and less able students; a winter tent and ski trip; 3 spring cabin trips, which stress environmental studies; and a 7-to-10 day summer adventure trip which involves canoeing, caving, rock-climbing, backpacking and biking.

These alternative approaches to educating special populations are not presently the norm in the United States. However, at the national level, an increasing concern has been expressed for reaching 'at risk' students with innovative programmes.

The most typical type of residential outdoor education programme is conducted at the 5 or 6 levels (age 10–12) for 2–3 days. During the elementary (primary) years, only one such residential experience is commonly provided. Usually, the school leases a summer camp or outdoor-environmental education centre and plans a balanced curriculum which incorporates several objectives. They include:

—learning a variety of subject matter (knowledge and skills)
—becoming aware of and appreciating natural and cultural systems
—increasing personal and social growth
—clarifying a personal environmental ethic
—enjoying the outdoors for recreational purposes

Frequently, students sleep in comfortable, heated or air-conditioned dormitories and have their meals served in a modern dining hall. Very seldom do students using these facilities prepare their own food, pitch a tent, build a fire, select what they want to learn or undergo much physical stress for long periods outdoors. The major focus is learning academic subjects and socialisation skills. The predominant subject is usually science, although history, art, math, and language arts are sometimes integrated into the learning experiences. Classroom teachers usually accompany the students to the outdoor school, but the amount of teaching they do varies. Some centres provide all the instruction, while others provide none. In many cases, outdoor specialists share instructional responsibilities with classroom teachers.

Teacher-training

A problem that has not been adequately addressed in most American colleges of education is the training of teachers for outdoor teaching roles. The ability to teach outdoors depends upon sufficient knowledge of ecological relationships, student organisation and management skills, minimal ability in identifying flora, fauna, and other natural objects, and knowledge of related subject matter content and activities.

Another problem is limited student access to outdoor educational opportunities. It is estimated that only 5–10 per cent of the American student population participates in residential outdoor education during the regular school year. This usually occurs once during the student's 13 years of formal education. Most of the students in large urban school districts do not participate because of limited funding or disinterest among the teachers and administrators.

One approach to alleviating these staffing problems is to require teachers to take outdoor education courses, either as undergraduates or graduates. Northern Illinois University is one of the few universities in the United States that is addressing the need for skilled outdoor teachers. However, it will take a more concerted effort by Federal and state Departments of Education in order to make significant gains in outdoor education across the nation.

To summarise the meaning of the term outdoor education in America: it's a process which:

—is conducted outside the school building to study phenomena within the context of natural or cultural communities (using a specific setting)
—employs direct observation and the use of other senses ιo involve students by investigating cultural and/or natural resources (applying a specific philosophy and related methods)
—is aimed at extending knowledge and skills within particular subject matter content (reaching cognitive goals and objectives)
—leads to positive attitudes and values about people and the environment and a desire to maintain or restore natural and cultural areas (reaching affective goals and objectives)

Historical Background

The idea for conducting outdoor learning did not originate in the United States. Long before schooling was institutionalised, most learning took place in communities and natural areas. Gradually, as education became more formalised, it was moved indoors for convenience and dealt primarily with media such as books, models, and writing implements and teaching methods which emphasised lectures, recitations, rote memorisation and reading and writing to gain and reinforce desired information, skills and attitudes. Students' contacts with the world outside the school became more indirect and lessons became separated from everyday applications outdoors. Teachers increasingly asked students to recall their contacts with past events and objects, rather than attempting to provide them with common experiences in natural contexts during school time.

One predictable fairly recent response to this situation was a growing dissatisfaction by some educators, who advocated changing the setting, teaching methods and goals. This dissatisfaction with traditional education still characterises many outdoor educators today. In the early years of American schooling, the writings of several European educators influenced school practice.

Early Educators and Philosophers

John Amos Comenius (1592–1670) advocated direct experience and activity as ways to achieve life-long, interdisciplinary learning (Minton 1980: 24). He wrote: 'Instruction must begin with actual inspection, not with verbal description of things. . .the object must be a real, useful thing, capable of making an impression upon the senses. . .' (Minton 1980: 28).

Jean-Jacques Rousseau (1712–78), influenced by Comenius, believed in discovering information rather than learning by rote, applying scientific processes rather than memorising facts, using common phenomena as media for learning and constructing one's own simple apparatus. His dictum was 'return to nature' (Minton 1980: 30–31). He wrote: 'Our first teachers are our feet, our hands and our eyes. To substitute books for all these. . .is but to teach us to use the reason of others' (Hammerman 1961: 88).

Johann Heinrich Pestalozzi (1746–1826), influenced by both Comenius and Rousseau, believed in replacing recitation with discussion, individual learning with group instruction. and inculcation of ideas with teaching students to think for themselves. He maintained that observation was the basis of all knowledge (Minton 1980: 32). He wrote: 'All instruction of man is then only the art of helping Nature find her own way' (Charles 1979: 17). Freidrich Froebel (1782–1852), a student of Pestalozzi's, believed in developing the inborn moral, social and intellectual capacities of the child through nature-study, gardening, and play. He emphasised sympathy and oneness with nature (Minton 1980: 33). He wrote: 'Take your little children by the hand; go with them into nature as into the house of God' (Vinal 1926: 178).

Today, outdoor education literature still reflects the basic philosophies expressed by these educators. Attempting to relate to the interests and needs of students and to motivate them through direct contact with nature persists. The often-quoted guiding principle stated by L.B. Sharp, a leading twentieth-century influence, encapsulates their philosophy: 'That which can best be learned inside the classroom should be learned there; and that which can best be learned through direct experience outside the classroom, in contact with native materials and life situations, should there be learned' (Sharp 1947: 43).

In the late 1960s and 1970s, the term environmental education appeared in the literature to capture the idea of teaching about natural resources and working towards a quality environment. According to Roth, this new term developed out of a need to bring together the diverse philosophies and goals of the nature-study, conservation education and outdoor education movements (Minton 1980: 140). One of the leading proponents of this movement was William Stapp, now of the University of Michigan. In the early 1970s, the US Office of Education published a lengthy definition of environmental education which incorporated some of the following points (Minton 1980: 145–46):

—education about humankind's relationship to the built and natural environment.
—experienced-based, life-long learning using the resources of the school and surrounding community as laboratories
—interdisciplinary approach involving all subjects to motivate society to take the responsibility for improving the quality of life

In some cases, the terms outdoor education and environmental education are used interchangeably. Sometimes, they are even combined ('outdoor-environmental education') because of the inter-relationship between the two constructs. The one distinction between the terms, however, is that environmental education takes place both indoors *and* outdoors, whereas outdoor education is always conducted outside the school building. Some have debated whether or not a field trip to study inside a building such as a fire station or a sewage treatment plant is outdoor education, but such debate seems to be a pointless exercise. The main point of outdoor education is that students are supplementing their vicarious classroom experiences with direct ones, to create improved learning whenever possible. Some students discover that their preferred learning styles are better suited to out-of-classroom learning. At the same time, some teachers discover that their preferred teaching style is also enhanced by venturing outside the school building.

Historical Roots of Outdoor-Environmental Education

The contemporary fields of outdoor-environmental education can be traced to their roots in several related movements: organised camping, nature-study, and conservation education.

Organised Camping

Two of the best sources of material for understanding the history of organised camping in the United States are a series of articles written by H.W. Gibson, appearing in *Camping Magazine* (1936), and Eleanor Eells' book, *History of Organised Camping: The First 100 Years* (1986). As the United States developed into an industrialised nation in the 1800s and urban centres became more crowded, youth became more used to indoor environments. The need for organised camping grew from a desire to also move youth outdoors. During the late 1800s, a small group of men became interested in providing boys with opportunities for camping during the summer. Their reasons for doing this varied, but most wanted to teach boys to be more self-reliant and to strengthen them physically and morally. Some leaders were reacting against the rigid structure of the school curriculum which resulted in boredom for some students. Organised camping developed because some adults did not agree with how the schools were approaching human development in youth activities. Early camp leaders believed they had found a better way of guiding youth. Their formula was to supply plenty of fresh air and activity in rural settings and to provide opportunities for fun and learning in simple and rugged communities of caring leaders and campers. In many ways the early camps reflected the pioneer life-styles that characterised the western expansion of the country. These early camps provided youth with a mixture of work projects, team sports and nature-study.

The first school sponsored camp was initiated by Joseph Cogswell and George Bancroft of the Round Hill School in Northampton, Massachusetts (1823–34) (Ford 1981: 21). Although there were other isolated examples of schools taking students outside on overnight trips before 1861, Frederick William Gunn and his wife were among the first educators to take the entire student body of the Gunnery School for Boys in Connecticut on a two-week Summer camping trip. The activity continued for eighteen years as an integral part of the school's curriculum and the event has been cited as the beginning of the organised American camping movement (Ulanoff 1968: 20–21). Organised camping was for boys only until Laura Mattoon took eight-year-old girls on an expedition to the wilderness in 1902 (Eells 1986: 12). Summer camping grew steadily to a point where it is now an important, multi-billion-dollar enterprise with over 11,000 camps in America (Editor 1984: 10).

Many of the leaders in outdoor education gained early experience in such summer camps. One was Lloyd B. Sharp, who reorganised *Life Magazine's* Fresh Air Camps in 1925. Sharp changed the programmes from formal, militaristic affairs to programmes in which campers and staff lived in small, family-like groups, with choices in the selection of their activities. These changes incorporated the beliefs of progressive educators and philosophers such as William James (1842–1910), John Dewey (1859–1952), Alfred North Whitehead (1861–1947) and William Heard Kilpatrick (1871–1965) (Hammerman 1980: xvi). Sharp and Julian Smith were influential leaders in the early school camping movement, Sharp demonstrating the educational values of camping to school leaders (Wiener 1966: 76, 262). Beginning in the early 1960s, the term school camping was replaced by 'resident outdoor education'.

Nature-study

The nature-study movement had its origin in the United States in the early 1800s with the writings of the literary naturalists. The early settlers of New England on the east coast, guided by the Old Testament, viewed nature as essentially, evil and certainly not worth saving. Writers such as Walt Whitman (*Leaves of Grass* 1855) and Ralph Waldo Emerson (*Nature* 1836) inspired Henry David Thoreau (*Walden* 1854), who was considered to be the father of the nature essay in America. Such essays were a powerful force in moving the American public toward an appreciation and understanding of the wilderness they had 'tamed'. The term nature-study was first used in 1884 by a teacher in Pennsylvania to replace other terms such as 'natural history' and 'object teaching'. Object teaching, or the use of concrete nature to focus attention, had been seen as 'emancipation from the words of textbooks'. The active phase of nature-study in American schools lasted from the 1890s to the 1920s and was all but dead by the early 1930s (Minton 1980: 72–139).

Nature-study was generally considered to be more than the study of natural objects, but there was little agreement on the exact definition of the term. According to Olmsted (1967: 66–67) it '. . .was a term in search of a definition'. Leaders agreed that it designated a plan for elementary school science instruction, but beyond that there was little consensus on the definition, purpose or methods. Some proponents maintained that nature-study should be directed toward developing the powers of young minds (faculty psychology), and not for providing information or for shaping attitudes (Olmsted 1967: 88). Others maintained that it should provide children with the motivation and methods needed for acquiring knowledge on their own initiative through objective and rational scientific inquiry (p. 91). Still more argued that nature-study should encourage children to love nature, something which would eventually lead to a caring attitude towards the rural environment. They assumed that children had an instinctive interest in nature (p. 116). Yet another group believed that nature-study should be the vehicle for bringing useful and essential information to children so they would live a healthy and prosperous life. They believed that practical knowledge, useful in everyday affairs as well as in adulthood, was most important (p. 129). Olmsted concluded (p. 189) that the nature-study movement was an important factor in the introduction of science into the elementary school curriculum and therefore influenced the shaping of American education.

Conservation Education

Before the idea of conservation was incorporated into the public school curriculum, American society dealt with several major controversies and catastrophes involving natural resource use. Funderburk (1948: 5–11) describes some of the early leaders of the conservation movement.George P. Marsh (*Man and Nature* 1864), after viewing the desolation of the once-bountiful Mediterranean area, wrote his monumental work about human impact on the land and the upsetting of the balance of nature.

In 1887, when Carl Schurz became the Secretary of the Interior he was responsible for administering the management of many of the United States' public lands. His aim of preserving the country's natural resources was severely criticised by the public, and finally rejected. Gifford Pinchot, President Theodore Roosevelt's chief adviser on matters of public use of natural resources, initiated the country's first systematic forestry practices in 1892. John Wesley Powell, author of an important monograph published in 1878, was instrumental in initiating legislation that 're-claimed' arid western lands by diverting water from river systems. Hugh H. Bennet, chief of the Soil Conservation Service, tried to call attention to soil erosion control in the early 1900s. At first the public was not interested in the problem, but finally, in 1928, Federal funds were given to set up regional erosion stations to measure soil and water losses. The information about the loss of these natural resources, along with mid-western dust storms in the early 1930s, convinced the public that something must be done about conservation. The Soil Conservation Service was created in 1935, and soil and water conservation gradually appeared in school curricula around the country. Charles Van Hise had published an important book on conservation as early as 1910, but other education materials did not begin to proliferate until the mid-1930s. By 1935, educators believed that schools should give attention to, and take responsibility for, current social and economic problems, including conservation. Educational journals began to carry more articles on the subject. From July 1935 to June 1938, the *Education Index* listed fifty such articles. In 1937, the Commissioner of Education called a national conference on conservation education and the Office of Education expanded its programmes. In 1938 four bibliographies of conservation material were issued (Funderburk 1948: 10–36).

By the late 1930s, schools were attempting to instil a consciousness of the necessity of the conservation of natural resources into America's youth. The conservation education movement filled in the gap left when the nature-study movement waned in the early 1930s. Although the term conservation education is still used today, outdoor-environmental education still predominates in the literature.

Changing Terminology

Even though the terminology has changed over the years, the careful observer can still find evidence of these earlier movements, the forerunners of contemporary outdoor-environmental programmes. One of the best articles describing the evolution of terminology in the field was written by Disinger and published by the ERIC Clearinghouse for Science, Mathematics and Environmental Education (1983). In 1986, Ford prepared a helpful publication outlining the definitional problem and clarifying the use of terms in the field. There is little doubt that leaders will continue to redefine and create new terminology to communicate more effectively as American society changes.

Trends and Projections

Recently there has been a trend away from the use of the term outdoor education and toward the use of environmental education. This could indicate greater acceptance of the outdoors in meeting educational goals. There may be less need to justify out-of-school learning activities by distinguishing them with a separate term. It has been said that it takes at least fifty years for an innovation to become accepted into the education system. Total acceptance has not yet occurred but there are indications that school leaders are recognising the values of outdoor education. One very successful supplementary environmental and conservation education programme, Project WILD, makes use of indoor *and* outdoor settings to '. . . assist learners of any age in developing awareness, knowledge, skills and commitment to result in informed decisions, responsible behaviour and constructive actions concerning wildlife and the environment upon which all life depends' (Western Regional Environmental Education Council 1986: vii). New outdoor-environmental education materials will continue to be integrated into existing curricula, rather than separate courses being created to reach the goals and objectives of the field. This infusion into several disciplines will increase the probability that outdoor-environmental education will remain in both private and public educational systems. Successful curricular innovations have always been characterised by carefully planned staff development strategies. Two of the most widespread environmental education programmes, Project WILD and Project Learning Tree, require that the teacher guides be distributed only through leadership workshops. Another trend is increased networking among professionals involved with the various approaches to the field. For example, the Conservation Education Association, the North American Association for Environmental Education, and the American Nature

Study Society have co-operated in holding joint meetings and other projects. Eventually these separate organisations may join and co-ordinate their efforts to a greater degree. Other indicators of co-operative networking efforts in the field are the Coalition for Education in the Outdoors (Department of Recreation and Leisure Studies, State University of New York, Cortland, NY 130450) and the Alliance for Environmental Education (Box 1040, 3421 M Street, NW Washington, DC 20007). Both of these 'organisations of organisations' are attempting to assist the diverse outdoor-environmental groups in communicating and co-ordinating their efforts.

As cities grow larger and technology increases, outdoor experiences are bound to become more popular. Schools will become increasingly aware of the potential of out-of-classroom learning as a motivational device for learning the basic subjects, as well as for educating youth for leisure activities.

Another trend is the recognition of the value of outdoor environments for learning human relations skills, building communities and achieving co-operation and even peaceful co-existence. Ecology will be viewed as including all humankind as well as other animals and plants in the biosphere. Humanity will be seen as integrally connected with the rest of the natural world and polluting the environment will be viewed as poisoning ourselves. The duality between 'man and nature' will gradually dissolve. Outdoor-environmental education will be fully integrated into the major disciplines and valued as necessary for quality living and survival on the planet. Perhaps some day in the future the existing professional terminology will disappear from educational jargon because the goals and objectives of present-day outdoor-environmental education will be fully accepted by society. Outdoor education in the United States is alive and well: our future is dependent upon its principles, methods, goals and objectives.

References

Charles, C.M., Gast, D.K., Servey, R.E. and Burnside, H.M. (1978) *Schooling, Teaching and Learning American Education*, C.V. Mosby, Saint Louis, USA.

Cornell, J.B. (1987) *Sharing Nature with Children*, Ananda Publications, Nevada City, California, USA.

—— (1987) *Listening to Nature: Daily Inspirational Quotations and Activities*, Dawn Publications, Nevada City, California, USA.

Disinger, J. (1983) 'Environmental Education's Definitional Problem', *ERIC Clearing House for Science, Mathematics and Environmental Education Information Bulletin* 2, Columbus, Ohio, USA.

Editor (1984) 'Camping's National Economic Estimate: Study discloses US has 11,200 Camps; Industry is $2.5 Billion Annually', *Camping Magazine*, May.

Eells, E. (1986), *History of Organised Camping: the first 100 years*, American Camping Association, Martinsville, Indiana, USA.

Fitzpatrick, C.N. (1968) 'Philosophy and Goals of Outdoor Education', Unpublished doctoral dissertation, Colorado State College, USA.

Ford, P.M. (1981) *Principles and Practices of Outdoor/Environmental*

Education, John Wiley, New York.

—— (1986) 'Outdoor Education: Definition and Philosophy', *ERIC Digest: Outdoor Education*, ERIC/CRESS, New Mexico State University, Las Cruces, USA.

Funderbunk, R.S. (1948) 'The History of Conservation Education in the United States', Unpublished doctoral dissertation, George Peabody Teachers College, Nashville, Tenn., USA.

Gibson, H.W. (1979) *The History of Organised Camping in the United States*, Reprinted with the permission of the American Camping Association by the Lorado Taft Field Campus of Northern Illinois University, Oregon, Illinois, USA.

Hammerman, D.R. (1961) 'A Historical Analysis of the Socio-cultural Factors that influenced the Development of Camping Education', Unpublished doctoral dissertation, Pennsylvania State, Institute of Education, USA.

Knapp, C.E. and Goodman, J. (1985) *Humanising Environmental Education: a Guide for Leading Nature and Human Nature Activities*, American Camping Association, Martinsville, Indiana, USA.

Minto, T.G. (1980) The History of the Nature-study Movement and its Role in the Development of Environmental Education', Unpublished doctoral dissertation, The University of Massachusetts, USA.

Olmsted, R.R. (1967) 'The Nature Study Movement in American Education', Unpublished doctoral dissertation, Indiana University, Bloomington, Ind., USA.

Sharp, L.B. (1947) 'Basic Considerations in Outdoor and Camping Education', *The Bulletin of the National Association of Secondary School Principals* 31.

Ulanoff, S.M. (1968) 'The Origins and Development of Organised Camping in the United States, 1901–61)', Unpublished doctoral dissertation, New York University, NY, USA.

Van Matre, S. (1972), *Acclimatization: A Sensory and Conceptual Approach to Ecological Involvement*, American Camping Association, Martinsville, Indiana, USA.

—— (1979) *Sunship Earth: an acclimatization programme for outdoor learning*, American Camping Association, Martinsville, Indiana, USA.

Vinal, W.G. (1926) *Nature Guiding*, Comstock Publishing, New York.

Western Regional Environmental Education Council (1986) *Project Wild: Elementary Education Guide*, WREEC, Boulder, Colorado, USA.

Wiener, M. (1965) 'Developing a Rationale for Outdoor Education', Unpublished doctoral dissertation, Michigan State University, USA.

3
Environmental Education

Annette Greenall Gough

Introduction

There are many similarities of interest between environmental education and outdoor education, and there are many misconceptions about the relationship between the two. The purpose of this chapter is to describe some aspects of the history of environmental education in Australia and to suggest some approaches to the incorporation of environmental education into the curriculum in ways which recognise its relationship with outdoor education.

What is Environmental Education?

The nature of environmental education has been the subject of much discussion and debate over the past two decades. Among the most commonly accepted goals, objectives and guiding principles for environmental education are those recommended and endorsed at the 1977 UNESCO-UNEP Intergovernmental Conference on Environmental Education in Tbilisi (UNESCO 1978) and subsequently re-endorsed at the 1987 UNESCO-UNEP International Congress on Environmental Education and Training in Moscow (UNESCO-UNEP 1988):

(1) The goals of environmental education are:
   (a) to foster clear awareness of, and concern about, economic, social political and ecological interdependence in urban and rural areas;
   (b) to provide every person with opportunities to acquire the knowledge, values, attitudes, commitment and skills needed to protect and improve the environment;
   (c) to create new patterns of behaviour of individuals, groups and society as a whole towards the environment.

(2) The categories of environmental education objectives:
   Awareness: to help social groups and individuals acquire an awareness of and sensitivity to the total environment and its allied problems.
   Knowledge: to help social groups and individuals gain a variety of experience in, and acquire a basic understanding of, the environment and its associate problems.
   Attitudes: to help social groups and individuals acquire a set of values and feelings of concern for the environment, and the motivation for actively participating in environmental improvement and protection.
   Skills: to help social groups and individuals acquire the skills for identifying and solving environmental problems.

41

Collaborating

Planning

> *Participation*: to provide social groups and individuals with an opportunity to be actively involved at all levels in working toward resolution of environmental problems. (UNESCO 1978: 26–27)

A version of these objectives was contained in *Environmental Education for Australian Schools* (Greenall 1980) which was distributed to all schools in 1980 as part of the Curriculum Development Centre's environmental education programme.

More recently, the Australian Association for Environmental Education (AAEE Inc. 1989) has described environmental education as:

an approach to learning that is useful to individuals and groups in coming to a better understanding of the inter-relationships between humans and environments. Environmental education encourages people to develop caring and committed attitudes that will foster the desire and ability to act responsibly in their relationships with environments. Thus, environmental education is concerned with knowledge, feelings, attitudes, skills and social action.

Rationale for Environmental Education: A Social Imperative

Early History

During the late 1960s and early 1970s, the mass media and popular authors, together with the scientific community, increasingly brought the threat of environmental degradation and the implications of human impact on the environment to the attention of the general public. Calls for a new ethic, based on an awareness of the inter-relationships between people and their environments, concern for the quality of the environment and commitment to the principle of environmental conservation, also drew attention to the need for education to develop a deeper and more effective environmental consciousness. For example, Ehrlich and Ehrlich criticised the 'almost total failure [of countries throughout the world] to prepare people to understand and make decisions relating to the population-environment crisis' (Ehrlich and Ehrlich 1972: 357). The environmental education movement grew out of this increased social awareness of environmental issues.

The term environmental education was first used in an official context in Australia at the Education and the Environmental Crisis national conference, which was convened by the Australian Academy of Science in April 1970. The purposes of the conference were to enquire into the extent to which education authorities, especially those in Australia, had responded to the perceived environmental crisis by introducing new educational programmes, and to promote an exchange of views about the responsibilities of educational institutions and the mass media towards the environment (Evans and Boyden 1970).

At this conference, O'Neill (1970) reported that environmental education in Australian schools was incidental and, in her opinion, totally inadequate. Some conservation education was included in primary school syllabuses and there was an increasing interest in ecology in biology syllabuses in secondary schools, but in no state was there any syllabus which had been designed specifically to increase environmental understanding and motivate students to become committed to environmental conservation and restoration. O'Neill argued that there was an urgent need for education authorities to assume a more positive role in response to the environmental crisis.

There was no immediate significant response to the conference from state education departments or teacher education institutions but, during the following years, a number of changes did occur within the various Australian education systems.

More Recent Developments

During the 1980s, environmental education has continued to be recognised as an essential component of the resolution of environmental problems.

In 1980 the International Union for the Conservation of Nature and Natural Resources (IUCN), together with the United Nations Environment Programme (UNEP) and the World Wildlife Fund (WWF), released the *World Conservation Strategy* (WCS). This document proposes three main objectives of living resource conservation:

— to maintain essential ecological processes and life-support systems
— to preserve genetic diversity
— to ensure the sustainable utilisation of species and ecosystems.

By its very existence, the WCS highlighted the continuing environmental crisis facing this planet and the need for action by all to resolve problems. The WCS is explicit about the role of education in achieving its objectives (IUCN 1980):

> Ultimately the behaviour of entire societies towards the biosphere must be transformed if the achievement of conservation objectives is to be assured. A new ethic, embracing plants and animals as well as people is required for human societies to live in harmony with the natural world on which they depend for survival and well-being. The long-term task of environmental education is to foster or reinforce attitudes and behaviours compatible with this new ethic.

This statement is important because it emphasises the role of environmental education in the formation of attitudes and behaviours. Environmental education is seen as being more than just increasing awareness and understanding about the environment.

The WCS urged each country to prepare and implement a national conservation strategy and this request was taken up by Australia. The WCS objectives, together with a fourth (to maintain and enhance environmental qualities), were adopted as the objectives of a National Conservation Strategy for Australia (NCSA) which was proposed by a national conference in 1983 and subsequently endorsed by the Commonwealth and most state and territory governments.

The NCSA listed education and training as the first priority national action for achieving its objectives and this was instrumental in raising hopes that the NCSA might provide 'a new direction, focus and hope for the future of environmental education in Australia' (Greenall 1985: 13) or, at least, a raised prominence for environmental education. However, some four years earlier, I had argued that environmental education had been subjected to incorporation within the existing hegemony of Australian schools in a neutralised form: the radical 'action' components of its aims had been deleted from school programmes while the less controversial cognitive and skill aims had been retained (Greenall 1981). The environmental education programmes encouraged by the NCSA are concerned with promoting 'an awareness of the inter-relationships between the elements of the life support systems and which encourage the practice of living resource conservation for sustainable development' (Department of Arts, Heritage and Environment 1984: 17). These statements do not explicitly support the attitudinal, behavioural and action-oriented aspects of environmental education.

Environmental education has also been given a prominent and more strongly worded place in the State Conservation Strategy for Victoria (1987), the Western Australian State Conservation Strategy (1987) and in a statement on the curriculum of South Australian schools (1987). Its role is also more clearly specified in all these documents.

The environmental education objectives of Victoria's conservation strategy are to increase community awareness and involvement in environmental matters, to promote a conservation ethic and encourage the adoption of environmentally responsible attitudes and life-styles and to ensure that the community has adequate opportunities for involvement in environmental decision-making.

The Western Australian strategy gives prominence to education, awareness and understanding. 'Fostering an environmental ethic through-out all sectors of the community' is seen as 'the most important aspect of the state strategy' (1987: 11).

The South Australian Education Department seeks 'to encourage schools to develop an environmental education orientation across the curriculum. It highlights 'the central importance to environmental education of the need to develop in students positive attitudes towards the environment ... [and] the need to develop the skills to enable students to take appropriate action in the interests of the environment' (1987: 2).

One of the most recent documents to describe the social imperative for environmental education is the report of the World Commission on Environment and Development (WCED). The Foreword by the Commission Chairman, Gro Harlem Brundtland (1987: xiv) gives education a vital role in achieving sustainable development:

> But first and foremost our message is directed towards people, whose well-being is the ultimate goal of all environment and development policies. In particular, the Commission is addressing the young. The world's teachers will have a crucial role to play in bringing this report to them.
>
> If we do not succeed in putting our message of urgency through to today's parents and decision-makers, we risk undermining our children's fundamental right to a healthy, life-enhancing environment. Unless we are able to translate our words into a language that can reach the minds and hearts of people young and old, we shall not be able to undertake the extensive social changes needed to correct the course of development.

There are a growing number of movements for such social change both in Australia and overseas. They stress an ecological way of looking at the world and broadly can be grouped under the heading of 'Green politics'. The Green movement in Australia, which has 'working towards a peaceful, sustainable and achievable future' (Hutton 1987) among its aims, recognises the importance of education in fostering an understanding of these issues, in changing human values and in developing a new world view in society. Green politics is a relatively recent development but it is a significant one, with relevance to, and with implications for, the future development of environmental education in schools.

The Current Status of Environmental Education in Australian Schools

The status of environmental education in Australian schools varies from state to state, from school to school and from teacher to teacher.

When environmental education first appeared on the educational agenda in the early 1970s, it was at the instigation of policy-makers outside the field of education itself and many educational bureaucrats did not see it as an educational priority: they saw the curriculum as already overcrowded and environmental education as being able to be catered for within existing areas. The situation seems hardly to have changed. In 1987 a New South Wales Department of Education officer (Cobbin 1987) noted that

> we all need to consider how we might best meet the challenge of changing teachers' attitudes towards environmental education in a climate where any perceived 'addition' is seen as a threat and regarded with hostility. I have a feeling that the environment movement is gaining momentum but that may not be enough to ensure willing acceptance to all schools.

While Cobbin was commenting on the situation in New South Wales, his observation that the whole formal education system seems to be lagging behind the environment movement in its involvement in environmental education appears to be true in other states and territories. The most recent overview of the state of current practices in environmental education in Australian schools comes from the proceedings of the Third National Environmental Education Seminar which was organised by the Commonwealth Department of Arts, Heritage and Environment in February 1987 (see also Greenall 1988).

Several states have environmental education policy statements of varying levels of prescription. The Western Australian policy statement from the Director-General of Education was issued in 1977 and this is still the basis for environmental education in that state. The South Australian policy statement referred to above seeks to raise awareness and to encourage schools to develop environmental education. In 1988, the New South Wales Higher Education Board released a document which established the parameters and goals of environmental education. The objectives outlined were based primarily on the earlier work of the Australian Curriculum Development Centre. The Queensland Department of Education first issued a policy statement in 1977, updating it in 1988. The Victorian Ministry of Education currently has a working party which is to make recommendations on the implementation of the State Conservation Strategy by the Ministry.

The Tasmanian Education Department states that it is 'very conscious of the needs of environmental education' (Greenall 1988: 56). Environmental education is supported in the Northern Territory through in-service education courses conducted by the Education Department and by the Conservation Commission, which has a teacher on its staff to prepare teaching materials. The Australian Capital Territory schools system is decentralised and some teachers offer environmental education programmes.

Most states and territories have field study centres or similar centres which assist teachers with out-of-school-grounds activities. Most also have government environment agencies and non-government environment groups which provide material and physical support for teachers on request. Several education systems also have nominated environmental education officers within their structures to assist teachers with developing and implementing environmental education programmes and activities.

Environmental Education in the Curriculum

Environmental education programmes occur in many places in the school curriculum. Their origins were in the scientific study of the environment through ecology. Subsequently, geography, social studies and outdoor education became involved, and nowadays it is possible to find programmes which are called environmental education in languages studies, music, media, history and many other areas.

Programmes have been introduced through

— the incidental provision of information in units organised around other topics
— activities integrated into subject areas traditionally associated with environmental matters
— using an environmental issue as an integrating theme for an interdisciplinary unit of work, drawing upon several subject areas
— the introduction of a separate subject

One trend in the developing practice of environmental education in schools has been for teachers to begin by teaching *about* the environment (usually in a classroom setting). They may then progress to teaching both about and *in* the environment, for example, by going outdoors to investigate environments through such activities as data collection. They may also progress to teaching *for* the environment, for example, by working with students on local environmental action projects (e.g. Malcolm 1988). A more radical 'ecopolitical pedagogy' which seeks to encourage learning *with* environments has also been suggested (see Gough 1987, 1989). However, teaching *for* the environment still seems to be uncommon and much encouragement is needed if more schools are to adopt this approach. The timidity of many teachers and schools in these matters is understandable (because environmental problems are invariably 'politically sensitive'), but their fears are often groundless (as is demonstrated in Malcolm 1988 and Robottom 1987).

The importance of the action component of environmental education programmes is now well recognised. For example, the South Australian Education Department (1987: 18) states that:

It is essential that the teaching approach selected leads the students to take action. Effective environmental education will not occur unless taking action happens as part of the learning process . . . This 'action' step is essential to the aims of environmental education since it seeks to generate the view that individuals and groups can change the course of events.

Such statements notwithstanding, observations to date indicate that while there has been an increase in student awareness of environmental problems and issues, there has not been a similar increase in active participation and practical problem-solving by students. Indeed, the increase in environmental awareness of students could well have been stimulated by sources other than schools.

The concept of the socially-critical school (Kemmis *et al.* 1983) is also relevant to the development and implementation of an action component for environmental education which, by its very nature, has a socially-

Figure 3.1 From Shallow Environmentalism to Deep Ecology

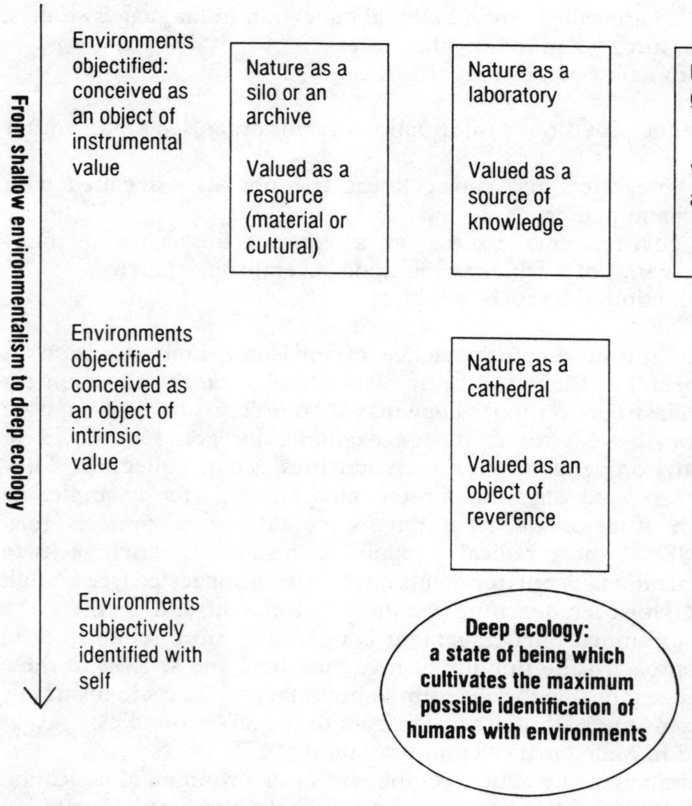

Source: Gough, N. (1989) 'Becoming Ecopolitical: Some Mythic Links in Curriculum Renewal', Paper presented to the Annual Meeting of the American Educational Research Association, San Francisco, USA, 27-31 March.

critical orientation. It is concerned with engaging students in social problems, tasks and issues and giving them experience in working on them, i.e., experience in critical reflection, social negotiation and the organisation of action, both individually and collectively. Such experiences must be an integral part of student learning: education must engage students in social practices and social structures immediately and not merely prepare them for later participation.

One example of an environment educational practice which embodies many of these characteristics is Earth Education. Earth Education aims to help learners 'to build a sense of relationship — through both feeling and understanding — with the natural world' and 'to interact more directly with the fascinating array of living things around them' (Van Matre 1979: 5–7). The activities encourage the development of sensory awareness and ecological concept-building, but more as tools for perceiving and searching the natural environment than as abstractions. They strive for the 'big picture' in understanding life. Earth Education explicitly rejects the 'shallow environmentalism' of much conventional 'nature-study' and seeks instead to develop the kind of *identification* of humans with nature that has become known as 'deep ecology' (see Figure 3.1). The most recent Earth Education programme, Earthkeepers, also contains a personal action components: participants must reflect and act on their personal practices to lessen their impact on the earth before they can complete the programme. This programme is described in the following case study.

Case Study: Earthkeepers

Introduction
Earthkeepers is one of several programmes developed by the Institute for Earth Education (IEE) and is suitable for use with primary school students.

An Earthkeeper is described as 'a person who has a special relationship — in both feelings and understandings — with the earth and its life'.

In the Earthkeeper's programme, students, both children and adults, undertake a number of activities towards earning K, E, Y and S keys and beads. K activities are concerned with *knowledge*: all living things on the earth are connected. E activities are concerned with *experience*: getting in touch with the earth is a good feeling. Y activities focus on *yourself*: your actions on the earth makes a difference. S activities are *sharing* tasks: helping others improve their relationship with the earth is an urgent task.

The activities are designed to teach the concepts of cycling, energy flow, inter-relationships and change, and to make students more aware of their own impact on the environment. The aims of the programme are to help students become Earthkeepers who

—understand how all life on the earth is tied together
—spend time outside in touch with the natural world
—try to do things that won't harm the systems of life and try not to do things that will harm other living things
—tell others about the importance of understanding and enjoying the natural world we share

In late 1988 the Melbourne and Metropolitan Board of Works (MMBW) staff at the Dandenong Valley Metropolitan Park ran a pilot three-day programme of Earthkeepers with local Year 6 children. The children visited the park three times, each visit being a week apart. Students earned their K and E keys during these activities (which made them 'apprentice Earthkeepers') and their Y and S keys and first bead through follow-up activities at school and at home, thus becoming 'Earthkeepers Level 1'.

The Case Study School

I followed the activities of one class of twenty-seven Year 6 students with their teacher from Jells Park Primary School. Two of the Year 6 teachers from the school had volunteered to undertake the programme as part of their Term 4 activities. The students came from a variety of ethnic backgrounds and had varying amounts of past experiences with the natural environment.

The Earthkeepers programme was conducted at the Earthkeepers Training Centre in Shepherds Bush, an area of the MMBW Park not far from the school (indeed several of the students told me that they rode their bikes through the area at weekends even though they knew that bike-riding was prohibited in this particular area).

The Programme

Day 1 of the programme started with an opening ceremony in 'E.M.'s Lab'. This is a magical place which is central to the programme. Here the programme was explained to the students and they received their Earthkeepers training manuals and diaries.

Following this introduction the students undertook two activities concerned with knowledge and with developing the concepts of energy flow and cycling. They also had an opportunity to discover and adopt their own 'magic spot' and start writing in their Earthkeepers diary. These activities captured the interest of the majority of students, including several who were usually regarded as inattentive in class: the magic seemed to be working. At the end of Day 1 the students who had successfully completed the two activities (all had, of course) received their first key (K) back in E.M.'s laboratory and opened the K box to learn the first meaning of E.M. This generated much excitement amongst even the cynical students.

On Day 2 of the programme the students continued their knowledge activities and learned of the concepts of inter-relationships and change. They also started on their E key activities by revisiting their magic spots to write in their diaries and by following a trail from E.M.'s diary. Some of the magic generated on Day 1 had been lost from the group by the end of Day 2. This could have been because the students had had a week to discuss among themselves what they thought E.M. meant, and whether or not E.M. was 'real', rather than the mystery continuing on successive days. Unfortunately some inattentiveness again arose among those who were so inclined, which was a disruptive influence on some of the other students.

Day 3 continued the experiential activities with an 'Earth Walk' to heighten observation skills. Sadly, some more magic had been lost in the intervening week and several students did not get into the spirit of this activity. Students who had successfully completed the E activities then received their E keys and learned another meaning of E.M. through opening the E box in E.M.'s laboratory. Once again they all received a key, which rekindled some of the excitement of the programme. After lunch the students were told about what they had to do to receive their Y and S keys. They decided which activities they would undertake to lessen their impact on the earth and deepen their feelings about it (to earn a Y key) and what knowledge and experience, gained in the programme, they would share to earn their S keys. They then pledged to complete these Y and S tasks back in class and at home over the following month.

At this stage, I interviewed the teachers and students about their impressions of the Earthkeepers programme. Overall, they were very positive. Both the Year 6 teachers commented that the students had enjoyed the experience and gained a better appreciation of nature and simple things, as well as improving their observation and social developmental skills. They thought the programme was suitable for Years 5 or 6, but would prefer to do it at the beginning of Year 6 rather than at the end, which they intended to do in subsequent years.

Students' comments included that they thought it was 'different' and 'fun' to do the activities by 'doing, not just listening'. Other comments included that they 'learned about the bush', 'wouldn't normally visit [these areas]', 'enjoyed the quiet atmosphere', 'looked at things from a different point of view' and 'liked being outdoors'. Many enjoyed the 'suspense of the boxes' and 'getting the keys', and the 'good feelings' of the magic spots. They would have liked more freedom to explore the bush on their own and did not like the 'veil of silence' which was invoked in some of the activities.

One month later I revisited the class to observe how they had progressed with completing their Y and S tasks as pledged back at the Earthkeepers Training Centre. Approximately half the class had completed them and were excited to receive their keys and bead and learn the last two meanings of E.M. Several of those who had completed the tasks were interested in continuing with other Earthkeepers activities at the park during the school holidays. Those who had not completed their pledges had a variety of reasons for not doing so, ranging from the unfortunate occurrences such as illness to scepticism about the whole exercise (the latter viewpoint being in the minority). However, given a second chance of gaining their keys the next day, several of the students promised to complete the tasks before then.

It was interesting to note the difference between the case study class and the other Year 6 class in the same school. There was an obvious difference in the level of teacher motivation in that only a quarter of the students in the other class had completed their pledges. There is an obvious need for teachers to reinforce the programme back in the classroom and, as several of the Y activities require behavioural changes at home, it would help if parents were also familiar with the programme.

Overall the programme must be gauged a success in that half the class being studied had maintained their interest in the programme and completed the activities, including some in their own time. There are some changes which could be made to add to its success, such as running it on successive days rather than over three weeks, but overall both the teacher and the students gained from it.

Conclusion

Contrary to much of its development to date, the objectives of environmental education are concerned with active (attitude and action-oriented) rather than passive (knowledge-oriented) education. While much education that occurs *in* the environment is concerned primarily with increasing student awareness and knowledge, it is possible for these experiences to also encourage attitudes and actions which are *for* the environment and to encourage students to learn *with* environments. Much depends on how humans conceive of their inter-relationships with nature. Five views of these inter-relationships are depicted in Figure 3.1.

Many conventional approaches to environmental education in classrooms treat nature as a silo or an archive, the contents of which are resources of knowledge. Education outside classrooms has frequently treated nature as a gymnasium or a laboratory in which exercises and investigations are to be conducted. These approaches conceive of nature as an object of instrumental value: something to be used. There are also forms of outdoor activity and education in which nature is conceived as an object of intrinsic value to be treated with reverence: a cathedral in which to worship, its contents sacred and therefore to be preserved.

Recent developments such as the World Conservation Strategy, but more particularly the report of the World Commission on Environment and Development, and the growth of Green political movements, have emphasised the need for a new approach to the environment, a new ethic which cultivates the identification of humans with their environments. The contemporary challenge for environmental education and outdoor education is to design learning programmes in which such identification is a credible and realistic outcome.

References

Australia, Department of Arts, Heritage and Environment (1984) *A National Conservation Strategy for Australia*, Australian Government Publishing Service, Canberra.

— (1987) *Environmental Education — Past, Present and Future*, Proceedings of the Third National Environmental Education Seminar and Workshops, Australian Government Publishing Service, Canberra.

Australian Association for Environmental Education Inc. (1989) Membership brochure.

Cobbin, A. (1987) 'Release of environmental policy', *Greenscene*, September.

Ehrlich, P.R. and Ehrlich, A.H. (1972) *Population/Resources/Environment: Issues in Human Ecology*, Freeman, San Francisco, USA.

Evans, J. and Boyden, S. (eds) (1970) *Education and the Environmental Crisis*, Australian Academy of Science, Canberra.

Gough, N. (1987) 'Learning with Environments: Towards an Ecological Paradigm for Education' in I. Robottom (ed.) *Environmental Education: Practice and Possibility*, Deakin University Press, Geelong.

— (1989) 'Becoming Ecopolitical: Some Mythic Links in Curriculum Renewal', Paper presented to the Annual Meeting of the American Educational Research Association, San Francisco, USA, 27–31 March.

Greenall, A. (1980), *Environmental Education for Schools*, Curriculum Development Centre, Canberra.

— (1981), *Environmental Education in Australia: Phenomenon of the Seventies*, a Case Study in National Curriculum Development, Curriculum Development Centre, Canberra.

— (1985), 'A New Beginning for Environmental Education in Australia', *Australian Journal of Environmental Education* 1 (2): 13–15.

— (1987), 'A Political History of Environmental Education in Australia: Snakes and Ladders' in I. Robottom (ed.), *Environmental Education: Practice and Possibility*, Deakin University Press, Geelong.

— (1988) 'Environmental Education' in T. Hundloe and R. Neumann (eds), *Environmental Practice in Australia*, Environment Institute of Australia Inc. with the Institute of Applied Environmental Research, Griffith University, Brisbane.

Hutton, D. (ed.) (1987) *Green Politics in Australia*, Angus and Robertson, Sydney.

Institute for Earth Education (1987) *Earthkeepers Training Manual*, The Institute for Earth Education, Warrenville, Ill., USA.

International Union for the Conservation of Nature and Natural Resources (IUCN) (1980) *World Conservation Strategy*, IUCN, Gland.

Kemmis, S., Cole, P. and Suggett, D. (1983) *Orientations to Curriculum and Transition: Towards the Socially-critical School*, Victorian Institute of Secondary Education, Melbourne.

Malcolm, S. (1988) *Local Action for a Better Environment*, Penguin, Ringwood.

O'Neill, B. (1970) 'Environmental Education in Australian Schools' in J. Evans and S. Boyden (eds), *Education and the Environmental Crisis*, Australian Academy of Science, Canberra.

Robottom, l. (ed.) (1987) *Environmental Education: Practice and Possibility*, Deakin University Press, Geelong.

South Australia Education Department (1987) *Environmental Education*, Adelaide.

UNESCO (1978) *Intergovernmental Conference on Environmental Education, Tbilisi (USSR), October 1977: Final Report*, Paris.

UNESCO-UNEP (1988) *International Strategy for Action in the Field of Environmental Education and Training for the 1990s*, Congress on Environmental Education and Training, Moscow, Paris and Nairobi.

Van Matre, S. (1979) *Sunship Earth: An Acclimatization Program for Outdoor Learning*, American Camping Association, Martinsville, Indiana, USA.

Victoria (1987) *Protecting the Environment: A Conservation Strategy for Victoria*, Melbourne.

Western Australia Department of Conservation and Environment (1987) *A State Conservation Strategy for Western Australia*, Bulletin 270, Perth.

World Commission on Environment and Development (1987) *Our Common Future*, Oxford University Press, Oxford.

4
Adventure Education

Bruce Hayllar

Introduction

For many educators the term adventure education conjures up images of students climbing vertical rock faces, careering down sharply inclined ropes (the 'flying fox' or 'zip wire'), or being tossed around in a bucking canoe by torrents of white surging foam. Simultaneously, and quite appropriately, it may foster other images and promote serious questioning. What have such activities got to do with the processes and practices of formal education? What educational objectives do they purport to meet? Why expend staff time, money and resources to undertake such activities? What about the risk, insurance and legal liability?

As well as addressing such issues, this chapter defines the term adventure education and develops a rationale for its inclusion as a legitimate and important part of outdoor education. Guidelines are provided for educators who wish to make their students' experiences in the outdoors more adventurous and the chapter concludes with a case study to illustrate the processes and practices of an adventure programme.

What is Adventure Education?

Adventure education is not easily defined. Many educators use the term interchangeably with other forms of outdoor educational experience and thus it has gained currency through common usage rather than as a particular form or type of educational practice. For example, the nature walk or field trip of a group of primary school children can be perceived as adventurous and indeed promoted as such by the teacher in an attempt to create interest or to make particular teaching points. In this particular educational experience the notion of adventure is usually less important than other educational objectives. Conversely, the type of activities outlined in the opening paragraph, where adventure is central to learning, contain opportunities for other educational outcomes to be achieved through the adventure experience. What, then, are the unique qualities of adventure education?

As has been historically the case with outdoor education, a universal definition of adventure education is problematic. It has been argued that all outdoor pursuits should be considered as adventure education and, to an extent, this position is defensible. 'Adventure' according to the *Macquarie Dictionary* is defined as 'participation in exciting undertakings and enterprises'. Accordingly, it could be argued that any well taught and structured outdoor programme could be defined as adventurous.

The dictionary, however, qualifies the term further: 'an undertaking of uncertain outcome; a hazardous enterprise, to take the chance; to dare; to take the risk involved'. Adventure in this sense goes beyond mere participation and introduces the dimensions of risk-taking and uncertainty. In adventure education programmes, risk-taking and the creation of hazard and uncertainty are deliberately incorporated within the educational objectives of the activity. Adventure education is thus conceptualised as an outdoor education programme 'that contains elements of real or apparent danger, in which the outcome while uncertain can be influenced by the actions of participants' (Ewart 1980: 2). Thus *perceptions of danger*, *risk* and *personal responsibility for outcomes* are inherent qualities of adventure education.

The Beginnings of Adventure Education

The practical origins of adventure education are in the work of the German educator Kurt Hahn, and his involvement in the development of the Salem School in Germany, Gordonstoun in Scotland and, arguably his most significant contribution, the founding of Outward Bound. On the other hand, the theoretical foundations are closely linked to the work of John Dewey, the American educationalist and philosopher.

Dewey was one of the earliest and most articulate proponents of an education based on experience. In Dewey's view, experience is necessary for real learning to take place. Only through experience, he argued, are individuals provided with the opportunity to develop original thoughts. In a powerful statement of his position (Dewey 1970: 27–28), he claimed that:

> No thought, no idea can possibly be conveyed as an idea from one person to another. When it is told, it is another given fact, not an idea. The communication may stimulate the other person to realise the question for himself and to think out a like idea, or it may smother his intellectual interest and suppress his dawning effort of thought. But what he directly gets cannot be an idea. Only by wrestling with the conditions at first hand, seeking and finding his own way out, does he think.

Dewey was also concerned with the methods and techniques of an education based on experience. In a cautionary note, a caution that has not been heeded sufficiently by many educators, he pointed out that an experience is not in itself sufficient to achieve the objectives of experiential education. The important variable for Dewey was the way in which the methods and techniques of the experiences were structured to provide a meaningful basis for future learning. For Dewey, the craft of the teacher in experiential learning situations lies in their ability to structure and interpret the experience with and for their students.

Hahn's approach to education parallels that of Dewey. However, his objectives for learning focus on what he called the 'Six Declines' which he considered were not being addressed by current schools-based education (Richards 1985: 9):

(1) A decline in fitness
(2) A decline in initiative and enterprise
(3) A decline in memory and imagination
(4) A decline in skill and care
(5) A decline in self-discipline
(6) A decline in compassion

His concern for the need to address these declines ultimately resulted in the establishment of the archetypal adventure programme, Outward Bound. Before this Hahn had, in the 1920s, been the Principal of an experimental 'modern' school in Germany, under the patronage of Prince Max of Baden, the East German Imperial Chancellor. He wanted to establish a school which had development of the self as its underlying principle. He believed that 'the aim of education is to impel people into value forming experiences . . . [and] to ensure the survival of these qualities: an enterprising curiosity; and undefeatable spirit; tenacity in pursuit; readiness for sensible self-denial and, above all, compassion' (Colorado Outward Bound 1981: 3).

In the early 1930s Hahn moved from Germany to Britain where his vision captured the imagination of influential British educators, and attracted the financial support needed to establish Gordonstoun. The Gordonstoun Programme provided a model for similar schools throughout the British Commonwealth, including Geelong Grammar's Timbertop in north-eastern Victoria.

The onset of World War II provided the inspiration for turning an experimental school into a world-wide movement. Laurence Holt, the owner of a merchant shipping line transporting war materials across the Atlantic, had become increasingly concerned at the losses of seamen following submarine attacks on his ships. A peculiar pattern emerged which puzzled him. Why was it that the older men in the ship's company had greater rates of survival than the younger and, logically, more physically able? Holt reasoned that because the young men had not previously been exposed to situations in which they had to face up to extreme hardship, i.e., to test their character against the elements, they were unaware of their inner strengths and ability to continue when all appeared lost. He argued that if Hahn's school could train men, both physically and psychologically to endure hardships and to overcome fear it would enhance their chances of survival. The first graduates of Hahn's Outward Bound School attested to the accuracy of Holt's thesis. From this beginning arose a world-wide movement of thirty-two schools.

Outward Bound is one example of the many adventure education programmes conducted world-wide. In Australia, adventure education principles are incorporated into the educational curricula of schools in all states and fulfil a diverse range of purposes and educational objectives. It is an interesting educational irony that the private school sector, which historically has been associated with educational 'basics' is the leading proponent of outdoor adventure education, a 'frill' in the eyes of many others.

A Rationale for Adventure Education

While the ideas of Hahn and Dewey have been incorporated into the curricula of a number of school-based programmes, there is still a need to more fully develop a rationale for adventure education. In what ways is an education based on adventurous experience justifiable in terms of its methods and outcomes? In response to this question, two specific areas for discussion emerge:

—the holistic nature of adventure education, and
—the role of adventure education as a vehicle for personal and social development and leisure education

Adventure Education as a Holistic Educational Process

Adventure education is holistic in approach in that it attempts to have an impact upon each of the behavioural domains which influence human growth and development: psychomotor, cognitive and affective. The potential for adventure education to make an impact on each of these is discussed below.

Psychomotor Impacts

Psychomotor or physical impacts relate to physical fitness (aerobic capacity, strength, flexibility and endurance) and to physical co-ordination.

Bushwalking

While all adventure education programmes should be developed according to the age and experience of the group, their demanding nature invariably requires some individual physical commitment. A walk through undulating bushland, a wade through a creek, a cross-country ski tour or an arduous rock climb, all demand varying levels of physical fitness and preparation.

Skiing

Rafting

Indeed, for some adventure programmes, the attainment of high levels of physical fitness may be an integral part of the curriculum. For example, it may be the psychological spur that encourages students to undertake a particular adventure. Furthermore, it may test students' levels of commitment to a programme: a certain level of fitness might be required before attendance is permitted. Finally, fitness may be a key element of a programme where health education/preventive health objectives are developed as part of the rationale for the adventure experience. Thus, a programme may contain mechanisms to establish an individual's current health status, the establishment of a training regimen, and a post-programme health and fitness assessment to ascertain changes over the programme's duration.

Adventure activities might also be used to develop psychomotor skills. Students' co-ordination might be improved by paddling a canoe or tying (and untying!) knots. Balance might be similarly improved through rock-climbing.

Two additional values of the physical aspect of adventure education relate to:

—the levelling nature of the activities. Thus, a student who may have had limited success in the past with physical (particularly sporting) activities has the opportunity to succeed in pursuits that in the main require no previous experience or particular physical attributes
—the non-sexist nature of the activities. In general terms, males are no better equipped physically to undertake adventure education programmes than females. Experience has often shown adventure programmes to be a humbling experience to a formerly macho male

Cognitive Impacts

The cognitive aspects of adventure education are an integral part of the learning process at all levels. Once the objectives of the programme are established, by the teacher and by students as they mature and gain experience and skills, attempts should be made to incorporate students at all levels of programme planning. For example, if a lengthy expedition entailing a number of nights away from home is to be incorporated, students should be involved at all stages of the decision-making process: planning, expedition and evaluation. What to take; how much to take; who will take what; which route to follow; how we get to there and home; where to camp; and what emergency procedures will be followed, are all matters for consideration and decision. Ultimately, the success of any programme will largely be determined by how effectively such questions are answered.

In terms of student interest, it is the immediacy of feedback and its relationship to 'survival' needs which gives adventure education its potential for cognitive development. Students experience the outcome of their efforts in a personal and meaningful way. For example, if inadequate preparation has gone into a bushwalking expedition, this lack of preparation becomes immediately obvious. There will be blisters because of poor foot-wear (or care), overtiredness through inadequate route-planning or physical preparation, and so on.

This notion of 'action: consequence' is a central theme of adventure education. While teachers may discuss with their students the need for adequate planning and the possible outcomes of poor preparation, the consequences of their not heeding such advice are not always apparent, particularly in the short term, in other forms of education. In an appropriately planned adventure education curriculum, however, consequences of action are immediate and relevant. Moreover, students cannot avoid accepting responsibility for such consequences. After all, it is their actions—or lack of them—which precipitate outcomes. The food may run out; they may have planned to walk too far; inadequate consideration may have been given to individual differences within the group; or an inappropriate camp-site may have been chosen. In each case, a lack of preparation and *their actions*, have consequences for which they must accept responsibility. Part of the craft of teaching through adventure is to ensure that students are given the opportunity to make meaningful decisions and thus are forced into the action: consequence framework, as illustrated below.

Figure 4.1   Action-Consequence Paradigm: A Theoretical Example

Action	Consequence
Inadequate:	
planning of nutritional needs and quantities	Hunger
planning of daily route	Exhaustion, Blisters
attention to individual differences	Loads too heavy for smaller group members
consideration of camp-site selection	Wet weather washes out two tents

On a cautionary note, it is essential that students are involved in decision-making processes only to the extent that their knowledge and skills has equipped them. Students should be involved in decision-making from the early primary years and gradually given more responsibility. The ultimate aim is to give them as much responsibility as possible. However, teachers need to remain aware that ultimate responsibility rests with those in authority.

Affective Impacts

The affective or emotional outcomes of adventure education have attracted considerable research interest. Affective outcomes generally revolve around the terms self-concept or self-esteem.

Self-concept refers to the ideas and attitudes we have about ourselves at any particular time. The acquisition of this self-concept is a continual process of defining and redefining our attitudes towards ourselves based upon our stage of development, environment and social situation. Thus, our self-concept is not static but is subject to change throughout our lives. According to Frost (1973: 35), the ideal self-concept is difficult to define but it 'must include a reasonable degree of self-confidence, enough self-esteem so that no-one is overwhelmed with feelings of guilt or inadequacy, and a knowledge that one is liked and respected by peers, teachers, parents and the many others with whom he comes into contact'. Experiential learning and the nature of the adventure experience can be powerful vehicles for developing this self-concept.

Perceived risk and/or danger are factors which give adventure education its unique character and distinguish it from other forms of outdoor education programming. At the core of a perceived risky or dangerous experience is the notion of stress. Stress in itself is a neutral term and may be of two types: eustress (or positive stress) and distress (or negative stress). The adventure educator's goal should be to promote situations that invoke positive stress-related experiences that, in a cumulative way, cause the individual to re-assess his or her particular view of him or herself. It is part of the art of teaching to make situations sufficiently challenging and stressful, to confront without defeating the individual, so that positive images of the self are enhanced. The experience has to be organised so that stress can be met, challenged and conquered in a sequential manner from its outset of the programme to its completion. Harris (1980: 159) calls this progression a spiralling of experiences. He notes:

> Decision-making plays an important role in one's involvement in risk-taking situations . . . After each new risk-taking experience, the calculated risks change as one increases in experience and confidence. As one increases . . . experience and frame of reference, the basis for making decisions and the trade-offs keep shifting . . . it takes more risks and greater risks as one's experience, expertise and confidence develop.

Maslow's work on self-actualisation and its potential for changing self-concept dovetails with the affective benefits of adventure education. Self-actualisation, or personality integration, is concerned with maximising the development of the individual. According to Maslow (cited in Graham and Klar 1979: 10):

> . . . every human being has two sets of forces within him. One set clings to safety and defensiveness out of fear, tending to regress backwards, hanging on to the past, afraid to jeopardise what he already has, afraid of independence, freedom and separateness. The other set of forces impels him forward toward wholeness of Self and uniqueness of Self toward full functioning of all his capacities, toward confidence in the face of the external world . . .

For Maslow, 'peak experiences' are vehicles for self-actualisation and are keys to self-discovery and awareness. Clearly, adventure education provides the opportunity for 'peak experiences' to be built into a programme at levels which are commensurate with the age, experience and expertise of students.

In this section, attention has been focused on providing an educational and philosophic framework for adventure education. Unlike classroom approaches which tend to focus on particular aspects at particular times, adventure education, integrates all aspects of learning, as depicted in Figure 4.2.

Figure 4.2   Conceptualisation of Adventure Education

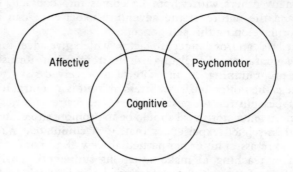

Planning for Adventure

Like all outdoor experiences, adventure education programmes require planning to ensure the effective conduct of the activities, the safety of the participants and staff and, ultimately, the realisation of programme objectives. However, in adventure programming, the degree of commitment to planning, staff selection, training and expertise, and student welfare have to meet the highest professional standards. While human nature and the outdoor environment are dynamic entities, thorough preparation at all levels can, to a large degree, minimise the apparent and real dangers of the programmed activities. The skill of the planner, and the delivery of the planned product through effective teaching, are central to ensuring that the inherent values of adventure are maintained without jeopardising the welfare of individuals or, ultimately, of adventure education itself.

Establishing Objectives

The objectives of an adventure education programme typically focus on personal and social development. Outward Bound (USA) (Colorado Outward Bound 1981: 4), for example, identifies its role in the following terms:

> To broaden enthusiasm for and understanding of self, others, and the environment. To enhance interpersonal communication and co-operation.

Their objectives are stated as follows:

—*Personal Development*: To extend the individual's self-awareness by identifying his personal limits, by clarifying his needs and goals and by helping him to recognise his role in society and to acknowledge a responsibility to himself and others. To have fun.

—*Interpersonal Effectiveness*: To expand the students' capacity for responding to others, to encourage open and effective communications, and to construct co-operative relationships around common projects, involvements and commitments.

—*Environmental Awareness*: To enhance students' understanding of the fragile nature of wild areas and to increase their sense of responsibility for their care and preservation.

—*Learning*: To create and maintain an environment and an attitude in which the emphasis is on experimentation and participation in experiential learning. To provide training in the skills essential to living and travelling in the mountains.

—*Philosophy and Values*: To provide situations and experiences in which the students can test and refine their personal values and which will stimulate them to examine and articulate their basic beliefs.

Harmon (1974) attempted to operationalise the broad objectives of Outward Bound by identifying specific observable behaviours which could be measured. Three broad areas were reported (psychomotor, cognitive and affective) and criterion objectives were developed for each. For example, the following criterion objectives were specifically developed for the affective domain (adapted from Harmon 1974):

Affective Objectives: Improvement in attitudes and values
(1) *Increased sense of personal worth and self-confidence*
    —Student willingly attempts previously untried experiences
    —Student willingly admits mistakes
    —Student accepts leadership and responsibility
    —Student accepts responsibility for his/her own actions
(2) *Improved interpersonal communications*
    —Student tries to resolve conflicts with others
    —Student shows concern for others' feelings
    —Student is willing to try another's ideas and/or adopt their plan of action
    —Student willingly recognises achievements of others
(3) *Improved group interaction skills*
    —Student is honest and open in his/her relationship to members of the group
    —Student listens to other points of view

While these objectives are specific they do clarify the kinds of behaviour which are anticipated and will be encouraged. The clear specifications of personal and social development objectives and of objectives involving outdoor skills, will help teachers develop effective adventure education programmes. Teachers are also encouraged to incorporate other objectives, including those relating to leisure education, into their programmes.

Caulfield Grammar in Victoria has developed a programme which illustrates how the various components of outdoor education can be integrated. Their objectives may be summarised as follows (adapted from Whitford, undated):

(1) *Personal and Social Development*
    —Helping an individual to become an integrated, contributing group member

—by working in small groups in which each individual needs to contribute

—by the provision of a variety of situations that involve group problem-solving and group interaction

—through the satisfying feelings of overcoming a difficult challenge

—by creating opportunities for group decision-making

—The development of trust, responsibility and self-motivation
  —by trusting students with real responsibilities
  —by the provision of situations that are free from staff supervision
  —by giving appropriate recognition for effort and diligence

—The development of the personal qualities necessary to overcome physical, mental, emotional and social challenges
  —by creating a positive atmosphere
  —by providing goals that extend the students, but which are achievable
  —through the satisfaction of hard-earned achievement

—Practice in decision-making, leadership and communication

(2) *Outdoor Skills*
  —The provision of the outdoor skills, knowledge and procedures to handle the particular challenges of the adventure activities, the Upper Yarra environment, and the winter weather
(3) *Environmental Education*
  —Experience in, and understanding of, winter farming
(4) *Inter-Curricular*
  —An introduction to local history

In establishing the framework for adventure education, it must be remembered that outdoor skills are considered as tools or means through which the other objectives may be realised and that they are not ends in themselves.

Sites for Adventure Education

The type of residential sites outlined in Chapter 9 may provide suitable venues and facilities for adventure education programmes. However, the level of physical infrastructure necessary will be largely determined by the design of the programme itself. The mobile concept, in which students are continually moving and living in tents, negates the need for a developed site. In school programmes it is more usual to have basic washing and cooking facilities at either a school-owned or leased site. The most important site consideration is the availability of a physical environment which provides the opportunity for the programme to be fully developed.

Urban or school-based environments may be useful in the training phases of an adventure programme. Some schools, for example Narrabundah College in Canberra, have climbing walls which can be used to practise climbing skills. Project Adventure in Hamilton, Massachusetts, USA, a leading proponent of adventure programmes for high school children, has produced a booklet on the construction of indoor ropes courses to facilitate urban adventures (High Profile 1981). In Britain, the Coventry Intermediate Treatment Association, an adventure programme working with young offenders, conducts its canoeing programme on the old industrial canals that weave their way through the Victorian back streets of the city (Sanders 1986). Thus, while the qualities of specific wilderness environments provide unique opportunities for adventure experiences, it is possible to develop adventure programmes in urban environments.

Programme Design

Programme design will largely depend on the objectives established and the human and physical resources available to meet them. Caulfield and Knox Grammars, for example, have both permanently employed outdoor education staff and operate well-established outdoor education centres which allow considerable flexibility. In school-based centres there is also the potential to make the programme cumulative over several years. This extended process is evident in Caulfield's programme which commences in Year 4 and progresses through to Year 10.

Whether the programme is to be a single experience or more long term, the principles of design remain fundamentally the same.

Selection of Activities

Adventure activities generally come from those groups identified by Darst and Armstrong (1980) as of medium and high-risk. Medium-risk activities are those which, while inherently dangerous, may be accomplished relatively safely with good leadership, instruction and training. Activities in this group would include bushwalking, flat water canoeing, cross-country skiing (day trips), low-level ropes course, estuarine or river sailing, cross-country orienteering and horse trekking. High-risk activities involve greater inherent dangers and, therefore, a heightened potential for threatening an individual's safety and well-being. Among this group would be included rock-climbing, mountaineering, white-water canoeing/kayaking, caving, cross-country skiing (overnight), a high level ropes course, extended bushwalking trips and open ocean sailing.

Grading Experiences

While some programmes are advantaged by having students for extended periods of time (allowing for skill progression), all must seek to ensure that experiences are graded according to factors such as maturation, previous experience and emotional and physical development. Experiences must be introduced logically and sequentially to ensure that success is achievable and that subsequent activities build on these skills and successes. The successful grading of experiences from the easy to the hard, from the low to the high risk, from the physically easy to the physically demanding, from the cognitively simple to the cognitively complex, and from the led to the leader, is an important part of programme design.

The Challenging Experience

In concert with the above, adventure education programmes typically attempt to incorporate cumulative activity which seeks to call on those physical, cognitive, and affective resources of the individual developed and nurtured throughout them. Again the nature of this final experience or challenge will depend on the characteristics of the group. The final expedition of Outward Bound, where small groups, generally unaccompanied, are responsible for safely travelling on a pre-determined route for a given period, would be an example of this challenge phase. In other programmes, participants might be asked to complete a particular rock climb, a 'solo' experience (time alone in the bush for personal reflection), or the negotiation of a set of difficult rapids. Primary school-aged children could also be involved in culminative activities providing that these were appropriate to the group and individual students.

Reflection and Synthesis

All programmes should allow time for individual reflection, evaluation and feedback. This is arguably the most important element of the programme with students being helped to interpret and clarify their relationships with their leader and peers. As this period draws to an end, it must be conducted in such a way to ensure that there is an effective and satisfying conclusion for each individual. Priest (1987: 32) calls this 'processing' the experience. According to Priest:

> it is important to remember that processing is merely a guide to more effective learning; it is not learning in itself. The experience of the initiative activity teaches the group about change; the facilitator merely clarifies the teaching. Some basic processing techniques, within the questioning framework, include self-disclosure of each individual as desired, confronting issues, reflecting on the activity and actively listening to each group member in turn. Tools such as humour, touching, and paraphrasing all help to draw connections between the actual occurrences and the objectives for learning.

Staffing

Adventure education processes require those staff who lead the programme to have adequate levels of both 'soft' and 'hard' skills. Soft skills refer to attributes such as interpersonal communication, empathy and understanding. Hard skills refer to the technical competencies necessary to conduct the programme efficiently and effectively. Zook (1986) suggests that leaders of adventure education programmes must:

—want to see participants develop their potential in an many dimensions as possible

—be able to teach using guided discovery, open-ended questions, and teachable moments to draw out of people the resources they possess below the surface

—be sensitive to human needs and predicaments by identifying with people without losing rationality, and by providing support without becoming condescending

—be willing and able to address adverse group behaviour

—listen

—have the technical knowledge and skill to lead groups in adventure activities, while ensuring that the perceived high-risk elements are safe

—employ a working knowledge of the sciences of nature

—maintain a current understanding and interpretation of relevant environmental issues

—lean towards simplicity

—possess the common sense to reduce situations, circumstances and life in general to their more basic issues

Liability and Safety

The spectre of litigation is beginning to haunt Australian society as it has in the United States. Therefore, in organising any outdoor education experience (and perhaps more so in adventure activities), teachers must recognise that litigation is always a possibility if they are negligent in their planning or in their supervision of the students. Experience, however, suggests that litigation is unlikely if key guidelines are followed.

In a review of over 100,000 thousand cases involving physical activity, Van Der Smissen (1975) concluded that only one, boxing, has been considered by the US judicial system to be inherently dangerous. It has not been the activities themselves that have brought forth the litigation, but rather negligence. Negligence occurs when the duty to protect people from unreasonable risks has not been adequately performed. Van Der Smissen (p. 12) added:

> As far as the basic principles of negligence are concerned, there is no difference between an adventure activity and any other activity being conducted. The very same principles for conducting these activities apply to all types of activities.

In Australia we have no consolidated data on the incidence of accidents or injury to participants through their involvement in adventure activities. However, two US studies provide some data.

The National (US) Safety Network was established in 1984 to address a number of issues related to safety in the adventure education and adventure camping industry. Their 1985 report was based on the responses from 18 different programmes with a total of 373,266 participant/activity days. This volume of programming is the approximate equivalent of operating an adventure programme every day of the year while enrolling 1,000 students. A summary table of their data appears in Table 4.1.

Table 4.1   Injuries by Activity (1985)[1]

Activity	Participants	Staff	Total
Backpacking/Hiking	18	2	20
Initiative games	10	2	12
Sports	11	2	13
Ropes course	10	2	12
Swimming/Snorkelling	4	0	4
Cabin/Bunk	5	2	7
Rock-climbing	2	1	3
Travel to site	3	1	4
Animal handling	2	1	3
Camp-site cooking	3	2	5
Unplanned day	3	0	3
Canoeing/Kayaking	2	1	3
Rock-hopping	1	0	1
Bicycling	1	0	1
Machine-operation	0	1	1
Work crew	1	0	1
Skiing	2	0	2
Fishing	1	0	1
Totals	79	17	96[2]

[1]This table does not, of course, purport to compare risks associated with the listed activities
[2]Of this total, 62 were considered *serious* which is defined as: an injury which causes a person to abstain from more than one half day of programming, must be treated by a doctor, or causes long-term medical complications for the injured

Given that these figures report in absolute numbers only, a more accurate assessment can be gained by examining the number of accidents per number of participant/staff days, calculated as:

$$\frac{\text{No. of Serious Injuries}}{\text{Combined Participants/Staff Days}} = \text{Rate of Injury}$$

Using this formula, the overall reported serious injury rate for staff and students participating in adventure activities is 20 for every 100,000 days of participation. This method of calculation also allows for comparison of activities. For example, programmes with a 'traditional' sports component, while having the same number of serious injuries as courses with a ropes courses component, have an injury rate 22 times greater.

A 10-year safety study by Project Adventure (1982) on 116 high schools with ropes courses reported 78 injuries. Of these, 55 were minor bruises and contusions. The remaining 23 were more serious strains and breaks, the majority of which occurred on the low elements. Using total hours of participation as the calculation base, this translates to 5.13 injuries per 100,000,000 hours of participation. The author concluded by noting that (Rohnke 1982: 3):

> this survey covering approximately 175,000 students over 10 years confirms what we at Project Adventure have long believed: the Programme properly implemented, is as safe as, or safer than, other physical education programmes for youth.

The above reports, while to some extent limited, are encouraging in terms of the overall safety of adventure education activities. This record is largely attributable to the high standards of safety adopted by the majority of agencies working in adventure education. In order to maintain this record, to ensure the safety of the participants and ultimately, to limit the likelihood of litigation, Williams (in Golins 1980: 49–50) recommended the following:

(1) See that a thorough safety policy is drawn up and adopted. Make sure that everyone along the 'chain of command' is familiar with the document and see that it is implemented in the field.
(2) See that everyone on the staff understands what their responsibility is and that that responsibility is not static: that as conditions of an activity change so does the responsibility.
(3) See that the instruction proceeds in an appropriate progression. Instructors should be sufficiently skilled to make these judgements.
(4) The instructor or leader must always be alert to the participants to be able to judge accurately the capacity and capabilities of the participants as conditions change.
(5) It is essential that persons trained in the practice of first aid and emergency are present during all activities.
(6) The participants must be fully informed of and understand any risks to which they are exposed.
(7) Act professionally, or as the law states: 'as a reasonable and prudent professional'. One must accurately judge one's own competence in any activity area where one accepts a leadership role. This means that, if you accept the position as a rock-climbing instructor, you are saying that you know proper, safe, current practice in rock-climbing. In the event of an accident, the instructor's qualifications will certainly be called into question.
(8) Since most lawsuits of the type we are considering are based on negligence, it is negligence that must be avoided. This can be described as a breach of duty—such as not protecting the student from a foreseeable hazard. If the hazard is not foreseeable, it is not negligence.

Case Study: Camp Knox

Introduction

A residential centre is, of course, not an essential ingredient of an adventure education programme. There are certainly real advantages in being able to use different wilderness and other outdoor settings which have no buildings or facilities. Indeed, some outdoor/adventure educators prefer this alternative. Camp Knox is described here, because it offers a cohesive and long-term programme which, in spite of its limitations (and all programmes have limitations), could provide some inspiration to those who want to develop something similar—whether they have access to a comparable facility or intend to use diverse, non-residential settings.

Camp Knox is situated on the Hawkesbury River at Fisherman's Point north of Sydney. The site, which is water-accessible only, was first used for outdoor education purposes in the 1950s by Outward Bound for their Australian school. Outward Bound remained there until 1973 when they moved to their existing site near Tharwa in the ACT. The centre was then purchased by commercial operators who established 'Camp Hawkesbury' as a holiday camp for children. In 1974, the site was acquired by Knox Grammar School with the aim of extending and developing the education of their students. The actual camp is located on a small site, but adjoins the Marra Marra National Park and Crown Land reserves. The camp thus has the availability of both suitable water and land resources on which to conduct its programmes.

Objectives

In the preamble to the objectives of the programme, the following is noted:

> The acquisition of skills and development of technical excellence in a particular activity are no justification for running outdoor education programmes and should not be seen as ends in themselves.

For Knox, outdoor activities are used as a mechanism to achieve the following objectives:

To develop:
—democratic group living skills
—co-operation with others
—responsibility for one's actions
—new friendships
—appreciation and awareness of the natural environment
—self-esteem and confidence
—respect for others

To encourage:
—leadership opportunities
—enjoyment and adventure
—perseverance
—common sense
—decision-making
—self-discipline
—communication

To teach:
—necessary skills
—safe practices and habits
—new recreational interests
—courtesy
—consideration for others

To provide:
—challenging and adventurous activities within a safe framework
—enough range of activity so that each student finds at least one area in which he is confident and proud of his achievements
—guidance, encouragement and discipline without domination, bullying or insensitivity
—opportunity for students to discover how they behave in difficult circumstances, as individuals and within a group.

Programme Design

With the exception of Kindergarten and Year 9 classes (the latter due to a required year in Cadets), all students attending Knox Grammar visit the centre at least once annually, up to and including Year 10. The objectives outlined above apply equally to all grades. The activities are graded according to maturational level and previous experience.

A brief overview of the programmes for each is as follows:

First and Second Grade: First and second grade programmes are of a day's duration. They tend to be informal and the programme will largely be the responsibility of the classroom teacher who attempts to link the visit with current curriculum needs. From the centre's perspective, these programmes serve as an introduction to the camp, its facilities and the bush. The programme generally takes the form of a bushwalk which incorporates some elementary environmental studies, a barbecue for lunch, and some activity directly linked with the school curriculum. This may be art, bushcraft, or an element within the social studies curriculum.

Third, Fourth and Fifth Grade: These programmes are of two days' duration and require the student to overnight in hut accommodation. A range of activities are offered and co-ordinated with the classroom teacher. At these levels students are more formally introduced to the adventure education programme and, in particular, to the safety aspects of the activities. A fifth grade programme typically contains: mapping exercises; low-level ropes course; abseiling; fishing; arts and crafts; general games; and canoeing.

Sixth Grade: The sixth grade programme, of three days' duration, is the students' first introduction to tenting and formal mapping work. Basic safety procedures commenced in the lower grades are more formally structured, as this grade is seen as the major entry point into the Knox programme. The sixth grade programme contains the following activities: first aid, ropes course, orienteering, abseiling, canoeing (canoe practice sessions as well as an overnight canoe tour to a neighbouring island) and tent camping.

Years 7, 8 and 10: The three high school years are designed to sequence logically together. The duration of the camps increase and the levels

Table 4.2   Knox Outdoor Education Programme Activities for Years 7-10

Year 7 (5 days)	Year 8 (7 days)	Year 10 (12 days)
Service	Service	Service
Canoeing	Canoeing	Canoeing
Abseiling	Abseiling	Abseiling
Bushcraft	Rock Climbing	Rock Climbing
Expedition (2 days)	Bushcraft	Bushcraft
Orienteering	Expedition (4 days)	Expedition (5 days)
Navigation	Orienteering	Solo (3 days)
First Aid	Navigation	Orienteering
Environmental Conservation	First Aid	Navigation
Initiative Tasks	Environmental Conservation	
Ropes Course (Low)	Initiative Tasks	
	Ropes Course (Low)	

of technical competence and individual responsibility heighten. The programmes become more field-based and small group-oriented. Students take more of the responsibility for planning, food and equipment, navigation and overall personal and group needs. The culmination of the outdoor education programme is the three-day 'solo' during the final expedition in Year 10. A summary of the high school programme is outlined in Table 4.2:

Staffing

Knox employs three permanent outdoor education staff (Director, Senior Instructor, Instructor) who are based at the centre. Additional casual staff are employed during the year to assist with the Year 10 programme. The advice given to Knox staff with respect to their responsibilities is valuable advice to all adventure education teachers:

—The attitude of staff to students, programmes and activities is of far more importance than their skill levels in outdoor activities. The most skilful and knowledgeable leaders will not achieve success with their groups unless they can balance the many requirements.

—The enthusiasm, commitment, and integrity of the instructors will be reflected in their groups. They must not only require a high standard of behaviour of their groups, but set the standards by example.

—The balance of adventure and safety in the programmes is largely weighted towards safety. To achieve adventure, the perceived risks and hardships must also be created in the minds of the students.

—Although an instructor's responsibility towards students must be safety, comfort and enjoyment in that order of importance, the student must experience this in reverse order: enjoyment, comfort and safety. If too much overt emphasis is placed on safety, the sense of adventure and achievement will be lost.

—An instructor's approach to the group must be flexible. The group will need nudging and coaxing and, at times, firm direction. However, domination of the group, and suppression of their ideas and actions that do not fall within the instructor's experience, is counter-productive to the aims of the programme.

—Instructors must be patient and sensitive to the individual needs of students in their care.

Conclusion

Adventure education is an holistic educational process which provides opportunity for the individual to develop physically, intellectually and emotionally. Its teaching environment is the outdoors and its basic tools are vigorous outdoor activities.

To maximise the potential of adventure education programmes for personal and social development (its primary objective) requires careful planning, committed and experienced staff and an understanding of the methods and processes necessary for achieving these objectives. To this end, the 'soft skills' of teaching are equally, if not more important, than technical excellence in selected outdoor pursuits.

If educators believe they have responsibilities to their students for more than just the transfer of information, and that this responsibility includes the provision of opportunities to think: about themselves, about relationships with other people, and about the natural world and their responsibilities toward it, then adventure education may be one vehicle for assuming that broader responsibility. Richards (1977: 93) writes:

> A certain degree of struggle and conflict is necessary to the life of any person, otherwise stagnation will ensue. Indeed as long as the conflicts encountered and the struggles engaged in are of a constructive kind . . . then they have many useful, if not vital, functions in the life of any person. For example, they stimulate curiosity and interest in problem-solving and they are the basis of much personal, organisational and social change. They also form part of the process of testing and assessing oneself, and consequently may be enjoyable as the pleasure of the full and active use of one's resources is experienced.

References

Colorado Outward Bound (1981) *Instructor's Manual*, Denver, USA.

Darst, P.W. and Armstrong, G.P. (1980) *Outdoor Adventure Activities for School and Recreation Programs*, Burgess, Minneapolis, USA.

Dewey, J. (1970) *Education and Experience*, Collier Macmillan, London.

Ewart, A. (1980) *Adventure Education: A Treatise*, Colorado Outward Bound, Denver, USA.

Frost, R.B. (1973) 'Physical Education and Self-concept', *Journal of Physical Education*: 35–37.

Golins, G.L. (1980) *Utilizing Adventure Education to Rehabilitate Juvenile Delinquents*, Eric Document 187501, New Mexico State University, USA.

Harmon, P. (1974) *The Measurement of Affective Education*, Outdoor Pursuits in Higher Education Conference, Appalachia University, USA.

Graham, P.J. and Klar, L.R. (1979) *Planning and Delivery of Leisure Services*, William Brown and Co., Dubuque, Iowa, USA.

Harris, B. and Wilson, D.M. (eds) (1980) *Adventure Programs for Human Services*, Colorado Outward Bound, Denver, USA.

Kesselheim, A.D. (1974) *A Rationale for Outdoor Activity as Experiential Education*, Conference on Outdoor Pursuits in Higher Education, Appalachia University, USA.

Kimball, R.O. (1980) *Wilderness/Adventure Programs for Juvenile Offenders*, Eric Document 196.586, New Mexico State University, USA.

Manning, R. (1985) *Camp Knox Instructor's Manual*.

National Safety Network (1986), *A Review of the Injury Data Base Developed from Injury and Close-Call Reports*, Ohio, USA.

Priest, S. (1980) 'Processing the Experience', *Adventure Education* 4 (1): 32–33.

Richards, A. (1985) 'An Experiential Base for Outdoor Pursuits Centres', *Adventure Education* 2 (3): 7–9.

Richards, G.E. (1977) *Educational Implications and Contributions of Outward Bound*, Australian Outward Bound, Canberra.

Rohnke, K. (1981) *High Profile*, Project Adventure, Hamilton.
—— (1982) *Ten Years' Safety Study*, Project Adventure, Hamilton.
Sanders, G. (1986) 'Coventry Intermediate Treatment Association — An Urban Approach', *Adventure Education* 3 (2) 33–35.
Tregonning, K.G. (undated) *Adventure Camps*, Hale School, Wembley Downs, WA.
Van Der Smissen, B. (1975) 'Legal Aspects of Adventure Activities', *Journal of Outdoor Education* 10: 12–15.
Whitford, I. (undated), *People, Situations, Recreations: An Approach to Outdoor Education*, Caulfield Grammar, Melbourne.
Zook, C.R. (1986) 'Outdoor Adventure Builds Character in Five Ways', *Parks and Recreation*, January: 54–57.

5
Integrated Outdoor Education

Keith McRae

Introduction

Throughout this book, the diverse nature of outdoor education purposes and practices is explored. Outdoor education is shown to include activities in the school playground; longer excursions into the community or to settings away from the school; visits to field study centres and resident outdoor education centres; camping expeditions of various kinds; and the use of natural environments for adventurous leisure pursuits. These experiences can be an approach to teaching and learning adopted by teachers at any level and in any curriculum area or they can be part of a programme to which the title outdoor education, or any of a number of other titles, can be given. Outdoor education experiences or programmes can range from a few minutes to a whole day, several days or to longer-term programmes lasting many weeks, months or even years. An outdoor education experience might simply involve an attempt to improve the learning of a particular concept or skill by providing students with appropriate, direct and first-hand experiences. On the other hand, a longer-term programme could involve an attempt to help students achieve a range of objectives in the cognitive, affective and psycho-motor domains.

In Chapter 1, a review of the definitions and practices of outdoor education helped to identify three of its forms. The central focus of *outdoor teaching and learning* was defined as the use of outdoor settings to enhance learning in any curriculum area. *Outdoor environmental education* was seen as emphasising the development of knowledge, skills, attitudes and values relating to the natural and built environments. The major thrust of *outdoor leisure education* was seen to be the development of the knowledge, skills and attitudes required to participate in a range of outdoor pursuits, and the provision of opportunities for the personal and social development of participants. This form of outdoor education increasingly seeks to help participants know, and be concerned about, protecting the natural environments in which they spend their leisure.

An Alternative Approach: Integrated Outdoor Education

In this chapter, it is argued that outdoor education teachers should attempt to develop alternative approaches to outdoor education which incorporate some or all of these diverse forms and practices. The extent to which a teacher is able to develop programmes which cover all the purposes of outdoor education will depend, of course, on answers to a number of key questions, including:

—Is the teacher interested and committed?
—Does the teacher have the knowledge and skills required to develop and implement the proposed programme?
—Are sufficient numbers of competent leaders available?
—Are key people and groups such as administrators, other staff, members of the community and the target populations supportive?
—Is the proposed programme appropriate to the developmental level of the potential participants?
—Are suitable outdoor settings readily accessible to the school or centre?
—Does the school or centre have access to adequate equipment?
—Can the school, centre and potential participants meet the costs involved

The Ideal Model?

Assuming positive responses can be obtained to these questions, it is suggested that outdoor education programmes should incorporate each of the identified forms. The proposal is regarded as an ideal and is based on four major premises. It is felt that outdoor education should:

(1) begin in the early years of formal schooling
(2) be developed as a discrete subject with clearly prescribed objectives, content, learning experiences and assessment/evaluation procedures
(3) be based on activities which foster the knowledge, skills and attitudes required to participate in a range of outdoor leisure activities considered appropriate for particular groups
(4) also include objectives and learning experiences designed to promote:
    —learning in a range of different curriculum areas
    —the development of a sound, morally-justifiable environmental ethic
    —personal qualities and capacities
    —the skills involved in social relations

Figure 5.1 illustrates the proposed alternative:

Central to the model of outdoor education shown in Figure 5.1 are adventurous leisure activities which take place in the outdoors. The activities selected should be appropriate to the age, interest and abilities of particular groups. The activities should be fun, enjoyable, satisfying, challenging and fulfilling. The focus should be placed on helping the students, as a result of the total programme, to acquire the technical and planning skills necessary to participate in these activities during their leisure for the rest of their lives. Importantly, however, the proposal places strong emphasis on the development of the leisure concepts and attitudes which form the foundation of the Leisure Education Advancement Project (See Chapter 1), including the recognition that leisure can be an avenue for personal satisfaction and enrichment and that it has an important function in today's complex society.

Figure 5.1   An Ideal Model for Integrated Outdoor Education

Teaching and learning across the curriculum

Environmental knowledge and ethics

Outdoor leisure knowledge, skills and attitudes

Social relations

Personal qualities and capacities

Students are more likely to grasp concepts and develop attitudes if they are exposed to more than just an occasional and brief outdoor leisure experience. A wide range of appropriate learning experiences which cut across the whole curriculum could be introduced prior to, during and after outdoor leisure activities.

Eating

Creating

Laughing

Integrated Learning Experience prior to Outdoor Activities

As preparation for a bushwalking and camping trip in a nearby national park, for example, a class of sixth graders could be involved in learning experiences designed to achieve objectives in a number of different curriculum areas, as shown in Table 5.1.

Table 5.1 Some Preparatory Activities for Outdoor Leisure Activities: Illustrated Learning Experiences and Objectives

Learning Experiences	Student Objectives	Curriculum Area(s)
Menu-planning	To develop, in groups, appropriate criteria for selecting items of food	Health
	To select food requirements: types, quantities, costs	Mathematics
	To develop abilities to communicate, co-operate, compromise	Social Studies
Fitness training	To acquire a level of fitness appropriate to the proposed activity	Physical Education
	To develop positive attitudes to physical fitness	Physical Education
Environmental activities	To acquire knowledge of key ecological concepts	Natural Science
	To understand the management policies of the national park authorities	Social Studies
	To develop a personal environmental ethic	Natural Science
	To be able to state the key guidelines for protecting natural environments and entities during leisure experiences	Natural Science
Map-reading and navigation	To take compass bearings	Mathematics
	To identify major land-form features on a map	Social Science
	To follow a compass bearing	Mathematics
Studies of the Aborigines of the local area	To locate appropriate resource material	Reading
	To select relevant data from books and other material	Reading
	To write a report about the traditions/lifestyles of local Aborigines	Social Studies/Writing
Local history studies	To become aware of the life-styles of early white settlers	Social Studies
	To compare the attitudes of Aborigines and early white settlers to environment	Social Studies
	To develop confidence through writing and participating in drama activities depicting an aspect of the life of early Aboriginal or white settlers	Social Studies/Drama
Leisure awareness activities	To clarify personal attitudes to participation in outdoor leisure activities	Leisure Education
	To identify the reasons for participation in regular leisure activities	Leisure Education

These learning experiences and related objectives are not meant to suggest that other experiences or objectives should not be included in a programme designed to prepare students for a bushwalking/camping expedition. This list is not comprehensive, but it does illustrate an approach which can be used to plan school-based learning experiences as preparation for outdoor activities. Each teacher, when planning an outdoor leisure experience, has the responsibility for identifying learning experiences and objectives which are appropriate to the students, the outdoor activity and the on-going curriculum.

Integrated Learning Experiences during Outdoor Activities

Learning experiences which involve a number of curriculum areas can also be introduced *during* outdoor activities. Keighley (1985: 26–30), a tutor in Outdoor Education in the Cumbria Local Education Authority in Britain, has written that:

> By means of a wide variety of experiences in the outdoors, through adventurous activities . . . young people can be introduced to a wide variety of themes which may either introduce or reinforce other areas of the curriculum. Outdoor education provides unique opportunities for integrating learning . . . it has many implications for a host of learning areas such as the sciences, the humanities, social studies, languages, the arts, health, physical education, music, mathematics and many others.

Keighley then demonstrated how outdoor activities could be used as vehicles for integrating learning. He suggested that numerous studies and projects could be undertaken by students during the outdoor activities which could also be designed to help them develop some important personal and social skills. These skills are discussed in greater detail later in this chapter. Without listing all of Keighley's suggestions, the basic approach is illustrated below:

Table 5.2   Outdoor Activities as Vehicles for Integrating Learning

Studies	Suggested Outdoor Leisure Activities
Coastal	Camping, Bushwalking, Canoeing, Sailing
Climatic	Camping, Bushwalking, Skiing, Caving
Drama activities	Camping, Bushwalking, Raft-building
Geology studies	Camping, Bushwalking, Caving
Creative Writing	Camping, Bushwalking, Canoeing

Keighley also claimed that most outdoor leisure activities can be used as vehicles for the promotion of a range of general educational skills including decision-making, problem-solving, listening and observing. Keighley does stress, however, that teachers 'should know exactly what it is they intend to draw out of the activity' and suggests that several questions will need to be resolved. For example, what are the specific objectives? What learning will take place? Will the experience reinforce learning already introduced?

Integrated Learning Experiences after Outdoor Activities

Keighley also stresses the importance of follow-up activities:

> Given the notion that outdoor education enables both individuals and groups to learn in a unique way, from their own experiences, it is essential that leaders structure programmes to ensure that adequate time be set aside for reviewing. So important is this process that leaders should regard it as an integral part in the organisation of any programme and not consider it merely as an appendage, to be fitted in if time permits.

It would seem axiomatic that an outdoor leisure activity should be followed by a range of learning experiences which are based on leisure and other experiences which the students undertake in the outdoors. Once again, it is obviously important that the teacher plans a total programme with a clear set of reasonably specific objectives which can be readily translated into learning experiences to be implemented on the completion of the outdoor section of the programme. Structured experiences which reflect or build on the outdoor activities, events, incidents and learning are essential if the learning is to be as effective as possible. However, it is also important for the teacher to be flexible enough to take advantage of unplanned and spontaneous events, discoveries and, of course, questions which occur to the students at any time during or after the outdoor programme.

Any list of possible post-programme learning experiences would depend on the objectives which were set down and implemented, but they could include:

—Class and group discussions of feelings and opinions which emerged during the course of the outdoor activity
—Values clarification exercises
—Debates on important environmental and other issues raised
—Project work relating to questions arising from the outdoor activity
—The taking of action regarded as necessary to help solve issues raised or problems observed
—Factual reporting for class or school magazines, newspapers
—Creative writing: stories, poems, plays
—Art work: drawing, painting, modelling
—The preparation of photographic displays or tape/slide presentations
—Revision and extension of concepts and skills drawn from those areas of the curriculum introduced prior to, or during, the outdoor activity

Integrating Outdoor Leisure and Other Elements of the Model

The adoption of a similar approach would be needed to integrate learning experiences relating to other elements into the model of outdoor education which has been proposed. The promotion of environmental knowledge and of an environmental ethic will be discussed in greater detail in Chapter 11. In integrating this aspect of outdoor education and the development of personal skills and social relations with outdoor leisure education programmes, teachers need to follow the procedure of:

—carefully selecting objectives appropriate to their students
—designing learning experiences which help students achieve these objectives
—determining whether the experiences will be implemented before, during or after the outdoor component of the programme

Objectives in Integrated Outdoor Education

It has been suggested in this chapter that the specification of objectives should be regarded as an essential starting point in the development of an integrated programme of outdoor education. This is not to deny the value of the spontaneous learning experiences which inevitably arise during outdoor leisure experiences. Neither does this imply that students will not benefit in many ways from participation in these experiences even when objectives are not specified or when planned learning experiences are not implemented. It is suggested, however, that the learning of students is likely to be more effective if teachers are clear about the outcomes they expect, and are able to develop and implement a comprehensive set of relevant, structured learning experiences.

Teachers may wish to base their integrated outdoor education programme around the following set of objectives. First, a few comments on the list are pertinent:

—It is long, but even so it is not claimed that it covers all objectives which could be included in an integrated programme
—Not all objectives will be appropriate to all programmes, all teachers or all students. For a number of reasons, teachers may prefer to omit or modify some specific objectives
—However, it is recommended that any programme in integrated outdoor education should include learning experiences designed to *help* students, whatever their age, prior experience, ability level, to achieve each of the broad objectives
—It is accepted that many of the objectives involve knowledge, skills and attitudes which are complex and difficult and, perhaps, beyond the capacity of younger students or students with little motivation or ability
—Teachers, especially those who work with junior primary school students, are, nevertheless, urged to introduce learning experiences which it is hoped will lead to eventual mastery of the knowledge, skills or attitudes involved in the broad objectives
—Teachers can take comfort from the experience of others who have already demonstrated that students can learn difficult concepts at an early age providing that the learning experiences in which they participate are interesting, challenging and appropriate to their age(s) and ability levels

Outdoor Leisure Skills

No attempt is made here to include objectives covering all outdoor leisure activities. Rather, bushwalking, camping and cross-country skiing are included as examples, together with other skill areas considered to be necessary, ultimately, if students are to be able to participate in outdoor activities independently, i.e., without the leadership provided by outdoor education teachers or other outdoor leaders. In the list, the broad objectives are highlighted and these are followed by more specific objectives. The programme will help students to:

(1) Enhance their abilities to plan outdoor experiences
    1.1   Plan a route for a bushwalk or other outdoor experience
    1.2   Select and organise appropriate and adequate clothing and equipment for an outdoor experience
    1.3   Select and organise suitable and adequate food and drink for an outdoor experience
(2) Develop basic skills in bushcraft and campcraft
    2.1   Apply criteria to be used in selecting and organising a camp-site
    2.2   Pack and organise equipment correctly
    2.3   Erect and dismantle a lightweight tent
    2.4   Cook meals in the bush
    2.5   Assess the quality and safety of water supply in the bush and render water safe to use
(3) Become proficient in the basic skills of map-reading and navigation
    3.1   Use a map and compass to work out a route
    3.2   Identify land-form features from a map
    3.3   Use a legend to interpret features on a map
    3.4   Identify distinct land-form features in the bush
    3.5   Work out a compass bearing on a distinct feature
    3.6   Walk on a compass bearing
    3.7   Use a map and compass to locate position in the bush
(4) Develop the basic skills required to participate in selected outdoor experiences, e.g., cross-country skiing
    4.1   Select equipment, clothing and food necessary for cross-country skiing
    4.2   Master the technique of diagonal striding
    4.3   Stay upright when skiing on a relatively flat surface
    4.4   Come to a stop without falling when skiing down a slope
    4.5   Master the technique of turning when skiing down a slope
    4.6   Camp comfortably in the snow
(5) Develop basic skills in first aid
    5.1   Explain the basic purposes of first aid
    5.2   Demonstrate the procedures for treating simple injuries or conditions likely to be encountered in the bush
    5.3   Describe the physiological effects of exposure to extremely cold conditions and recommended methods of prevention and treatment

5.4   Describe the physiological effects of exposure to extremely hot conditions and recommended methods of prevention and treatment

5.5   Describe the recommended methods of treatment of venomous bites and stings

(6) Cope with emergencies in the bush

6.1   Describe relevant regulations and practices required to prevent bushfires

6.2   Describe the steps required when faced with a bushfire

6.3   Identify signs indicating the onset of adverse weather conditions

6.4   Describe procedures for surviving in extremely cold conditions during outdoor experiences

6.5   Describe procedures for surviving in extremely hot conditions during outdoor experiences

6.6   Describe recommended procedures to be followed if lost in the bush

6.7   Describe recommended procedures to be followed in evacuating a member of a party who is injured or ill

Other Leisure-related Objectives

(7) Develop positive attitudes to leisure

7.1   Recognise that leisure is an avenue for personal satisfaction and enrichment

7.2   Be aware of the many valuable leisure opportunities available in the outdoors

7.3   Understand the significance of leisure to society

7.4   Appreciate natural resources and their relationship to leisure and life quality

7.5   Develop the knowledge, skills and attitudes that will assist in making leisure satisfying

7.6   Be able to make responsible decisions regarding leisure

7.7   Enjoy and find satisfaction in outdoor leisure activities

7.8   Develop long-term commitment to participation in outdoor leisure activities

Personal Development

Some outdoor education teachers/educators may feel that broad objective 8, below, with its focus on the physical fitness aspect of good health, is too narrow. This merely illustrates the point that the list is not exhaustive. Each person responsible for the development of a programme will need to choose or develop appropriate and desirable objectives.

(8) Develop positive attitudes towards physical fitness

8.1   Appreciate the contribution physical fitness can make to increasing the level of enjoyment and satisfaction to be achieved in outdoor experiences

8.2 Develop a personal commitment to improving physical fitness
(9) Enhance personal qualities and abilities
    9.1 Make a realistic assessment of the extent to which they have the knowledge and skills required to participate in selected outdoor experiences
    9.2 Be committed to improving their capacity to participate in selected outdoor experiences
    9.3 Develop confidence and expertise in collecting information relevant to outdoor experiences
    9.4 Develop the ability to examine critically their own decisions, actions and feelings, including those involving stress and hardship
    9.5 Develop a willingness to accept and act upon advice about ways to improve personal performance in outdoor experiences
    9.6 Develop self-reliance in relation to participation in outdoor experiences
    9.7 Develop confidence to cope with outdoor experiences in natural environments
    9.8 Be willing to try new outdoor experiences even if these appear to be difficult or even daunting
    9.9 Use initiative in coping with problems or difficult situations during outdoor experiences
    9.10 Gain a sense of achievement from their participation in outdoor experiences
    9.11 Test and refine personal attitudes and values
    9.12 Improve their level of physical fitness
    9.13 Improve their capacity to participate in outdoor experiences which are physically demanding and/or involve stress or hardship

These objectives involve the development of personal qualities and abilities needed to maximise the value to be obtained from participation in outdoor leisure experiences. Although it is hoped that such qualities and abilities will transfer to other life situations, the decision was made to make them as realistic as possible and to relate them directly to outdoor leisure experiences.

There is, of course, no universally agreed upon set of objectives relating to personal development. Different concepts are often selected and the words used to determine objectives vary considerably from one person to another. Keighley, for example, included the following personal constructs:

Motivation	Challenge	Adaptability/flexibility
Tolerance	Self-reliance	Responsibility for self
Self-discipline	Self-awareness	Self-responsibility
Trust	Interaction	Environmental awareness

Other constructs such as self-concept, self-esteem, self-image and self-efficacy are often included in lists of outdoor education objectives. Given the range of possible objectives, it is necessary to repeat that those listed above should be regarded as merely an idiosyncratic selection.

Social Development

Again, there is frequent disagreement about the objectives which should be included in this category. Additionally, there is often confusion about whether particular objectives should be included in the personal or social development categories. Keighley, for example, included a number of objectives in the social development category which might more logically, have been placed under personal development. However, this is not the place to engage in a debate on this matter. Keighley's social development objectives (social constructs) are:

Knowing one another	Group cohesion	Responsibility for others
Team Spirit	Group co-operation	Leadership
Taking orders	Sharing	Compromising
Negotiation		

The social development objectives suggested here as appropriate for integrated outdoor leisure education are:

(10) Enhance relations with others
- 10.1 Identify the benefits of group planning, decision-making and action
- 10.2 Value participation in group activities
- 10.3 Communicate ideas, opinions and feelings
- 10.4 Value the sharing of thoughts and feelings arising from outdoor experiences
- 10.5 Co-operate with others
- 10.6 Act with responsibility towards others in the outdoors
- 10.7 Recognise, value and acknowledge the qualities and abilities of others
- 10.8 Tolerate any different ideas, opinions and feelings of others
- 10.9 Contribute effectively to the resolution of differences of opinion or conflict among peers
- 10.10 Make new friends
- 10.11 Relate more effectively and meaningfully to leaders

Across-the-curriculum Learning

It is not possible, of course, to identify all the objectives which might be selected for integrated outdoor education programmes. Each teacher will choose objectives from a range of curriculum areas as these appear appropriate to particular outdoor experiences. The following objectives are, consequently, very general:

(11) Enhance learning in a range of curriculum areas
- 11.1 Enhance the learning of concepts, skills and attitudes in a range of curriculum areas

11.2 Develop a positive attitude to school attendance and participation

11.3 Develop a greater interest in learning generally

Environmental Knowledge and Ethics

As with the previous category, it is not possible to list all the specific objectives relating to the promotion of environmental concepts. Key concepts are included in Chapter 11 and these should form a necessary element in integrated outdoor education programmes. The following objectives are also regarded as essential:

(12) Become environmentally concerned

12.1 Understand key ecological concepts

12.2 Develop a sense of respect for natural environments and entities

12.3 Recognise the capacity of human beings to alter or damage fragile natural environments and entities

12.4 Appreciate the need to take individual responsibility for the protection of natural environments and entities

12.5 Avoid or minimise damage to natural environments and entities during outdoor experiences

12.6 Develop a commitment to supporting social policies and practices designed to protect or improve natural environments

12.7 Develop the knowledge and skills necessary to identify and resolve potential threats to natural environments

Using the Objectives: A Framework for Developing an Ideal Integrated Programme in Outdoor Education

It is beyond the scope of this book to set out a complete and detailed curriculum in integrated outdoor education encompassing content, learning experiences, teaching-learning materials and assessment/evaluation procedures as well as objectives. It would also be a fruitless and impertinent exercise. No programme developed in isolation from a particular school and community can be entirely relevant to their needs, and nor should it be adopted without the major modifications needed to make it appropriate to the students who would undertake it. It is also recognised that many experienced teachers of outdoor education have the knowledge and skills to flesh-out the bare bones of a set of objectives into programmes which are relevant to particular groups of students and the communities in which they live. The ideas which appear below are provided for the benefit of teachers who may be a little uncertain.

It was suggested earlier that integrated outdoor education should begin as early as possible in the primary school and continue through the remaining years of formal schooling. It would certainly be highly desirable if students could undertake a rigorous and systematic programme in integrated outdoor education which was designed to achieve the objectives outlined, beginning in Kindergarten and ending in Year 12. A number of factors militate against the realisation of this ideal, including, amongst others, the pressures already faced by schools and teachers to cope with new subjects in a curriculum perceived as being overcrowded, and a shortage of teachers with the necessary knowledge, skills and experience to develop programmes. But, assuming that the teachers in, for example, a primary school have the interest, commitment, expertise and experience required, how do they proceed?

A number of questions need to be addressed although not necessarily in the order presented. Initially, only objectives relating to outdoor leisure, environmental knowledge and ethics, and personal and social development should be considered. Across-the-curriculum objectives should be addressed when initial decisions about the objectives, content, learning experiences and outdoor settings to be included in the core programme have been made. The development of a curriculum is a dynamic process and it will be essential for teachers to re-assess decisions on a continuing basis.

Time and Funds
(1)   Provisionally, how much time and what funds will be allocated to integrated outdoor education for classroom lessons in each grade each week, term or year?

Objectives
(2)   Which of the suggested objectives are appropriate?
(3)   Which objectives need to be modified?
(4)   Which other objectives should be included?
(5)   Which objectives would be better achieved in (a) classrooms (b) the outdoors and (c) both indoors and outdoors?
(6)   Which objectives would be better introduced, for the first time, in each of the grades?

Previous learning
(7)   What knowledge, skills and attitudes related to the objectives will the students bring to the programme?

Adventure Activities
(8)   Which adventurous outdoor leisure activities will be introduced to the students in each of the grades?

Course content
(9)   What specific content (concepts, skills, attitudes) should be included in learning experiences designed to achieve the objectives selected or developed in each of the grades?

Learning experiences
(10) What learning experiences should be implemented to help the students achieve the objectives selected for each grade?
(11) Which of these learning experiences should be implemented in classrooms?
(12) In what order will the classroom learning experiences be implemented in each grade?

Outdoor settings
(13) What outdoor settings are available:

—on the school site?
—on the local community?
—on nearby farms?
—at field study and resident centres?
—in accessible natural areas such as forests, rivers, creeks, ponds?
—in accessible national parks?

Outdoor learning experiences
  (14) Which of these learning experiences should be implemented in the outdoors?
  (15) How many excursions, field trips and longer outdoor experiences should be included in the programme for each grade?
  (16) What adventurous outdoor leisure activities will be undertaken during these experiences?
  (17) What objectives, drawn from other areas of the curriculum, could be achieved during outdoor experiences?
  (18) How long should each of the outdoor experiences last?
  (19) When will the outdoor experiences be implemented in each grade?

Leadership
  (20) Can all safety guidelines be met during the outdoor experiences?
  (21) Are additional leaders needed for the outdoor trips? What competencies are required? Are suitable leaders available?
  (22) How will teachers or other leaders gain the knowledge and skills not already held?
  (23) To what extent and in what capacity will parents be invited to be involved in the programme?

Integration of classroom and outdoor experiences
  (24) Are the classroom learning experiences associated with the integrated programme adequately integrated with those to be implemented during outdoor experiences?

Integration of outdoor education programme and wider curriculum
  (25) Are opportunities taken to relate the objectives and learning experiences of the outdoor education programme to the wider curriculum?

Teaching-learning materials
  (26) What teaching-learning materials are available or need to be developed for classroom lessons and outdoor experiences?
  (27) Is all the required equipment available?
  (28) Is suitable transport available?
  (29) Can all costs of materials, equipment and transport be met?

Assessment/evaluation procedures
  (30) What procedures should be adopted to assess the extent to which the students achieve the objectives set for each grade?
  (31) How will the overall programme be evaluated to ensure that improvements are made?

Modifying the draft curriculum
  (32) Can all the planned (classroom and outdoor) learning experiences be implemented in the time and with the money allocated for each grade? If not, can the time allocation be increased or, given that this is not possible, what modifications need to be made to the programme?

An Impossible Ideal?

Realistically, the number of schools in Australia likely to be able to mount an ideal programme in integrated outdoor education is, at the present time in any case, quite small. The framework presented above can, however, be used by individuals or groups of teachers who want to mount such a programme in primary and secondary schools. A first or third grade primary teacher, for example, could use the framework to develop a year-long programme. Fifth and sixth grade teachers could develop a more comprehensive programme which lasted two years. A group of secondary school teachers, preferably drawn from a number of different curriculum areas, could develop a subject called Outdoor Education. Alternatively, one or more teachers from subjects such as physical education, science, geography, history (or any other area) could develop an integrated programme as an elective.

In addition, many of the questions could be used by those responsible for developing, implementing and evaluating programmes in resident outdoor education centres or by organisations other than schools which offer outdoor education programmes. Although some of the questions will be inappropriate and others may need to be modified, the basic framework will assist in the development of a systematic, comprehensive and integrated programme.

Further Help

Outdoor education teachers and outdoor educators who require additional help in the development of an integrated outdoor education programme or who need ideas, for example, for learning experiences or materials, have a wide range of possible sources available to them, including:

—Outdoor or environmental education consultants in the local education department or authority or private consultants
—Relevant officers in other government departments and instrumentalities
—Members of outdoor or environmental education associations and conferences organised by these groups
—Experienced teachers in other schools or centres
—Tertiary educators who teach outdoor/environmental education
—Books, journals and curriculum documents which are available through libraries
—Clubs or societies with interest or expertise in an aspect of the programme
—Parents with knowledge or skills
—Relevant companies and organisations

Conclusion

The purpose of this chapter has been to encourage schools and teachers to give serious thought to the implementation of a comprehensive programme in integrated outdoor education. Teachers are also encouraged to do two further things:

(1) To be aware of the deficiencies they may have and the need to develop and implement programmes which are within their competencies; and
(2) To make every effort to improve their level of knowledge and skills in order that they may expand the scope of any programme in which they are or may be involved.

Reference

Keighley, P. (1985) 'Using the Potential of Outdoor Education as a Vehicle for Integrated Learning', *Adventure Education* 2 (4/5).

6
The Use of School Sites for Educational Purposes

Elizabeth Liebing

Benefits

While much can be learned from text books, teacher talks and discussions, opportunities for students to learn directly from the environment as well as about it are invaluable in the learning process. The view of Fein (1988) that 'the Australian environment, be it a city street, a beach, a farm or a forest, can be used to give reality, relevance and practical experience to learning', reflects the views of many outdoor education writers. Irrespective of the subject area, studies of researchers' and teachers' reports show that children learn best when learning involves more than just books and blackboards.

A key objective of outdoor education, as discussed in this book, is that students gain understanding of Australia's natural environment. This chapter will concentrate on how we can provide stimulating opportunities within schools for students to gain such understanding. The classroom and the school grounds can both be used to provide these opportunities. As school programmes are often the only opportunity provided for young people to learn how they depend on natural resources and how our use and care of soil, water and air affect our environment, it is essential that we maximise the use of outdoor learning environments.

Using the classroom and/or developing an outdoor classroom in the school grounds expands the learning environment readily accessible to teachers and students. Their use requires no permit, no time-consuming transport arrangements, no interruptions to the timetable and no special arrangements for lunch, toilet facilities or inclement weather. The value of creating an outdoor classroom on site is that it is immediately available for continuous studies, for unexpected observation, for individual study projects and for capitalising on the 'teachable moment'. In such environments, working with natural resources, learning takes on new dimensions. Students gain not only essential learning skills but begin to develop concepts about how components of the natural world operate and interact, as well as how humans relate to and have an impact on this environment.

Outdoor classrooms also provide children with a variety of learning experiences from sensory to formal, using soil, water, plants and animals. Such experiences are needed to develop a personal value system that gives priority to behaviour consistent with rational and prudent use of our natural resources. Our attitudes are shaped early in life, and the value of experiences in the classroom or the school grounds related to gaining understanding of the natural world for our future citizens is extremely important.

Research by two Americans, Falk and Balling (1980), show that young children actually learn best when field work is conducted close to home. They compared two groups of students studying the same phenomena. One group, third graders, used the woods adjacent to the school, while the other, fifth graders, went on an all-day field trip to a nature centre. Both groups retained much of what they learned, but of particular interest was the finding that 'third graders learned more in the non-disruptive, relatively familiar setting of the woods, whereas fifth graders found the unfamiliar, more novel field trip away from the school more conducive to learning'. Thus Falk and Balling recommended shorter, close-to-home field trips for younger students.

Their study showed that the 'novelty factor' can interfere with learning in environments new to children. My personal experience suggests that this could be overcome, to some extent, if children are familiar with the techniques of outdoor field work. Regularly using such techniques in familiar environments can do much to enhance the quality of excursions and camps to more distant locations.

Unfortunately, it is not practical for each school to create 'mini-Australias' in their grounds for outdoor learning. Each outdoor classroom needs to be an individual project, planned according to the size and shape of the area available and to other factors such as topography, geography and climate. Examples discussed in this chapter will provide some insight into ways of developing exciting outdoor learning environments.

Developing Outdoor Learning Environments

Bringing the Outdoors Indoors

The classroom can be successfully used to enrich learning and gain understanding of the natural world. Teachers can expose students to a variety of mini-environments through, for example, using aquariums and terrariums. Establishing and maintaining an aquarium can enable students to become immersed in fresh-water studies in such a way that they will be able to experience some of the subtleties of a fresh-water web of life. Questions related to species selection, water quality, diet and shelter will need to be investigated and appropriate answers resolved if the aquarium is to become a viable habitat. Experiences like this enable students to begin to develop understanding of how a particular ecosystem operates. Such learning in this 'first-hand' manner will progressively mature into concepts that in later life will enable participants to be better informed on various issues that periodically confront the outdoor environment. As Hasset and Weisberg (1972) point out: 'A child who has had the responsibility for planning, setting up and maintaining an aquarium in the classroom is better equipped to understand the problems of water pollution in terms of his own experiences.'

In South Australia, the Nature Education Centre, a volunteer service for schools, enables teachers to create exciting learning environments in their classrooms. Part of the centre's service enables teachers to either hire or buy a variety of animals including Green Tree Frogs, Eastern Plains Rats and Spinifex Hopping Mice. Through using this facility, teachers can provide a range of creative learning environments. Students can, for example, become involved in establishing a viable habitat for Spinifex Hopping Mice. Through this activity, they will become more aware of the particular characteristics and needs of these mice, a species children are not likely to encounter in their daily life. Longer-term projects of this nature provide opportunities for students to gain practical experience that will better enable them to interpret concepts related to our natural world. Outdoor educators are in the business of assisting children to understand the workings of the outdoor environment. Classroom projects that the Nature Education Centre helps establish are a significant and valuable beginning to that process. Such projects will also greatly enhance learning that then occurs in the outdoors.

Using the School Grounds

The school grounds are the most frequented site for students, yet as an educational resource, they are often untapped. The development of school grounds to provide a variety of learning environments is a very logical, cost-effective programme to undertake. Unfortunately, the decision to create an outdoor classroom in the school grounds usually comes long after school buildings and facilities are in place. However, unused areas of the

Investigating

site, perhaps those considered too hilly, too wet or otherwise undesirable, may be ideal for outdoor classrooms.

A South Australian school, Paradise Primary, provides an example of the development of an outdoor classroom immediately after the school was completed. The school ground development was not part of the original plan, but when plans for manicured lawns were mooted, one teacher, Paul Lindus, a keen environmentalist, suggested a project that he thought would help the school community unify and develop an identity out of the available, standardised brickwork, asphalt, grass, and brightly coloured furnishings. Lindus embarked on a project with students and the school community that changed an area covered in Salvation Jane and dandelions into one rich with studies for the whole community. The objective of the project was to return the area to its pre-European settlement days.

The Native Flora Area as it became known, was planted with trees and shrubs indigenous to the site. It was envisaged that it would provide a haven for native birds and hence diversify study options for students. A special club of children assisted by community working bees maintained the area during the early growing days.

The area flourished into a superb outdoor classroom. Seasonal, self-guiding learning trails were developed for lower, middle and upper primary students, and the creation of a pond introduced fresh-water studies to the area. Within three years, the number and variety of native birds visiting the area increased considerably. 'To walk into the middle of the area gives one the opportunity to almost forget they are in a school yard' (Lindus 1983). Besides enhancing the environs of the school, a significant impact had been made on the learning environments for Paradise Primary students. Here was a readily accessible site, where students could become involved in long-term projects, gaining skills and understanding of a particular outdoor environment that no text book could match.

As part of the project, students contributed to a publication describing the area's flora and fauna. This booklet became generally available to the wider community, many of whom visited the area during the day or prior to collecting students.

Paradise Primary outdoor classroom also became a stepping stone for students into the wider outdoor community. Students used the knowledge and skills gained to begin a revegetation programme in a nearby native flora park. Lindus comments on this extension support the value of developing school grounds for outdoor learning:

> Teaching about the environment became much easier. Students were completing tasks in the park not because teachers wanted them to, but because they had meaning. Their experiences at school had provided a sound basis for becoming involved in the park project and they have developed a special affinity for the area.

A similar, but more diverse school ground development has occurred at another South Australian Primary School, Modbury West. Planned as a 'school circumference learning trail', the area was designed for 'hands-on experiences' to enhance student learning. The development included:

—*copse plantings* to provide a place to hide, to be in close contact with the bush, and for 'sensory walks'

—a *pond* for aquatic ecology activities to provide opportunities for close examination of species

—an *arid zone* to include a map of Australia showing 80 per cent of Australia as belonging to the arid zone in order to provide a comparison with respect to plant species

—a *Melaleuca and Eucalyptus Garden* to provide variety of leaf, habit, flower, and bark within a species and to attract native birds

—a *Bird Sanctuary* to be planted so that year-long flowering would provide a variety of species for students to observe. A *Bird Hide* built in this area has greatly enhanced student learning

As the outdoor classroom developed, a key teacher was released from classroom duties to co-ordinate an overall programme of activities for the area. Units of work were designed and the teacher worked with classes and their teachers. This method helped ensure that experiences in the school grounds were developed in the context of classroom work and that teachers developed their own personal skills and confidence in using the outdoor classroom.

It is always interesting to contemplate how much outdoor educators do influence students through the experiences they provide. In my teaching at Arbury Park Outdoor School, I met a Year 7 country girl whose knowledge about the outdoor environment set her apart from classmates. In chatting to her, I discovered that she had attended Modbury West Primary for three years. Her enthusiasm and excitement for the place, two years later, was obvious. She talked non-stop about the 'great grounds' they had and the activities in which they had engaged. Her comments were not limited to these, but included comments on 'how great the yard was to play in at lunchtime, much better than where I am now'. I came away from the conversation feeling that here was one outdoor classroom that had certainly had an impact.

The value of developing school grounds into outdoor classrooms cannot, as shown in the above examples, be underestimated. Vanden Hazel and Benson (1973) in their book, *Teaching Outdoors*, give a case study where a primary school teacher at an urban school embarked upon a program of outdoor studies in the school grounds. His children were, to use his description, 'lively'. They organised themselves into interest groups ranging in size from two to six pupils, and conducted weather, soil, insect, plant and rock studies in the school yard and a nearby park. The results were apparently outstanding. Vanden Hazel and Benson continue:

> The children not only improved their academic work, as was to be expected, but also changed their attitude towards school and towards each other.

More importantly, the authors pointed out that:

> These benefits of out-of-school education are intangible and difficult to measure, but they may change the classroom atmosphere as the youngsters find out that what they are learning at school is really related to their own lives.

Outdoor Recreation in the School Grounds

Most often the emphasis of activities in outdoor classrooms is on learning about our natural environment. However, they can also be used to introduce students to outdoor recreation skills such as fire-lighting, tent-pitching and using a map and compass. A grassy patch, or ideally a little grove of scrub, as part of the outdoor classroom would enable the skills of minimum-impact camping to be taught, and for students to become well-versed in their usage.

These skills, combined with understanding of outdoor environments, will begin to develop a personal environmental ethic amongst students.

General Principles for Developing School Sites

Smith and Wilson (1981) in *Environmental Education: A Sourcebook for Primary Education*, provide a comprehensive chapter on school ground development. It is not envisaged that their materials be reprinted here. However, some general principles for developing outdoor classrooms will be briefly addressed.

Although the idea of developing the school site into an outdoor classroom may come from an individual or group of people, approval and support of the school administration and community is essential before detailed planning can begin.

Preparing a proposal should involve:

—Clearly stating educational objectives after consultation with staff
—Details of costing, both immediate, and proposed future needs
—Consulting with appropriate resource specialists for ideas and information
—A rough design of the proposed development

After approval to proceed has been granted, the most efficient and practical way to deal with the development is through a small committee that represents teachers, resource specialists, school maintenance staff, students, parents and, if appropriate, community groups.

Agreement must then be reached between users of the area, and a final concept plan, showing the stages of development, should be drawn up and displayed. Prior to the first pick ripping into the soil, a calendar of events should detail when activities are to occur, so that work takes place in the most appropriate season.

During the development phase there will be opportunities for students to become involved. For example, they can:

—compile an inventory of the site prior to development
—record the history of the outdoor classroom development through slides, tapes and videos; permanent photographic points could be established
—design and build learning trail markers, signs and benches

Once begun, the committee should assess progress regularly, report to the school body as required, and ensure that features of the area are not overlooked. The latter point will depend on geographic location and the size of the site, but developers should keep a watchful eye for existing phenomena that could be easily destroyed: for example, animal habitats (nesting trees, old stumps, fallen logs); historical remnants (fences, ruins, trees); exposed soil profiles and sites that would be appropriate for learning trails, with study areas and listening posts for ponds and wet areas. As each stage is completed, students could organise a special event to celebrate the occasion.

Conclusion

The school environment has long been neglected as an outdoor education resource. In this chapter, I have endeavoured to show that this need no longer be the case. Approaches as described show the educational utility of such developments. In addition, the site development that accompanies such education programmes makes the school a much more pleasant environment to be in.

It is also important to note that where students are involved in developing, managing and pursuing long-term projects in the area, they gain a real sense of identity with their school. In days when school vandalism and the negative attitudes of children towards school are problems, a feeling of such identity is of great value.

References

Falk, J.H. and Balling, J.D. (1980) 'School Field Trips: Where You Go Makes the Difference', *Science and Children* 17 (6).

Fien, J. (1988) *Education for the Australian Environment*, Curriculum Development Centre, Canberra.

Hasset, J.D. and Weisberg, A. (1972) *Open Education—Alternatives within our Traditions*, Prentice-Hall, New Jersey, USA.

Lindus, P. (1983) 'Paradise Recreated?—A Project of Unification', Paradise Primary School, South Australia.

Smith, J.H. and Wilson, J.R. (1981) 'Developing School Grounds for Environmental Education' in *Environmental Education: a Sourcebook for Primary Education*, Curriculum Development Centre, Canberra.

Vanden Hazel, B. and Benson, D. (1983) *Teaching Outdoors: How, Why, When and Where?*, McGraw-Hill, New York, USA.

7
Field Trips and Excursions: Using Outdoor Settings in and around the Local Community

Robert Hogan

Introduction

In this chapter, as the title implies, we are looking mainly at the benefits of field work as an adjunct to classroom learning. Making use of appropriate settings in the local community serves, it is generally agreed, to enhance the treatment of subject matter and improve the quality of the overall learning experience. A significant advantage of using the local area is that it is a readily accessible resource and can be used at little expense and on a number of occasions. Before looking at how we could select and use such settings we should briefly examine the benefits of providing field trips or excursions.

The Purposes of Field Trips and Excursions

Much has been written about the potential for field experiences to enhance the learning process. In Chapter 1, McRae summarises the results of a review undertaken by Swan (1986) of research into the effectiveness of field work. Swan's findings are relevant here. Swan concluded that field work can play an important role in:

—improving the learning of concepts in virtually all subject areas
—fostering higher-order learning skills such as the ability to apply knowledge, to analyse real-life situations, to develop solutions to problems and to make decisions
—helping students to clarify attitudes and values
—improving understanding and relationships between students and between teachers and students
—fostering such personal and social traits as self-esteem, co-operation and leadership
—developing positive attitudes to learning generally

A number of anecdotal accounts support such findings and claim even greater benefits for field work. Hannaford (1986: 122), retired Principal of Marion High School in South Australia, justifies the importance of field work in a restructured approach to secondary school education when he says:

Remembering that the learning rate on a well-planned field trip might be six times the best rate the same teachers can achieve in the classroom, the effort and

Exploring

the time involved is well spent. Although there will inevitably be some interference with the normal timetable, the cognitive and affective learning benefits to the students justify field work as an integral part of the programme.

Hannaford (1986: 123) reports an experience at his own school to support his claim:

> A teacher was teaching geography and finding the class to be flat as they waded through highly theoretical chapters which the students thought were irrelevant. Against the teacher's judgement, the field team persuaded him to share two study trips and a week-long study camp with them. Reluctantly the teacher helped plan each occasion. He returned from each event astounded by the enthusiasm and productivity of the students. The relationship between himself and the students was better and the students' attitudes to study had improved.
>
> Repeatedly we have found difficult students respond atypically at a study camp. They are notably less difficult afterwards. Their cries of 'boring' and 'why should I have to do this?' come less frequently, and overall the quality and quantity of their work increase dramatically. In our example, the prediction of a poor test result was astray, and the teacher was won to a new approach which both restored and maintained him, and also lifted his students.

This raises the question of spin-off benefits, an area addressed by many writers in the field. Hammerman and Hammerman (1973: 12) summarised this area well when they wrote:

> Out-of-classroom learning has a way of producing numerous gains, many of which defy measurement in terms of producing visible or tangible results. Among the list of intangible gains is the improved relationship that invariably develops between teacher and pupils. In the free atmosphere of the outdoor laboratory, unrestricted by the formalities of the schoolroom, pupils frequently view their teacher for the first time as an honest-to-goodness human being.

Outdoor learning environments provide a setting which enables the teacher to observe his/her pupils in a variety of conditions in which he would not ordinarily see them. Under these circumstances a different sort of pupil-teacher relationship is bound to be established.

Both research and anecdotal evidence, then, support the view that outdoor field work can both enhance the learning of the subject matter being studied, and generally improve the quality of the learning environment.

Before proceeding, however, a note of caution should be added. Despite the evidence of what field work can achieve, a number of writers are critical of approaches taken to field work in some settings. Hannaford (1986: 123) writes:

Do we treat a field trip as a study trip naturally incorporated in the flow of study? Around the world I have observed hundreds of school trips where the students are just fooling about, waiting for the next shop or entertainment parlour. Occasionally, one sees students rapt in their study experience, excited by each discovery and thirsting for more. In every success story, there is a teacher well prepared and ready to share in the excitement.

Clearly, then, it's not the fact of taking students on a field trip itself which counts, but what one actually does and how it is done. Gough (1985: 66) makes the same point as Hannaford, but perhaps a little more directly when he states:

On many conventional field trips, students are no more than tourists and the potential for practical learning is minimal. Whether or not field trips encourage practical learning depends on the reasons for the trip and the nature of the learner's activity at the field site.

Liebing carried out a series of observation visits at Cleland Conservation Park's fauna enclosure as one aspect of her thesis 'Educational Excursions and Diversions'. Her (1975: 1) report of her first day of observation appears to substantiate such claims and provides a glimpse of a popular excursion venue:

The head ranger had informed me that four schools were booked in to visit the park that day, so on my arrival at Cleland I tried to ascertain some of the objectives and goals each of the classes had for their excursion. After speaking with the teachers and many of the students, I found it very difficult to discover any educational reasons for bringing two hundred primary and high school students to Cleland that day. As I proceeded around the park, I made the following observations:

—students wandering around aimlessly, looking bored and saying there was nothing to do
—students far removed from adult supervision (many using the kiosk for a coffee break)
—excited students running around throwing objects, teasing and imitating the animals
—a general lack of direction and motivation for all students.

On conferring with the staff of the park, I learned that this type of activity was quite common, and that it may be observed on many weekdays during the year.

From this and other similar experiences since that visit, it has been my observation that many teachers who take students outdoors do not take advantage of the experience, and look on it just as a recreational break from the classroom for themselves and their students. These teachers are content to let children roam unguided while they have a rest. It is from this type of situation that education in the outdoors loses all value and effectiveness.

While we may like to think that things have improved since 1975 (and in some quarters it undoubtedly has), it is still true that a great many teachers have had little training in the area of outdoor field work and do not fully understand its potential.

Before commencing a field trip, then, we should look at the factors important in its planning and conduct.

Selected Research into Outdoor Field Work

American researchers Falk and Balling (1980), working from a field studies centre in Chesapeake Bay, investigated the effect of field work on a series of lessons concerned with the biology of trees. Using experimental groups of third and fifth grade students, they found that field work in the school ground and on a full day trip to a nearby nature centre did lead to significant learning taking place. However, based on the response of the younger children to the field study centre, and on subsequent studies (see Falk and Balling 1982), they postulated that only when students are familiar with a setting, and comfortable with it, is learning facilitated. When students are placed in an unfamiliar setting, the 'novelty' of it can, in fact, disrupt learning.

This is in itself a strong argument for using local outdoor settings rather than distant ones. Local settings will either be more familiar to students, or the possibility of repeat visits allows time for exploration and familiarisation prior to introducing learning tasks. In general, distant settings will be more novel and, due to the cost involved in reaching them, are rarely visited more than once. The time which can be spent in the familiarisation phase is thus minimised.

An Australian study by MacKenzie and White (1982) investigated not only the use of field work, but also compared two field work approaches. To help students learn about coastal land-forms and associated flora, they first used programmed instructional materials supplemented with photographic slides of geographic features. For one-third of the group, the control group, this was all the exposure to the topic they had. The remaining two-thirds took a half-day field trip to a nearby coastal area. There they were divided into two groups. One group went on a 'traditional' field trip, dominated by the teacher who called their attention to the feature they were to observe and then asked them to complete the relevant section of a work booklet.

The second field trip group had a more 'active' field trip and were involved in tasks involving observation, recording and sketching, and a variety of 'unusual' tasks. For instance, to estimate salinity they walked through the mud to a mangrove shoreline and tasted the foliage! In addition to generating information from these tasks, the teacher gave answers to questions raised along the way. While the time spent in the field was identical for each group, the second group was required to perform more physical and mental activities. Each group took an achievement test immediately following their experience, and a retention test some months later. The results of this test are shown in Table 7.1.

Table 7.1 Mean Test Scores (Maximum 35) of Three Geography Classes

	Test 1	Test 2
Group 1	26.3	13.5
Group 2	29.2	17.2
Group 3	33.1	29.7

Source: MacKenzie and White 1982

Clearly the active field trip learners achieved the best score in both cases. It is the retention test that is most striking, however. The active group retained 90 per cent of the information learned, whereas both other groups had forgotten so much that their results were both below 50 per cent achievement. The active group not only learned more, they learned it better.

A detailed discussion of these results is beyond the scope of this chapter, but it does seem reasonable to postulate that where students are physically and mentally involved in the learning process, especially when there is direct interaction with the outdoor environment, they learn more and are more likely to retain the new knowledge.

Planning and Structuring the Field Trip Experience

Where You Go Makes the Difference

Anecdotal evidence indicates that sites selected should be good examples of what you want to show, or good settings for what it is you want the children to experience. The work of Falk and Balling suggests that particularly with young children more familiar environments give the best results.

How You Do It is Important

Just to take students outdoors does not guarantee a hands-on, practical learning experience. Teacher talk outdoors is probably about as effective (or ineffective) as teacher talk indoors. The work of MacKenzie and White (1982), for instance, casts serious doubt on the effectiveness of the 'tour guide' approach. For field work to be effective, the teacher must create an active learning environment. Whether using verbal cues (teacher talk) or written cues (student worksheets), the bulk of the excursion should be student activity centred around interactions with the environment.

The inquiry approach to learning, where children are involved in observing, recording, discovering and generating their own information has long been recommended as being the more satisfactory approach to field work. Where students are working on designated tasks they should generally be in small groups. This not only makes teacher control easier, but also maximises involvement in the experience.

The study by MacKenzie and White suggests that 'unusual episodes' in this interaction with the environment can be important to field work effectiveness. Their discussion argues that such an approach is based on the model of memory proposed by Gagne and White (1978) who postulate that newly-acquired knowledge will be better retained if it is associated with an easily recalled 'episode'. These could be unusual or striking events that occur on a field trip, such as the walking through mudflats and the tasting of foliage described in the MacKenzie and White study. These events are novel and can be easily recalled. The associated concepts are, therefore, also likely to be recalled.

To this end, the unique approaches to environmental interpretation contained in Van Matre's books *Acclimatisation* (1972) and *Acclimatising* (1974), and Cornell's *Sharing Nature with Children* (1979) have been used to great effect by teachers seeking environmental interaction and a lively atmosphere in their field work.

Having a Clear Context is Crucial to Success

Students should clearly understand how the field trip relates to classroom work. As in the classroom, if students have no idea of the purpose of the activity, it is unlikely they will gain a great deal from it. Moreover, in the case of an excursion, it could be seen by the students simply as a break from learning or an amusing dimension, given the many distractions possible in an outdoor setting. Stoddard (1961 cited in Smith *et al.* 1973: 40) reflects the results of research into effective teaching practices when he says that: 'It is educational only if the experience is progressively structured into an intellectual whole that is perceived by the participant.'

The teacher's role here is critical. The teacher should fully brief the class as to the purpose of the field trip and its context in relation to classroom work. Once the children are working on the activities set, the teacher should act as a resource person to assist where necessary. At the conclusion of the unit of work relevant to the excursion, the teacher should draw the threads of all work done together by linking the experiences in the field and the classroom so that students clearly understand the overall concepts. If students see the field trip as an isolated experience one would expect gains to be minimal.

Students should be Familiar with Field Work Skills

It seems reasonable to extrapolate from the work of Falk and Balling that familiarity with field work techniques or routine is an important factor in effective field work. Just as students need particular skills to operate in the classroom, they need skills specific to the outdoor setting. Familiarity with at least the field work techniques could help to overcome problems of setting novelty.

Field work, then, needs thorough and detailed planning. It should not be seen as a break from classroom routine (even though it is) by teachers or students. While many teachers plead problems of time in preparing for excursions, this should not be a great problem when using the local area. Such an area is accessible for planning and, providing the teacher stays at the school, it is likely to be used for similar units in subsequent years.

Some Practical Aspects

A whole list of organisational matters needs to be attended to in order to maximise the possibility of a smoothly-run field trip. Transport to the venue, if needed, must be organised well ahead, consent notices sent home to parents, and students briefed as to special requirements for the trip.

One must always remember that, when on an outdoor field trip, one is exposed to the elements much more so than when in the school itself and it is essential that this is taken into account when determining clothing requirements. Generally, field work requires more 'dirt-tolerant' clothing. If the possibility of rain exists, students should have water-proof parkas, or teachers should select a venue where shelter is available. Similarly, in hot weather, hats and sunburn cream are advisable. If, of course, the weather is particularly inclement, it may be necessary to postpone the field trip altogether. A certain degree of flexibility is essential in all outdoor programmes.

If the field trip is a full-day one, it is probable that you will need to have students bring packed lunches and, often, drinks. You should also check and see what toilet facilities exist at or near the field trip venue. Even for a half-day excursion, these can be needed by some students. 'Bush toileting' may be a little difficult on a trip to the local area.

At the excursion venue, students should be familiarised with the location. Boundaries should be clearly delineated, the location of any relevant facilities indicated, and any special instructions for working given.

References

Cornell, J.B. (1979) *Sharing Nature with Children*, Ananda Publications, Nevada City, California, USA.

Falk, J. and Balling, J. (1980) 'The School Field Trip: Where You Go Makes the Difference', *Science and Children* 17 (6).

—— and Balling, J. (1982) 'The Field Trip Milieu: Learning and Behaviour as a Function of Contextual Events', *Journal of Educational Research* 76 (1).

Gough, N. (1985) *Curriculum Programmes for Practical Learning*, Curriculum Branch, Curriculum Programmes Section, Department of Education, Melbourne, Victoria.

Hammerman, D.R. and Hammerman, W.M. (1973) *Teaching in the Outdoors*, Burgess, Minneapolis, Minnesota, USA.

Hannaford, B.D. (1986) *A Risky Business—Changing a Secondary School*, Pagel, Adelaide.

Liebing, E.L. (1975) 'Educational Excursions and Diversions', Unpublished thesis, Advanced Diploma in Teaching, South Australia College of Advanced Education, Adelaide.

Mackenzie, A.A. and White, R. (1982) 'Field Work in Geography and

Long-term Memory Structures', *American Education Research Journal* 99.

McRae, K. (1986) 'Outdoor Education 'Down Under': Diversity, Direction?', *Adventure Education* 3 (3).

Smith, J., Carlson, R., Donaldson, G. and Masters, H. (1973) *Outdoor Education*, Prentice-Hall, Englewood Cliffs, NJ, USA.

Stoddard, G.D. (1961) 'Educating People for Outdoor Recreation', Paper presented to the Conference of State Inter-agency Committees on Recreation, Bean Mountain, New York, USA, 23 May.

Swan, M.D. (1986) Various unpublished papers on research studies in outdoor education, Lorado Taft Field Campus, Northern Illinois University, USA.

Van Matre, S. (1974) *Acclimatisation*, American Camping Association, Martinsville, Indiana, USA.

8
Off-School Field Centres for Environmental Education

Joan Webb

Defining the Centre for Environmental Education

One recognisable component of outdoor education is environmental education which aims at increasing awareness of, and concern for, the environment. It entails practice in decision-making in order to solve current environmental problems and to prevent the development of new ones. It is clear that environmental education must, of necessity, be directed towards the development of attitudes and skills appropriate to the maintenance and improvement of the quality of the whole environment.

School-based environmental education is discussed in detail in Chapter 3, but for the purposes of this chapter, it is desirable to identify certain key elements which should be present in any programme. They are:

—its integrated nature
—a concern for the development of environmental awareness
—a problem-solving and activity-centred orientation, and
—its decision-making component

It is also essential to recognise that for the purposes of environmental education in Australian schools today, environment should be taken to mean the total surroundings of all people and other living things. As such, it has many facets including natural systems and human constructions, as well as cultural, social, historical, economic, aesthetic and political components.

The rapid growth of environmental concern during the 1970s led to the establishment of a number of field studies centres in Australia, following similar trends in Britain and the United States. Field studies, particularly in the natural environment, were early seen as an important component of environmental education. Today the classic 'field studies centre' or 'nature centre' is more likely to be seen as a vehicle of the broad concept of environmental education. A variety of off-school centres, out of the classic field studies centre mould, also contributes towards the dissemination of environmental education in schools and the general community. A significant indicator of this trend was the proposal in NSW in 1987 to change the title of the Department of Education Field Studies Centres to Environmental Education Centres.

For the purpose of this chapter, the following criteria are used in order to identify a facility as a 'centre for environmental education':

Sharing

(1) an area of accessible environmental resources of a natural, semi-natural, or man-made character suitable for the study of any aspect of the environment

(2) leadership by an autonomous, professional director, the allocation of trained teaching staff to implement programmes, and of support staff to help in management

(3) a clearly-defined educational policy and one of more programmes aimed at those either within the formal education system and/or outside it in order to increase their awareness and understanding of the environment

The application of these criteria led to the recognition of a number of centres or facilities as potential vehicles for the promotion of environmental education, differing according to the nature of the resource, the kind of programme being offered, the type of administration under which the centre operates, and whether they are residential or day centres.

Classification According to Administration

(1) *Centres supported and staffed by the state Department of Education*
Examples: Queensland Field Study Centres such as Pullenvale (day) and Numinbah Valley (residential).
New South Wales Field Studies Centres such as Field of Mars (day) and Wambangalang (residential); Whipstick (Bendigo, Victoria, residential); Arbury Park (South Australia, residential); Marine Studies Centre (Woodbridge, Tasmania, day).

(2) *Centres staffed by Department of Education but supported by another government department or community group*
Examples: National Parks and Wildlife Service support St Helena Island in Queensland; Royal Field Studies Centre in New South Wales; the Zoological Board of Victoria supports Melbourne Zoo and Healesville Sanctuary; the Shortland Wetlands Centre (Newcastle) is supported by the Hunter Wetlands Trust; the Rottnest Island Authority Supports the Kingstown Environmental Education Centre on Rottnest Island, Western Australia.

(3) *Centres administered by tertiary institutions*
Examples: Crommelin Biological Field Station of the University of Sydney, Pearl Beach, New South Wales.

(4) *Centres administered by private bodies or private individuals*
Examples: Binna Burra Environmental Centre, Queensland, supported by the Lamington Natural History Association; Chakola (Kangaroo Valley, New South Wales); Wangat Lodge (Dungog, New South Wales); Yarrahapinni (Kempsey, New South Wales); Merribrook (Margaret River, Western Australia).

(5) *Centres administered by the Department of Sport and Recreation*
Example: Broken Bay Sport and Recreation Centre, New South Wales.

(6) *Centres controlled by individual schools*
(a) Government, for example, Bumberry, (New South Wales) attached to Dulwich High School; Mt Cameron Field Study Centre, attached to Scottsdale High School (Tasmania).
(b) Private, for example, Camp Knox (New South Wales) attached to Knox Grammar School, and Timbertop (Victoria) attached to Geelong Grammar School.

Classification According to Programmes

Grade 4   Programmes have a strong emphasis on adventure-type pursuits and/or development of social skills; environmental education is incidental
Examples: Camp Knox; Bumberry

Grade 3   Programme   has   a   balance   of   adventure/socialisation/

environmental education activities

Examples: New South Wales Sport and Recreation Centres; Chakola

Grade 2   Programmes are concerned with academic or interest studies of biological phenomena or landscape, for example, marine studies, animal behaviour in a zoo, the strata displayed in a local quarry; programmes also extend the studies to include environmental issues and environmental management

Examples: Melbourne Zoo Education Centre, Marine Studies Centre (Victoria)

Grade 1   Programmes contribute not only to a knowledge of the environment, but encourage an awareness of, and a concern for, the environment; programmes interdisciplinary in nature

Examples: Timbertop (Victoria); Yarrahapinni (New South Wales); Arbury Park (South Australia); Queensland Department of Education Field Study Centres; New South Wales Department of Education Field Studies Centres; Wangat Lodge (New South Wales); Mt Cameron (Tasmania); Kingstown Environmental Education Centre (Rottnest Island, Western Australia).

The Role of the Off-School Centre

A satisfied teacher wrote to the teacher-in-charge at Yarrahapinni Ecology Study Centre after a visit to the centre:

> Many thanks for your assistance during our visit last week at Yarrahapinni. The overwhelming reaction of students and parents to our camp has been tremendous. The Principal has received a number of letters and a great many phone calls expressing appreciation that the school offered such an experience—the kids are still on a high and getting a great buzz out of it. We've done a brainstorm recall session on what they learned, and we are really quite surprised at how much they got out of the environmental experience. We will be putting on a slide display and talk at the next P&C meeting—so we are very hopeful of returning next year.

Yarrahapinni Ecology Study Centre at Grassy Head, near Kempsey, New South Wales is just one of a number of off-school field centres in Australia which aim to provide support for environmental education programmes developed by schools. It is obvious from the detailed inter-disciplinary and long-term nature of environmental education that an effective programme must be whole-school based. However, study units or themes developed in the school can be enriched by specialised activities and field work in a field study centre. Field study centres/environmental centres can only complement, not replace, a school programme of environmental education.

The policy on environmental education for department schools in Queensland (1987: 4) states:

> A visit to a field study centre should not be seen as an end in itself, or even as a total experience for the learner. Such a visit must be regarded as an integral part of the programme offered by the school. The special role of the field study

centre rests upon it capacity to provide learning activities which cannot readily be developed within the resources of an individual school.

A specific example of such specialised roles for off-school centres is the St Helena Island Education Unit, Queensland, which is responsible, through the Queensland National Parks and Wildlife Service, for scheduling school groups wishing to visit the island and providing programmes, in a range of disciplines, for the visiting students. St Helena is an historic site, and the ruins of its penal establishment have great historical significance, providing an opportunity for students to gain an insight into the past, the way of life in the prison, the establishment of a settlement, the problems encountered, and the way in which they were overcome.

Through these and other studies, students can become increasingly aware of social attitudes of an era, current influences and the impact of humans on their environment.

What is provided by centres like Yarrahapinni and St Helena that makes them so worthwhile as resources for environmental education?

First, they provide specialised environmental encounters that the school cannot provide; second, they have expert staff who can not only provide expertise during the actual visit, but who also assist teachers in the planning and implementation of work units for which the visit is only one part; and third, in the case of Yarrahapinni, there is the advantage of residential facilities.

The functions of an off-school centre often extend beyond these three basic provisions. The Field of Mars Field Studies Centre at Ryde, New South Wales, for example:

—is a resource centre for environmental education and provides library facilities for teachers and students
—provides sites for students from Kindergarten to Year 12 to undertake field work relating to all areas of the curriculum
—assists teachers to design and carry out field work at the sites selected by them
—acts as a venue for staff development, in-service courses and seminars (student and teacher)
—assists teachers with implementation of environmental education
—writes and produces resource material

Two innovative approaches to the use of an off-school centre have been developed at the Shortland Wetlands Centre in Newcastle, New South Wales. The establishment in 1985 of the Shortland Wetlands Centre by the Hunter Wetlands Trust, the staffing of the Centre by the Teacher-in-Charge of the New South Wales Education Department's Awakabal Field Studies Centre and the provision of an additional teacher at Awakabal, all enabled the pioneering of a teacher education programme in environmental education at the University of Newcastle. It aims to develop the basic teaching skills required of any pre-service teacher training programme to provide students with a licence to teach. However, emphasis is placed on practical work in the environment, with continued stress on using it as a resource across all aspects of the curriculum and with carry-over into the classroom in a well-defined school-wide programme.

The teacher training programme involves visits to the centre, a workshop conducted by staff, assistance by students in school excursions, and the option of a four-week practice teaching block jointly at the Shortland Wetlands Centre and the Awakabal Field Studies Centre at Dudley. Readers are invited to consult the paper by Maddock (June 1986) for further details on this initiative.

Another initiative taken by the staff and management at Shortland is a broad community-based approach in which whole families are encouraged to visit the centre and take part in programmes. The staff members believe that desirable attitudes cannot develop in isolation from the family situation. The community emphasis is extended to the encouragement of tourists, radio programmes, newspaper articles, and an outreach team of visiting speakers, all play a part in bringing uncommitted people into the centre.

Two important aspects of the use of off-school centres need to be considered: first, the organisation of the visit to achieve maximum benefits, and second, the development of field centres by schools and/or the community. Before discussing these two elements of field centre use, a number of existing centres will be described and presented as examples to illustrate the variety of centres which exist, with particular reference to the nature of sites, types of management and programmes available.

Centres in Australia

The *Arbury Park Outdoor School* is owned and operated by the Education Department of South Australia and was funded partly by a Schools Commission innovations grant in 1975 of $220,000, with the balance of approximately $500,000 coming from state revenue. It is situated 23 kilometres from Adelaide, near the township of Bridgewater in the Adelaide Hills. It caters for both primary and secondary students, with their teachers, either on a Monday-to-Friday basis, or over a weekend. The site is in use every week of the school year and demand for its use is approximately four times that which can be accommodated.

The facilities, designed to cater for up to ninety-six children plus teachers, include dormitory units, a gymnasium, teacher's residence, tennis court and a main building which has withdrawal rooms, wet areas, general purpose dining area, kitchen, laundry and offices.

The ninety-four hectares of land include natural bush, de-natured areas, dams, a nursery of European trees and Cox's Creek, which was used in earlier days to operate the flour mill at Bridgewater. The area abounds in bird and insect life. The four broad aims of the Arbury Park Outdoor School are as follows:

(1) To provide experiences for children which will enable them to develop positive attitudes to, and respect for, the environment.
(2) In a setting which is different from the normal school, to give teachers opportunities to relate curriculum directions to real life

situations, and to assist them in programming with ideas and resource material.

(3) To introduce children to new choices of leisure activities centred on the outdoors.

(4) With special programme components, to improve interpersonal skills amongst children, and between staff and children, taking advantage of the already improved relationships which result from the residential nature of the course.

The Outdoor School develops and trials innovative techniques, including simulation and conflict games in natural settings; long-term studies in monitoring natural phenomena; Earth Education sensory programmes; major landscaping projects; and wood-lot development and management.

Like St Helena in Queensland, the *Royal National Park Field Studies Centre* near Sydney, New South Wales, is a joint venture between the National Parks and Wildlife Service and the Department of Education. Facilities are provided by the service and staff supplied by the New South Wales Education Department. The teacher-in-charge, Mr John Critchlow, believes that this joint venture is a successful one; the field studies centre is not a separate entity, but forms part of the service complex (facilities are shared), and free communication occurs between rangers and the field centre staff. In general, as is the case with all centres staffed by the Department of Education, use is restricted to four days a week during school terms, and bookings are restricted to government schools, because of the high demand. Critchlow does take a number of TAFE groups on weekends, and occasional Girl Guide and church groups, but the general policy is to exclude weekend and school holiday use. The Education Department pays the salaries of two teachers, and a part-time secretary and general assistant. Programmes tend to have an ecological emphasis and promote national park policy in terms of awareness, responsibility and management problems.

For twelve years, the *Fortitude Valley Field Study Centre* has been providing assistance to schools undertaking urban studies in Brisbane, Queensland. Initially located in the Fortitude Valley State School, the centre concentrated on primary level programmes in the surrounding area. Since moving to Spring Hill, the range of programmes available has been expanded to include a number of units especially developed for secondary levels and based on field work in the central area of Brisbane. A comprehensive programme includes such topics as:

—studies of the composition, structure and form of the art and architecture of the city (Art)

—studies of aspects of town planning in Brisbane, including development control plans (Design in Action)

—the use of the city area as a location for the production of documentary-type video programmes, possibly relating to issues covered in other subject areas (Film and Television)

—urban quality surveys; building and area impact studies (Social Science)

—studies relating to Brisbane architecture (Manual Arts)

Fortitude Valley Field Study Centre is just one of fifteen field study centres in Queensland, with a total staff of almost forty teachers and a commitment by the Queensland Department of Education to ensure that every school in the state has reasonable access to a centre. Programmes vary from an emphasis on marine studies in Cairns, to historical programmes at Pullenvale (Brisbane) and St Helena, to rain-forest studies at Paluma, up in the hills ninety kilometres north-west of Townsville.

A field centre with a difference is the *Whipstick Environment Centre* at Bendigo in Victoria. A submission was made to the Schools Commission in 1974 to use the local closed school. Work started in 1977, a mud-brick toilet block was built, and the centre officially opened in November 1978, as the only centre of its kind in Victoria. The centre is only a mile from a section of Whipstick mallee, the closest mallee to Melbourne. Historically it is an interesting farming area. An ironbark forest and box forest are close by. Historical urban studies of the gold-rush era are possible inclusions in a study programme. Bird life is prolific.

A mud-brick dining and storage area is now on the site, but the four to five day camps are still accommodated in tents; cooking is on an open fire. The teacher-in-charge, Mr John Lindner, agrees that the site is not the ideal one for a camp-site, due to its open setting but its potential as a rural semi-wilderness experience for the urban child is not in doubt. It is an ideal centre for combining the outdoor experience with environmental education: the camping experience, the bicycle rides to study areas, the historic farming and gold-mining sites, the mallee, the nearby eucalyptus distillery—an integrated experience which is ideal for the primary child.

The *Kerang Environmental Study Centre* is a privately established centre in Victoria on a farm, Macropus Park, which is fifty-five hectare mixed irrigation enterprise joining the Appin State Forest and Appin Recreation Reserve. This centre not only provides work in environmental education in all subject areas for primary, secondary and tertiary students, but provides accommodation facilities and guided tours for family holidays and social groups within the Kerang region.

The facilities consist of two accommodation buildings, totalling eight bedrooms, each with en suite toilet/shower. Each bedroom has three double bunks, and each building has two small teacher rooms. The Ernest Jackson Field Laboratory/Library provides a large area for lectures, discussion groups and basic laboratory work. All meals are prepared on-site at the centre and are provided all-inclusive with the accommodation tariff.

The *Molesworth Environment Centre* is a day-visit centre in a small rural valley approximately thirty minutes from Hobart. The actual centre is a base from which a number of environmental trails and walks spread out through the valley. These trails encompass a wide variety of habitats and provide an ideal vantage point from which to study the whole spectrum of environmental education. The centre's main aim is to develop curiosity, care and concern for the environment by providing teachers with the necessary skills and back-up to conduct effective environmental education experiences with their children in a variety of outdoor settings. These include dry sclerophyll forest, streams and ponds, sandstone cave areas, farms, hills and rock formations. Seminars are held on a regular basis for teachers and parents; schools book the centre out a year in advance on every school day for class excursions.

One initiative developed by the Molesworth Centre is the setting up of a problem-solving trail in a disused hop field adjacent to the centre. Use of this trail is designed to develop in children:

—an increased familiarity and identification with the natural world
—increased sense of confidence and self-esteem
—increased co-operation and natural support between members of a group
—increased joy in being themselves as part of a group solving problems together in the environment
—language and problem-solving abilities through discussion of various tasks
—a feeling of ease in their environment through their senses and through their understanding, making them more aware of their ultimate dependence on the natural environment

The *Mt Cameron Field Study Centre* is located in the Mt Cameron Range, 145 kilometres and 2½ hours from Launceston in Tasmania. It was established as a result of an innovations grant in 1976 and was built and developed by the staff of Scottsdale High School, the people of Scottsdale in general, and their service clubs in particular. It is run by a management committee consisting of staff representatives and interested individuals from the community. Booking of the centre and hire of equipment is made through the Bursar, Scottsdale High School. A number of programmes have been developed for the Mt Cameron area and are available to the users of the centre on request. These include, for Year 8, a hike involving land-mark identification, navigation, local mining history, and plant identification. Mapping exercises and orienteering courses are also available. For Grade 9, notes on a challenging obstacle course, local history, geology and botany are available. For Grade 10, resources and notes for a detailed study of the wild-life and water environment in the north-east have been prepared. A handbook is available for conducting a survival camp.

Yarrahapinni is the ideal environmental study site for outback New South Wales children. The privately-run centre is on a unique beachfront property of seventy-two acres located near the north arm of the Macleay River between Kempsey and Nambucca Heads. Study programmes cover such topics as rain-forest, wet and open forest, banana plantation, fresh-water creek and lagoon, paper-bark swamp, reefs, ocean beach, salt-water river, mangroves, stable and unstable sand dunes, flora and fauna. The habitats covered by the study programme are found on or within 800 metres of the camp. The camp can accommodate 104 people in bunk-houses containing 16 rooms, to house from 2 to 9.

Dorroughby, near Lismore, is a residential New South Wales Department of Education Centre with an excellent programme that combines studies in the environment with adventure pursuits, personal and social development, and arts/crafts. The teacher-in-charge, Mr Ian Clements, believes that even in an inter-disciplinary programme, the children need to be confronted with the fundamentals of environmental education and how to deal with environmental issues. It is essential that pupils are given sufficient instruction to develop skills they will use on their field visit;

activities in the school grounds should precede any excursion to a field centre in order to receive maximum benefit from a trip which is often costly in terms of time and money.

The *Townsville Environmental Education Centre*, whose field centre is at Paluma, in the hills, sends the classroom teacher a plan of the unit to be covered, with activities for the pre-excursion, the week of the excursion and the post-excursion. Under the headings of 'concept', 'learning experience' and 'resources', the teacher, working on a dry forest unit, for example, can cover the birds of the forest, poetry, songs, first aid, and so on, on the week before the visit. The week of the visit includes forestry and conservation, language arts, mathematics, a forest walk, sensory awareness activities, a leaf litter study and research on forests. Post-excursion activities include art/craft, drama, music, planting trees, role-play in an environmental issue and production of a small newspaper—all related to the forest experience.

An essential prerequisite, of course, is the forward planning that includes a booking at the centre (often six months ahead), permission from the school principal and parents, liaison with centre staff, transport arrangements and perhaps purchase of food.

Establishing a Field Study Centre

An off-school field study centre has four basic elements: land, building, people and programmes.

Land

There are three important factors in selecting a site:

(1) Ideally the land should be as varied as possible to allow for a diversity of studies, to maintain interest for all kinds of people and to allow for lay-over areas which prevent over-use.
(2) In times of rising transport costs, a centre should be ideally placed near a railway station, or within a short distance of one, so that local bus companies can transport the group at low cost.
(3) The site should be accessible at all times; the building/camping site should be carefully considered in terms of aspect, drainage, shelter, water and electricity.

Problems with location often arise in centres developed from closed schools. For example, the Whipstick Environment Centre at Bendigo is in an area of great potential, but the actual camp-site, chosen because of the availability of a weatherboard classroom from the Neilborough East Closed School, is most uninviting. The site is too exposed, especially in hot months; drinking water is a problem, and a location closer to the range of habitats available would have been better.

Another problem concerning location is the siting of Muogamarra Field Studies Centre in New South Wales in a nature reserve. For several months of the year, due to safety precautions in relation to bushfires, the centre is inaccessible to schools. Furthermore, while it is commendable that the reserve is being used for educational purposes, adults, many encouraged by their children who have visited the centre, try to enter at the weekend when the reserve is closed. If a field studies centre is placed in a closed reserve, ideally there should be a ranger on duty at weekends so that programmes can be available for the general community.

However, for those wishing to establish a centre with minimum costs, wise consideration of closed sites on Department of Education land, or that of other government departments, such as Forestry, can be profitable.

Dulwich High School in Sydney, New South Wales, has an annex at Bumberry, thirty kilometres from Parkes, in the buildings of a small school closed in 1971. It was taken over by Dulwich High School in 1974 after submissions from the then-headmaster, Mr W. Miles. The school organises at least six trips a year from its junior forms, and senior classes use it as a base for ecological studies.

The school population is more than 90 per cent migrant and the staff sees the centre more as an opportunity for developing socialisation skills and helping in adjustment than for environmental education. An unstructured but active programme is conducted throughout the four-day stay; from Bumberry there is access to the Parkes Telescope, the Lachlan Village, dams, hikes over the mountains to quarry sites, local farms and the landscape of the west.

Recently Dulwich High received some Disadvantaged Schools' money for renovation: new toilets, roof repairs and verandahs and washrooms. The centre consists of boys' and girls' sleeping quarters (mattresses on the floor), a storeroom off each sleeping quarter, and a washroom in between. Cooking facilities are all outdoors.

Even with its emphasis on the socialisation experience, at Bumberry there is an opportunity for city children to have a real outback experience, perhaps their first environmental encounter.

Programmes and Buildings

After acquisition of the land, the most sensible approach is to plan the programme and then fit the building to the programme. The plan of activities and the development of the property and buildings should be related. It cannot be too heavily stressed that people familiar with the proposed programme and with school and community visitor needs, must liaise with the architect. Among other things, for example, thought must be given to:

(1) The main building, which should contain space for exhibits, a library, office, rest-rooms, an assembly room (which can double for audio-visual displays) and a visitor workshop or laboratory
(2) Toilet facilities, which, if possible, should have access to the outside and the interior
(3) An entrance area which can cope with thirty wet or muddy children
(4) Enough wall space for exhibits and notice-boards
(5) Outdoor assembly areas: log seating, space for camp-fire
(6) Working space for the staff essential for preparation and printing of written materials, and preparation of interpretive devices and exhibits
(7) Maintenance and storage space, an essential either inside or outside the main building

(8) Provision for resources such as gardens of native plants, small demonstration plots of crops, beehives, and bird-feeding stations

There are examples of field centres in Australia which are dysfunctional because planning facilities and the programmes did not go hand in hand and do not reflect the needs of staff or users. This is not the case with the programmes in environmental education developed for pupils at Geelong Grammar School in Victoria.

A few kilometres out of Mansfield, on the edge of the mountains, is *Timbertop*, a residential school for the whole of Year 9 boys and girls enrolled at Geelong Grammar School. Here is a school whose policy and objectives for its fourteen to fifteen year-old students reflect a commitment to environmental education, and one also to the physical, moral and social development of the individual child. Science, geography and history are very heavily oriented towards the study of local environmental issues, and 140 students of the 200 in residence took the environmental studies option in 1987. The integrated nature of the curriculum, the outdoor pursuits, the stress on developing skills necessary for communal living and the site itself, combine to make living together in this particular environment the most important part of a school experience.

The successful field study centre network developed by the Queensland Department of Education has expanded over the past fourteen years as a result of careful planning and management policy by Mr Jack Althaus, a Senior Adviser in Agricultural and Environmental Education. Mr Althaus would carefully inspect any schools or forestry sites being considered for closure and would accept or reject them on criteria such as have already been discussed. His policy was not initially to allocate fancy buildings, but to choose an ideal site with a range of habitats, and then erect essentials such as toilet blocks, and appoint selected, trained staff.

People

The success or failure of a field studies centre may depend on the quality of its staff. A centre ideally needs a trained educational director, one or more assistants, a secretary, and a caretaker or groundsman. With centres supported by the Education Department in each state, such staffing is possible. However, the educational staff are still expected to be a jack-of-all-trades, specialists in landscaping, gardening, general maintenance, field work, first aid, and so on. This presents an even greater problem for the private operator who attempts to be both manager and teacher, and sometimes fails to meet the demands of 7-day a week, on-call 24 hours life-style.

The ideal enterprise may be a joint venture, with community or private sponsorship, and the Department of Education supplying the staff. This is the situation at the *Shortland Wetlands Centre*, Newcastle, already referred to, a centre which is a co-operative venture between the Education Department, community groups, the University and the College of Advanced Education. Corporate sponsors (such as BHP), the Newcastle City Council, a CEP grant, and support from the members of the Hunter Wetlands Trust, all combined to find the resources to buy the land and establish a suitable building. However, such an enterprise is not possible without the dedication, initiative and forward thinking of a few key people who go out and seek support, lay the foundations, establish policies and make the dream become a reality.

It would be difficult to identify the typical or ideal person to fill the role of director for a centre. The ideal residential centre needs a manager as well as an educational director; the centre which operates for day visits could only function with its teacher-in-charge as director, but needs secretarial and other ancillary staff as support. Given that different people can operate just as effectively even if their methods differ, it is suggested that certain characteristics mark a successful director:

—a broadly-based academic training
—experience in both teaching and some other occupation
—a holistic approach to the study of the environment
—an interest in the needs of the local community
—time and a creative flair for preparing suitable written materials
—practical common sense
—tolerance, flexibility, initiative, enthusiasm, persistence and a sense of humour

Teaching in an Off-School Field Centre

It would be impossible to present a typical model for the Australian off-school field centre and the kind of teaching and programmes which are conducted there. As indicated above, locations vary from the urban environment to the farm, from the coral island to the dry whipstick mallee. Similarly, teaching varies, with teachers being supported by a number of administrative and/or other ancillary staff in some centres, while other teachers/directors need to be on call twenty-four hours a day, seven days a week, to serve as a jack-of-all-trades. Programmes also differ from centre to centre, reflecting not only the diversity in habitats, but differences in teaching styles and personalities of the people in charge.

Mr Jack Althaus has the responsibility for co-ordinating the field centre network in that state. He has stated (personal communication, 1987) that within the guidelines of a basic policy he allows his teacher-in-charge to operate with a certain degree of freedom and flexibility; he is satisfied that the staff of the different centres enjoy not only variety in habitats, but an individuality of teaching styles.

It is, however, possible to make a number of generalisations about teaching in the off-school field centre:

— over the past ten years, centres have made a role change from a facility providing specialised studies, mainly of an ecological nature, to a learning or resource centre providing integrated programmes, issue-oriented and less structured
— programmes emphasise concept and skills development; simulation activities are used; the programme at the centre is integrated with an extended school-based programme
— the number of worksheets has been greatly reduced: emphasis is on the experiential

— staff are capable, dedicated and experienced, but have to display a flexibility that fits them for any task
— teaching staff in centres often have little opportunity for professional development; only Queensland provides pre-service and in-service courses for government field study centres, and in New South Wales the Department of Sport and Recreation provides in-service training for staff in their centres

Comments from several people who have worked in the same centre for eight to ten years are of particular interest. M. Keith Enchelmaier of the Fortitude Valley Urban Field Study Centre, Queensland, said (personal communication, 1986) he now tries to relate his work to large-scale issues, meaning that he looks first at the level of student development and the things which relate to young people, and moves from there to more global concerns.

Content is not as important; awareness and sensitivity, especially with the lower grades, now take precedence. Programmes are better developed, walks are shorter, the field studies visit is only part of a larger unit, and the use of structured worksheets is kept to a minimum.

Mr David Kennelly of Thalgarrah, New South Wales believes there is value in staying over a period of time; he is part of the local community, and the increase in knowledge of the local area leads to more relaxed and authoritative teaching. The structure is less formal, and some time is set aside for playing environmental games, allowing children to enjoy themselves in the new environment.

Mr Terry Parkhouse of Yarrahapinni, New South Wales has not changed his policy over the years, but is continually updating his materials. At the personal level he is now advocating that knowledge should result in action, and he introduces the study of issues where appropriate.

Conclusion

For those teachers convinced of the value of outdoor education, the ideal programme should involve a comprehensive set of in-school learning experiences, but it is recommended that such a programme is complemented, supported and enriched by one or more experiences at an off-school centre and in other appropriate outdoor settings. A number of benefits may be gained from the inclusion of off-school visits in the total school programme, especially in the area of environmental education. First, there is no way that any state system could move directly to school-based environmental education without the in-servicing of teachers in the field, and that would operate best through the field studies centre network where teachers can see the way in which their pupils are changed by the field experience, and learn from the teaching methods of personnel operating the centre. Second, even if classroom teachers reached the point where they could effectively conduct their own school-based environmental programmes, there would still be a place for the experience of visiting a particular centre or facility such as St Helena Historic Site, the rain-forest at Paluma or Binna Burra in Queensland, the coastal eco-systems of Yarrahapinni in New South Wales and places like Dubbo Zoo.

For the city child, an experience of a dry inland environment such as Whipstick in Victoria or Wambanalang in New South Wales might well be thought to be highly desirable. Third, the advantage of a residential site with a balanced programme of environmental education and adventure pursuits such as Chakola, New South Wales has tremendous potential as a socialising experience.

In the off-school centre, the classroom teacher and the interested individual have the opportunity to sample an environment different from the local one, to make use of resources perhaps not available elsewhere, and to benefit from the expertise of enthusiastic and skilled staff. Teachers have a wide variety of facilities and expertise from which to choose, and the growth of private and community sponsored centres over the last few years will help spread the message that outdoor education is not just for children.

Reference

Webb, J.B.A. (1980) *Survey of Field Studies Centres in Australia*, ANPWS and (1988) *Survey of Environmental Education Centres in Eastern Australia*, ANPWS.

List of Centres

Arbury Park Outdoor School,
Arbury Park Road,
Bridgewater, SA 5155.
Phone: (08) 339 3987

Binna Burra Environmental Studies Centre,
c/- Binna Burra Lodge,
Lamington National Park,
via Beechmont, Qld 4211.
Phone: (075) 33 3574

Broken Bay Sport and Recreation Centre
c/- PO Brooklyn, NSW 2253.
Phone: (043) 79 1101

Bumberry,
c/- Dulwich High School,
Seaview Street,
Dulwich Hill, NSW 2203.
Phone: (02) 560 7299

Camp Knox,
c/- Knox Grammar School,
Pacific Highway,

Wahroonga, NSW 2076.
Phone: (02) 487 0122

Chakola,
PO Box 24,
Kangaroo Valley, NSW 2577.
Phone: (044) 65 1222

Crommelin Biological Research Station,
75 Crystal Avenue,
Pearl Beach, NSW 2256.
Phone: (043) 41 8007

Dharnya Centre,
c/- Department of Conservation, Forests and Lands,
Sand Ridge Track,
Barmah, Vic. 3639.
Phone: (058) 69 3302

Dorroughby Field Studies Centre,
Mullumbimby Road,
Dorroughby NSW 2480.
Phone: (066) 89 5286

Field of Mars Field Studies Centre,
Field of Mars Reserve,
Pittwater Road,
East Ryde, NSW 2113.
Phone: (02) 816 1298

Fortitude Valley Field Study Centre,
c/- Department of Education,
PO Box 33,
North Quay, Qld 4002.
Phone: (07) 224 7035

Kerang Environmental Study Centre,
Macropus Park,
Appin, Victoria;
PO Box 248,
Kerang, Vic. 3579
Phone: (054) 57 6222

Kingstown Environmental Education Centre,
Rottnest Island, WA 6161.
Phone: (09) 292 5152

Marine Studies Centre,
Jetty Road,
Woodbridge, Tas. 7162.
Phone: (002) 67 4649

Molesworth Environment Centre,
c/- Molesworth Primary School,
Molesworth, Tas. 7140.
Phone: (002) 61 2091

Mt Cameron Field Study Centre,
c/- Scottsdale Primary School,
Scottsdale, Tas. 7260.
Phone: (003) 52 2477 (School) or (003) 55 2215 (Mt Cameron)

Merribrook,
Margaret River,
c/- PO Cowaramup, WA 6289.
Phone: (097) 55 5490

Numinbah Valley Field Study Centre,
MS 208 Numinbah Valley, via Nerang, Qld.
Phone: (075) 33 4148

Pullenvale Field Study Centre,
250 Grandview Road,
Pullenvale, Qld 4069.
Phone: (07) 374 1002

Royal National Park Field Studies Centre,
PO Box 41,
Sutherland, NSW 2232.
Phone: (02) 542 1951

Shortland Wetlands Centre,
PO Box 130,
Wallsend, NSW 2287.
Phone: (049) 51 6446

St Helena Island Education Unit,
c/- Darling Point Special School,
368 The Esplanade,
Manly, Qld 4179.
Phone: (07) 396 0754

Thalgarrah Field Studies Centre,
Rockvale Road,
Armidale, NSW 2350.
Phone: (067) 75 1736

Timbertop,
c/- PO Mansfield, Vic. 3722.
Phone: (057) 77 5503

Townsville Environmental Education Centre,
c/- Vincent State School,

PO Box 415,
Aitkenvale, Qld 4814.
Phone: (077) 75 7233

Wambangalang Field Studies Centre,
Obley Road,
Dubbo, NSW 2830.
Phone: (068) 87 7209

Wangat Lodge,
Chichester Dam Road,
via Dungog, NSW 2420.
Phone: (049) 95 9275

Whipstick Environment Centre,
c/- Ministry of Education,
PO Box 442,
Bendigo, Vic. 3550.
Phone: (054) 40 3111

Yarrahapinni Ecology Centre,
Grassy Head,
via Stuart's Point, NSW 2441.
Phone: (065) 69 0771

9
Residential Outdoor Education

Bruce Hayllar

Introduction

This form of outdoor education refers to programmes which take place at established centres with residential accommodation. Residential centres vary greatly in terms of ownership, programme objectives and development, levels of physical infrastructure and the potential offered by their immediate and regional environments for outdoor education experiences. This chapter considers different types of residential centres, details examples of different programmes and provides guidelines for planning outdoor education experiences in residential settings.

Residential Outdoor Education: Types, Purposes, Programmes

Centres are owned by individual schools (both private and public), state departments of education and other government instrumentalities, commercial operators, church-affiliated organisations and voluntary associations. Programmes vary from the highly-structured and centrally organised, to the decentralised, dynamic and student-centred. Objectives include personal and social development, environmental awareness, the learning of outdoor skills and inter-curricular activities. Levels of development and standards of accommodation range from the relatively primitive to the luxurious. Physical environments extend from mountainous alpine regions to beach-fronts, from inland lakes to coastal estuaries and from isolated rural sites to the urban fringes of major capital cities. Staffing levels range from sites with non-resident caretakers to centres with complete administrative, programme and maintenance staff.

Given the diversity of services and facilities offered by the large number of residential sites situated throughout Australia (Victoria alone has over 300), it is not surprising that centre-based programmes are the predominant form of outdoor educational experience available to students of all ages. Their popularity is attributable to a number of factors including:

Access: the large number of residential centres makes them relatively accessible to most schools
Organisation: the existence of accommodation, catering and programme facilities on site can take much of the organisational burden from the leaders of visiting groups

Incremental experiences: residential sites provide a good point of entry for student's early experiences in the outdoors. (The existence of an established facility with basic conveniences may also be attractive to the hesitant parent)

Staff demands: many sites have existing programmes or can provide support for visiting staff who are attempting to develop their own programmes. This is particularly important where staff members are interested in providing outdoor education experiences for their students, but lack confidence in their existing skills and expertise

Cost: although costs vary widely between centres, they are nevertheless market-oriented and thus provide facilities and services at competitive rates

Establishment factors: because most residential centres have well-established facilities and programme resources, schools can have an annual outdoor education experience without incurring the costs of purchasing individual or group equipment

Weather: residential programmes are less influenced by existing or changing weather patterns. Thus the opportunity for year round programming is available

The following section reviews examples of different types of outdoor residential centres. While not exhaustive, it provides insight into the diversity of these operations in selected states of Australia.

Centres Owned by State Governments

Highly developed and well established residential outdoor education centres exist in all states. Extensive state-funded networks exist in Victoria, controlled by the Ministry of Education and the Department of Sport and Recreation; in New South Wales, through the Departments of Sport and Recreation and Education; and in Queensland by the Queensland Recreation Council.

The New South Wales Department of Sport and Recreation conducts the largest centrally administered public sector residential camping programme in Australia. The primary objective of the NSW centres is to extend, reinforce and supplement the formal education of students in the areas of living skills, the environment and recreation activities. The objectives for each of these areas illustrate the broad goals of outdoor education in the residential setting (Policy Document, NSW Department of Sport and Recreation):

Environmental education: The primary aim of environmental education at centres is to provide children with opportunities to develop an understanding of the broad environmental inter-relationships and interdependency between vegetation, physical-environment, climate, Man and animal life. This is achieved by providing:
—opportunities for direct experiences in outdoor living
—activities which will enable the student to experience directly the 'living environment' and use senses in the discovery and appreciation of the environment

—activities which develop an awareness of the relationship between man and his environment

Recreation education: The aim of recreation activities at centres is to provide opportunities for children to participate in a variety of leisure-time activities with the overall purpose of developing positive attitudes towards recreation participation by providing activities which:

—develop a range of physical and recreation skills
—introduce and extend knowledge of creative and/or recreational activities
—facilitate enjoyable participation in recreational activities
—increase safety awareness

Social living skills education: The aim of social education activities at centres is to develop a knowledge of the factors affecting the relationship between the individual and society with the purpose of developing a commitment to work within accepted community standards by providing opportunities for:

—children to participate in activities where a successful completion of the activity depends on individuals working effectively within a group

Trusting

—children to express, develop and test their ideas in a group environment
—developing leadership skills and responsibility

These objectives guide the operation of twelve residential outdoor education centres situated throughout New South Wales. This state-wide system of centres has grown from the original and rustic Broken Bay National Fitness Camp of the 1940s (built largely by voluntary labour), to a modern network with highly-developed sites, an extensive range of programmes and permanent, full-time teaching and administrative staff. These centres are used throughout the school year for residential outdoor education programmes and in school vacation times for holiday camping. Two different programme structures operate during the school term — whole-school camping and Primary Outdoor Education Programs. The exceptions to this are the secondary school Field Studies Programme operating at the Lake Jindabyne Centre in the Snowy Mountains, and the junior secondary Field Studies and Outdoor Skills Programme operating at the Little Wobby Centre on the Hawkesbury River, north of Sydney.

Whole-school camping is conducted at five centres: Borambola, near Wagga-Wagga in south-western New South Wales; Lake Burrendong, near Wellington in the west of the state; Newnes Forest, near Lithgow in the Blue Mountains west of Sydney; Milson Island on the Hawkesbury River; and the Sydney metropolitan centre of Narrabeen, situated on the northern urban rim. As the name suggests these centres cater specifically for whole-school groups. Schools are formally required to bring their own teaching staff at a ratio of 1:20 students. The programme is conducted under the direction of the resident instructional staff who are employed by

Table 9.1 Five-Day Outdoor Education Programme, Borambola Centre

Monday	Tuesday	Wednesday	Thursday	Friday	
Camp entry	Bike education	Archery	Bivouac	Canoeing	MORNING
Banking	Bike education	Archery	Bivouac	Canoeing	
Orientation					
	Craft	Bivouac	Horse-riding	Grass Ski	AFTERNOON
Boomerangs	Craft	Bivouac	Horse-riding	Grass Ski	
EVENING ACTIVITIES (all groups)					

Note: Morning and afternoon sessions are of 2 hours duration the Department of Sport and Recreation — typically at the ratio of 3 to every 100 participants. Programmes may be of 5 or 7 days duration, although the vast majority of schools attend during the school week only. An example of a whole-school camp programme is outlined in Table 9.1: Primary Outdoor Education Programmes (POEP) are conducted at Lake Keepit, near Tamworth in the north-west of New South Wales; Lake Ainsworth on the far north coast; Myuna Bay and Point Wolstoncroft on Lake Macquarie near Newcastle; and Broken Bay, situated at the mouth of the Hawkesbury River. Individual classes from different schools attend with their own class teacher, again on a 1:20 student ratio. However, POEP centres, unlike whole-school camps, are staffed at the same ratio and with teachers employed by the NSW Department of Education.

Lake Jindabyne Centre is predominantly used by secondary students and focuses on environmental education. Webb (1980: 62) noted that:

> The academic programme is an integrated approach to the environment, carefully balanced in terms of difficulty and nature of the activity, based almost completely on student observation and inference and tied together by looking at man's impact on the environment.

The centre is staffed by secondary school science teachers employed by the Department of Education.

Little Wobby is the smallest centre and takes one or two class groups of junior secondary students with their teachers. Their programme combines field studies and an outdoor skills programme of three to five duration.

As Figure 9.1 suggests, sport and recreation centres, with the exception of Lake Jindabyne and to some extent Little Wobby, direct their programmes towards the teaching of physical recreation and outdoor skills. Social and personal development, environmental and inter-curricular objectives are also evident but are of less importance. The programmes are generally teacher-centred and tend to rely heavily upon the extensive physical facilities and resources developed at the sites. Webb (1980) has argued that this concentration on facilities has in fact hindered the development of the type of programmes which could make use of the varied natural environments in which the centres are located.

The Victorian Ministry of Education has the direct control of three school camps and, through individual school or regionally-controlled centres, the overall responsibility for an additional forty centres. The three Ministry of Education camps: Rubicon School Camp, near Lake Eildon in northern Victoria; Bogong School Camp near Falls Creek in the north-east; and Somers Childrens' Camp on Westernport Bay, south of Melbourne, are fully staffed by qualified outdoor education teachers. Bogong and Rubicon accommodate secondary schools while Somers is for primary school children only. Each of these camps is of the whole-school variety, and visiting teachers are expected to play an active role in the programme. The objectives and programmes of these centres reveal a conscious attempt to meet a range of educational objectives. Like the New South Wales system, there is an emphasis on outdoor recreation activities.

According to its 1988 policy statement, the Bogong School Camp views its educational role as providing:

Figure 9.1   NSW Department of Sport and Recreation Centres, Programme Summary

Activity	Borambola	Broken Bay	Lake Ainsworth	Lake Burrendong	Lake Jindabyne	Lake Keepit	Little Wobby	Milson Island	Myuna Bay	Narrabeen Lakes	Newnes Forest	Point Wolstoncroft
Water Safety and Resuscitation					•							
Windsurfer Sailing												
Tennis	•	•	•	•	•	•	•	•	•	•	•	•
Swimming Pool	•		•	•	•					•	•	•
Swimming	•	•		•				•			•	•
Surf Lifesaving	•	•	•	•	•	•	•	•	•	•	•	•
Snorkelling				•								
Skiing (Snow)					•							
Skiing (Grass)												
Sailing	•							•		•	•	•
Rope Safety										•	•	•
Ropes Course			•		•	•	•	•		•	•	•
Orienteering			•							•	•	
Indoor Games	•	•	•	•	•	•	•	•	•		•	•
Horse Riding	•											
Gymnasium/Gymnastics	•				•							
Golf/Mini-Golf	•				•					•	•	
Gliding							•					
Fun and Fitness Track	•				•					•		•
Fishing	•								•	•		•
Field Games	•	•	•	•	•	•	•	•	•	•	•	•
Fencing	•	•	•	•	•	•	•	•	•	•	•	•
Environmental Education	•	•	•	•	•	•	•	•	•	•	•	•
Dancing	•	•	•	•	•	•	•	•	•	•	•	•
Cricket Nets	•	•		•				•		•		•
Canoeing	•	•	•	•		•	•	•	•	•		•
Bushcraft	•		•	•	•				•	•	•	•
Bushwalking	•	•	•	•	•	•	•	•	•	•	•	•
Boomerang Throwing	•	•	•	•							•	•
BMX Cycling	•	•	•	•	•	•	•	•	•		•	•
Bivouac			•	•					•	•	•	•
Beach Activities		•	•					•	•	•		•
Athletic Track		•	•				•					
Archery	•	•	•	•	•	•	•	•		•	•	•
Air Rifles	•			•		•			•			

a unique educational experience by developing programmes that contain a balanced blend of interacting environmental, outdoor recreational and adventure activities. These activities should enable individuals to learn about themselves, the environment and other people, through guided direct experiences, away from the usual settings of school and home. Through such experiences the students should develop independence, confidence and self-esteem while promoting co-operation, communication and tolerance within groups.

This policy is achieved through a programme which follows two separate yet inter-related directions:

(1) *Designated environmental education sessions*
These sessions should develop within participating students an awareness and sensitivity to the total environment; help students acquire social values and strong feelings of concern for the environment; and encourage them to relate this awareness to the manner in which the total environment is used.

(2) *Outdoor recreation and adventure activities*
These sessions concentrate on the growth and development of such things as student self-esteem, confidence, independence, initiative, reliance, co-operation, tolerance, patience and communication.

They should also stimulate interest in outdoor activities suitable for life-long pursuits. The acquisition of specific recreational skills may be seen as a consequence of these activities.

These sessions should also provide a variety of challenging outdoor activities to fulfil the needs of the students for adventure and excitement and to ensure that all individuals will experience success at one or more of these activities.

This approach of using outdoor recreational and adventure activities as mediums for personal development, environmental education and awareness, should filter through all activities on the programme and should extend into the general socializing and co-operative atmosphere that camp life offers.

Rubicon School Camp draws to the students' attention the broader attributes of the camp experience which they intend to offer and develop with them. Indeed the values espoused are relevant to all residential experiences:

Challenge: a little stress and tension as problems are met and overcome on new activities
Harmony: the ability to live and work together, socialising and making friends away from the usual environment
Respect: for the environment, equipment, and other people
Initiative: at all times, but particularly when under pressure and in demonstrating leadership
Safety: features of which are built into all activities, but not such that they detract from the challenge of the activity

Figure 9.2   Bogong Camp Programme

A   Daily Timetable for a Typical Working Day at the Camp

7.00 am	Lights On
7.10 am	Morning Run
7.20 am	Meal Duty Group to Dining Room
7.45 am	Weather Recording
8.00 am	Breakfast
8.40 am	Dormitory Inspection
9.00 am	Morning Assembly
9.05 am to 12.05 pm	Morning Activity Session
12.20 pm	Meal Duty Group to Dining Room
1.00 pm	Lunch
1.55 pm	Afternoon Assembly
2.00 pm to 5.00 pm	Afternoon Activity Session
5.20 pm	Meal Duty Group to Dining Room
5.30 pm	Weather Recording
6.00 pm	Dinner
7.30 pm to 8.30 pm	Evening Activity Session
8.30 pm	Canteen
9.40 pm	Students into Own Rooms
9.45 pm	Students in Bed
10.00 pm	Lights Out

B   Activities Conducted at Camp

A: Summer Camps (10 days)
B: Spring Camps (8 days)
C: Winter Camps (5 days)

Activities	A	B	C
(i) *Morning and Afternoon Activity Sessions (3 hours)*			
Rockclimbing and Abseiling	•	•	•
Orienteering	•	•	•
Canoeing	•	•	
Ropes Course	•		•
Hike Preparation	•	•	•
Pioneering	•		
Field Studies	•	•	•
Initiative Activities	•	•	•
Introduction to the Environment	•	•	•
(ii) *Evening Session*			
Indoor Games	•	•	•
Night Hike	•	•	•
Survival	•		
Film	•	•	•
Bush Dancing	•	•	•
Disco (Last Night)	•	•	•
Rogaining Preparation	•		•
(iii) Two-day hike	•		
(iv) Downhill Skiing			•
(v) Cross-country Skiing			•
(vi) Rogaining (Full Day)	•	•	•

Note: Visiting Teachers are responsible for the supervising of students between Lights Out (10.00 pm) and 7.00 am the next morning

Our ski camps are aimed at beginners. Students who can ski will not find our programme suitable for them, and by attending they will deprive a non-skier of an ideal introduction to skiing.

The Victorian Department of Sport and Recreation is the other significant government provider of residential facilities, with centres at Anglesea, Bacchus Marsh, Falls Creek, Mt Eliza and Mt Evelyn. In each case, these centres provide a range of facilities and opportunities for residential outdoor education. No programme staff are provided directly by the Department. However, up-to-date records are maintained by specialist staff who may be available to assist teachers with their programmes. In general terms, the Department sees its role as one of providing access to residential experiences and relies on facility users to shape programmes according to their specific educational or recreational needs.

The operational philosophy and management structures of the Victorian Department of Sport and Recreation are similar to those of the Queensland Recreation Council, which maintains thirteen Recreation Camps throughout the state. The Maroon Outdoor Education Centre is the only Education Department Centre operated in Queensland. Situated on the Maroon Dam site, this centre combines an outdoor skills adventure programme with a strong environmental studies element.

The system of dual Department responsibility for residential outdoor education is also evident in Tasmania, which has both Education Department and Division of Recreation centres. Western Australia has five school camps under the direct responsibility of the state Department of Education.

South Australia, like Victoria, has numerous schools with their own outdoor education centres. The Arbury Park Outdoor School, situated in the Adelaide Hills, is owned and operated by the South Australian Department of Education and is the state's only centrally-funded outdoor education centre. The centre is in great demand from primary and secondary schools all over South Australia. While the school is residential, the staff are also conscious of their role to produce resources for teachers so that the impact of the visit carries over to school-based studies. The stated objectives of Arbury Park reflect a recognition of the potential for learning offered by the outdoors:

—to provide experiences for children which will enable them to develop positive attitudes to, and respect for, the environment

—in a setting which is different from the normal school, to give teachers opportunities to relate curriculum directions to real-life situations, and to assist them in programming with ideas and resource material

—to introduce children to new choices of leisure activities centred on the outdoors

—with special programme components, to improve inter-personal skills amongst children, and between staff and children, taking advantage of the already improved relationships which result from the residential nature of the course

Church/Religious-based Facilities

Facilities owned by various denominational groups provide a major resource for residential experiences in all states. Unlike publicly-owned facilities, which tend to be of a uniformly high standard, there is great variance in this sector, from the modern, fully-catered and administered facility to the basic self-catering establishment with an on-site caretaker.

Many of these sites were originally established by central church agencies to provide holiday and retreat venues for members of their congregations. In particular, their pastoral care and youth ministries saw a particular need to provide inexpensive accommodation at sites with opportunities for outdoor recreation and group fellowship. While still maintaining their original mission, most church sites are now available for hire by schools and other organisations, thus providing an excellent resource for residential programmes. Many centres, conscious of the need to attract a broader audience, now trade as Conference Centres. In the Sydney area alone, the Uniting Church has nine such centres.

School-owned or Operated Centres

Independently-owned residential centres, operated by both primary and high schools, have historically been considered the preserve of private schools. However, these days, many state schools have established outdoor education centres of their own. Unlike private schools, which typically have staff dedicated to the centres' operation, it is unusual for state schools to have permanent residential staff. As a consequence, they tend to rely on non-specialist school staff to service their programmes.

The educational philosophies which underpin the operation of the two systems differ quite markedly. Private schools tend to focus their objectives on the personal and social development aspects of outdoor education. This development is based largely on British traditions where private schools, such as Scotland's Gordonstoun, have directed their programmes towards 'character development' through vigorous outdoor pursuits.

In comparison, state school centres, while acknowledging the personal and social development aspects of outdoor education, tend to emphasise the building of inter-curricular relationships and environmental concepts and values. Given the expense of operating such centres, the linkages between the outdoor experience and the regular curriculum need to be emphasised to attract ongoing parental and departmental support. The following examples illustrate these differences:

Marion High School is seen by Webb (1988: 41) as having the most developed secondary outdoor education programme in South Australia. Marion has its own bus, camping and outdoor recreation equipment, as well as its own residential site at Cape Jervis, south of Adelaide. The seventy hectare site overlooks Kangaroo Island and has a small building on site which accommodates up to forty-two students. Their programme seeks to provide students with the opportunity to:

—become aware of the natural environment
—recognise the need for conservation
—improve their observational skills and their ability to record information
—experience new sensory impressions of the natural environment
—be involved in a variety of studies relating to the natural enviroment
—appreciate more fully the beauties of nature

Caulfield Grammar, a private school, has its own outdoor education centre at Yarra Junction. The development of this centre began in 1944 and now comprises 135 hectares, of which 100 are used to support a commercial dairy farm. The property adjoins the Little Yarra River and has immediate access to the Yarra State Forest, as well as the neighbouring Warburton Mountains.

The aims of the Caulfield Grammar programme reflect a commitment to the personal and social development of students through residential outdoor education. While specific objectives are documented for each grade, the general aims of the Mandatory Program are as follows (Whitford undated):

(1) To provide specific situations that will assist an individual to understand himself/herself

(2) To help an individual to relate to his/her peers and with other people

(3) To provide an understanding of, and experience in, community living.

(4) To help an individual to cope with the 'pressures of living' e.g. responsibility, competition, failure, success, fear

(5) To encourage self-reliance, resourcefulness, and the ability to make effective decisions

(6) To spend time away from the comforts of home, the luxuries of modern living and the care of parents

(7) To develop an awareness and understanding of, and respect for, the Australian bush and its inhabitants

(8) To experience life on a farm

(9) To provide some experience in outdoor activities and initiate skills that individuals may wish to pursue as healthy recreational activities

Commercial Residential Outdoor Centres

There has been considerable growth in the number of commercially-operated centres providing residential outdoor education facilities and programmes. The diversity of programme type, standard of facilities, support services and staffing arrangements, reflect the breadth of outdoor education.

The nature of commercial operation (to make a profit), suggests that these centres will be more expensive to attend than those of other organisations. However, most operators are aware of the 'market-place' and attempt to keep costs and services within the reach of their various client groups. This market orientation is reflected in the flexibility of their operations and programmes. Programme flexibility of this type is not always evident within other sectors, particularly in public sector programmes where schools may find it difficult to negotiate programmes to suit their particular needs. By contrast, commercial operators need to be aware of, and be able to adapt to, the requirements and desires of their client groups. The degree of freedom enjoyed by the private sector is, in part, an outcome of their management structures, which are usually owner-operated.

Flexibility in staffing is also apparent. State-run sites tend to employ only qualified and registered teachers, for industrial as well as pedagogical reasons. Private operators are not constrained by this requirement and, therefore, tend to draw their instructors from a diverse range of backgrounds in different disciplines and with expertise in different curriculum areas.

Typically, though, commercial centres tend to focus on accommodation, and the provision of programme opportunity, rather than conducting instructional sessions themselves. Thus, while many supply equipment and programme resources, fully-staffed centres are the exception. When such centres do have permanent instructional staff, their programmes tend to concentrate on the teaching of outdoor skills. The following examples illustrate the range of programmes in the commercial area.

Camp Somerset, situated on the Colo River, and adjacent to Wollemi National Park, west of Sydney, is promoted as a multi-purpose outdoor education centre. It has the facilities to provide accommodation with full catering and complete instruction and supervision of outdoor pursuits programmes, including abseiling, rock-climbing, canoeing, orienteering, survival training and bushcraft.

By contrast, Vivonne Bay Outdoor Education Centre ('The Living Classroom') is a unique commercial venture. Situated on Kangaroo Island, twelve kilometres from the South Australian mainland, it uses the unique natural, cultural, and historic features of the island for the purposes of meeting environmental education and inter-curricular objectives. The programme is 'ranger-led' by the husband-and-wife team who operate the centre.

Variety in programme opportunities, pricing structures, venues and an orientation to the needs of their consumers, are the distinguishing features of commercial operations.

Voluntary/Non-profit Associations

There are many voluntary/non-profit organisations, like the YMCA, Scout Associations, the Youth Hostels Association, and Police and Citizens Clubs which have venues and facilities for residential outdoor education.

The Australian Youth Hostels Association has over 120 hostels Australia-wide and these are generally situated in areas of social, cultural, historic and environmental interest. The hostels vary in size, accessibility and available facilities. However, they are uniformly clean and friendly places, and certainly provide the opportunity for social interaction with individuals from diverse age groups, backgrounds and nationalities. They are generally self-catering. Their main value for outdoor education purposes is the provision of a 'base' from which a programme can operate.

The Scout Association of Australia has a number of metropolitan and regional training centres. These centres are multi-purpose facilities which provide both a training function for scout leaders and a venue for scout camping. Most centres are situated in ideal environments for outdoor education programmes, and most operate on a self-catering basis.

The above overview of residential outdoor education gives some insight into the range of programmes and potential opportunities available.

Clearly, for those teachers who wish to use residential facilities as a component of their outdoor education programmes, the range of options in terms of location, standards of accommodation, cost, personnel, physical environments and programme types, provides great potential for shaping the outdoor experiences around their particular educational objectives.

Planning the Experience

The type of outdoor residential experience undertaken will depend on a range of factors including: the educational objectives established for the programme; the expertise and experience of staff (and perhaps parents); and the age, experience, training, background and physical and emotional capabilities of the students. In addition to pedagogical and human resource considerations, cost, equipment requirements, catering and transport also need to be taken into account. When planning programmes, attempts should be made to involve students at all levels of the process. This can be achieved in a number of ways including (Outdoor Education Unit Guidelines, South Australia):

—discussion of suitable venues and possible sites for the programme
—calculating the costs and logistics of transport. If a bus is to be hired, children could make the initial contact with the company. (It is important that a plan of the information required is developed beforehand and that practice in using the telephone is undertaken before the call is finally made)
—students corresponding with site owners and other key resource people who may be used during the programme, e.g., a letter to parents or the state Forestry Department
—planning the journey. Students could be given the responsibility for determining:
    —departure/arrival times
    —route
    —visits on the way
    —suitable rest stops
    —individual and group responsibilities on arrival at the site

—timetable preparation. Students, in consultation with teaching staff and the residential site staff, could prepare a timetable for:
    —meals
    —recreation activities
    —cleaning rosters
    —activity times

—developing clothing and equipment lists
—discussing and developing rules for outdoor living
—checking and maintenance of any necessary equipment before camp
—arranging a pre-camp meeting with parents to discuss all aspects of the programme

—preparing a camp booklet
—researching the history of the area to be visited and interviewing any staff or students who may have previously used the centre
—organising of fund-raising activities, if necessary

Setting Objectives

In Chapter 10, a planning framework for under-canvas camping is established and used for setting objectives around four main areas of outdoor education. It is suggested here that the same broad framework be applied to residential outdoor education programmes. A set of objectives for a Grade 6, four-day residential experience might be structured in terms of:

Inter-curricular objectives
On the completion of the camp the students will have:
—developed a resource folio which traces the development of Camp Winterton from its beginning as a forestry workers' camp to the present day
—developed a series of creative writing ideas based on the theme of Nature vs Humanity for completion on their return to school
—constructed, in a small group, a map and interpretive three-dimensional collage of Camp Winterton, using only natural, non-living materials

Personal and social development objectives
On the completion of the camp the students will have:
—developed an understanding of the need for working co-operatively to achieve both group and personal goals
—participated in the preparation of food, cleaning of dormitories, and maintenance of the general amenity of the camp environment
—undertaken a minimum of one hour's 'camp service'

Outdoor skills
On the completion of the camp the students will have participated in the following outdoor recreation activities:
—orienteering
—canoeing
—abseiling
—bushwalking

Environmental education
On completion of the camp the students will have:
—investigated the ecosystem of Koala Creek and discussed and recorded the impact that human habitation and upstream development is having on the creek's natural processes
—compiled a folio of the common plants and animals of the dry-leaf forest
—calculated the height of a tree using transact lines and quadrants to demonstrate plant succession and distribution

Selecting the Site

Once the objectives for the camp have been established, a venue or site for the programme needs to be established. Distance to be travelled, cost, available facilities and staffing will clearly influence site selection. However, when undertaking this process consideration should be given to investigating and checking the following (adapted from *Safety in Outdoor Adventure Activities* 1982):

(1) *Buildings*: safety hazards, adequate facilities for wet weather, roof leaks, adequate space for programme needs, ventilation, hygiene and heating
(2) *Accommodation*: suitability for mixed groups, necessity of sharing with other potential users, availability and conditions of beds, blankets, pillows, and mattresses
(3) *Power supply*: lighting, switches, power points and electrical appliances should all be in safe working order
(4) *Water supply*: taps, plumbing, quality, quantity and storage
(5) *Shower and toilet facilities*: numbers, cleanliness, state of repair, availability of *hot* water
(6) *Kitchen*: cooking facilities, fuel supply (gas, oil, wood, electricity), food storage (refrigerators and cupboards), food preparation areas, washing-up facilities, cleaning facilities (mops, brooms, buckets), rubbish disposal and suitability of menu. If the camp is being serviced by an outside caterer, check their willingness and ability to provide for any special food requirements for the group
(7) *Dining room*: sufficient tables, chairs, eating utensils and storage facilities
(8) *Fire safety equipment*: availability and condition of extinguishers, hoses, knapsacks and hydrants
(9) *Grounds*: suitability for planned programme
(10) *Equipment*: condition and suitability of equipment available at the site for programme use (e.g., canoes, ropes, compasses and maps)
(11) *Emergency facilities*: location and telephone number of police, doctor, ambulance and hospital should be noted. A vehicle should be available at the camp in case of emergencies
(12) *First aid equipment*: check the availability at the centre. Additional first aid kits for off-site activities should be taken to camp

The degree of detail required in the site selection process will largely depend on the type of residential venue chosen or on previous experience with their operation. For example, in most state-owned camps and commercial concerns with established credentials, one can usually make assumptions about safety and accommodation standards. As a general rule, it is always worthwhile speaking to someone who has been there before to discuss their experiences so that informed decisions can be made.

Programme Design

In designing programmes, teachers should be aware of the educational objectives established for the experience. In those residential centres which have an established programme and teaching staff, this task is considerably easier, as there should be a match between objectives and the programme on offer. However, where the school has complete responsibility for programme development, the design process is more complex. In developing a programme, consideration should be given to:

(1) *Staff*: experience, training, interests and enthusiasm of those in attendance. Where possible use staff in areas where they have expertise, and support those who are using the experience as a learning tool. Without doubt, effective and capable staff are the prime ingredient for programme success.

(2) *Students*: age, previous camp experience, prior training, particular interests, and perceived physical capabilities. Ideally, students will have considerable input into the programme design during the build-up to the residential experience. For older students with previous experience this role might involve considerable responsibility in overall planning

(3) *Facilities, equipment, and environment of camp*: any programme design must reflect the capacity of the site and its facilities to fulfil objectives.

(4) *Timing*: consideration needs to be given to both the structured and informal programme. Obviously, the first priority is to develop the programme around the formal activities. However, time should be allowed for such things as: student-free time to allow for informal interaction; non-scheduled periods for staff (where practicable); and time to undertake tasks such as food preparation, clearing up and personal ablutions. While the daily programme should make best use of the available time, the schedule should be not so rigorous that people are gulping food, running to make the next activity or having little time for socialising (both staff and students). Timing should also take into account the season, available hours of daylight, meal-times, rising and retiring times for different age groups, and the duration of the camp.

Role of Teachers

The role of teachers will depend largely on the type of residential programme being undertaken. At fully-staffed and programmed outdoor education centres, teachers generally accompany their class and act as an adjunct to existing instructional staff. At other centres, they may assume complete responsibility for both teaching and supervision in non-scheduled periods.

The Visiting Teacher (*Centres with Permanent Instructional Staff*)

At centres with instructional staff, the role of the visiting teacher is generally to support the existing programme and its personnel. (This is certainly the case in the Victorian Ministry of Education Camps and in NSW Department of Sport and Recreation Centres.) Unless teachers have specific skills, their responsibilities generally revolve around matters of student welfare: supervision in the evening and in periods of non-scheduled activity and supervision of general camp duties (cleaning, tidying and care of the facilities). At Rubicon School Camp, for example, visiting teachers are responsible for the organisation of evening activities.

A guide to lesson planning for these activities is forwarded to visiting teachers prior to their visit so preparation can take place. In addition, teachers usually assist with the general educational programme, which can be invaluable in-service training in outdoor education.

The classroom teacher is also in a unique position as an observer of the personal and social development of students throughout the programme. This may give valuable insights into children's needs and provide information for counselling of individual students on their return to school. During the camp, the visiting teacher may also offer permanent staff background information into the behaviour of particular students and, ideally, discuss with them the linkages between the centre programme and curriculum areas currently being taught. In both cases, the building of a relationship between the camp experience and the regular school curriculum is essential and helps to ensure the continuity of the benefits of the outdoor programme.

The Teacher at Camp (*Centres without Permanent Staff*)

The role of a teacher at a resident centre is more demanding than the role of the classroom teacher. Not only does the teacher have responsibility for the educational component of the programme but, additionally, he or she has to be concerned with student welfare and the traumas that being away from home (sometimes for the first time) can bring. Homesickness, bed-wetting, special dietary requirements, individual religious practices, physical impairment, and emotional problems are all matters with which the teacher may have to deal at a centre. Of course, the potential for these interrupting the programme is greatly lessened if adequate planning and organisation precedes the camp.

The main advantages of teachers staffing their own programme include:

—familiarity with their students
—optimal use being made of pre-camp and post-camp time for programme orientation, evaluation and follow-up activities

Possible disadvantages include:

—lack of expertise in the subject or skill areas
—the amount of time taken in organisation
—difficulty sometimes experienced in adjusting from teaching strategies used in the classroom to the less formal teaching methods that outdoor teaching necessarily requires

However, taking a class into the outdoors, in whatever capacity, is invaluable in itself. As Ford (1981: 193) notes:

> . . . one of the strongest reasons for using the classroom teacher in the outdoors relates to the social-living skills that are inevitable in the informal setting. Dressing in jeans and boots, handling plants, analysing soil, singing at a camp fire, eating with students, slipping in the mud, and actually being an integral part of a total living situation all make teachers seem more human than does the

sterile atmosphere of the four walls of a classroom. The teacher is viewed as a friend, companion and equal, rather than as an authority, disciplinarian and adult. Many youngsters have never known adults as anything other than as authority figures, and the resident outdoor program induces an equalising effect wherein adults and youth can relate to each other co-operatively

Case Study: Vivonne Bay Outdoor Education Centre

Introduction

The programme of Vivonne Bay Outdoor Education Centre, which is deliberately structured to build relationships between the natural environment and the in-school curriculum, evolved from the concerns of the manager about the general educational standards of children visiting the centre. In response to this, discussions were held with teachers before they came to the centre in an attempt to bring the in-school curriculum to the field, and to undertake learning in their natural locations. The first field trials were held with students from Year 7 to Year 10. The results from the trials were extremely positive and led to the development of 'The Living Classroom' programme at Vivonne Bay.

The Programme

The programme is normally of five days duration and is led by centre staff. Programmes from ten days to six weeks are provided for overseas students. Each programme is designed to complement the existing state syllabus for each grade and is progressive. Each day attempts to build on the skills and knowledge developed previously. Subjects are many and varied and include:

Natural History
Aboriginal Occupation: History and Mystery
European Occupation
Biology and Physiology
Botany
Ornithology: bird mist netting and banding
Marine Studies
Zoology particularly, on-going research with the Echidna and Australian Sea Lions
Geography
Geology
Herpetology
Major land-clearing project, 1952 to 1963
Land Management
Acidity and Salinity due to Land Clearing
Sand Dune Studies, consolidated and un-consolidated
The International Lighthouse System
The National Parks, Their Purpose and Role
Cave Tours and Exploration
Canoeing and Water Safety

Palaeontology
Art: Drawing, Painting, Drama
Marine and Freshwater Field Sampling Studies
Bushwalking and Camping

The programme is structured from these field opportunities and depends on the age of the students and the particular curriculum emphases required by the school in attendance.

Conclusion

Residential outdoor education provides the potential for achieving each of the broad objectives of outdoor education. The particular type of residential experience selected by teachers will, in large measure, be determined by the educational needs of their students. Once selected, the extent to which these needs will be met depends on teachers who, working with their students and other resource people, have the responsibility for planning, implementing and evaluating the programme. In accepting this responsibility, the words of the educational philosopher Dewey (1970: 26–27) present a challenge to outdoor educators:

> It is not enough to insist upon the necessity of experience, nor even of activity in experience. Everything depends on the *quality* of the experience which is had. The quality of any experience has two aspects. There is an immediate aspect of agreeableness or disagreeableness, and there is its influence on later experiences. The first is obvious and easy to judge. The effect of an experience is not borne on its face. It sets a problem to the educator. It is his business to arrange the kind of experiences which, while they do not repel the student but rather engage his activities are, nevertheless, more than immediately enjoyable because they promote having desirable future experiences. Just as no man lives or dies to himself, so no experience lives or dies to itself. Wholly independent of desire or intent, every experience lives on in future experiences. *Hence the central problem of an education based on experience is to select the kind of present experiences that live fruitfully and creatively in subsequent experiences.* (emphasis added)

References

Dewey, J. (1970) *Education and Experience*, Collier-Macmillan, London.
Ford, P.M. (1981) *Principles and Practices of Outdoor Environmental Education*, John Wiley, New York, USA.
Hogan, R.A. (1984) 'The Emergence of Outdoor Education in the South Australia State Secondary School System: A Case Study in Curriculum Innovation', Unpublished MEd. thesis, Flinders University.
New South Wales Department of Sport and Recreation (1988) *Policy Statement for Sport and Recreation Centres*, Sydney.
South Australian Department of Education, Outdoor Education Unit, *Outdoor Living Series: Student Involvement*, Curriculum Services Unit, Adelaide.
Rees, G. (1988) *Vivonne Bay Outdoor Education Centre*, personal correspondence.

Rubicon School Camp (1988) *Students' Guide*.

Victorian Department of Education (1982) *Safety in Outdoor Adventure Activities*, Publications and Information Branch, Melbourne.

Victorian Ministry of Education (1988) *Bogong School Camp Policy Statements*.

Webb, J. (1980) *A Survey of Field Studies Centres in Australia*, Australian Government Publishing Service, Canberra.

Whitford, I. (undated), *People, Situations, Reactions: An Approach to Outdoor Educations, Caulfield Grammar*.

10
Camping and the Curriculum

Bruce Hayllar

Introduction

Camping broadly involves planned outdoor education programme which uses under-canvas (tent) camping experiences primarily for the achievement of objectives related to the general school curriculum.

The incorporation of tent camping into the curriculum of a class or school is, by necessity, a formally organised and structured process. The level of preparation and pre-planning required, the intensity of spending at least one night with a group outdoors and the time and energy needed to follow up and evaluate the experience on its completion, all point to the necessity for establishing clear objectives and expectations from the outset. This is necessary to ensure that the considerable effort of both students and staff involved is rewarded educationally, professionally and personally.

Taking a group under canvas for even one night involves the teacher in a range of organisational considerations beyond normal class or curriculum-based activities, including arranging for the hire, loan or scrounging of equipment; the organisation of transport; consideration of departmental policies on field trips and different outdoor activities; enlisting the assistance and support of parents; arranging for release from other school duties and so on. Although some of the responsibility for these tasks can be delegated to the students, overall co-ordination and responsibility ultimately rests with the teacher. In this chapter, it will be argued that the effort involved in organising this form of outdoor education experience is ultimately worthwhile.

This chapter offers guidelines on how to structure tent camping experiences with regard to both curriculum and broad organisational considerations. It includes selected examples of different approaches to using camping experiences in the school curriculum.

Conceptual Framework

The conceptual framework for tent camping is based on the ideal model of outdoor education proposed by McRae in Chapter 5. Outdoor education, within the context of the current chapter, is seen as an experience-based educational process which uses the outdoor environment for the realisation of inter-curricular, leisure education (outdoor skills/outdoor pursuits/adventure education/outdoor recreation), and personal and social development, and environmental objectives.

In general terms, the inter-curricular objectives of outdoor education involve the use of outdoor settings for learning experiences designed to facilitate the acquisition of concepts, skills and attitudes drawn from all curriculum areas.

Outdoor education can also be specifically oriented towards developing an understanding of natural environmental processes and of the impact of human beings on these.

The outdoor skills objectives of outdoor education involve the acquisition of the knowledge, skills and attitudes required by students to participate in selected activities in outdoor education programmes and during their leisure.

Personal and social development can be realised by students who are involved in formally structured 'adventure' experiences or in informal 'teachable moments' in the outdoors. Outdoor adventure education programmes, as discussed in Chapter 4, can be a catalyst for the self-appraisal

Sawing

required to bring about profound changes in the way individuals perceive themselves and in their relationships with others.

Camping and the Curriculum: Integrated Learning

It is useful, for the purposes of definition and clarification, to separate the objectives of outdoor education. However, in practical terms, it is desirable that attempts should be made to integrate them into a cohesive programme. Indeed, it is strongly recommended that outdoor education should be viewed holistically as it has an important role to play in the broader curriculum.

Navigating

Tent camping provides many opportunities for realising the objectives of outdoor education. While the primary purpose of a camping trip may be to investigate coastal land-forms or to determine the environmental impact of the timber industry, it should be recognised that the educational experience should not be confined to, or by, these objectives. When a class encounters the outdoor environment, the dynamics of everyday living and the relationships between students, and students and teachers, are altered by the demands that group outdoor living imposes. Individuals or groups need to co-operate to choose a camp-site; to pitch their tents; to cook their food; to make themselves comfortable for the night; to entertain each other without the aid of electronic means; to live with peers they may not know; and to live and work with an adult who knows them as a student, not necessarily as a person. Clearly such an experience is more than just an element of the curriculum being taught out-of-doors. It is incumbent on the teacher to recognise the various dimensions of the outdoor experience from the outset and incorporate them into objectives of the programme.

By way of example, a Year 9 history teacher took her class to visit the old Kiandra gold-fields which are situated on the western edge of Kosciusko National Park in southern New South Wales. In preparing for this journey, it became obvious that an overnight camp was necessary to visit the most interesting sites at the old diggings. Thus, while the curriculum objectives were directed toward historical and cultural aspects, other objectives in the outdoor education process could also be addressed:

> *The Development of Outdoor Skills*
> —organisation of personal equipment including clothing, foot-wear, and rucksacks
> —pace and rhythm when walking to the site
> —map-reading and navigation to the site
> —establishing the camp-site, including pitching of tents, dedication and preparation of ablution areas
> —catering (including menus, food-ordering and preparation)
>
> *Incorporating Elements of Environmental Education*
> —selection of camp-site and establishing procedures to minimise impact (and why this is necessary)
> —informal investigation of specific fauna and flora in the area, through tracks, traces and direct observation
> —identifying the impacts of humankind on the natural environment through the processes of hydraulic mining
>
> *Personal and Social Development*
> —facilitating interaction and co-operation between group members
> —observing the behavioural dynamics of individuals within the group and intervening where necessary

Outdoor education can thus be approached in an holistic way, and can provide opportunities to achieve objectives beyond those primarily identified.

Planning the Camping Experience

Programme Approach

In order to plan a camping experience and fully develop its potential, teachers should firstly clarify their educational objectives. By definition, camping and the curriculum has its primary focus on achieving general curriculum objectives, i.e., the use of the outdoors to enhance, enrich or extend learning in areas of the 'regular' curriculum. This approach to the use of camping experiences may be grouped into three areas: disciplinary, inter-disciplinary and thematic.

Disciplinary

In this approach, the objectives of the camping programme are primarily focused on a single discipline. Hamilton Technical School in Victoria, for example, conducted a two day Maths Camp in the Grampians. The principal purpose of this was to provide opportunities for the experiential learning of mathematical concepts.

The camp-site was located on a farm in the Victoria Valley and many of the activities used the resources in the immediate vicinity – hay sheds, dams and trees. These provided the experiential basis for disciplinary learning. Excerpts from the programme document demonstrate one of the methods used to achieve their curriculum objectives.

Figure 10.1   Hamilton Technical School Maths Camp

Concept: 'Finding Volumes'

Aims:(1) To determine the volumes of a hay shed, and calculate how many bales it would hold
　　　(2) To determine the volume of a cylindrical tank

Prior Knowledge:(1) Area and volume formulae
　　　　　　　　　(2) Use of four-figure tables
　　　　　　　　　(3) Properties of similar triangles

Location: Position (A) on the layout plan
Equipment:(1) Four-figure tables
　　　　　　(2) Tape measure
　　　　　　(3) Range pole
Method:
　A: The Hay Shed
Step 1
　—Measure the dimensions of the hay shed and, from this information, calculate the volume. You may require a special process to find the heights of the shed.
　—In your calculations take particular care with the shape of the roof
Step 2
　—Now measure a bale of hay and find its volume. Are all the bales the same? What size will you use?
　—Determine how many bales will fit into the shed

　B: The Water Tank
Step 1
　—Measure the circumference and height of the tank. Using the circumference, calculate the outside diameter of the tank
　—The wall of the tank is 6 cm thick. What will the diameter be inside the tank?
　—Determine how much water the tank will hold

Interdisciplinary

In this approach, the camping programme is designed to meet the curriculum objectives of a number of disciplines. St Brigid's Catholic Primary School in Sydney, for example, conducts three-day camping programmes each year for classes within each grade at camp-sites within a 150 km radius of the school. The interdisciplinary nature of their Year 6 camp, held at The Basin, a water-accessible camp-site on Pittwater within the Kuring-gai Chase National Park, is reflected in their programme outline (Figure 10.2):

An interesting example of the interdisciplinary approach is reported by Lentz *et al.* (1976: 68). The programme was conducted with high school students in the north-eastern United States. Ostensibly a high school biology camp to Cape Cod, this programme draws staff from the English, maths, and physical education departments in addition to the science staff. The theme of the three-day camping trip is a multi-disciplinary exploration of Cape Cod. Lentz also notes that, beyond their academic goals, they

> . . . were concerned that the students had a chance to move beyond the ordered, the rational and explainable. We wanted them to have a chance to experience for themselves (many for the first time) the varied rhythm of the waves, the density of life within a salt marsh and the grandeur of the Great Dunes. We wanted the students to directly come up against such primary forces as life and violent death; forces which one inevitably comes up against on any long walk along an open bench.

Figure 10.2   St Brigids Primary School Year 6 Camp

Mathematics:
An orienteering programme to incorporate the mathematical principles and properties of the compass: circles and semi-circles, degrees, angles, circumference. Elementary mapping, three dimensions to the plane

Environmental Studies:
Rock platform and fresh-water organism studies

Art/Craft:
Using natural materials located at the site for individual and group projects

Dance/Drama:
Developing performances for presentation at the evening camp-fire. These performances relate to themes developed from the immediate camp environment and to both its natural and cultural history

Thematic

The thematic approach is similar to the interdisciplinary method but differs in that it attempts to draw together each of the disciplines under one generic theme. For example, an Aboriginal Theme could have been developed quite simply and appropriately in the St Brigid's camp. The purpose would be to identify relationships between each of the disciplines and the theme. This is a particularly valuable use of camping as the experience from the camp can be completely integrated into a unit of work, thus providing an experiential basis for the classroom programme.

An example of this approach was a programme conducted with a group of tertiary students at Jenolan Caves. An historical theme, Bushranging, was the focus of the weekend. The bushrangers, whose exploits reputedly led to the discovery of the cave system, provided excellent scope for the students to develop thematic-based resource material.

The first phase of the planning process, then, is the identification of the programme focus and the particular curriculum approach to be taken.

Programme Format: Base and Mobile Camping

Tent camping may have a number of different formats. In general terms, these may be broadly divided into base or mobile camping. Base camping involves the establishment of the camp on one site for the duration of the programme. The group may leave the site for day excursions or concentrate the programme in the immediate environment and spend each night at the same site. Base camps are usually established in recognised camping areas, which typically have vehicle access. The advantages of base camping primarily relate to this accessibility:

—Motor vehicle access makes the transportation of students and equipment simpler.
—It provides the opportunity of bringing to the site larger 'family' tents and camping equipment such as gas stoves, inflatable mattresses and portable cooler boxes.
—It allows staffing to be more flexible. People may come and go when their specific tasks have been completed. This is particularly useful when outside specialists are being used. (There is also a potential disadvantage to programme continuity, however, if teachers are constantly changing.)
—It is reassuring to younger students and parents, in terms of overall safety and security, if there is ready access. This is particularly important if it is the first programme of its type.
—It can be a valuable first step for the introduction of a more adventurous outdoor experience at a later time.
—Generally, a lower level of outdoor skill is required by staff.

The disadvantages of base camping include:

—Programme limitations imposed by one site
—A site which is too accessible may have to be shared with other groups whose objectives, age, standards of conduct etc. may be totally different from those of the group
—It is sometimes difficult to create a 'spirit of adventure' in a well-used or developed site

Mobile camping involves the use of a number of sites. Students may be personally responsible for transporting their own equipment and food.
The advantages of mobile camping include:

—Access to a greater diversity of environments to facilitate the achievement of different curriculum objectives
—The opportunity to develop outdoor skills in a progressive way, as part of a comprehensive programme
—A source of motivation and inspiration for students
—Additional opportunities to include an 'adventure' component in programmes

The disadvantages of mobile camping programmes relate, in the main to the advantages of base camping:

—A lack of specialised equipment may be restrictive
—A high level of staff expertise and commitment may be required
—The level of outdoor skills required by students may cause this aspect to dominate those curriculum goals which are the primary focus

Programme Objectives

Having identified the approach, format and broad direction of the programme, the next stage is to clearly articulate specific objectives and identify the staffing resources necessary to achieve these. A planning matrix is useful for these purposes.

Figure 10.3   Planning Matrix for the Outdoor Experience

Outdoor Education Objectives	Camping Programme Objectives	Teaching strategies	Staff skills/Staff member
Inter-curricular Environmental Education Outdoor Skills Personal and Social Development			

The primary purpose of the planning matrix is to clearly identify the objectives to be achieved and their relationship to the overall objectives of outdoor education. However, it may also serve other purposes:

Staffing: It assists in identifying the teaching resources necessary to implement the programme. Thus, a teacher may seek the assistance of a parent or colleague who has particular skills, or the support of outside staff (e.g., a national parks officer) to enable the objectives of the programme to be attained.

Programming: It aids in structuring the format and time-frame of the programme. It assists in answering the question of how best to use the available time to attain the objectives established.

Preparing the Students: It enables the teacher to identify, in advance, the skills required by the children to undertake such a programme, particularly in the area of outdoor skills.

Venue or Camp-site: It helps to identify the type of site(s) or areas that are required and available within distance, time and cost constraints.

Planning Considerations

Once the general parameters have been established, detailed planning of the experience then needs to take place. Among the broad considerations are:

Staffing

The School Principal: Teachers should approach the school Principal in the next stage of their planning to help his or her support. The Principal and, ultimately, the parents, need to be confident that:

—clearly defined educational objectives have been identified and appropriate learning experiences planned
—the planning and conduct of the programme is in the hands of competent staff
—the staff have adequately assessed the students' capacities, interests and needs
—adequate preparation has been undertaken in both educational and logistical terms
—consideration has been given to the effect staff absences may have on the operation of the school curriculum
—appropriate avenues of communication have been established between parents and the school with respect to items such as medical and permission forms, insurance, detailed information on the camping programme, emergency procedures and contact numbers

Teaching Staff: In organising staff, four main areas need to be considered:

—Knowledge and skills: Do the teachers have experience, knowledge and skills of the relevant curriculum area(s) to implement the programme as identified through the objectives?
—Understanding and empathy: Conducting a tent camping program with students of any age can be viewed as a great teaching opportunity or an unnecessary burden to already overworked staff. For these reasons it is important that, when selecting staff, they are fully aware of the demands that will be placed on them.
—Fitness: This refers to the ability to 'endure', on a twenty-four hour a day basis, the strains of caring for others, while at the same time seeing to one's own personal needs, surviving without tobacco or alcohol, and having the physical and emotional staying power to keep interested and physically active over the duration of the camp. If the programme is to be successful, staff should be clearly aware of these extraordinary demands.
—Ratios: A 1:10 ratio for overnight camping is recommended.

Parents: Interested parents can assist with meeting the desired ratios. Experience has shown that parents can be extremely valuable or a significant drain on the programme. Careful consideration, therefore, needs to be given to selecting suitable parents. The process used for selecting staff might be the first step in determining a parents' suitability

(adapted from guidelines of the Outdoor Education Unit, Department of Education, Victoria, undated)

Equipment

Equipment needs can usually be divided into items required by individuals and by groups. Many schools have their own equipment. Some states, the New South Wales Department of Education, for example, have regional resources with equipment for group (tents, cooking equipment etc.) and personal needs (rucksacks, sleeping bags and the like). Before purchasing any equipment, it is strongly recommended that alternative sources of supply be investigated.

The type and quantity of equipment will largely depend on the format of the programme, base or mobile. In planning equipment requirements, consideration needs to be given to accommodation (tents, sleeping bags, ground-sheets etc.); catering (food quantity, quality, procurement and preparation); the programme (specialist equipment and teaching aids); and personal needs (clothing, foot-wear, washing kits etc.) The Catholic Archdiocese of Sydney encourage base camping and, through their Disadvantaged Schools Programme, have established an equipment pool for the use of selected schools. Their equipment, based on forty students, includes the following.

Figure 10.4   Base Camp Equipment, Disadvantaged Schools Programme

Tents: Marquee: for cooking, eating, group meetings (in inclement weather)
　　　　Pyramids: 4-person, for sleeping
Cooking: Twin-burner gas stoves
　　　　Billies, hand grillers, camp ovens
Food storage: Portable coolers (45 and 65 litre)
　　　　　　　Water containers
Lighting: Gas lamps (6 x 2kg)
Sleeping: Sleeping bags, air mattresses, inner sheets, ground-sheets
Rucksacks: Day packs for all participants
Miscellaneous: Wash-up basins, camp shovels, tent-peg mallets, folding tables, bush saws

Accommodation, catering, programme and personal considerations apply equally to mobile programmes. In addition, equipment will need to be both portable and lightweight.

Catering

The type of catering arrangements undertaken will depend on the programme format, available facilities and the ability, age and experience of those who will primarily be responsible for food preparation—ideally, the students! Food cooked out-of-doors need not be monotonous, dull, dirty or all three. It is essential that menus be prepared beforehand and specific ingredients and quantities determined to ensure correct nutrition and quality and to prevent waste.

On-Site Considerations: Safety and Hygiene

It is imperative that the camp site or sites should be inspected beforehand to identify potential hazards, to plan the layout and to determine the contact numbers and availability of emergency services. On arrival at the site, areas for cooking, ablutions and the layout of the general camp site should be clearly defined.

Students must be made aware and adhere to acceptable standards of cleanliness both in the preparation of food and personal hygiene. (Parents rarely appreciate their offspring returning from a week away from home with 'camp belly' and appearing as though they've been dragged through a swamp!)

Other Considerations

First Aid: A comprehensive first aid kit is essential for base camps. More lightweight, compact and robust kits are necessary for mobile programmes. Staff members should be conversant with first aid practices. A St John's Ambulance or Red Cross certificate is required by some educational authorities. Staff should be particularly aware of their own limitations to deal with accidents or illness during the camp. Accurate records should be kept of any first aid rendered or medication prescribed.

Authorisation: Permission for students to attend a camp is usually obtained from parents in writing. It is common to combine the camp information, payment and authorisation in the one document.

Evaluation: The evaluation of the camping programme should relate specifically to the extent to which established objectives have been met. To this end the objectives established early in the planning stages should be realistic and to a great extent measurable or observable. Evaluation is the most neglected element of planning and yet, in many cases, it is the most important. If outdoor educators can provide evidence of the 'success' of their programmes, this will go a considerable way towards ensuring their continuation.

Conclusion

Outdoor education experiences have the potential to bring the classroom alive. Tent camping is a fundamental experience in making this happen. It provides opportunities to:

- —complement and supplement the in-school curriculum
- —integrate the in-school curriculum in areas such as history, English expression, mathematics, geography, geology, physical education and social studies
- —experience group living, sharing and co-operation
- —learn new, and enhance previously learnt, outdoor skills
- —explore the natural world through meaningful experiences
- —gain a greater understanding of human relationships and an individual's role and responsibility in shaping these relationships

If we as educators fail to grasp the nettle and recognise and respond to these opportunities, we deny our students a unique educational experience; one that is meaningful, natural, stimulating, diverse, enjoyable and most of all, relevant.

References

Bewsher, W. *et al.* (1981) *Report of the Committee to Study the Alternatives in Outdoor Education*, Education Department of Victoria, Melbourne.
Dingle, P. (1988) Outdoor Education and Curriculum Integration, personal correspondence.
Hamacheck, D. (1973) *Encounters With The Self*, Holt, Rinehart and Winston, New York, USA.
Hopkins, D. (1985) 'Self-concept and Adventure: The Process of Change', *Adventure Education* 2 (1).
Keighley, P. (1980) 'Using the Potential of Outdoor Education as a Vehicle for Integrated Learning', *Adventure Education* 2 (4/5).
Lentz, R. *et al.* (1976) *Teaching through Adventure*, Project Adventure, Hamilton, Mass., USA.
Lyon, W. (1987) *Disadvantaged Schools Programme: Outdoor Education . . . A Resource*, Catholic Archdiocese of Sydney, Sydney.
Mortlock, C. (1982) *The Adventure Alternative*, Cicerone, Milnthorpe, England.
Rathore, A. *et al.* (1988) *Policy and Guidelines on Environmental Education*, NSW Higher Education Board, Sydney.
Outdoor Education Unit (undated) *Guidelines in Program Organisation*, Victorian Department of Education, Melbourne.

11
Fostering an Environmental Ethic in Outdoor Education

Keith McRae

Introduction

The upsurge of interest in outdoor leisure activities and the increased use of natural environments for outdoor education purposes is applauded and encouraged by outdoor educators. There has been increased participation in programmes organised by educational institutions, commercial and non-profit-making groups. Some accessible outdoor settings have become so popular that the ecological health of some natural environments and particular natural entities has become endangered. Less accessible wilderness areas have become more frequently visited. Two problems arise as a result of this increased human involvement in natural environments. First, there is an increased risk of danger to natural environments as a result of the impact of greater numbers of people of all ages who have not developed a commitment to environmental protection or, at least, to causing minimal impact; or those who are unaware of practices which can minimise the impact of human behaviour on natural entities and communities. Second, there is a danger that teachers and others will respond to the growing interest by organising outdoor education programmes even though they do not have the leadership competencies necessary to ensure the accomplishment of the goals of the programme or to avoid negative outcomes for participants or the environment.

Research on the Impact of Recreational Activities in Natural Environments

The findings of research on the impact of recreational activities in natural environments in the United States and Britain and of case studies of outdoor education programmes in Australia provide ample justification for concern and for attempts to improve the competencies of leaders including their ability to organise and implement programmes which do not damage natural environments.

Recreation impact research findings indicate strongly the potential for environmental damage. Bogucki *et al.* (1975), Legg and Schnieder (1977), Young (1978) and others have shown even that light to moderate use of camp-sites and trails can lead to the physical degradation of the environment: soil compaction, the removal of ground-cover and soil erosion. Leonard (1979) noted problems of human waste in camp-sites located on shallow soil and warned that heavy 'use of such sites has created more human waste than can be assimilated by the soil'. Researchers including Liddle (1975) and Cole (1977) have found that the recreational activities of humans can have a serious effect on plants and natural ecosystems. Barton (1969) expressed concern about the effect of the human presence on the quality of water in dispersed recreation areas. According to Ream (1979), wildlife 'is increasingly threatened by growing numbers of backcountry recreationists' and numerous articles and reports by writers such as Giest (1975), Gilbert (1976) and Schultz and Bailey (1978) have reported on the deleterious effects of human recreational behaviour on particular wild-life species.

The Need for Environmental Guidelines

Case studies of outdoor education programmes undertaken in the ACT in 1985 and 1986 suggested, in broad terms, that many outdoor educators tend to:

(a) lack the awareness and knowledge of environmental, ecological and biological concepts necessary to provide a basis for informed decision-making, responsible behaviour and constructive actions concerning natural environments; and
(b) have an inadequate grounding in other environmental sciences which help to provide a comprehensive understanding of natural phenomena.

The general and broad nature of these findings may mask their seriousness, but their implications are made clear by situations which are far too common in Australian outdoor education, such as careless camping habits and damage to fragile natural communities, the pollution of water courses and the widespread littering of wilderness areas. As desirable as it may be, it is obviously unrealistic to require outdoor education leaders to have completed tertiary studies in appropriate environmental sciences. However, it is important that leaders are committed to protecting natural environments and to implementing sound outdoor practices. All outdoor education programmes should be based solidly on an environmental ethic which has philosophical justification and which provides clear guidelines for participants.

Concerned environmentalists who have ventured into national parks or wilderness areas in Australia have often been appalled at the thoughtless behaviour of some individuals, groups and outdoor education parties who use natural environments for leisure purposes: the discarded tins or plastic wrapping; the broken bottles; branches broken off living trees and cast aside; scraps of food in a small creek. Concern to eliminate such anti-environmental behaviour has prompted various organisations through the world to promulgate behavioural guidelines directed towards those who want to visit environments in their natural state.

Although some differences and contradictory guidelines do exist in the various codes, there is also much that is common. Each of the codes has deficiencies, important omissions and, arguably, some unsound recommendations. Some codes were compiled after examination of contemporary research on the ecological impact of outdoor leisure activities while others were based on the conservation practices and experiences of environmentally aware individuals and groups. Many of the guidelines are oriented to the interests of human beings. It can be argued, of course, that the only acceptable approach to environmental protection involves the prohibition of all human activity in natural environments. This position has much justification in certain fragile environments, but there are areas which are sufficiently resilient to sustain careful and controlled usage. It can also be argued that the prospect of natural areas being protected is enhanced if those who visit these areas follow sound practices based on knowledge and become committed to environmental protection.

There is certainly a need for environmental guidelines. These need to be based solidly on an environmental ethic which has sound philosophical justification. The guidelines need to be regarded as essential by outdoor education leaders and teachers and by all users of outdoor settings in order to ensure that natural environments are protected from human impact.

An Environmental Ethic for Outdoor Education

An environmental ethic or ecological attitude is a central part of the conceptual framework of every reasonable argument concerning environmental issues. No reasonable argument contends that the destruction of natural forces, processes or life forms is a primary end or the pre-eminent goal of human behaviour. Even arguments which advocate the destruction of the natural environment do so only because they cite a higher or more important goal. Or so they would have us believe.

This basic ecological attitude no doubt has many psychological and sociological sources. It is obvious, at least, that all people desire clear air to breathe, unpolluted water to drink and healthy food to eat. Among all reasonable people there is a basic, although sometimes minimal, respect for the environment in which they live. In addition, the vast environmental literature and the continuous accounts of various environmental crises serve to create an environmental consciousness in human thought. It has, however, become difficult to avoid the conclusion that the present state of the relationship between human beings and the environment is, at the very least, uncertain. The fouling of the ocean shoreline, harbours and rivers, the elimination of species of animals and plants, the destruction of rain-forests, and the contamination of the air by a variety of pollutants, have all become serious issues of public debate. All arguments concerning these and other environmental problems have begun, it seems, with a basic respect for natural processes and life forms and the issues debated have involved arguments between competing relevant interests. Ecological problems have become conflicts between competing and ethical priorities. Those who want to build a dam for the purpose of producing hydro-electricity, for example, are not necessarily 'against nature'. They could simply believe that the benefits to humankind from the development of the dam outweigh the benefits of the protection of wild rivers and endangered flora and fauna. Those who wish to retain rivers for leisure purposes or to protect endangered species have different sets of priorities, or different evaluations of the benefits and costs of the project. Thus, an ecological problem with ethical implications is a problem of competing interests, values and goods. Coincidentally, the problem has certain scientific-ecological facts as its substantive background.

Since ecological problems involve the competition of moral values, it is possible to examine the moral claims made in various arguments to see if they are justifiable in regard to the protection of the natural environment. Do certain moral values, moral arguments, or competing material benefits better serve to justify a policy of environmental protection?

Rational arguments concerning the protection of natural environments generally begin with questions of direct human interest. Given an action that will benefit human beings and that may cause harm to the environment, one can ask: could any purpose be served from refraining from the action and, instead, protecting the environment? Could the protection of the environment itself directly benefit the lives of the human beings concerned with the questionable action? If so, do the benefits gained by protecting the environment outweigh the benefits of performing the action? These are the types of questions that environmentalists have been asking in an attempt to illuminate the relevance of the science of ecology to human action, and in their effort to convince people that they are not acting in their best interests in respect to nature.

Opponents of Environmental Protection

Before examining the arguments of environmentalists more closely, it is prudent to begin with an opponent of environmental protection, for example, an industrialist or an engineer or a developer—someone who wishes to use natural resources for the benefit of individuals, a particular community or even humankind as a whole. This opponent of environmentalism might not see any need to protect the environment. He might think it permissible, for example, to dump industrial chemicals into rivers, to burn coal which is high in sulphur content, to destroy rain-forests, or to build a dam and possibly eliminate species of flora and fauna. However, he might not commit these actions as a result of malice and he might not consider them to be acts of wanton destruction. On the contrary, many cogent arguments might be put forward to morally justify these actions. One argument might point to the personal economic benefits which could accrue to the agent and to others involved, benefits that are considered to outweigh any harm to the environment. Another might cite the inviolability of individual property rights and the need for protection of these rights. Still another might be based on the benefits of economic development for the society as a whole. Flourishing industries, even with pollutants, are commonly seen as a sign of a prosperous society. Even social justice might be used as an argument. Before all members of a society can have a decent share of society's products, there must be enough products to go around. These products are seen as being the result of the utilisation of natural resources.

These opponents of environmentalism can claim in various ways that the enhancement of human life requires the utilisation and, in some places, the destruction, of the natural environment. If this were the predominant view concerning the relationship between human beings and the environment, there would be little protection of natural resources. Any human benefit would over-ride the need for protection.

The Human Survival Argument

Environmentalists have answered the arguments of the opponents of environmental protection by claiming that they are misguided in their sense of what is actually in their best interests as human beings. These people, it is argued, fail to realise that the primary interest of humankind is its own survival. To preserve human existence, the preservation of the life-supporting features of the natural environment is seen as being essential.

This argument has strong emotional appeal and may well, in the end, be true. However, the extrapolations that environmentalists use in their predictions are vulnerable to criticism because they assume that certain practices and growth rates will remain roughly constant. There is also a tendency to ignore the development of new technologies and social institutions which could make continued human existence possible in spite of the degradation of the natural environment. The survival of human beings does not necessarily depend on the total functioning of the natural ecosystem, the continued existence of all species of life. The health and stability of the natural environment might be threatened; the future may be different; the quality of the future may be seriously impaired; but there could still be a future. It is also argued that, since human beings live in the environment, they must use it to some extent. The obligation to protect the environment arises only when its utilisation threatens an ecological collapse which will harm humankind. But this means that if humankind is no longer in danger of making the planet uninhabitable, then its obligation to ensure the protection of nature vanishes. This is not what is meant by a serious obligation to protect the environment. It does not provide sufficient basis for an environmental ethic. A justifiable argument would have to include support for the preservation of all forms of life.

Perhaps the most important question that needs to be asked is not whether human survival is at stake. Human beings are very flexible, inventive and adaptable animals, and there would seem to be little doubt that new cultural patterns would emerge even if the natural environment were seriously depleted, damaged or even destroyed. The more important issue is whether the quality of life offered by such a degraded environment would be tolerable. The answer to that question has to be resoundingly in the negative. This leads to a second argument adopted by environmentalists.

Other Human Interest Arguments for Environmental Protection

Environmentalists commonly argue that there are human interests such as beauty, leisure and science which justify protecting the natural environment. This position actually comprises a variety of related arguments, for different observers consider different aspects of the natural world to be most important, valuable or beneficial to human beings. In spite of their differences, however, they all contain one point which goes beyond the survival arguments, in that they find an object or value in nature worth preserving. However, the object or value in nature is always important to human beings. The motivation behind these arguments could be termed 'enlightened self-interest' as opposed to the crass self-interest of human survival. The interest transcends the basic need for survival and focuses on objects and concerns which are not strictly necessary for human survival.

In the strictest sense, the argument for protecting the environment for human interests other than survival cannot be substantiated logically. For example, beauty of some kind could remain in the world even if the natural environment was destroyed. Scientific endeavours would continue. Other settings for leisure activities would be available. While the argument does have some logical flaws, it remains important for the formation of an environment ethic. The loss of the beauty of the natural environment cannot be replaced by other forms of beauty and this loss would be a lamentable occurrence. Scientific endeavours which provide insights into the way human beings degrade the environment generally and the natural environment in particular cannot be conducted if there is no point of comparison. Obviously other forms of leisure activities could replace those which take place in natural environments. They would be different and, for some people, inferior and incapable of providing the enjoyment and satisfaction, the sense of achievement, or the wonder to be found in nature. We have reverted here to questions relating to quality of life and these are subjective matters, involving perception, feelings and values rather than narrow, rational, logical argument. They are matters of personal belief and judgement.

The weakness of this position is that it fails to go far enough. People who pursue 'enlightened self-interest' in a natural environment can be seriously, if slowly, affecting the balance of that environment and be unwittingly helping to cause irrecoverable damage. The human interest argument alone cannot ensure the preservation of the natural environment. There are too many people who have too many interests and too little understanding of the impact of their presence for preservation to be likely. Action which affects the natural environment cannot be evaluated solely in terms of the amount of human satisfaction which results from the action. The interests of non-human natural entities must be given moral value if an environmental ethic is to provide the securing of an obligation to protect the natural environment.

The Future Generation's Argument for Environmental Protection

The basic human interest arguments relating to survival, beauty, recreation and science can be used with more force by introducing the notion of future generations of humans. It can be argued that, even if the destruction of a certain area of the natural environment or the elimination of a certain endangered species would increase immediate human benefit, the long-term consequences for future generations would be a loss of benefit. A major problem arises with this utilitarian 'future generations' argument. Given the limitations of present-day information, the utilitarian really does not know how the actions of humans on the environment will affect the future. Without clear assessment of the utility of an action for future generations, the utilitarian environmentalist will be unable to defeat arguments which are based on an increase in immediate human benefit.

Touching

A Secure Foundation for Environmental Protection

To provide a secure foundation for environmental protection, it is necessary to move away from the vagaries of human interests while remembering that some human activities may be more inherently valuable, tolerable and more morally justifiable than others. It is necessary to examine a completely different kind of theory of moral value, one in which the interests of humans are not given special consideration and in which ecological values are recognised as independent of humans and significant in themselves.

The central concept in the establishment of an environmental ethic is considered to be the interdependent natural community. Humans do not live isolated from other natural entities and thus they must treat other members of their natural community with moral consideration. The concept of a natural community is the most plausible basis of an environmental ethic because it avoids many of the problems associated with the more common approach in which individuals are conceived as having moral rights. Trees, kangaroos and lizards cannot individually be said to have moral rights but, because they are part of a moral-natural community, they deserve respect and consideration.

The basis of this environmental ethic is a new moral framework in which the good of the community, rather than the interests of its individual members, is given pre-eminence in moral evaluation. This new framework based on communal ends and good is contrasted with the liberal tradition of emphasising individual rights and interests, but it is also opposed to the utilitarian goal of maximising individual satisfactions. The greatest satisfaction of interests for the greatest number of individuals is not the end of moral action. Rather its end is the good of the entire biotic community, the quality of the integrated whole. The concept of community does preserve the value of individual entities by relating their worth to community function.

The inspiration for this new environmental/ecological ethic is Aldo Leopold's almost visionary 'land ethic'. He extends the moral community, by means of ecological science, to include animals, plants, soil and water: the entire natural community. This ethic offers a rationale, and a justification or the protection of the natural environment. Humans protect the natural environment because the entities of nature are 'fellow-travellers', members of the same community. Thus, an environmental ethic and a policy of environmental protection is simply the correct manner of acting towards members of one's moral community. It may well be true that the interests and biases of humans cannot be ignored or eliminated totally. It is also true that ecological principles such as the health, stability and integrity of the natural community place a limitation of human action and eventually on human civilisation itself.

This environmental ethic and the concept of ecological health, and the subsidiary principles of ecological science provide a standard for human action, for human intervention in the environment. Only by means of this ethic, a system of moral rules which recognises the existence of value in the natural community, a community encompassing both human and non-human entities, can a policy of environmental protection be rationally and morally justified.

The environmental ethic also provides a realistic and soundly-based set of environmental protection guidelines which will empower the ethic. The implementation of these is of critical importance for those who wish to use a natural environment for leisure or educational purposes. All outdoor education programmes must be founded on a soundly-based ethic and on consequential guidelines designed to protect the natural environments in which the programmes are implemented.

The environmental ethic which has been outlined provides a basis for decisions about the value of different types of human actions; it justifies participation by humans in educational and leisure experiences in natural environments providing that the ecological health of those environments is not impaired; and it provides guidelines for the practical implementation of a policy in relation to the environmental protection. It is recognised, however, that people need to be educated *about* natural environments if the moral justification of the ethic is to remain empowered.

Environmental Guidelines for Outdoor Education

These guidelines should be regarded as the minimum requirements. Outdoor educators should be prepared to implement more stringent restrictions if these are necessary. There may well be circumstances in which the condition of particular environments will require a decision to abandon plans for outdoor education experiences. The guidelines will, however, serve to indicate behaviour which is acceptable in most situations.

Outdoor education teachers and leaders are urged to ensure that participants are acquainted with the guidelines before programmes are implemented. Ideally, participants will not only be aware of the guidelines but will be able to explain the reasons why they are considered essential.

Planning

(1) Consult with relevant authorities and other knowledgeable persons about management guidelines; prevailing and developing conditions (for example, weather, fire, water); particular precautions and care required both for the environment (for example, endangered species, compacted camp-sites), and the participants (for example, overgrown tracks, polluted water, baited areas); and other matters of interest or concern.

(2) Keep the group size small enough to protect the particular environment(s) involved. Remember, however, that the ecological impact of a group is not necessarily a function of numbers. One or two careless people can cause far more damage than twelve or more careful ones.

(3) Undertake a careful reconnoitre of the proposed route (close to the time of the event), locate suitable and sound camp-sites and assess the environmental implications of any proposed activity.

(4) Ensure that at least two party members have a sound basic bushcraft knowledge (for example, first aid, map reading and navigation, emergency procedures).

(5) Conduct pre-trip discussions and instruction so that all members of the group are aware of the requirements of minimum impact camping, the trip plan, and of the food, clothing and equipment needed. The environment should not be relied upon to keep people dry, warm, well-fed or comfortable.

(6) Consult with authorities at the completion of each trip about conditions and problems encountered and suggest any follow-up activity required to protect the area.

Travelling

(1) Move in a group of four to six people at the most if you are travelling with a large group. Four is the optimum number for off-the-track travel. Smaller units minimise environmental impact and maximise enjoyment and self-reliance.

(2) Resist the temptation to take short-cuts on zig-zag tracks. Keeping to track is important particularly in areas used by large numbers of people. Vegetation can be damaged and erosion can result.

(3) Follow wild-life tracks wherever possible.

(4) Select foot-wear appropriate to safety, comfort and the terrain. Heavy, studded boots may have an adverse effect on fragile environments. Use lightweight footwear wherever possible. Tread carefully and, if possible, walk on boulders and stony ground.

(5) Consider carefully the environmental implications of travelling in areas which have no previously used tracks. Such movement requires experience and extra sensitivity to the needs of the environment.

(6) Travel quietly in the bush, whether using an established track or following your route. You will see more of the environment, the wild-life will be less intimidated and other people will appreciate the quiet. Speak softly and save rowdy songs and games for other times.

Camp-sites

(1) Locate the camp-site at least thirty metres away from natural water sources. The choicest camp-sites are often frequently visited by wild-life so extra care should be taken to seek out a camouflaged area.

(2) Avoid tall trees, high knolls (lightning) and cliff bottoms (falling rocks) when selecting a site.

(3) Choose a resilient site which is non-flammable and non-scarring.

(4) Avoid areas of fragile vegetation which can be easily trampled, or slopes on which erosion is likely, or wet sites on which there is likely to be soil and vegetation compaction.

(5) Pitch tents in areas where there are ample organic materials or in sandy areas if possible.

(6) Use an existing camp-site rather than make a new one in the same area providing that the area is not in danger of being heavily compacted. In

either situation, disperse use throughout the area to avoid soil or vegetation compaction resulting from a concentration of activities in a confined area, but avoid expanding the camp-site.

(7) Avoid digging ditches, especially in delicate areas. Use natural drainage or tents with ground-covers.

(8) Refrain from using rocks or digging up soil or sod to hold pegs or tent flaps, and from landscaping the camp-site by cutting live branches, removing rocks or pulling up plants. If sleeping areas need to be cleared of twigs or small rocks, scatter these items over the area before leaving.

(9) Select and set up the chosen camp-site as early as possible to minimise unintended impact on the environment.

(10) Avoid spending more than two days at any one camp-site unless it is an already established site. Even then, be conscientious about moving the camp-site to avoid damage. In pristine areas (that is, those never previously used), it may be desirable to limit stays to one night.

Fires and Firewood

(1) Use stoves where law and local regulations dictate; where there is a fire hazard; where serious danger to the ecosystem exists; or where there is little or no firewood. Except where firewood is abundant, burning wood interrupts the natural cycle in which nutrients taken from the soil are returned by the decay processes.

(2) Use an existing fireplace if available providing that it is not too full of wood ash or the area over-trampled or scarred.

(3) Select a site (providing that fires are permitted and conditions are suitable) which is away from decaying matter, tents, trees, branches, shrubs or underground root systems. If ground cover or leaf or forest litter exist, clear the area thoroughly and dig well into the mineral soil. Dousing vegetation in the vicinity of a fire should be considered, particularly in dry conditions.

(4) Avoid ringing fires with rocks or building them against reflecting rocks in order to prevent permanent blackening and unnatural exfoliation.

(5) Use fires only in areas with a plentiful supply of firewood and rapid resource replenishment. The firewood should be selected from small diameter wood lying loosely on the ground in order to ensure complete and efficient burning. Never cut live wood for fires.

(6) Avoid wasting firewood on unnecessarily large fires. It is a valuable and often scarce resource as well as having an important role in the natural cycle. Fires should be kept small, that is, only large enough for important and immediate needs.

(7) Burn all wood as completely as possible. Plan ahead to ensure that only logs which are needed and which will burn to a white ash are placed on the fire.

(8) Douse the fire thoroughly when it has burnt down, until it is completely extinguished. Retrieve non-burnables such as foil, tin cans and plastics so that they can be carried out in a litter bag (glass should not be carried *in*). Scatter widely as much of the cold, white ash as possible to avoid an unnatural concentration of minerals in the fireplace.

(9) Restore the fireplace area and leave as few traces as possible. Scatter any unburnt firewood.

Human Waste

(1) Use 'cat-holes' in preference to latrines unless the number of people in the party exceeds fifteen or the camping areas are frequently visited. If latrines have to be used, they should be located well away from water sources (fifty metres) to allow human waste to decay and filter through the soil without polluting.

(2) Dig latrines to a maximum depth of 300mm but not deeper than the organic soil. The latrines should be buried before they are 50-100mm from full. Deeper burial prevents adequate decomposition, while shallower burial can foul the air and encourage animals to dig up the latrine.

(3) Cover faeces with topsoil after each usage and compress with foot or shovel. The soil is necessary to ensure decomposition.

(4) Dig individual 'cat-holes' (with trowel or heel of boot) in soil layers with high organism populations and in areas at least fifty metres from water sources, walking and other tracks and the camp-site. Forest and other litter and ground-covers should be carefully removed and a hole of 100-200mm deep dug. As soil bacteria constitutes the major decomposing agent, the faeces should be mixed with soil before litter and ground-cover is replaced.

(5) Urinate in areas with thick humus layers but avoid fragile vegetation because the acidity of urine can affect plant growth and the salt attracts plant-eating animals.

(6) Use single-ply white toilet paper and then burn it if possible or bury it along with the waste. In low moisture and high fire hazard areas, toilet paper should be put in a bag and carried out if burning or deep burial is not possible.

(7) In sterile soils and harsh environments sunlight, precipitation and temperature changes become the principal break-down agents. Hence, faeces should have shallower burial or even be left on the ground surface providing that there is little risk of water contamination or the unburied waste being encountered.

(8) Tampons burn only slowly on an extremely hot fire. In most cases, they should be carried out.

Litter

(1) Aim always to carry as few rubbish-producing materials as possible. Rubbish problems can be reduced by careful planning. Food should be repackaged in plastic bags or reusable containers. Food leftovers can be avoided by careful planning of meals.

(2) Keep the bush, tracks and camp-site litter-free by carrying out all rubbish in a litter bag. Rubbish includes such items as orange peel (which rots or burns very slowly), paper products, plastic, tins and aluminium foil.

(3) Avoid burying food scraps, leaving them lying around or throwing them into the bush or behind rocks. Non-soluble and coherent food particles (for example, macaroni or noodles) which inevitably occur in some dish-washing should be treated like bulk leftovers and packed up and carried out. Partial burning of food scraps is inadequate. Food scraps will soon be recovered by small animals and may contain organisms which are dangerous.

(4) Refrain from burying litter in snow. It will reappear in the spring.

(5) Pick up and carry out litter as you encounter it.

Washing

(1) Use biodegradable soap (if soap is used at all) and wash yourself and cooking and eating equipment at least thirty metres from water sources. Even biodegradable soap is a stress on the environment so as much of the washing as possible should be done with soapless hot water. A soapless wash will suffice for all but the most persistent dirt.

(2) Refrain from using soap to wash clothes. A soapless wash will suffice and residual soap in clothes can cause skin irritations.

(3) Carry water away from the source. If using soap, lather up and then rinse off the soap. Pour any soapy water left in containers into absorbent soil. This allows the biodegradable soap particles to break down and filter through the soil before reaching the water source.

Special Protection Measures

(1) Resist the temptation to feed birds and animals which appear curious or hungry. Even in low-impact areas, the feeding of wild-life can upset the natural balance of the food chain and alter feeding habits, migration patterns and reproduction levels and ultimately result in changed species composition. In addition, left-overs may carry bacteria harmful to the wild-life.

(2) Respect the needs of birds and animals for undisturbed territory and privacy. When tracking wild-life for a photograph or a closer look, stay downwind, avoid sudden motion and never chase or charge *any* animal.

(3) Leave undisturbed all insects and reptiles including those which bite and cause pain. Apart from being acceptable behaviour towards the inhabitants of a visited area, it will also lessen the risk to visitors.

(4) Avoid damaging plants, particularly in fragile areas. For example in the shade of some forest floors plants have a very slow growth rate and in sub-alpine areas they may be fragile and slow-growing. Particular care should also be taken in sand dunes and alpine marshes. It may take years to repair damage caused by just walking through such areas.

(5) Refrain from picking or uprooting plants. If a record is required, take a photograph.

(6) Refrain from using natural materials for shelter except in emergency situations and never cut down vegetation for unnecessary purposes such as furniture or bedding. Sleep on a single-cell foam mat or your softer hiking gear if necessary.

(7) Try to avoid difficult and persistent bush-bashing since this can cause considerable damage as well as placing a strain on inexperienced members of the party.

(8) Refrain from marking trees, building stone piles or leaving messages in the dirt. Other people can be confused by unanticipated markers and these signs of prior travel can make their wilderness experience less enjoyable.

(9) Keep to tracks when they exist. Cutting corners or avoiding muddy sections by walking in the vegetation causes erosion, unsightly multiple troughs and damage to plants.

(10) Avoid descending steep slopes if possible (i.e., seek out an easier route). In steep terrain, descending will compact the soil more and cause greater damage to plants than ascending.

(11) Leave pets at home.

Finally, in summary:

> Avoid wilfully damaging or destroying any living or non-living part of the ecological community in which you are a 'fellow-traveller', a 'visitor', a member of a community charged with responsibility for protecting all other entities.

Promoting an Environmental Ethic in Outdoor Education Programmes

Introducing the Environmental Code

The environmental code which has been outlined is detailed and comprehensive, but it may not, as it stands, but suitable for introduction to all age groups or in all programmes or natural settings. Without watering down any of the guidelines, outdoor educators or teachers who utilise outdoor settings for any educational purpose should select those items which are appropriate to the particular programme and participants. Teaching-learning experiences which aim to ensure that the participants are familiar with the guidelines and the reasons for their inclusion in the code should be designed and introduced.

The guidelines of the code can be introduced at one or more of three stages. Suitable learning activities could be undertaken in the classroom or in nearby natural settings prior to an outdoor experience in order to ensure that students are acquainted with the guidelines before needing to put them into practice. The activities could be implemented during an outdoor experience when the guidelines would be most meaningful. In some circumstances, it may be considered advantageous to introduce the activities as a follow-up to the outdoor experience. Ideally, appropriate learning experiences would be implemented at all three stages.

Two key questions need to be considered by teachers in deciding when the learning activities should be introduced: First, when do the learning activities need to be introduced in order to minimise the impact of the outdoor education experience on the environment? The obvious answer is that students must, at least, be acquainted with the principal guidelines before such an experience. Second, at what stage and in what circumstances would the learning activities be likely to be most effective? The answer to this question is more complex. The research evidence suggests that learning is most effective if students are involved in preliminary activities which promote a general awareness of the need to protect natural environments, introducing them to key guidelines which are followed up by activities in the field.

Withholding the implementation of learning activities until the outdoor experience was completed could have both a positive and a negative consequence. Students would be able to draw on their experiences when discussing the guidelines and the potential for learning would therefore be enhanced. On the other hand, it could be considered an abrogation of environmental responsibility on behalf of the teachers to create a situation in which students could cause, perhaps unknowingly, environmental damage, because of their lack of knowledge about environmentally-sound ways of behaving in natural environments.

Approaches to introducing the guidelines of the code could include direct instruction and/or class discussions. The choice of approach will depend on such factors as the age and ability of the students, the preferred teaching styles of the teacher and students, and the time available. Research findings and the experience of successful outdoor/environmental educators would suggest that the active involvement of the students in the learning process, plus some combination of the two approaches, is likely to produce the most profound cognitive and affective learning, providing that adequate time is available.

A number of factors could be influential in determining whether or not *direct instruction* would be effective either prior to or during an outdoor experience. The teacher would need to:

—be respected, perceived as knowledgeable, and as a role-model deserving emulation
—utilise the prior knowledge of the students, as the learning of new material is more effective if students are able to relate it to a conceptual framework that has already been established
—motivate students by enlisting their curiosity, provoking their interest or creating conceptual conflict
—utilise suitable teaching materials in order to assist the process of instruction
—punctuate the instruction with questions designed to relate the new material to previous knowledge, to maintain interest and to provide feedback about the extent to which learning is taking place
—introduce the new material in 'digestible bits', i.e., the quality of information and the pace at which it is introduced must be appropriate to the abilities of the learners

Class or group discussions would seem to be an effective means of helping students learn the guidelines. The approach adopted could be more or less directive, but the teacher must be well-prepared with a systematic series of specific questions. Although general questions would also be necessary to introduce the discussions, the key questions would flow directly from the guidelines of the code. The teacher could ask open questions such as:

—Should bushwalkers bury all their rubbish? Why? Why not?
—Should campers wash themselves with soap in creeks? Why? Why not?
—Should walkers keep to established tracks? When? Why? Why not?

Alternatively, the questions should be mixed so that each item calls for either a negative or a positive response. The questions could be framed in such as way that they require TRUE/FALSE answers or answers chosen from a Likert-type scale. Examples of questions could be:

—Bushwalkers should bury all rubbish   SA A U D SD or T F
—Campers should keep themselves clean
  by washing with soap in creeks   SA A U D SD or T F
—Walkers should keep to established
  tracks   SA A U D SD or T F

Armed with a list of questions, the teacher would be in a position to adopt a number of approaches. Each question could be directed at the whole class or group. The teacher should be prepared to:

—allow students to explain, clarify or qualify their initial responses

—allow other students to comment upon or raise questions about the initial responses of others or provide and explain alternative answers
—allow students to engage in lively dialogue about answers which are different
—provide and explain environmentally-sound answers if these do not emerge from the discussion.

Alternatively, the teacher could divide the class into small groups of three to five students. Each group could be asked to discuss all questions or some portion of the full set of questions, to allow each group member to provide and explain an answer and then to attempt to reach agreement within the group. When the groups have completed their discussions, each could then be asked to present a report in which the reasons for their answers are outlined as well as the reasons why they rejected other possible answers. Minority reports could also be presented. Once again, the teacher might be obliged to provide environmentally-sound answers. Obviously, some sensitivity would be required by the teacher who was in a position of having to reject an incorrect answer provided by students.

Fostering the Environmental Ethic

The mere ability of students to recall the guidelines of the code would not, of course, mean that they were committed to an environmental ethic which was based on the concept of ecological community. Nor would it guarantee that students would be committed to behaving according to the guidelines or, indeed, that they would do so. More is required. Two tasks must be accomplished. It is critical that students are helped to understand and accept the reasons why each guideline needs to be adopted. It is also critical that they comprehend the concept of the natural community and are committed to behaving as a member of that community. If students are committed to behaving in an environmentally-sound manner in natural environments, they are well on the way to embracing the ethic. It is suggested, however, that students also need to be given a thorough grounding in the ecological concepts which form the basis of the ethic, including the following:

adaptation	biodegradable	biotic community
competition	conservation	ecological entity
ecological health	ecological niche	ecosystem
endangered species	habitat	interdependency
natural community	non-renewable resource	preservation

These concepts can be addressed in any subject or curriculum area. Most likely they would be included in biology, ecology or in general science programmes. Or they could be introduced in any of the different kinds of outdoor education courses which have become accepted in recent years in many Australian schools. The earlier the concepts can be introduced to students, through classroom and outdoor learning experiences, the more likely it is that they will be understood.

No comprehensive curriculum materials suitable for use in Australian primary and secondary schools are yet available, although the Deep Ecology course, Values and Human Ecology, developed for the Victorian Higher School Certificate is a promising beginning. Courses in outdoor education offered at Colleges of Advanced Education in the various states also include some emphasis on an environmental ethic. What is required, however, is a move towards the development of the sort of programmes of curriculum materials which have emerged in the United States over recent years. Four programmes are particularly noteworthy. The aim of *Project Wild* is

> to assist learners of any age to develop awareness, knowledge, skills, and commitment to result in informed decisions, responsible behaviour, and constructive actions concerning wild-life and the environment upon which all life depends.

It is an interdisciplinary, environmental and conservation education programme which emphasises wild-life. The programme was developed, trialled and evaluated as a joint project of the Western Association of Fish and Wild-life Agencies and the Western Regional Environmental Education Council. In its preface it is stated that the programme is:

> ... based on the premiss that young people and their teachers have a vital interest in learning about the earth as home for people and wild-life. The programme emphasises wild-life because of its intrinsic ecological and other values as well as its importance as a basis for understanding the fragile grounds upon which all life rests. Project Wild is designed to prepare young people for decisions affecting people, wild-life and their shared home, earth. In the face of pressures of all kinds affecting the quality and sustainability of life on earth as we know it, Project Wild addresses the need for human beings to develop as responsible members of the ecosystem.

Project Wild is available for use by teachers, future teachers and representatives of any community group providing that they undertake a training programme which deals with the essential concepts and with the recommended approach to introducing the many learning activities which make up the programme. The programme features a carefully designed conceptual framework with seven sections:

Section 1: Awareness and appreciation of wild-life
Section 2: Human values and the wild-life resource
Section 3: Wild-life and ecological systems
Section 4: Wild-life conservation
Section 5: Cultural and social interaction
Section 6: Wild-life issues and trends — alternatives and consequences
Section 7: Wild-life, ecological systems and responsible human actions

The activities are set out in separate volumes for elementary (primary) and secondary schools and categorised according to:

—their suitability for different grade levels (Elementary: grades from Kindergarten to Grade 6; Secondary: Grades 7 to 12)

—subject areas (from anthropology to world history)
—skills (such as analysis, application, evaluation, inference, problem-solving and reporting), and
—topics (from adaptation to wild-life as an indicator of environmental quality)

The way the activities are categorised makes the programme extremely flexible and teachers of all grade levels and subject areas could use the activities. The programme is not as preservationist as many environmentalists would like and the activities are all based on wild-life found in North America. It does, however, provide a model which could be used in the development of an Australian programme and a set of activities which would help foster the development of a sound environmental ethic. The Tasmanian Wilderness Education Project and the appointment of an education officer by the Australian Parks and Wild-life Services give promise of the appearance of suitable Australian materials in the not-too-distant future.

Other American programmes include *Project Learning Tree* which is similar in structure to Project Wild and is designed to develop 'awareness, knowledge and skills related to understanding of renewable and non-renewable resources on a finite planet'. The *Class Project*, developed by the National Wild-life Federation, under a grant from the National Science Foundation, is another project with laudable aims. Students are expected to:

—acquire knowledge about environmental concepts
—learn to observe, measure, collect data, classify, hypothesise, make value judgements, communicate and solve problems concerning environmental issues
—develop an environmental ethic
—use acquired skills and concepts in taking thoughtful, positive action that will protect and enhance the natural environment.

Better known and more readily available in Australia are the environmental awareness activities developed and publicised by Van Matre.

An Inventory of Environmental Concern

In the absence of suitable curriculum materials, classroom teacher and outdoor educators can still help students develop an environmental ethic by helping students explore the concepts and issues involved in the items which make up the following inventory of environmental concern:

(1)   Protecting natural environments is more than
saving the jobs of timber workers   SA A U D SD
(2)   The benefits of modern consumer goods
outweigh the disadvantages of the pollution
caused by their production and use   SA A U D SD
(3)   Australians are lucky because they have
an unlimited supply of good water   SA A U D SD

(4) People who deliberately harm native plants or wild-life should be heavily fined   SA A U D SD

(5) Although dams destroy natural habitats, they must be built because they provide water, electricity and recreation areas   SA A U D SD

(6) If public transport were more efficient, I would encourage my parents to use the family car less often than they do now   SA A U D SD

(7) Australians are lucky because they have an unlimited supply of firewood   SA A U D SD

(8) Governments set aside some natural areas as reserves in which no human activity is allowed   SA A U D SD

(9) No logging or wood-chipping should be permitted in rain-forests even if the companies plant new trees   SA A U D SD

(10) My life is not affected by pollution   SA A U D SD

(11) Australians are lucky because they have an unlimited supply of energy sources   SA A U D SD

(12) National parks should be open only to people who are prepared to walk rather than drive in them   SA A U D SD

(13) Mining should be permitted in national parks because it provides jobs, profits and export earnings   SA A U D SD

(14) Nature will soon return polluted water and air to normal   SA A U D SD

(15) There are too many problems in recycling waste material for it to be worthwhile   SA A U D SD

(16) The government should limit the number of people in national parks even if the amount of environmental damage is small   SA A U D SD

(17) The need to produce food justifies the expansion of farms into forests and the killing of wild-life that damage crops   SA A U D SD

(18) The use of pesticides and insecticides do not pose an environmental threat   SA A U D SD

(19) I would be willing to act as a volunteer for an organisation which encourages the wise use of natural resources   SA A U D SD

(20) More roads should be built in national parks so that more people can enjoy them   SA A U D SD

(21) Native wild-life has just as much right to live as human beings   SA A U D SD

(22) The government should shut down factories which continue to pollute the environment   SA A U D SD

(23) Courses about the conservation of natural resources should be compulsory in schools   SA A U D SD

(24) Trail bikes and four-wheel drive vehicles should be banned from national parks   SA A U D SD

Clarifying Values

The approach to dealing with these items should be similar to that suggested for the discussions on the guidelines of the environmental code. The enthusiastic and creative teacher might be able to find the time and energy to go one step further than discussing the items with students. Each of the items involves important concepts and important real world issues. Womersley and Stokes (1981) have suggested problem-solving and values clarification approaches which could be used to study these concepts and issues. It was Stapp (1974) who identified seven steps in the problem-solving process:

—identifying and defining the environmental issue
—collecting, organising and analysing data related to the issue
—generating and evaluating alternative solutions
—selecting the best solution generated
—developing a plan of action
—implementing a plan of action
—evaluating the implementation process

Careful selection of the issue to be explored and the problem to be solved would make it possible for this approach to be used at any grade level. Although on the surface the skills involved would seem to be more appropriate to senior primary or high school students, it is recommended that junior primary school children are introduced to it. For example, Grade 2 children in an inner city school might address the problem caused by increased traffic flow and the parking of commuters' cars in the streets surrounding the school. The problem is a real one and it affects children personally. A teacher could sensitively guide the students through at least the first four steps in the problem-solving process. The level of sophistication displayed in problem definition, data collection, organisation, analysis and evaluation may not equal that which could be obtained from older and more mature students, but students will be gaining experience in the process and developing important skills.

As part of the problem-solving process the children will necessarily be involved in personal values clarification which is an integral part of the process of developing and refining an environmental ethic. Stapp (1974) suggested that five steps are involved in the process of values clarification:

—students and teachers identify an issue
—students suggest alternative solutions
—students consider the consequences of each alternative
—students express their feelings about each alternative
—students make a free choice of the alternatives

Three quotations from Womersley and Stokes highlight the purposes of values clarification and the role of the teacher:

> This process helps learners become aware of personal beliefs, attitudes, values and behaviours which they prize and are committed to both in and out of the classroom.

> By considering alternatives, the consequences of these and their own personal

feelings towards each, learners begin to refine and develop their own set of values.

An important part of the teacher's role in this process is to help learners consider whether their stated beliefs, attitudes and values are congruent with their actions.

These quotations are important because of the implied recognition that the process of promoting environmental attitudes and values is complex, difficult and requires time. Teachers must be prepared to begin the process early in the education of the children and to take every opportunity to foster the learning outcomes sought.

Environmental Ethics and Outdoor Leisure Education

In a recent articles, Simpson (1985: 25-28) suggested that 'in spite of the intentions and enthusiasm of the instructors, the short-term wilderness trip may not be a means of creating a positive environmental ethic in the value systems of trip participants'. Simpson implied that there were a number of reasons why the teaching of environmental ethics is often neglected or ineffective on a wilderness trip:

(1) The ability to teach and a knowledge of ecological and biological concepts do not have a high priority in the selection of wilderness trip leaders
(2) Objectives relating to environmental education/ethics often have a low priority in the planning and implementation of many outdoor experiential education trips
(3) The realities of excursion management may induce a leader to forego activities designed to foster environmental goals
(4) many wilderness leaders seem to believe or hope that trip participants will develop a sound environmental ethic as a result of mere exposure to the overwhelming beauty of the wilderness.

There is no doubt that most outdoor education trips to wilderness areas offered by schools and colleges in Australia are deficient in the attention that is given to promoting environmental awareness and in the development of an environmental ethic. Although the programmes vary considerably, the majority give greater emphasis to the development of leisure, personal and social skills than to environmental objectives, even when frequent visits are made to natural environments.

The development of an environmental ethic is unlikely to be fully achieved as a result of a single, short-term wilderness trip or a camping programme in a wilderness area, but there is not doubt that such experiences can make a worthwhile contribution, providing that appropriate environmental goals and activities are given strong emphasis in the planning and execution of the trips or camps. There is real merit in any proposal for teachers to provide increased opportunities for students to acquire the understanding, motivation and skills which would help them to make informed decisions about actions required to protect and improve their environment. Although a wilderness trip could have a strong impact on the attitudes and values of the participants, profound and long-term attitude change is obviously more likely if the trip is part of a systematic and comprehensive programme designed to help students acquire a sensitivity to their environment by using appropriate urban settings over an extended period of time. School grounds could be developed for environmental education purposes. Field trips could be made to a local park, a polluted river, a crowded shopping centre, a vacant lot or any other setting which offers opportunities for understanding the relationship between human beings and their environment. Such experiences are potentially important in promoting environmental awareness and, perhaps, in the development of a broadly-based environmental ethic.

Increasing interest and participation in recreational activities in natural environments poses a threat to these environments, creates a dilemma for those charged with responsibilities for the provision of recreational opportunities and for environmental protection and presents another reason why education about natural environments needs to be given increased rather than diminished emphasis. While taking into account the legitimate recreational needs of human beings, students could consider the impact of large-scale recreational developments and of wilderness trips in natural areas. The attitudes and behaviour and environmental impact of the people who are attracted by the facilities offered by a resort and those wanting a 'genuine' wilderness experience could be compared. It can readily be demonstrated that the activities of both groups can have an adverse effect on the environment even if the extent of the damage is different. Approaches which can be adopted by governmental agencies and by individuals and groups to minimise environmental damage could be explored. Students could also investigate the need for the promulgation and enforcement of restrictions on recreational behaviour in natural environments. These activities involve cognitive and affective learning of a high level. However, it does not necessarily follow that the activities need to be delayed until the latter years of formal education. Indeed, experience and research in Australia would seem to indicate that:

(1) the abilities and attitudes are more likely to be developed if they are built up systematically over an extended period.in a programme beginning in primary school grades
(2) students are more likely to develop a commitment to protecting natural environments if they participate in a systematic programme of environmental activities involving multiple trips to various settings in which natural entities and communities can be explored and in appropriate preparatory and follow-up learning experiences in classrooms
(3) students who develop understanding of, and sensitivity towards, natural environments are also likely to be concerned about improving the total environment.

The implication of these findings is not the abandonment of experiences which do not in themselves achieve the highest goals of environmental education. Rather, outdoor educators should be seeking to promote a wide variety of experiences and programmes which will make some contribution to the development of the knowledge, skills and attitudes considered desirable.

The Australian Experience: Practices and Possibilities

Over recent years, case studies have been undertaken of four wilderness trips, four short-term (three to five days) outdoor education experiences involving sixth grade children in wilderness areas, and of five longer-term outdoor education programmes offered in educational institutions at various levels. The author and outdoor education students at the Canberra College of Advanced Education interviewed participants, systematically observed behaviour and used a variety of other data-collecting methods including instruments designed to measure changes in knowledge, skills, attitudes and values. Each instrument was 'custom-made' in the sense that an attempt was made to make it relevant to the particular group and programme being investigated. It was considered that none of the available instruments were appropriate. In all cases, data collection was spread over a comparatively long period of time (three to fifteen months) in an attempt to avoid the deficiencies of research efforts which have attempted to measure changes without trying to:

—establish the extent and nature of existing knowledge and attitudes
—determine whether the changes were retained over time
—account for all the factors which may have been influential in the outcomes

The Australian case studies were not flawless in design or in execution. Indeed, each study had some blatant deficiencies. Detailed research reports have yet to be published, but some useful if tentative findings seem to have emerged and are relevant here.

Short-term Wilderness Trips

The four wilderness trips studied involved groups of 10 to 15 junior high school students under the leadership of 4 different groups of 3 or 4 leaders (senior undergraduate students in education who were taking a semester-length course in outdoor education in which they were required to gain experience in planning, implementing and evaluating an outdoor education experience). The high school student participants were volunteers and had had no previous experience in wilderness areas. Care was taken to ensure that the leader groups were comparable in terms of enthusiasm, competencies, confidence and level of maturity. Guidance and supervision was provided by the writer but was rarely required.

Contact between the leaders and the student-participants prior to the trip was limited in time and purpose. Three one-hour familiarisation meetings took place in which the leaders and students talked, generally about their backgrounds and interests. An attempt was made to determine the knowledge and attitudes of students to a number of concepts and issues relating to natural environments, and trip arrangements were discussed.

The explicit goals of two trips (for the 'recreationists') were basically recreational and social. The leaders were expected to model environmentally-sound camping practices but these were not to be discussed with the participants. For the other two trips (for the 'environmentalists'), environmental goals and activities were added as a major focus. In addition, the leaders of the latter two groups were expected to implement minimum impact camping guidelines and to discuss the reasons for these at 'opportune moments'. No follow-up was planned by the leaders or classroom teachers. The students were interviewed a week after the trip by the leaders and subsequent interviews were conducted by the writer a year later.

For various reasons, 8 of the 49 students did not feel positive about the experience. Most described them as 'fun', 'great' or 'excellent' or other words which indicated satisfaction. A week after the trips, all students felt that they would be prepared or keen to take part in a similar experience if they had an opportunity. After a year, 18 (4 of 22 'recreationists' and 14 of 27 'environmentalists') had participated in at least one other wilderness experience. One group of 7 'environmentalists' had organised 3 limited and safe trips by themselves. Nine students, including 6 of the 8 students who were initially negative, had no intention of participating in wilderness experiences a year after the trips. The other 22 were still interested, but either did not feel confident or competent to organise their own trips or had not had an opportunity to take part in such a trip.

A week after the trips, there appeared to be some positive change in the environmental knowledge and attitudes of students in all four groups. For example, the students were more aware of, and prepared to put into practice, minimum impact camping guidelines. During the trips, the commitment to the guidelines was more obvious in the students who belonged to the 'environmentalist' groups. These students also were inclined to hold protectionist views more strongly and to argue them more coherently a week later. The commitment to behaviour designed to minimise impact was still held by the majority of students a year later, although this commitment was most strongly expressed by those students who had been involved in further wilderness experiences. The absence of reinforcement, however, had the effect of creating some uncertainty or confusion about appropriate behaviour which was environmentally sound.

A perhaps surprising effect of the wilderness trips was a significant growth of interest in environmental concerns and issues generally. A year after the trips, most of the students were much more aware of local, regional, national and international issues than they had been before the trips. Although none of the students had subsequently been involved in relevant planned learning experiences in schools, they were more attentive to media reports, more inclined to seek out information on their own behalf, more knowledgeable about alternative perspectives and more likely to support arguments designed to protect and to improve the total environment. Not surprisingly, the arguments tended to be lacking in depth and sophistication but at least there was evidence of positive changes. Although the wilderness trips seem to have been instrumental in promoting environmental interest, there was obviously a need for comprehensive environmental education programmes which could have built on this base.

Short-term Outdoor (Wilderness) Education Experiences

The four programmes studied were similar to the wilderness trips in the sense that they were short-term. Preparatory work in the schools was limited to instruction in basic campcraft knowledge and skills. Follow-up activity was also limited in time and scope and involved reporting and evaluation activities only. The programmes involved younger children (Grade 6) and lasted from 3 to 5 days. The students were city-dwellers with no prior camping experience in wilderness areas. The goals of each camp were determined by the senior education students who were to act as leaders of small groups (a male and a female leader for each mixed group of ten sixth graders). With some minor variations, the purpose of each camp was to provide an outdoor leisure, environmental and educational experience for the children which would:

—provide fun, enjoyment and challenge in the outdoors
—help develop competency in basic bushwalking and camping skills
—help develop an awareness and appreciation of, and respect for, bush environments, especially in terms of their use and conservation
—help them become more aware of a range of outdoor leisure activities
—make learning more direct and meaningful
—help promote positive attitudes to physical fitness, nutrition, health and well-being-
—help them develop self-reliance, confidence and self-esteem by living in, and coping with, an unfamiliar environment
—help them become more caring, co-operative and tolerant in group situations

The goals are not new. The emphasis on environmental objectives, however, was central to each programme. During the whole experience, the students were involved in a variety of activities designed to achieve programme goals. Environmental goals permeated the total programme and over half the activities were specifically directed at promoting environmental knowledge and attitudes. In each case, a base camp was established in a wilderness area where the students were expected to make decisions about, and take responsibility for, most aspects of the camping experience, such as selecting sites for tents, collecting firewood and water, lighting fires, cooking food, and cleaning and tidying up. Each group walked through the bush to previously selected and different sites for an overnight experience in an isolated area.

With the exception of a few individuals who were pleased to return to the 'comforts' of home, students were very positive about their experiences immediately afterwards. A week later, all students felt that the experience had been worthwhile and enjoyable. A year later, the 'camps' were perceived as being a highlight of their schooling experience. An overall evaluation of the experiences is not relevant here. In terms of changes in environmental knowledge and goals, the camping experiences produced similar short-term effects to the wilderness trips. However, long-term retention tended to be less for the younger students involved in the camps than for the high school students who participated in the wilderness trips. There was a general and significant growth in environmental awareness and interest immediately after the camping programmes but, a year later, fewer than a quarter of the students had retained any active interest in natural environments and most of the gains in knowledge had been lost. The students were, however, more inclined to make environmentally-sound decisions when presented with value alternatives relating to real or hypothetical environmental issues. Nevertheless, it would seem that short-term outdoor education experiences need to be integrated into a longer-term and cohesive programme if maximum benefit is to be obtained from the increased motivation and positive attitudes generated by camping experiences, but not reinforced by subsequent learning experiences. This would seem to be particularly important for younger students who are unable to organise their own experiences.

Long-term Outdoor Education Programmes

Short-term wilderness trips and camps can have important and worthwhile effects on the attitudes of participants, but it is obvious that changes are likely to be greater and more lasting in longer-term programmes given a similar level of expertise and enthusiasm on the part of teachers or leaders. It would be anticipated that the longer, more rigorous and comprehensive a programme, the more likely it is that the higher level environmental abilities outlined previously would be developed and the greater the potential for developing a sound environmental ethic.

The following is but one example of Australian programmes which have been implemented at different levels and which appear to have resulted in significant and lasting changes in environmental knowledge and attitudes and in the development of the sort of ethic which Simpson is seeking.

A One-year Primary School Programme

This sixth grade programme was designed to provide an enjoyable leisure experience in the outdoors, to develop outdoor leisure knowledge and skills and to investigate the environmental effects of human beings on the mountainous area to the south of Canberra in the ACT. The area has been recently proclaimed as a national park. The first management plan for the park was released after the programme had been completed. The programme involved inquiry learning and values clarification approaches. Students sought to gain an understanding of the status and nature of the natural environment prior to the arrival of European settlers. The interaction of the original Aboriginal inhabitants with the natural environment and their impact on it was explored and compared with the effects of later inhabitants. The students interviewed people with an interest in the area; they were involved in weekly (half-day to three-day) visits to different locations; they were introduced to key ecological concepts; and they studied Australian and overseas examples of areas which had been established as national parks. They then set about developing a set of principles which would direct their attempts to produce a management plan which reflected their decisions about the use and protection of the park. The draft plan was discussed with representatives of numerous community groups and subsequently amended after consider-able conflict amongst interest groups (small groups of 'developers' and 'preservationists' and a larger group of 'protectionists') which had emerged within the class. The final plan was then submitted to the relevant authorities.

The students have moved on to high schools and will not have an opportunity to consider the official management plan as a class. In interviews, individual and small groups of students were advised of the major provisions of the plan. The 'preservationists' were disappointed that the plan did not contain the stringent limitations and controls they had recommended. The 'protectionists' were generally pleased that the park was to be protected from excessive human exploitation, although there was some concern that some of the provisions were open to interpretation. They felt that the provisions embodied in their own plan were more clear-cut and more likely to ensure the long-term protection of natural entities and communities. The 'developers' were disappointed that the park was not going to be opened up for wide community use, that facilities were not planned, and that economic exploitation was not given any emphasis.

The interviews and questionnaires undertaken at the completion of the programme and eight months afterwards revealed a remarkable growth of knowledge about natural environments, an increased capacity to identify and justify personal values and to account for alternative points of view, and a growth of interest in environmental issues generally. There were a few students who had rejected the basic tenets of an environmental ethic based on human beings being only a part of the natural community. They argued strongly that the interests of human beings should generally be paramount. In the main, however, the students were quick to proclaim themselves as environmentalists and, for sixth graders, they appeared to have a sound grasp of key ecological concepts.

It must be said that this exemplary programme is not common or typical. Most schools do not have such a programme. It is longer than most. The teacher is knowledgeable, enthusiastic, committed and an excellent role model. The principal, teachers and parents were ideologically and financially supportive. There was ready access to the area which became the park and to other appropriate settings within the city such as the National Botanical Gardens and city parks. All these factors were influential in determining the outcomes. Comparable outcomes may still be possible even in the absence of one or more of the factors. The crucial elements would seem to be the knowledge, enthusiasm, energy and creativity of the teacher.

References

Barton, M. (1969) 'Water Pollution in Remote Recreation Areas', *Journal of Soil and Water Conservation* 24 (4).
Bogucki, D.J., Molanchuk, J.L. and Schenck, T.E. (1975) 'Impact of Short-term Camping on Ground-level Vegetation', *Journal of Soil and Water Conservation* 30 (5).
Cole, D.N. (1977) 'Man's Impact on Wilderness Vegetation: An Example from Eagle Cap Wilderness, Northeast Oregon', Unpublished doctoral dissertation, University of Oregon, USA.

Giest, V. (1975) *Mountain Sheep and Man in Northern Wilds*, Cornell University Press, Ithica, New York, USA.

Gilbert, B. (1976) 'The Great Grizzly Controversy', *Audobon* 78 (1).

Legg, M.H. and Schneider, G. (1977) 'Soil Deterioration on Camp-sites: Northern Forest Types', *Soil Science Society of America Journal* 41 (2), USA.

Leonard, R.E. and Plumley, H.J. (1979) 'The Use of Soils Information for Dispersed Recreation Planning' in Ittner, R., Potter, D.R., Agee, J.K. and Anschell, S., *Recreation Impact on Wildlands, Conference Proceedings*, US Forest Service, Seattle, USA.

Leopold, A. (1970) *A Sand County Almanac*, Ballantine, New York, USA.

Liddle, M.J. (1975) 'A Selective Review of the Ecological Effects of human Tramping on Natural Ecosystems', *Biol. Conserv.* 7 (1).

Ream, C.H. (1979) 'Human-wildlife Conflicts in Backcountry: Possible Solutions' in Ittner, R., Potter, D.R., Agee, J.K. and Anschell, S., *Recreation Impact on Wildlands, Conference Proceedings*, US Forest Service, Seattle, USA.

Schultz, R.D. and Bailey, J.A. (1976) 'Responses of National Park Elk to Human Activity', *Journal of Wildlife Management* 42 (1).

Simpson, S. (1985) 'Short-term Wilderness Experiences and Environmental Ethics', *Journal of Experiential Education* 8 (3).

Young, R.A. (1978) 'Camping Intensity Effects on Vegetative Groundcover in Illinois Campgrounds', *Journal of Soil and Water Conservation* 33 (1), USA.

12
Outdoor Education and Special Groups

Bruce Hayllar

Introduction

Some outdoor education programmes involve groups or individuals for whom access to, and opportunity for, outdoor-based experiences are limited by a range of factors. These may include physical or emotional disability, social and cultural value systems, and social, economic or experiential disadvantage. Outdoor education programmes with specific population groups generally connect three separate yet inter-related themes:

(1) The provision of *opportunity* for outdoors experience where opportunity has previously been limited or denied, with disabled or socially disadvantaged groups
(2) The use of the outdoors for directed *therapeutic* purposes, e.g., with senior adults, or children with chronic illness
(3) *Integrative* programmes which draw on the previous two, e.g., those catering for youth-at-risk.

The evolution of special services for these groups has been the result of a gradual change in social attitudes which hitherto constrained opportunity through indifference, intolerance, and inadequate funding. These factors often result in limiting educational opportunity and employment prospects, and reducing access to community-provided leisure opportunities. They also lead to an emphasis on state institutions, in their various forms, as the simplistic response to a series of complex issues.

The late 1970s and the 1980s, however, witnessed a growing recognition and acceptance that quality of life, and the factors that contribute to this (e.g., housing and education), should be available to disadvantaged groups just as they are for the population at large. As a result, there has been growth in publicly-funded programmes attempting to improve access and opportunity through a range of initiatives.

While housing and employment were obvious targets for intervention, the contemporary awareness of the role that leisure plays in contributing to an individual's overall well-being have also been acknowledged. Thus, leisure-related programmes now play an increasingly significant role for this sector of the community. The development of outdoor programmes has been part of this trend.

Specific Programmes, Specific Purposes, Specific Groups

Outdoor education programmes with specific populations may take place in residential or non-residential settings or in a combination of both. They may range in length from one day to many weeks. They may take place in urban or wilderness environments, above the ground or below, on the water or the land. They may be conducted by schools, state-controlled agencies, by voluntary or private associations, or by commercial operators. In short, these programmes, in their broadest terms, are subject to the same operational opportunities and constraints as those for the population at large. However, what distinguishes them from the mainstream are the diversity of needs, demands, desires and expectations of the participants. These particular needs also require creative approaches to programme design, skilled and empathetic staff, and the encouragement of leadership qualities in participants. The ultimate goal of such programmes should be to help people move from dependency to independence. The rest of this chapter will review four different types of programme to demonstrate the diverse roles and purposes of outdoor education with specific groups. It concludes with a case study of an adventure-based programme for youth-at-risk.

A Bush Experience for Young Migrants

In 1985, the Brisbane Forest Park Administration received an innovative recreation programme grant from the government for newly-arrived migrant and refugee children. The programme was designed to provide opportunities for these children to experience the bush and 'typical' Australian pastimes through a range of outdoor activities.

The programme had four specific objectives (Programme Manual 1988):

—to promote positive attitudes towards the environment so that children can learn to value, wonder at and enjoy the Australian bush
—to increase children's English language skills by introducing them to new environmental concepts and contexts
—to provide a link to motivate children's families to explore new attitudes to their surroundings
—to provide the children with common experiences to facilitate assimilation with Australian children

The Bush Experience for Young Migrants programme was conducted in Queensland, at the Brisbane Forest Park, a 25,000 hectare area west of the city. It is an area characterised by open eucalypt and rain forest, and by creeks and rivers.

Participants were selected from students and staff of the Milpera Special School and Oxley Migrant Education Unit. The students were drawn from 28 different language groups and their ages ranged from 11 to 18. Over half the participants were Indo-Chinese, many of them orphans.

The programme focused on environment-related activities which were used primarily as media for language-based studies. The programme contained five elements, which are summarised below:

—*Residential Camp*: Two residential camps (of three and five days respectively) were held.
—*Tent camping*: Four two-day camps were conducted. The programme included campcraft and nature interpretation.
—*Nature-study days*: Sixteen half-day nature-study days took place. These days incorporated both in-field and class-based activities at the Brisbane Forest Park Headquarters.
—*Bush picnic days*: These days were social outings at a venue which provided a range of resources for active and passive recreation, including an adventure playground, a self-guiding nature circuit, a creek and an open playing field.
—*Ropes adventure course*: The ropes course was a series of timber, wire and rope obstacles built among the eucalypts. It was chosen to provide physical activity as an alternative to the environmental emphasis of the other elements.

The Principal of Milpera Special School felt that the programme both facilitated and accelerated language-based learning because:

—it provided a beautiful, natural and real context for language learning
—it provided a multi-faceted shared experience which was not a 'one-off' situation
—participants 'shared' experiences—with each other, with Forest Park personnel and, at a later stage, with their parents. (The programme has subsequently led to family outings and picnics in the forests)
—structured and unstructured activities helped the students become part of the Australian natural environment and sensitive to its needs
—it developed students socially and culturally as well as linguistically
—it enabled students to participate creatively in activities

Senior Adult Camping

If education is considered to be a life-long process, then educating individuals to derive pleasure and skills from outdoor experiences should not cease at the end of one's formal education. In recognition of this, and the long-term value of the outdoors to individuals, the New South Wales Department of Health launched its Senior Adult Camping Programme.

The rationale for this is based on the notion of preventive health care. While this is central, other aspects are also included. The residential camping experience seeks to:

—teach senior adults the value and methods of regular appropriate exercise
—provide guidance on nutrition
—introduce them to outdoor recreation activities
—increase self-esteem
—provide opportunities for socialising amongst a diverse range of senior adults

Having Fun

The camping programmes take place at residential sites throughout New South Wales. These may be state-owned centres or sites owned by commercial operators and religious organisations. The main consideration is that the centres should be relatively accessible in terms of physical layout, location, and a range of opportunities for recreational experiences.

The participants are drawn from a diverse range of backgrounds and have varying levels of health status. The programme seeks to involve participants with critical disabilities: e.g., individuals with sensory motor dysfunction which manifests itself in limitations with walking or lifting heavy objects, and with social disabilities: e.g., individuals who have difficulty in fulfilling social roles such as house-keeping, food preparation, grocery-shopping and social interaction with peers.

The average programme lasts 4 days and involves 6 staff and approximately 50–55 participants. It revolves around health-related seminars/workshops and outdoor recreation. A typical programme would include canoeing, bushwalking, archery, bush dancing and health-related activities.

Follow-up questionnaires are distributed on the completion of each camp. In 1988, a report (Whitfield) was produced which documented the findings from the evaluations of 1,200 ex-campers. It concluded that the camps had been a major influence on the lives of those who attended. Many had adopted the positive health and activity habits commenced at camp; friendships made during camp were continued; and an ex-campers association had been formed, on their initiative.

It is clear that senior adult camping brings enjoyment and pleasure to those who attend and the values espoused during the camp have a positive impact on post-camp life-styles.

A Caving Adventure

The Jenolan Caves are a series of limestone caves operated by the NSW Tourism Commission. Aside from the 'tourist' caves, there are more than 100 'adventure caves' available to organised speleological groups. The NSW Society for Crippled Children conducts twice-yearly caving 'expeditions' to the Jenolan Caves in the Blue Mountains west of Sydney.

Three specific objectives are established for these programmes:

—to provide disabled people with the opportunity to participate in the same type of activities available to the able-bodied

Caving

—to enhance self-concept and self-esteem through participation in a challenging, adventurous activity
—to promote public awareness of the abilities, rather than disabilities, of disabled people

Small groups of 6–8 men and women ranging in age from 15–18 attend these 2-day programmes. All of those who attend are confined to wheelchairs and are disabled by either spina bifida or cerebral palsy. Caves are selected according to their physical attributes, as participants need either to drag themselves or crawl through the system. Wheelchair access to cave entrances is also important. Due to these extreme physical demands only one cave is attempted during each programme.

Informal evaluations held with each group have shown a positive response to the programme. Participants particularly like the idea of demonstrating their abilities to the able-bodied. This process of informal public education is enhanced when tourists are confronted by speleologists in wheelchairs as the two groups emerge from their respective visits underground.

Outdoor Education for Youth at Risk

Introduction

The examples cited above with different groups further illustrate the diversity of outdoor education and its purposes. However, one of the most significant uses of outdoor programmes have involved those with young offenders and youth at risk. In Australia, programmes have operated in all states through direct government funding: e.g., the Cobham Survival Program conducted by the NSW Department of Youth and Community Services; through grant funding to specific organisations: e.g., Project Hahn in Tasmania (sponsored by the Federal and state governments and private enterprise); and by voluntary agencies using both grant funding and their own resources: e.g., the Sydney City Mission's 'Wilderness Project'. Adventure-based programmes with youth at risk primarily use vigorous outdoor activities as the therapeutic medium. Their aim is to use challenging and personally meaningful experiences to enhance inter and intra-group development, self-concept and self-esteem, and to engender within the participant pro-social attitudes and behaviours. The remainder of the chapter focuses on these types of programmes.

The use of adventure programmes for the rehabilitation of young offenders is generally recognised as having commenced with the work of Kelly and Baer, two psychologists working with the Massachusetts, USA, Department of Corrections. Early in the 1960s, Kelly argued that the 'warehousing' of delinquents in training centres was dehumanising, costly, and ineffective. Recidivism rates, the levels at which people returned to training institutions, were consistently high. He theorised that delinquent behaviour was a manifestation of:

—an adolescent identity crisis which was exacerbated by the absence of clear-cut 'rites of passage' into adult society, and
—a decline in the authority of the father figure

To test his theory, Kelly arranged for 5 delinquent youths to attend an Outward Bound programme which, he argued, would help resolve their identity crisis and provide them with the coping strategies necessary for more socially adaptive behaviour. Encouraged by the results of this programme, a further 40 young people were sent to Outward Bound and a 6-month follow-up was conducted to ascertain their recidivism rates. Only 4 returned to the training institutions, compared with the 15 or 16 expected at the usual recidivism rates. The final step was to send a further 60 (randomly selected) youths and to compare these with a similarly matched comparison group who remained at the training school. The results, after a year, showed a 20 per cent recidivism rate for the Outward Bound group and 42 per cent in the control group. Kelly's research pioneered the use of adventure programmes by numerous agencies throughout the USA (Golins 1980).

Research Findings

With the growth in adventure programmes for these groups, many research projects have been undertaken to assess their effectiveness. Typically, these involve investigations in the areas of personality, recidivism and cost-benefit analysis. Additionally, the research has sought to identify those factors contributing to the change process.

Personality Attributes

Self-concept measures have played an important part in the evaluation of programmes with young offenders. As discussed in Chapter 4, the notion of self-concept primarily refers to the way we perceive ourselves and, more importantly in terms of these programmes, how such perceptions are manifested in behaviour.

Although self-concept undergoes change over time, the potential for change is critical at different periods. Up to the age of 10, self-concept is ill-defined and somewhat unstable. However, by the ages of 11 or 12, stability becomes more characteristic (Piers 1969). Montemayor and Eisen (1977) reported on the way self-concept alters between childhood and adolescence. From a study of a group of 262 adolescents (average age 13.9), they concluded that, with increasing age, an individual's self-concept becomes more abstract and less concrete. The younger subjects in the study were primarily concerned with describing themselves in objective categories such as physical appearance and play activities, whereas the older group became more subjective and provided abstract descriptions of personal beliefs and critical self-evaluations.

The results are not surprising in themselves, as one would intuitively assume that with increasing age the ability to verbalise and communicate self-perceptions would also increase. But, as Rosenberg (1979: 217) states: 'the reason that the older child is more aware of a psychological interior is that he is capable of introspection, of reflecting on, and reacting to, his inner cognitive, affective and cognitive processes'. The nature and structure of outdoor adventure programmes suggests they have great potential for influencing these self-evaluative processes. Two examples from the literature, cited below, support such reasoning.

Kelly and Baer (1971) followed up their earlier work with a study of 120 young offenders. This group was compared with a matched group of offenders who were placed in correctional institutions. Following their Outward Bound experience, this group showed significant improvement in their general self-concept; an increase in levels of aspiration and maturity; reduced feelings of bravado; and increased personal identification with socially-acceptable behaviour.

Cave (1979) examined the effects of a wilderness adventure programme using two experimental and one comparison group. The two experimental groups attended an adventure programme with one group participating in a low-stress programme and the other in a high-stress course. Substantial reductions in maladaptive behaviours (produced by feelings of mistrust, shame, doubt, guilt, inferiority and role confusion) resulted. Noteworthy, from both programming and research perspectives, was the finding that the results in the high-stress group were more significant than for the low-stress participants.

Recidivism

In their 1971 study, Kelly and Baer defined recidivism as a return to a correctional institution for a new offence. Their data indicate a re-offending rate of non-participants over participants of approximately 2:1.

Cytrynbaun and Kerr (1971) studied juveniles who participated in the Connecticut Wilderness School Programme. The study noted a greater decrease in arrests, drug and alcohol abuse, and systems dependency on social service agencies in the six months following the programme. In comparison to an established control group, the data indicated that 11 per cent of programme graduates as opposed to 30 per cent of the comparison group were arrested during the same period.

The Underway Programme at Southern Illinois University was found by Hileman (1979) to produce a positive effect on recidivism rates. Twenty-two per cent of the 48 delinquents participating in the programme re-offended within 7 months compared with 40 per cent of a matched group provided with advocacy, counselling, alternative education and placements in group homes. Hileman also considered the seriousness of the recidivists' offences. Crimes committed by the Underway graduates were all misdemeanours and were significantly less serious than those committed by a control group (Kimball 1980: 23).

Kelly's 5-year follow-up of the first subjects in his study revealed that differences in recidivism rates were not statistically significant after that period. However, the direction, 38 to 57 per cent, was favourable towards the wilderness programme participants. Significantly, the greatest increase in recidivism occurred at the end of the second year of parole for the wilderness group, rather than the first 6 months as with comparison group members. This suggests that the programme had the effect of enabling the young people to sustain themselves in the community for a longer period. Implicit in this finding is the need for continuous community-based follow-up. Golins, however, tempers this finding with a cautionary note to practitioners:

Practitioners may have gone overboard on follow-up. The issue of follow-up has become a sacred cow. . . some of the more zealous adherents even go so far as to deny the efficacy of utilizing adventure education at all for troubled youth unless it is coupled with a panoply of supportive after-care services . . . What I have decided is that the need to follow-up is relative to the individual needs . . . Follow-up can be useful but not neccessarily so . . . Over-responding to a kid's troubles can be just as harmful as under responding. It can breed a feeling of needing help.

Cost-benefit Analysis

This criterion for evaluation has received little attention in the past. One notable exception is an evaluation of Michigan Expeditions, an adventure programme conducted by the Michigan Department of Social Services in the USA. Savings were calculated by:

—totalling the cost of the adventure
—determining post-placement cost for the period between programme completion and the average length of stay (based on institutional averages), and
—determining what placements would have cost if the youth had not been diverted

It was calculated that in one year a total of $230,580 was saved by the Department in conducting their adventure programmes (Golins 1980).

In their review of current programmes, Bagby and Chavarria (1980: 3) suggested that the adventure process helps the adolescent to:

deal with frustration and stress using determination and self-discipline. The delinquent sees the value of forethought and planned action over impulsivity. He must achieve beyond his preconceived limits demonstrating his competence by action, in terms he can comprehend. He takes satisfaction from his improved physical condition. More self-confident, he is better able to interact and depend on others. The constant self-examination results in greater self-awareness, more accurate self-perceptions and improved self-concept.

Why Use Adventure Programmes for Youth at Risk?

The research into adventure-based programmes is generally supportive of their effectiveness as a therapeutic tool. This effectiveness, it is argued, is attributable to six basic elements inherent in such programmes, which, in combination, provide a unique therapeutic environment. These key elements are: an emphasis on action; the use of the outdoor environment; the formation of a co-operative community; programmed success; an emphasis on stress; and the nature of staff/participant relationships.

An Emphasis on Action

The use of adventure activities contrasts with more usual 'talking therapies'. 'Wilderness programmes assume that experience is more therapeutic than analysis' writes Kimball (1980: 7). In a survival programme, the role of analysis takes place within the experiential framework, and emanates from *shared* experiences between counsellor and counselled.

Parker (in Cousineau 1978: 3) comments that the most precious power of the individual is the power to make choices. He notes that: 'control from without the person to choose, for whatever reason, neglects the development of self-control within. Control from within can only develop in situations in which the individual can make his own choices, act on them and learn their consequences.'

The Use of the Outdoors

The outdoors is an alien environment, and survival a novel concept to the majority of young offenders. By being impelled into the unfamiliar, the juvenile is forced to adopt new and appropriate behavioural norms conducive to cognitive and physical 'survival'. As such, new perspectives may be gained as old patterns and assumptions are challenged.

The outdoor environment is in sharp juxtaposition to the traditional training school or remand centre. Whereas the institutional setting demands that a young person functions in an adult world of rules, regulations and conformity, adventure programmes are structured differently. Individual responsibility at a concrete level is a key component. The special demands of the natural environment dictate the necessity of responding in an appropriate manner. If they fail to do so, the consequences are immediate and meaningful. For example, if the tent is not erected correctly, they get wet. If the saddle is not placed correctly on the horse, they fall off. When outdoor skills are learnt at an incremental rate, from novice to higher levels, life (in the microcosm of the adventure programme) becomes more manageable and relatively simple. With such positive outcomes, young people start to take cognitive control once again. They are then, it is hoped, in a better position to be responsive to matters of control as they relate to hoped, their roles and expectations in the wider community.

Co-operative Community

The challenges of an adventure programme dictate that individuals subsume themselves within a group context. Programmed experiences (and incidental occurrences) seek to develop feelings of group interdependence. The result of such interdependence is a form of group rapport that provides a therapeutic environment conducive to emotional expression and sharing—important elements of the therapeutic process.

While conflict within such groups is inevitable, the supportive group atmosphere helps to resolve these conflicts in a socially responsible manner. For many individuals, this experience is unique, and in stark contrast to typical delinquent behaviour.

Programmed Success

Adventure programmes are designed to ensure an individual achieves success. Although delinquent youth who have been habituated to failure often reject success, the 'novelty' of a wilderness programme helps to address this. The concrete nature of the experiences, coupled with a supportive staff and peer environment, act as dynamic forces that induce an individual to *accept* success in spite of the conditioned response of rejection. Success is tangible and unavoidably recognisable, according to Kimball (1980: 11).

Stress

Stress-inducing activity is at the core of an adventure programme. By successfully meeting difficult challenges and by overcoming induced stressful situations, an individual's perception of his or her personal abilities undergoes re-evaluation. Cave (1979) argues that the greater the stress the greater the development of social bonding, an important element in establishing a 'co-operative community'.

Staff/Participant Relationships

Effective staff/participant relationships are central to the success of these programmes. Both theoretically and practically, all other programme elements are linked by this relationship. Without effective relationships, the adventure programme is at best weakened and at worst irrelevant.

In the initial stages of the programme, staff competence (in contrast to the general incompetence of the participants in this environment) is an effective means of control. The authority and power of staff members does not come from a custodial structure, but rather from superior knowledge and experience. Given that personal self-worth is largely defined by the outcomes of social interaction, staff members must assist participants to interpret the significance of their newly-learned behaviours and achievements.

Lewin and Schein (1972 in Ewart 1980) have conceptualised these notions into a three-stage process of change (see Figure 12.1)—a change in perceptions which can be orchestrated by staff members. Stage 1 is the 'unfreezing' of certain attitudes, values, perceptions and behaviours as a result of disconformation or lack of conformation from others present in the change situation. Stage 2 represents a change through cognitive redefinition of assumptions previously held and analysis of information from others in the situation. Stage 3 is a 'refreezing' as a result of acceptance and reinforcement of the value of those changes.

Figure 12.1   Theory of Personal Change Through Survival Programme

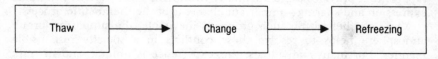

Source: Lewin and Schein in Ewart 1980

Conclusion

Golins (1980: 37) suggests that because of these elements and the mechanisms and properties inherent within them, the young person is seduced into achievement, in spite of himself. This 'seduction' process, he argues, is inevitable because of the delinquent's characteristic behaviour. Three principal characteristics stand out:

First, delinquents typically display an extreme unwillingness to assume socially acceptable types of responsibility for themselves or others. They live in an oceanic world where their wants and needs have few boundaries. They resist holding themselves (or being held) accountable. Delinquents have few functional values. At the heart of the matter is a failure of will-power and concurrent resentment for having to accept one's fate and earn one's keep. He takes his rage out on himself and on others. In terms of Kohlberg's theory of moral development, the delinquent tends to exist at a preconventional level—he finds it difficult to take another's perspective and follows his own impulses in preference to socially accepted rules.

Second, the delinquent is a limited learner. His thinking process seems to be overly concrete for his age. In Piagetian terms, delinquents commonly function at the concrete operations stage of cognitive development. He collects information without properly weighing it, consolidating it, or generalising from it to subsequent experience. He needs concrete models.

Third, his affective posture is debilitating. He lacks confidence in himself and others. As a result, his motivation to learn is low. Moreover, he resists learning from others, especially authority figures.

The picture I have painted is bleak and extreme. There are obviously degrees. Nonetheless, the delinquent is an extremist. His lack of responsibility and limited cognitive development carry him outside the law and into trouble.

Fortunately, there is in most delinquents a contrary desire to reconcile themselves to the demands of society and achieve success within its appropriate conventions. Moreover, being essentially normal human beings, they will naturally develop greater cognitive and affective sophistication if placed in the proper learning environment. This tendency to develop, coupled with a desire to reconcile themselves, exist as potential energy to be tapped. The delinquent experiences the dilemma of acting out his anger at society while simultaneously recognising on some murky level that his only hope is in joining it. He is looking for a way to join without losing too much face. *Adventure based education allows the delinquent to integrate himself into society in an acceptable way.* (emphasis added)

Case Study: The Cobham Survival Programme

The Survival Programme was initially conceived in 1981 by staff at the Cobham Remand Centre in Sydney's outer western suburbs.

At this time, it was recognised that the range of alternatives available to both the magistracy and the workers in the centre were extremely limited. Based on literature available from the United States, the Survival Programme was developed as the first of many new options available for institutionalised young people.

Objectives

The Cobham Survival Programme aimed at increasing the ability of the young offender to cope more effectively in his community by:

—providing opportunities for spontaneous interactions with, and the development of, counselling relationships between, participants and staff

—developing positive interpersonal relationships that would enable realistic, worthwhile assessment to facilitate the development of appropriate strategies for the ongoing support of each participant
—developing each participant's self-esteem and self-worth through involvement in challenging activities and self-awareness workshops
—developing leadership, organisational and living skills through the involvement of participants in fund-raising activities, an expedition and living skills workshop
—broadening each participant's awareness of worthwhile leisure and recreational pursuits

Programme Phases

The programme was implemented in three phases, as shown in Figure 12.2:

Figure 12.2   Survival Programme: Phases Overview

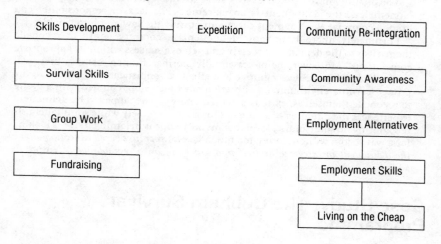

Phase 1: Skills Development

The Skills Development phase incorporated three specific areas:

Survival Skills

This stage was designed to equip programme participants with basic bushcraft knowledge and instruction in the specific outdoor pursuits necessary to undertake the Expedition Phase. The following skill areas were covered:

—Map-reading and compass work
—Menu-planning and cooking
—Bushwalking techniques
—Overnight camping
—Caving skills; abseiling
—Rock-climbing

—Horse-riding
—Expedition preparation
—First aid

Group Work

Group work sessions were designed to:

—establish inclusiveness and equip the participants with communication skills
—develop interpersonal communication skills: self-disclosure and feedback
—develop a good self-concept in the areas of identity, affiliation with others and sense of personal worth
—assist participants to assume responsibility for their own lives and the decisions they make

The construction of family support systems around the participants was an integral component. Two days after the programme commenced, the participants and their families met informally with staff members for a barbecue. At this time, the objectives and processes of the survival programme were discussed with all family members. The need for the family to make a commitment to their child's participation was emphasised. This was done in order to begin the necessary redirection of power away from the 'system' and back to the levels of corporate (family) and individual responsibility. The belief that, ultimately, the programme's success rested on community re-integration, necessitated the consolidation of support networks to facilitate this process. Where a family structure was not present, the existing living system was similarly developed.

Incorporated within the groupwork were a series of personal development workshops. These workshops provided participants with information on human sexuality, contraception and personal relationships and provided a forum for individuals to explore and develop their attitudes toward these issues.

Fund raising

Central to the programme philosophy was the notion that participants must be 'encouraged' to achieve, within the group context, a specific monetary target. Inherent was the assumption that 'no money meant no trip'. Ultimately over $2,000 was earned by participants. The specific objectives of this component were:

—to foster the development of positive work habits
—to encourage participants to 'earn what they get'
—to develop organisational and leadership skills
—to promote a positive image amongst the community

Work tasks included rock-collecting, land-clearing, window-washing, lawn-mowing and car-washing.

Phase 2: Expedition

The Expedition Phase was the key therapeutic intervention of the survival programme. Three specific outdoor pursuits were covered within the two-week period, namely:

—Skiing: three days skiing at Perisher Valley and Smiggins Holes
—Horse trekking: a four-day cross-country expedition onto the Snowy High Plains
—Caving: three days of caving at Wee Jasper, near Yass

The expedition was completed by a 'marathon' run and a final day in Canberra sightseeing. A formal evening meal at a local restaurant was the culminating event of the expedition.

Phase 3: Community Re-integration

The Community Re-integration Phase was designed as the bridge between the survival programme and the community which all participants would re-enter. In practical terms, the success of this phase was the gauge by which the programme would be judged. The components of this phase were:

Community Awareness

The objective of Community Awareness was to acquaint participants with the support services available to them in their local area. Groups visited and familiarised themselves with staff, transport systems and procedures at: alternative accommodation venues (refuges, communal houses, etc.); hospitals and medical services; social welfare support agencies (Youth and Community Services, Social Security and other non-government welfare agencies); and recreational and leisure facilities (e.g. Bidwell Community Centre).

Staff members were allocated to groups of participants within specified geographical zones.

Alternatives to Traditional Employment

The objectives of this component were to help participants

—to develop a number of alternate strategies to employment for each person
—to become aware of the variety of alternatives in each person's local community

These objectives were achieved through small group discussions, visits to alternate work settings within their community; visits to leisure activities within their local environment; practical workshops on the establishment of work co-operatives; and similar employment-generating activities.

As a consequence of this component, a number of participants, working together with staff members, established a 'work collective'. This undertook to complete tasks commenced during the skills phase. At the same time, a permanent organisational structure was established which enabled the collective to respond, on an *ad hoc* basis, to the needs of participants.

Employment Skills

The objectives of this component were to help participants:

—to develop and practise skills for finding and maintaining employment
—to visit potential employment centres in each person's community environment

Living on the Cheap

The objectives of this component were to help participants:

—to be aware of services available from government departments and other community agencies
—to be able to identify and locate appropriate accommodation in their local communities
—to be aware of cheap sources of clothing and consumer durables within their local community

The Therapeutic Environment

The establishment of a therapeutic environment to counsel participants throughout these phases was essential. This environment was structured on the dependence/interdependence/independence paradigm (see Figure 12.3).

Figure 12.3   Dependence, Interdependence and Independence Paradigms

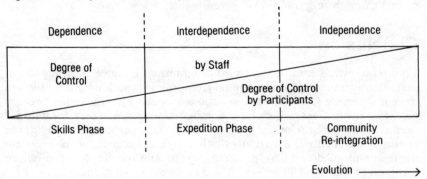

This paradigm suggests that in order to facilitate the development of the therapeutic community some degree of dependency (on staff) in the Skills Phase is desirable. As the programme evolves and moves into the Expedition Phase, the relationship becomes one of interdependence as the co-operative community forms. Finally, the therapeutic environment becomes less important with the commencement of Community Re-integration. These changing relationships are depicted in the figure.

Summary

In combination, the three phases attempt to equip participants with competencies commensurate with the progressive achievement of programme objectives. As a consequence, perceptions of previous abilities are constantly challenged. The reconciliation of these challenges into the formulation of new and more personally and socially constructive attitudes and behaviours is the essence of the Survival Programme.

Evaluation

Many positive examples of change and growth were evident throughout the programme:

—Introspective and intolerant young men commenced offering their feelings to the group and finding acceptance

—Hardened delinquents and resident cynics started to acquiesce, albeit grudgingly

—Individuals started to accept responsibility for their actions and to look less for scapegoats

—The group began to function as a *group* in tasks that, in the early days of the programme, had to be enforced

—Confrontations with authority were resolved by socially-acceptable means

—The modelling of behaviour on staff norms and not delinquent expectations became apparent

While the general evaluation revealed some key areas in which the programme had an impact, recidivist data was particularly encouraging. Statistics for the Survival Programme indicated a rate of 25 per cent after nine months, approximately half that of the other young people who moved through the 'traditional' juvenile justice system.

Conclusion

The trend toward community based programmes for specific groups is, in part, an outcome of an international trend towards seeking alternatives to large congregate facilities: de-institutionalisation. This movement recognises that institutions, which have dominated the human services field for over a century, are no longer appropriate. Clearly, the notions that 'insane asylums' would cure the mentally ill, that 'training schools' would educate the feeble-minded and that 'penitentiaries' would reform the criminal, so common in the late 1800s, have failed to meet expectations.

As outdoor educators, the opportunity to be part of this movement is increasing. Our services should recognise the special needs of these groups and respond with empathy, understanding and integrity.

References

Department of the Arts, Sport and the Environment, Tourism and Territories (1988) *A Bush Experience for Young Migrants: Program Manual*, Australian Government Publishing Service, Canberra.

Bagby, S. and Chavarria, L.S. (1980) *Important Issues in Outdoor Education*, Eric Document 191639, USA.

Cave, S.E. (1979) 'Evaluation of Level of Stress and Group Cohesiveness in the Wilderness Experience', Unpublished doctoral dissertation, University of New Mexico, USA.

Cousineau, C. (1978) *The Nature of Adventure Education*, Eric Document, 171474, USA.

Cytrynbaum, S. and Kerr, K. (1975) *The Connecticut Wilderness Program: A Preliminary Evaluation Report*, Connecticut Council of Human Services, USA.

Ewart, A. (1980) *Adventure Education: A Treatise*, Colorado Outward Bound, Denver, USA.

Ewart, A. (1977) *The Effect of Adventure Activities on Self Concept*, Eric Document 178261, USA.

Hileman, M. (1979) '*The Shortcomings of the Typical Recidivism—Study Design*', Paper presented at Adventure Alternatives in Corrections Conference, Colorado, USA.

Golins, G.L. (1980) *Utilizing Adventure Education to Rehabilitate Juvenile Delinquents*, New Mexico State University, Eric Document 187501, USA.

Kelly, F.J. and Baer, D.J. (1971) 'Physical Challenge as a Treatment for Delinquency', *Crime and Delinquency*, October.

Kelly, F.J. (1974) 'Outward Bound and Delinquency: A Ten Year Experience', Paper presented at the Conference on Experiential Education, Colorado, USA.

Kimball, R.O. (1980) *Wilderness/Adventure Programs for Juvenile Offenders*, Eric Document 196586, USA.

Montemayor, R. and Eisen, M. (1977) 'The Development of Self Conceptions from Childhood to Adolescence', *Developmental Psychology* 13 (4): 314–19.

Rosenberg, M. (1979) *Conceiving the Self*, Freeman and Co., San Francisco, USA.

Whitfield, B. (1988) 'The Relationship between Health and Life-style: An Evaluation of Healthcraft, Residential Programmes for Senior Adults, NSW Department of Health, Sydney.

13
Programme Evaluation in Outdoor Education

Norm McIntyre

Introduction

This book has shown that outdoor education can take many forms. One teacher may use appropriate outdoor settings in the school grounds, the local community, a farm or the bush, to provide first-hand experiences for students. Another may take students on a three-day bush camp or to a resident outdoor centre to participate in a range of activities drawn from a number of different curriculum areas. Others may take students on a four-day wilderness experience involving bushwalking, lightweight camping and learning activities designed to develop understanding of key ecological concepts and to promote environmental awareness. This experience could be a one-off event or may be part of a much more extensive outdoor education programme designed to develop outdoor skills and environmental knowledge and attitudes. Each of these forms of outdoor education needs to be evaluated.

Outdoor education can be difficult to get started in a school as teachers are often required to justify the introduction of any outdoor activity or programme. This is particularly the case when a teacher wants to introduce outdoor education as a subject within the already overcrowded school curriculum. To begin with, the very nature of outdoor education makes it difficult to assign it to a particular department or curriculum area within the school. Hence, it can suffer from lack of recognition. In addition, there is a widespread perception that outdoor education activities and programmes can be expensive and disruptive to the school programme. To overcome these difficulties and perceptions, teachers are required to specify the contribution that outdoor education has made in similar circumstances in other schools and demonstrate, through evaluation, that outdoor education programmes are as effective in their own situation. Even if teachers are not required by the school or other authorities to evaluate outdoor education programmes and activities, there are compelling reasons why outdoor education should be subject to constant and rigorous evaluation.

In the first instance, all outdoor educators need to be concerned to determine the extent to which their students are achieving the objectives specified for an activity or programme. It is important to know what changes, if any, are occurring in the students' knowledge, skills and attitudes. Only in this way can the effectiveness and the value of outdoor education programmes and strategies be demonstrated. Outdoor educators must, therefore, accept the task of determining what settings, experiences, strategies, materials and insights from other areas of the curriculum are most applicable to outdoor education. They must also begin to develop and evaluate those contributions that are unique to outdoor education. Further, they must make use of the embryonic networks provided by state associations and conferences to disseminate such information to others in the field.

What is Evaluation?

The evaluation process involves the teacher in collecting information and presenting this in a form which is useful. The basic purposes of evaluation are two-fold. It can provide information and insights that will help the teacher both to assess student entry points and progression, and to determine the effectiveness of the learning experiences.

In the first instance, the teacher is concerned about the following outcomes:

Discussing

(1) diagnosing learning outcomes
(2) identifying suitable remedial measures
(3) assessing student mastery of a particular learning task
(4) placing a student at an appropriate learning level in a programme

Teachers are also concerned about the suitability of the learning experiences for a particular age group or type of student; the usefulness of the materials used; the appropriateness of the settings selected; the time allocated or the time of year chosen; and any other matter which might have an influence on the outcomes. In this instance, evaluation enables the teacher to identify aspects of the programme which need to be improved and to suggest the means by which such improvements can be made. This will apply equally to those situations where a programme is being modified and to those where a new programme is being developed.

The achievement of these purposes will also enable a teacher to meet another expectation: that of accountability. If a teacher is able to show that the claims made for outdoor education are substantiated and that stated objectives are being achieved, then this information can be used to help justify outdoor education to interested people (the school principal, other teachers, parents, prospective students, members of the community) and to interested and concerned authorities.

Evaluation Methodologies

Traditional evaluation studies have favoured experimental designs in data collection. Such designs usually involve quantitative measurements involving randomly selected participants under controlled conditions and are useful only when applied to events where cause and effect relationships can be clearly isolated. Such ideal situations rarely occur because students in outdoor education classes are not, as a rule, randomly selected and the programmes they undertake are normally quite complex and involved. Hence, while studies based on experimental designs have produced some useful insights in appropriate situations, they are of little practical value to teachers involved in programme evaluation.

In recognition of the difficulties presented by true experimental designs, researchers and evaluators have sought less rigorous approaches which are more flexible and accepting of the complexity of the outdoor education experience. These are called quasi-experimental designs and have been used in situations where true experimental control is difficult or impossible.

Campbell and Stanley (1963) have described a wide variety of such designs, many of which have been used extensively in outdoor education in recent times. However, if they are to be at all credible, these designs must be complex. Hence, they are difficult to implement effectively and generally require quite sophisticated statistical analysis.

The aim of both of these designs is to add to our general understanding of the processes and effects of outdoor education: hence the need to control for as many factors as possible in order to allow for maximum generalisation. Such designs are more the province of the researcher and graduate student than the teacher, who is more concerned with the impacts of his or her programme on a particular group of students.

A recent survey of evaluation practices at residential centres in the United States (Chenery and Hammerman 1985) has revealed that 'observation of the programme' and 'group discussions with participants' were used as evaluation tools in 90 per cent and 79 per cent of outdoor education centres respectively. This observation suggests that more informal approaches to evaluation than those previously described are favoured by practising teachers at such centres. It is evident that they have recognised the difficulties of implementing the approaches advocated by researchers and have rejected them in favour of a more holistic and pragmatic approach to evaluation. Such an approach accepts that the outdoor education programme must be treated as a whole rather than manipulated or fragmented into experimental bits. This process seeks to describe and analyse the true richness and complexity of the outdoor education experience. In some cases, the evaluator may use interviews, written records, participant observation and case histories to view the experience through the eyes of the participant. At other times, questionnaires, observation of activities and discussions with groups may be more appropriate.

Reviewing

These methods typify the 'naturalistic' approach to evaluation, which is characterised by qualitative measurement of changes and their effect over time. It relies on an ongoing analysis of the complex interplay of the learner, the teacher and the setting for its relevance, and avoids attempts to control, manipulate or eliminate developments. The evaluation thus aims to provide an accurate and realistic picture of the processes and outcomes of the outdoor education experience.

This approach generally relies on a close interaction with the programme and participants over an extended period of time. Hence teachers are in an ideal position to be involved in data collection as a normal part of their duties. Many of the methods used are unobtrusive and can be incorporated into the regular programme with a minimum of disruption. Proponents argue that the information collected is especially relevant to outdoor education programmes because it documents what actually happens and, therefore, aids in the understanding of processes as well as outcomes. In this context Staley (1980) has commented:

A non-experimental (naturalistic) design is ideal for the evaluation of most outdoor education programmes because it provides information that is useful for making decisions about programme effectiveness. It thus contributes to programme development, not its labelling of successes or failures.

Experimental and quasi-experimental designs have been used extensively by research workers who have had the time and expertise to develop and implement such sophisticated approaches to evaluation. They have used a variety of appropriate research methods to collect data, and they have analysed the data carefully and produced research papers based on the results. Outdoor educators rarely have the time to match such efforts. However, the teacher or outdoor educator can still evaluate their own programmes by using the less formalised naturalistic approach and, in this way, produce information that is of direct relevance to their particular programme and students.

Design of an Evaluation Plan

Ideally, evaluation should be seen as an integral part of the process of pro-gramme development. This is not always the case, because evaluation is both difficult and time-consuming and is commonly viewed as something best avoided until the necessity arises. Alternatively, it is viewed in the rather restrictive sense of a measure of student achievement rather than as a means of programme improvement.

distinction between summative and formative evaluation. The former deals with the completed programme and may include judgements about student achievement and the relative merits of different programmes or programme offerings. Formative evaluation, on the other hand, is concerned with the improvement of learning opportunities, programmes and courses. A further distinction is that formative evaluation mainly serves the needs of outdoor education teachers, curriculum-developers and decision-makers ('insiders'), and summative evaluation mainly satisfies the accountability requirements of 'outsiders'. In both cases, essentially the same data may be collected, and while the use of the information in the summative sense is one of the realities of outdoor education, arguably its main use should be for ensuring that the best strategies are used and that there is a close match between programme objectives and outcomes.

Many evaluation projects are ineffective in that the results are never used. The major reasons for this are that the information provided fails to address issues and concerns of relevance to those involved and that the need to develop grass-roots support for the evaluation process is ignored so that the problems of suspicion and anxiety that the process can raise remain unresolved.

In summary, programme evaluation is seen as a formative process concerned principally with programme improvement, and as such it is a continuous, interactive process of collecting relevant information about processes and participants in order to increase programme effectiveness.

The evaluation strategy proposed in this section emphasises the formative use of the resulting information and is developed from a combination of the 'responsive evaluation model' of Stake (1975) and the 'direct evaluation model' of Nowak (1984). It is a pragmatic strategy tailored to meet the needs of teachers and outdoor educators who have limited time, money and research experience.

The strategy is comprised of four stages:

(1) identification of issues and problems and/or clarification of goals and objectives of the programme
(2) choice of methods of data collection
(3) data collection and analysis
(4) reporting of information

Stage 1 is probably the most important part of the process. At this stage, information is collected from as many people involved in the programme as possible including participants, programme staff, parents, teachers, programme sponsors and others. This is essentially an interactive process, the end result of which should be a clear understanding of the programme and its stated and unstated purposes, and a familiarity with the main issues and concerns of the groups and individuals affected. The major purpose at this stage is to ensure that the evaluation process is seeking answers to questions that are relevant to the programme managers and that it will ultimately bring about an improvement in the effectiveness of programme outcomes.

The next stage involves deciding what data is required to address the issues and concerns raised in Stage 1. It determines the appropriate means by which the data should be collected. The 'direct' method of data collection is probably the most appropriate in situations where the evaluation is being conducted by the teacher or outdoor centre staff. Nowak (1984) has described this method as simply:

> ... asking what you want to know! If you want to know how well a session is working, ask the question directly ... Many management questions which can have a dramatic effect on programme quality can be answered in a direct fashion.

This approach is likely to be useful in most evaluation situations encountered by teachers in programme justification, modification and evolution such as measures of satisfaction with programmes of facilities provided and participant attitudes and learning.

Observation, questionnaires, case studies, group discussions, participant journals, interviews or some combination of these various methods of data collection would be preferred, because they are easy to implement, can be locally designed and produced and deal with the real world of the programme. In general terms, the aim of this stage is to choose whatever methods seem suitable to the information needs of the situation.

Statistical analysis of the data should, in most cases, be limited to the calculation of summary statistics such as the total response, frequency of response to particular questions, mean score and standard deviation. These statistics are easily interpreted and understood by most audiences and require minimal statistical expertise and a simple calculator to derive them.

After collecting and processing the data, the next stage concerns communicating the resulting information in such a way as to maximise its usefulness. While a formal report may be required as part of the evaluation study, it should not be seen as the only, nor in many cases the most appropriate, means of communicating information. Round-table discussions among staff, audio-visual presentations, exhibits and many other methods may be more useful in disseminating the results of the evaluation to appropriate audiences both within the school or centre and beyond to the general community. The following example describes the evaluation of a 4-day camping experience for 72 Grade 6 (9–10 years old) children from an Brisbane inner-city school. The camp was situated in a rural setting on the banks of the Brisbane River. The students were accommodated in 4-person tents and eating, toilet and shower facilities were available on-site. As this was the first school camping experience for many of the students, and for some the very first ever, each group of 12 students was supervised by a helper (a tertiary student from a local teacher's college). The class teachers took an advisory and trouble-shooting role in the camp.

Some weeks prior to the camp, class teachers and helpers met to discuss the goals of the camp. A series of such meetings suggested that, given the length of the camp and the relative inexperience of the students, the following goals and objectives were realistic:

Goals

—co–operation among all participants
—the children will have an enjoyable experience that extends them both mentally and physically.

Objectives

At the end of the camp the children should have:

—enjoyed the camping experience
—made new friends and got to know their teachers better
—experienced new and challenging activities
—learned new things about the natural environment
—been involved in a variety of activities requiring a co–operative effort among staff, helpers and children

Apart from decisions about the goals of the camp, concern was expressed about the need to communicate the outcomes of the camp to other teachers in the school, to the principal and to the parents of the children.

Having set a series of goals and objectives for the camp, the next stage was to decide the methods by which the goals could be evaluated. An essential aspect of the direct method of evaluation is to express the objectives, issues and so on in statements that are sufficiently specific to allow for measurement. The objectives relating to enjoyment, challenge (mental and physical), co-operation and activities were evaluated using a student questionnaire, an observation schedule (refer to the following section on Observation for discussion of the latter) and a questionnaire for parents. The evaluation instruments developed by the teachers are shown in Figures 13.1 and 13.2; each of the questions are keyed to the specific objectives (the actual design of such questionnaires is discussed in the section on Self-administered Instruments).

Figure 13.1   Student Questionnaire

Read each of the following statements carefully. Decide how you feel about and circle one of the three signs to the right of the statement. If you agree with the statement then it means you are 'for' it. If you disagree with the statement it means you are 'against' it. The three signs are explained below:

D   you disagree or are 'against' it
?   you don't know if you agree or not
A   you agree or are 'for' it

An example of what you do is this:

  Good camps are long camps   D   ?   Ⓐ

In this example, the person agreed with the statement because he or she thought that long camps were good.

Read each statement carefully and circle one of the three signs. There are no correct answers, as in a test; you should answer according to how you feel. We want to know your feelings about the camp, so please do not give answers that you think we (your teachers) might want. You do not have to put your name on the paper.

(1)	I enjoyed the camp (1)	D	?	A
(2)	Camp activities are fun to do together (5)	D	?	A
(3)	I didn't do many new activities at camp (3)	D	?	A
(4)	I got to know my teachers better (2)	D D	?	A
(5)	I would not like to go on another camp like this one (1)	D	?	A
(6)	I like working with the other kids at the camp (5)	D	?	A
(7)	I learned new things about plants, animals, rocks and stars (4)	D	?	A
(8)	Camp duties were easy because we all worked together (5)	D	?	A
(9)	I didn't make any new friends at camp (2)	D	?	A	A
(10)	Some of the activities we did were a bit scary, but I'm glad we did them (3)	D	?	A

In addition to the questionnaire administered to the children at the end of the camp, a series of questions were given to parents approximately two weeks after the camp to gauge the effect on the children as viewed by the parents. The general formal of the parent questionnaire is shown in Figure 13.2.

To meet the needs of the communication aspect of the evaluation, a video recording of each part of the programme was made, incorporating not only the different activities but also ensuring an adequate coverage of all children involved. In addition, a series of 35mm colour transparencies were prepared and the children were given a number of opportunities to express feelings about the experiences of the camp through drawing, poetry and writing. All of these communication methods provided useful materials for the school display and parents' evening.

Figure 13.2   Parent Questionnaire

Dear parent,
Your daughter or son has just returned from a camp. We used the few days at camp to provide what we thought were worthwhile educational experiences which could not be provided in the normal school environment.
   We are most interested in your reaction to the experience for your child (or children) and in your suggestions for improvement. In this regard your responses to the following questions, as well as any general comments you might like to make, will be most helpful.
Thank you.
....
Principal

Section A

	Yes	Not Sure	No
(1) Has your child been to an outdoor camp before? (1)	....	....	....
(2) Was your child enthusiastic about the camp BEFORE attending? (1)	....	....	....
(3) Was your child enthusiastic about the camp AFTER attending? (1)	....	....	....
(4) Has your child discussed the camp in detail with you? (1)	....	....	....
(5) Did your child make any new friends at camp? (2)	....	....	....

Section B
(1) What part of the experience do you feel was most valuable for your child? (3)

....
....
....
....

(2) Which of the following do you think should be the main aim of the sixth grade school camp? (Please mark what you consider should be the major aim)
   (a) fun (1)   ....
   (b) adventure (3)   ....
   (c) academic (outdoor lessons)(4)   ....
   (d) social (2,5)   ....

The final stage was the communication of the evaluation results to the various interested parties. These comprised the following events:

(1) a meeting of all staff and helpers to discuss the results of the evaluation and to consider possible modifications to the programme, venue and so on for the next year

(2) a written report of the results, with comments on (1) and illustrated by student work, presented to the Principal and the Regional Director, with copies placed in the school and teacher college libraries

(3) a display of student work and photographs of the camp in the school library

(4) a parent, children, staff and helper evening at a local hall

In some cases, where an outsider with appropriate skills is available, a completely external evaluation may be possible. This approach means that the 'outsider' must develop a familiarity with the programme and its processes and outcomes through interaction with staff, participants and relevant others. Programme goals, issues and problems should arise out of this process of familiarisation. Such an objective view has much to recommend it, as this type of evaluation, when undertaken by an experienced and sensitive individual, can reveal much about the programme and its impacts previously unnoticed by the staff. The resulting information is invaluable and can provide a strong basis for the continuous process of programme improvement. While the advantages of the approach are manifest, a high level of trust and a strong commitment to the process by those who have an interest in its outcomes are essential.

The evaluation strategy described in this section depends for its relevance on staff familiarity with the programme and, consequently, an appreciation of its strengths and weaknesses combined with a commitment to programme improvement through the formal process of evaluation. What this approach may lack in apparent objectivity, it makes up for in ease of implementation, relatively low costs in actual money terms and in staff time, and in the immediacy of the information.

Methods of Data Collection

This section initially discusses a number of general issues related to data collection. It then addresses actual methods of collection that have been or could be used in outdoor education and provides appropriate examples in an Australian context.

A broad range of measurement possibilities are available to the teacher. This is demonstrated by the types of data that can be collected: that on knowledge, skills, attitudes and behaviours; accompanying teachers, parents, teachers in other classes and independent judges; and the variety of methods that can be used to collect each type of data: multiple-choice tests, camper self-rating, observation, rating scales, group discussions, interview and questionnaire.

Cheney and Hammerman (1985) discovered that the most frequently evaluated aspects of outdoor education programmes at residential centres in the United States were as follows:

'students' and teachers' satisfaction with the programmes (85 per cent of all centres); operational aspects of the programmes (80 per cent); students' attitudes to the environment (71 per cent); effectiveness of staff (70 per cent); and students' attitudes to others (54 per cent). However, student achievement in academic subjects was evaluated in only 25 per cent of the centres.

These same authors noted that, although accompanying teachers and students were the most usual source of data, outdoor centre staff, administrators and parents were used frequently as alternative sources of information. The majority of evaluation is internal, as outside evaluators were employed in only 7 per cent of the centres. While written evaluation instruments were most popular (62 per cent of the centres), a wide variety of other measures were used as additional or alternative methods of evaluation, including observation of the programme, group discussion with participants, individual discussion, logs or journals, self-designed and standardised tests and audio-visual methods.

While many evaluation methods may seem attractive after discussion with others or from descriptions in the literature, it is essential that the methods chosen are both feasible and cost-effective for the programme in question. Consequently, a number of questions about the chosen methods of evaluation should be considered:

—What disruptive effect, if any, is data collection likely to have on the participants?
—Can the staff resources handle the instrument design, data collection and analysis, or is outside assistance likely to be required?
—Can staff be made available to oversee and implement the process, at least initially?
—Is the resulting information likely to be of sufficient use to be implemented?

Many evaluation studies incorporate a number of data collection methods and sources of information to study the same programme outcome. This approach, called triangulation, relies on the assumption that information derived by one method of data collection (or from one source) is much more certain if substantiated by one or more other methods (or sources).

The study discussed in the previous section, for example, used student questionnaires, data from parents, observation and student work to examine the effectiveness of the programme. In another instance, a standardise test of self-concept, an observation schedule and an interview with selected students were all used to examine the change in self-image of 14–17 years olds, as a result of a 7-week residential outdoor experience (McIntyre 1987)

Evaluation is an essential facet of programme development. The key to success is in matching the methods of evaluation to available resources, the needs of the stake-holders and to staff talents and capabilities.

Self-administered Instruments

These are usually printed forms which ask questions of individuals or use some sort of scale to measure attitudes or levels of satisfaction. The important feature of such tests is that they are completed by an individual without assistance from others or from the evaluator (apart from basic instructions), in much the same way as an examination. Such instruments are very popular because so many are available for a wide diversity of requirements; they are generally simple to administer and score; and they minimise bias likely to arise in other methods through evaluator/participant interaction or evaluator subjectivity.

Many 'standardised tests' are available, especially in the area of 'attitude assessment'. These have been used on large numbers of people from a diversity of backgrounds, hence the reliability and validity of the measures have been established for general populations. The Tennessee Self-concept Test, the Nowicki-Strickland Locus of Control Test, the Jessness Inventory and the Millward-Ginter Outdoor Attitude Inventory are a few of the standardised tests that have been used to evaluate various aspects of outdoor education. The most complete guide to such tests is the *Mental Measurements Yearbook* by O.K. Buros (see References) which can be found in the reference section of most libraries; this does not deal specifically with outdoor education. Staley (1980) has compiled a list of tests used previously in outdoor education and, his articles provides a useful starting point.

A cautionary note must be sounded about the indiscriminate use of such tests. The fact that they have demonstrated high reliability and validity for general populations does not guarantee that they are appropriate for participants in outdoor education programmes. In addition, the characteristics of the programme and participants may be such that the content and style of items in specific standardised instruments may be unsuitable.

The Nowicki-Strickland Locus of Control Scale has been advocated as an appropriate instrument for a wide variety of outdoor education situations (Crompton and Sellar 1981). The complete scale consists of 40 items, but the authors have suggested a shorter form comprising 21 items, which is suitable for secondary school students (Figure 13.3).

The evaluation of 'attitudes and personal and social outcomes' is frequently the focus of standardised tests and it is in this most important area that an appropriate match between programme outcomes and measuring instrument is most difficult to achieve. Usually standardised tests are used in their original form or are modified for use with specific programmes and this approach does not create large problems as long as appropriate safeguards are implemented: According to Staley (1980):

> Anyone beginning a programme in outdoor education with an evaluation component should first make a careful analysis of what the programme is designed to achieve ... Then search to find or develop valid and reliable instruments appropriate for measuring the anticipated (and perhaps unanticipated) outcomes that can occur. Reversing the process by finding a measurement instrument first and then trying to fit it to the programme often proves disastrous.

Figure 13.3   Nowicki-Strickland Locus of Control Scale

(Items are answered 'yes' or 'no')

(1) Do you believe that most problems will solve themselves if you don't fool with them?
(2) Are you often blamed for things that just aren't your fault?
(3) Do you feel that most of the time it doesn't pay to try too hard because things never turn out right anyway?
(4) Do you feel that most of the time parents listen to what their children have to say?
(5) When you get punished does it usually seem it's for no good reason at all?
(6) Most of the time do you find it hard to change a friend's opinion?
(7) Do you feel that it is nearly impossible to change your parent's mind about anything?
(8) Do you feel that when you do something wrong there's very little you can do to make it right?
(9) Do you believe that most kids are just born good at sports?
(10) Do you feel that the best way to handle most problems is just not to think about them?
(11) Do you feel that when a kid your age decides to hit you, there's little you can do about it?
(12) Have you felt that when people were mean to you it was usually for no reason at all?
(13) Most of the time do you feel that you can change what happens tomorrow by what you do today?
(14) Do you believe that when bad things are going to happen they are just going to happen no matter what you do to try to stop them?
(15) Most of the time do you find it useless to try to get your own way at home?
(16) Do you feel that when somebody your age wants to be your enemy there's little you can do to change things?
(17) Do you usually feel that you have little to say about what you get to eat at home?
(18) Do you feel that when someone doesn't like you there's little you can do about it?
(19) Do you feel that it's almost useless to try at school because most other children are just plain smarter than you are?
(20) Are you the kind of person who believes that planning ahead makes things turn out better?
(21) Most of the time, do you feel that you have little to say about what your family decides to do?

An alternative approach is for teachers to construct their own instruments that are appropriate to the content and objectives of the programme and to try them out with a sample of the target group prior to general use. This strategy is used extensively in the evaluation of programme specific outcomes, such as students' and teachers' overall satisfaction with the programme.

The following questionnaire (Figure 13.4) was developed for a Grade 11 (16–17 years) residential camp. It is relatively short and takes only a brief time to complete. The aim of the survey is to get feedback on students' perception of the camp programme and its setting. As the students are fairly mature, the questions can be open-ended and the students asked to express their perceptions in their own words, rather than simply marking appropriate boxes. The purpose of the questions is simply to provide a structure to guide the students in giving their impressions of the camp. While this type of survey is perhaps more difficult to score due to the broad range of possible answers, the potential for providing relevant information is enhanced.

In a study for the Third National Conference in Outdoor Education 1981, Simpson details the results of a mailed questionnaire used as a follow-up for Project Arcadia, some 4 years after the event. Project Arcadia involved taking selected 16–17-year-old students from Queensland schools for a 10-day back-packing trip into the Carnarvon Ranges of western Queensland.

This is one of the few studies which have attempted to evaluate the long-term effects of a wilderness experience on participants. Simpson reports that all who replied had a high regard for the programme and significant numbers of these considered that the experience had strongly influenced their career choice. Almost all indicated it had an effect on their leisure interests and environmental attitudes. While the results cannot be accepted uncritically, because it is likely that only those with a high regard for the programme would bother to return the questionnaire, it is a remarkable comment on its effectiveness that almost half of the participants did actually respond.

Figure 13.4 Camp Assessment Questionnaire (for Grade 11 Residential Camp)

(1)   Were you generally satisfied with the camp? YES ..... NO .....
      Comment ....

      ....

      ....

(2)   Were you satisfied with the catering? YES ..... NO .....
      Comment ....

      ....

      ....

(3)   Comments on the camp-site and its surroundings.

      ....

      ....

      ....

(4)   How do you rate the MIX of activities provided at the camp?
      Poor ..... Fair ..... Good .....
      Comment ....

      ....

      ....

(5)   How do you rate the TYPES of activities provided at the camp?
      Poor ..... Fair ..... Good .....
      Comment ....

      ....

      ....

Figure 13.4 Camp Assessment Questionnaire (for Grade 11 Residential Camp)

(6)   What was the BEST thing about the camp?

....

....

....

7)   What was the WORST thing about the camp?

....

....

....

(8)   What benefits did you get from the camp?

....

....

....

(9)   Any other comments?

....

....

....

The questionnaire used in this study is typical of the purpose-built variety, where each item consists of a question, a series of scaled answers, and room for comment. For example:

Q   To what extent has the Project Arcadia experience contributed towards your present career interest?

A   Greatly   ☐ Somewhat   ☐ a little   ☐ not at all

Comment ....

....

....

In this example, the respondent is asked to rate the influence the experience of participating in Project Arcadia had on career choice.

Inviting a comment also allows for expansion on the answer, and frequently provides additional information in the form of actual career choice, reasons for the choice, and so on. The results of the mail-back questionnaire were tallied and the percentage response to each question was used along with comments to provide a measure of the success of the programme in achieving its aims.

In another situation, a similar style of questionnaire was designed to measure staff satisfaction with various aspects of a Youth Conservation Programme in the United States. However, in this case, the results of the evaluation were used as a focus for staff discussion about problem areas perceived by all staff and also on problems about which there was some disagreement. With slight modification, this same instrument was administered to participants to gauge their level of satisfaction with the same aspects of the programme and in this way a different perspective could be added to the staff discussions.

Scaling Systems

The scaling systems used in the above situations are typical of those commonly used in the evaluation of attitudes, beliefs and judgements, where a simple 'yes' or 'no' answer would be inappropriate.

As teachers and others are frequently interested in such measures, a brief introduction to the main characteristics of these scales is provided.

Three types of scale are commonly used in measures of attitude, belief or judgement: the Thurstone Scale, the Likert Scale and the Semantic Differential. Of these the latter two are the easiest to the construct and the most popular and for these reasons are discussed more fully below.

The Likert Scale: This is a 5-point scale which is used to indicate the respondents level of agreement with a particular statement (Figure 13.5) which might express a belief, attitude or judgement. Although a 5-point interval is normal, 3–7-point interval scales have also been used. The 3-point scale is preferable in those situations where children are the respondents (Figure 13.1) and, in such cases, a pictorial scale might even be better; the 7-point scale has been found to be no more reliable than the 5, so the latter is generally recommended for use. Respondents indicate their level of agreement by circling or marking the appropriate position on the scale. Generally a high scale score (5) is used to indicate 'strong agreement' and a low scale score (1) indicates 'strong disagreement' with the statement. However, in the case of negative items, the score is reversed, so that the total score is a measure of the positive agreement with the subject in question.

Item development consists of preparing a series of statements which relate to the objectives of a camp. Such statements may be derived from discussions among staff and/or from student comments and logs. Both positive (pro) and negative (con) statements should be included to reduce the possibility of students marking all items in the same way. Where possible, a number of items should be developed which measure the achievement of the same objective (Figures 13.1 and 13.2), to provide a check on the consistency of the responses.

Figure 13.5   Likert Scale Example

Camping in the outdoors is fun

strongly agree (5)	agree (4)	undecided (3)	disagree (2)	strongly disagree (1)

The Semantic Differential: The scale consists of a number of 7-point rating scales, each of which is made up of a pair of bipolar adjectives: for example, strong/weak, cold/warm, timid/adventurous. These are scored on a 1-7 basis, with the latter being the most positive. Adjective pairs are listed in both directions to minimise bias. The respondent is asked to judge the subject in question (THE LEADER, Figure 13.6) on each of the bipolar adjective scales by placing a mark on one of the spaces on the scale.

Figure 13.6   The Semantic Differential

The Leader

fun:	:	:	:	:	:	:	:boring
confident:	:	:	:	:	:	:	:insecure
friendly:	:	:	:	:	:	:	:unfriendly
authoritarian:	:	:	:	:	:	:	:democratic
physically fit:	:	:	:	:	:	:	:unfit

and so on

The development of such scales is relatively easy and many books have been written on the subject of item and scale development; some of the most useful are listed in the References at the end of this chapter. With a little extra effort and access to modest computing facilities, the reliability of the instrument can be improved. This is achieved by initially preparing more items than is required for the final test, administering them to a pilot group and subsequently eliminating those of lowest reliability by item analysis (Tuckman 1978: Chapter 8).

Written evaluation measures are the most popular way of evaluating outdoor education programmes and most teachers will make use of them on their own or (preferably) in concert with some other method. This section has emphasised that the indiscriminate use of standardised tests should be avoided and that teachers should instead develop their own measures which then assure a close match between the evaluation instrument and the particular objectives and special circumstances of their programme.

Observation

Although not used very frequently in a systematic way, observation has high potential as an evaluation method in outdoor education. While many teachers tend to avoid the use of observation because it is perceived to be time-consuming or lacking in the quantitative respectability of written measures, there are compelling reasons why this method should be considered:

(1) because of its highly practical nature, outdoor education lends itself well to observation of student behaviour
(2) observation can be carried out as part of the normal outdoor education programme
(3) as observation can be integrated into the normal programme, students are less tense and respond more naturally than in a conventional test situation
(4) observation can produce data that is available in no other way.

The most common strategy used in observation is for one or more people to observe aspects of an outdoor activity or programme in order to view at first hand the behaviour of participants. In some cases, the observations are guided by some sort of check-list, and focus on particular behaviours or interactions.

One of the many classroom interaction scales could be adapted to examine participant/instructor interactions during an outdoor teaching session. This strategy was used to examine the four-day camp for Grade 6 mentioned previously; there a teacher observed the activity of the students during a variety of camp activities including meal-preparation, tent-pitching, washing-up and so on. The criteria used are listed in Figure 13.7 and the observation schedule is shown in Figure 13.8.

Figure 13.7 Observation Criteria to Examine Task Orientation at Grade 6 Camp

(1) Task Oriented: intent on activity
(2) Social Task Oriented: any social remark or interchange that is activity oriented
(3) Social Friendly Behaviour: social remark or interchange unconnected with the activity
(4) Intent Other Task: working but not on the activity with which the group is involved
(5) Intent Non-Task: intent on a non-work activity
(6) Wandering: looks around, strolls or watches others without purpose, day-dreaming
(7) Non-task Disruptive: behaviour unrelated to the task at hand and detrimental to successful completion

Systematic observation of participants in a 'group initiative activity' can provide a useful assessment of entry capabilities of individuals. Subsequently, this baseline data can be used to assess individual improvement as a result of participation in the programme. While the observations made in such situations can be largely unstructured in the early stages of development of the evaluation process, it is important that the recording of the data be formalised by making field notes at the time. Initially, note down the things that kids are doing: participating; making suggestions; standing around; trying things out; looking bored; watching; helping; leading; following and so on. This initial survey is useful when you are trying to establish appropriate categories for the development of a checklist of behaviours. These categories will form the basis of an observational instrument which can be used by any staff member in a similar situation.

A sample observation schedule is shown in Figure 13.8. In this case, a group of students could be involved in a group activity and one or more teachers could observe them using a checklist comprised of behavioural categories etc. (see Figure 13.7). One of the group members (ABC and so on) is observed just long enough to note what he or she is doing and the behaviour(s) marked (X) in the appropriate position on the schedule; then a second student is observed and so on until the whole group is completed and the process can begin again. Hence, every individual in the group can be observed in a short period of time. At the end of the observation period, the individual scores are tallied and a pattern of individual behaviour as defined by the predetermined categories is revealed.

Figure 13.8   Observation Schedule

	Location		Date..
1	Activity		Start time ....
	Group...		End time...
	Observer		Duration ....

Category Name	1	2	3	4	and so on
A	XXXX	XXX	XX	XXXXX	
B	XXX	XXXX	XXXXX	XX	
C	XXXXXX	XXXXX	XXX	X	XXXXX
D			and so on		

Alternatively the group activity can be videotaped and the schedule used by a number of teachers at some later date. In addition, the videotape can function as a training device for staff prior to field observation, as a means of checking reliability of observations among different staff or can be used as an integral part of the development of the categories comprising the schedule.

In some instances, direct observation of the students may yield more reliable data on the effect of a particular programme or strategy than other methods commonly used. Self-report measures can be unreliable if, for example, students can write down what they should do but for a variety of reasons do not match their words with appropriate action. This is an issue that can be addressed most appropriately in the practical setting of many outdoor activities.

A common goal of many outdoor camping programmes is to develop low impact camping behaviours through classwork and camping experiences. In many instances, a written test is used to evaluate these behaviours. Unfortunately, success in this test offers no surety that the students do in actual fact exhibit the desired behaviours. Casual observation also does not provide a satisfactory answer. However, a systematic, direct approach to this problem can provide a sensitive measure of student performance as well as a focus for effective programme development. The next example suggests how such an approach might be implemented.

A Grade 10 (14–15-years-olds) outdoor education programme has as one of its goals the development of environmentally appropriate camping behaviours. The programme consists of classwork and three weekend camping experiences in remote to semi-remote areas.

On the basis of their own experience and a study of relevant literature, the staff involved in the programme develop a checklist of low impact behaviours appropriate to the settings to be used for the camps. In the first instance, each staff member produces his or her own list. Subsequently the lists can be discussed by all the staff and consensus reached on appropriate behaviours in any areas of contention.

At the first camp, each staff member is assigned a group of no more than eight to ten students whom they are required to observe during the weekend, systematically noting by means of the checklist the frequency of occurrence of particular behaviours in the context of minimal impact. This can be done when camp is being set up or dismantled. Teachers would normally watch students at these times, offering advice, assisting and so on. All that is suggested here is that this process be systematised and used as a basis for evaluating a major goal of the programme. The camping area should also be examined carefully prior to departure for litter, foodscraps, damage to vegetation and so on, and any such evidence noted. After the trip, once the data has been processed, staff can meet to identify any problems in implementation and to refine the checklist as required.

Once the instrument has been perfected, it can be used on the following two camps, and any subsequent camps with other groups, to identify changes in the frequency of detrimental behaviour and to highlight any particular behaviours which might require special emphasis in the programme. The information could be further refined by examining the degree of correlation between an individual's score on a written assessment and his or her observed behaviour.

The approaches outlined above place the evaluator firmly in the position of an observer. However, in some instances, the observer can also be a participant, actively involved as a member of the group, in a way that non-participant observation cannot. In other words he or she can capture the phenomenon in its own terms.

One study of this type has been described in outdoor education. It was used as one of a series of methods in a comprehensive study of Outward Bound (Smith *et al.* 1973). In this case the individual had no previous experience with Outward Bound, was typical of individuals who participated in Outward Bound courses, and had some training in the behavioural sciences. He was sent on the Outward Bound course to describe what he experienced, and what he saw others experiencing and the effect these experiences had on himself and others in the course.

While such a study would be difficult for the ordinary teacher to duplicate, might it not be possible for him/her to use the basic principles of participant observation to obtain relevant observational data? Most outdoor education teachers do in fact share in the outdoor experiences with their students, and hence the opportunity to observe them is frequently available. For example, each teacher on an extended bushwalk of, say, five day's duration, could aim to write one or two significant statements or observations on each student each day. At the end of the trip, these could be pooled by the various staff to provide an insight on the various ways an individual student responded to the experience. Again, this sort of information is noted by staff, but generally is done in a rather haphazard manner. The above strategy suggests how this process may be systematised to yield appropriate information that can form the basis of student reports and/or be instrumental in programme improvement.

Devices such as cameras, video and audio recorders are being used increasingly in an evaluation role. Unlike other means of observation, they provide a permanent record which can be re-examined and reviewed by the evaluator and others at will. The value of portable video devices in remedial skills development in, for example, canoe stroke correction is well established. However, the potential of these same devices in the examination of small group interaction and teaching strategies in outdoor situations is yet to be explored.

This section has suggested that outdoor education teachers are in a unique position as regards their interaction with students because of the activity-based nature of the outdoor programmes in which they are involved. Under such circumstances, systematic observation of such things as student skill development, behaviours and interactions with staff and other students would seem to require only a simple refinement of present practices.

Written Records

Participants' comments in written records such as daily logs, diaries, journals, narrative accounts and expressive writings are used frequently as sources of information on the success of a programme and its impact on participants. Such records also provide comments which describe the participants' experiences during the programme and their feelings about them. They are an invaluable source of anecdotes for evaluation reports informing parents, sponsors and in some cases the general public about the results of a programme in a way that both entertains and informs. A good example of such a publication is the Jubilee Youth Trek Report from South Australia.

Excerpts from student diaries were used by Simpson in his initial evaluative report on Project Arcadia. The following entry was made by one of the students on the last night of the camp and provides strong evidence of the group feeling developed during such activities:

> Already the second last day of the expedition has come and almost gone. I am saddened to think that it will soon be all over and know that this is the common feeling amongst the crowd. During the past few days we have developed strong friendships between us. Although in a way, in respect to the walking, I will be glad to see the bus tomorrow, I will also be unhappy at the thought that the bus signifies the subsequent breakup of the party.

A daily diary, designed for a four-day residential camp for blind and partially-sighted children, encouraged them to express their feelings about the various activities and to write a short poem or draw a picture about the day. One of the children wrote the following about the walk to the top of a nearby hill they named Mt Smartie:

> We went on a mountain, we went
> up high, we went right up to the sky
> We climbed and climbed, we're all wrung out
> of time, we saw a tree and then we saw
> Smarties, I had lunch, I want to give you a Punch.

Today was fun, it was as pretty as a bun.
We had to climb because the teacher said
Let's go down now, and we had fun going
down, slipping and sliding on the ground.

I liked today but we had to go away.

Amanda, who wrote the poem, is eight years old and totally blind.

The Outline of the Camp Diary

(This outline was varied each day to reflect the activities undertaken by the children.)

How did you sleep last night? ....

Did you feel homesick? ....

Where did you go for your hike? ....

Write about an interesting thing that happened on your hike

....

....

What feelings did you have when you were doing the ropes course?

....

....

Draw a picture, tell a story, write a poem about TODAY.

Teaching through Adventure — A Practical Approach illustrates another use of student reports which can be used to gain invaluable information about student responses to, and feelings about, outdoor education activities. This book is a guide to Project Adventure, a programme which used a variety of outdoor adventure experiences, from a visit to a swamp to abseiling, as foci for creative expression in prose, poetry, art and drama.

A diary outline is useful for younger students. However, with increasing maturity, the outline could be simply reduced to a series of brief headings. In some cases, a quotation may be appropriate to set the tone of the day, to initiate discussion on the day's activity or to act as inspiration for the day ahead. These last informal structures provide complete freedom of expression for the students and thus have the potential to elicit the most candid and useful evaluation information. However, to access such data it is necessary to give participants the opportunity to write about their experiences and feelings in an atmosphere of trust. Anonymity, restricted access and privacy are all part of this process.

Written reports of a quite complex nature can be analysed systematically by the process of content analysis. Such analysis is a rule-guided systematic process of document evaluation. It involves defining the evaluation problem in terms of categories that, in the simplest approach, can be counted: for example, statements about the group, about the camp ground, about activities, feelings about oneself or others, or descriptions of the natural environment. The categories should:

—relate to the purposes of the evaluation
—be exhaustive
—be mutually exclusive

Developing the categories is a trial and error process involving a number of readings of the documents (logs, diaries, records of interviews or unstructured observations). Data that can be collected by this method may relate to the presence of the object of the evaluation: for example, is there any mention in the account of the natural environment?; the frequency of occurrence; the emotional context (favourable, unfavourable, humorous, serious); and the intensity of the statement (strong, weak, neutral).

The process as discussed here, while useful in the situations indicated and certainly better than 'a quick glance through', is relatively unsophisticated. Those readers who wish to review the full potential of this method or who make extensive use of student journals or diaries in evaluation are referred to the classic text by O.R. Holsti, *Content Analysis for the Social Sciences and Humanities*.

This section indicates that a variety of sources of unstructured comments are produced as a by-product of the outdoor experience. Such information, analysed systematically, can provide insights into the effects of the experience on an individual or a group often inaccessible by any other method.

Group Discussions

Discussions with participants during an extended outdoor experience are frequently used as a means of adapting the programme to changes in circumstances or to meet the developing needs of participants. Similar sessions at the end of the experience can provide a forum for discussion of overall perceptions, crucial incidents and learnings, suggested changes and personal outcomes, to name but a few of the likely topics.

The following strategy has been found to be useful in debrief sessions at the end of major expeditions. Participants and staff gather at an informal venue, immediately following the experience. The discussions are free-ranging and unstructured except that everyone is encouraged to participate by having an initial opener during which each individual in turn is invited to express an opinion or feeling about any aspect of the expedition. Subsequent discussion elaborates on issues raised or can range over a wide variety of topics related to the expedition. Staff act as catalysts, inviting comment, seeking clarification of comments and opinions and raising issues of interest to themselves as participants and as leaders.

In many instances this is the only form of evaluation and, while full meeting practices are generally unnecessary, some written account is desirable. This can be done during the discussions in the form of brief summary statements. If this strategy is adopted, it is necessary to verify these statements at appropriate intervals in much the same way as the chairperson of a meeting summarises the main points of discussion prior to voting. Otherwise, brief notes are made after the meeting and compared with those of any other staff involved in the discussions. Such accurate records of the group discussions provide a valuable source of evaluation data for subsequent course improvement.

Discussions can be carried on with students in the classroom on return to school after the outdoor experience. Points raised by students are written on the board and opened up for general discussion. An assessment of numbers agreeing with certain statements or sharing particular perceptions may be assessed on a show of hands or used as the content for a simple questionnaire. This latter approach has the advantage that the questions used as a focus for the evaluation are grounded in the concerns of the students.

Some situations, such as wilderness camps, lend themselves to discussion sessions at the end of each day during which leaders can gain insights into students' feelings about the events of the day and so provide some measure of programme effectiveness. Such sessions are probably best conducted in the evening, around the camp-fire with a group of no more than ten students. The leader opens the discussion by completing the statement: 'The thing I enjoyed most about today was . . . ' and invites each student in turn to complete this same statement in his or her own way. The first round invites the students to respond at the factual level and hence creates little threat to the individual. The leader initiates the second round by completing the statement 'I enjoyed it because it made me feel . . . ' Both the leader's response to this statement and the way it is worded encourages students to share how they felt at the time. The discussion can continue in the same vein, examining such things as the happiest event; the worst event; the scariest event; and so on. Generally, the formalised part of the session should be fairly brief (about fifteen minutes), although informal discussion of the day's events, stimulated by the initial session, may continue for some time.

Tape recorders provide one means by which a permanent and complete record of the discussion can be obtained and analysed at some later time. This is certainly a convenient way to record the information. However, the convenience must be weighed against the likely inhibitory effect the device will have on the discussion (students' permission to tape the session would be essential) and the likelihood that the analysis will join the other 'jobs I'll do one of these days'.

This section has detailed some of the ways in which teachers/outdoor educators may elicit information in a relatively informal way. Such information can aid in the understanding of the ways in which young people respond to outdoor experiences and so contribute to more effective programmes and strategies. Again it is emphasised that some means should be employed by the leader to document the discussion. The role of the leader in the discussion is to be responsive to, and accepting of, participants' comments. This is not the time to justify or defend the programme or strategies, no matter how critical the students' comments may seem at the time.

Interviews

Generally seen as the oldest form of data collection and commonly categorised as 'conversations with a purpose', interviews may be very structured or loose and unstructured. In the former, identical questions are asked of a number of individuals. In effect, it is a verbally-administered questionnaire. At the other end of the spectrum, unstructured interviews follow where the respondent leads and are typically conducted with individuals who have special knowledge or experience.

The most common use of interviews in outdoor education is in conjunction with other methods of data collection. In this role, they add the perspective of individual perception to otherwise statistically-dominated data. Despite the obvious value of the technique, they are very time-consuming and, for this reason, a sample of interviews with selected students or with accompanying staff at an outdoor centre would probably be more realistic than an attempt to interview all participants. Prior to an outdoor experience, interviews with some of the participants on their expectations will assist in the development of appropriate items for an evaluation instrument. The exploratory nature of such interviews means that they can be quite short and unstructured. On the other hand, structured interviews are frequently used to test the understanding and content of the questions comprising an instrument before it is used in the field.

In some situations, a small number of specially selected individuals may be interviewed, in depth, either during or at the end of an outdoor experience. These individuals may be targeted as a result of observations by staff or performance on a standardised instrument, or may be randomly selected from participants. As the main purpose of such interviews is to match the standardised test, the interview should be designed to address similar outcomes. This approach was used in the study by McIntyre (1987), where selected students were observed interacting with their peers and staff. In addition, these same students were tested with a standardised instrument and interviewed using a series of predetermined questions.

Figure 13.9   Semi-structured Interview Schedule

(1)   What did you enjoy most about your stay?
(2)   Can you tell me about it in a bit more detail?
(3)   What did you enjoy least about your stay?
(4)   Can you tell me a bit more about it?
(5)   What did you expect to get out of being here?
(6)   Did it work out that way?
(7)   Did you make any new friends?
(8)   What was it about them that made them your friends?
(9)   How did you get on with the other students?
(10) What sort of changes did you have to make in the way you usually did things to get on with other students?
(11) In what ways do you think you have changed as a result of your stay here?

The advantage of this approach lay in the fact that it was possible to clarify the questions and probe more deeply where appropriate and so elicit much more information than could have been gained by other methods.

In a study investigating the relationships of fear during rock-climbing and self-actualisation, Davis asked Outward Bound graduates to reflect upon their feelings of fear prior to, during and after their first rock climbing and abseiling experience. He compared these verbal reports with the individuals' scores on a rating scale which indicated their levels of fear at specific times during this experience. Among other things, the results suggested that overcoming fear caused a positive change in self-awareness and self-confidence.

This type of evaluative research has reinforced the long-established belief that activities with a high perceived risk, such as rock-climbing and abseiling, have a central role in outdoor education programmes designed to enhance participants' self-concept.

In the context of evaluation, interviews are seen as a method of trialling questions, as a device for checking the reliability of data from small numbers of selected individuals and as a substitute for other measures where these are inadequate, for example, where individuals cannot read questions or write answers.

Summary and Conclusions

Evaluation is a systematic process of gathering information, primarily for the purposes of programme improvement. This process is guided by the information needs of those involved in, or affected by, the programme. Consequently, an early part of the evaluation process is the clarification of those needs and their transformation into appropriate questions. Once this has been accomplished, data collection may proceed. In recognition of the true complexity of the outdoor education process and setting, a variety of methods of data collection have been detailed, including interviews, discussions, teacher-designed instruments, systematic observation and written records. The choice of the method(s) to be used is determined principally by a combination of its ability to generate the desired data and its feasibility in terms of implementation and cost. In the final stages of the evaluation, the type of data analysis and the style of reporting selected depends on the characteristics of the target audience. For some, a full statistical report may be necessary. For others, a few well-selected bar graphs and an informal briefing may suffice.

Staley (1980) has argued that outdoor educators in the United States have done a good job of evaluating their programmes. They have been, in his words, 'quite accountable in this age of accountability'. However, this chapter has suggested that accountability is only one function of evaluation and, arguably, the least important in terms of programme development (though perhaps not in terms of programme survival!) Do pressures for accountability create an environment where the easy things are measured and the more difficult are ignored?

Cheney and Hammerman's 1981–82 study of evaluation practices in outdoor centres in the United States would suggest that this is the case. The most common evaluation studies reported are 'satisfaction' measures and the most needed studies, according to the respondents, are the 'effects of the camping experience' and the 'effects of the outdoor education programme on the attitudes of campers'. These more difficult questions are the ones that, perhaps, must be tackled. In the final judgement, the answers to such questions will probably do more to justify the money and effort expended in outdoor education than numbers of satisfaction measurements of specific programmes.

What is the present position in Australia? At a 1987 Perth conference, a number of different studies were described (McRae, McIntyre, O'Brien and Richards) that have begun to look at some fundamental questions about the effectiveness of outdoor education programmes. This indicates that the Australian (and New Zealand) scene is beginning to move from its previous fascination with programme description, and exhortation, to an empirical stage which attempts to examine the process of outdoor education and its impact on participants.

The researchers are not alone in recognising that programme development depends on a deeper understanding of the effects of outdoor education experiences on the participants and on establishing a clearer picture of the link between programme content and outcomes. Outdoor education teachers are aware of these same needs, as demonstrated by the current interest in evaluation methods in schools and outdoor centres.

This chapter has attempted to demystify the process of evaluation by demonstrating that instrument design, and the collection, analysis and use of evaluation data are within the capabilities of every outdoor education teacher. Commitment to this process gives access to the benefits that arise from systematic evaluation, including: improved programmes; better content; appropriate facilities; sensitive and responsive leaders; an enhanced understanding of the effects of the programme on participants, and consequently an improved ability to manipulate the programme content to best meet their needs; more efficient use of scarce resources; and greater satisfaction with programme outcomes on the part of participants and leaders.

References

Brandt, R.M. (1978) *Studying Behaviour in Social Settings*, Holt, Rinehart and Winston, New York, USA. (A useful reference for techniques in observation)

Buros, O.K. (ed.) (1972) *The Seventh Mental Measurements Yearbook*, Gryphon Press, NJ, USA.

Campbell, D.T. and Stanley, J.C. (1963) *Experimental and Quasi-experimental Designs for Research*, Houghton Mifflin, USA.

Chenery, M.F. and Hammerman, W. (1985) 'Current Practice in the Evaluation of Resident Outdoor Education Programmes: Report of a National Survey', *Journal of Environmental Education* 16 (12)

Crompton, J.L. and Sellar, C. (1981) 'Do Outdoor Experiences Contribute to Positive Development in the Affective Domain', *Journal of Environmental Education* 12 (4).

Guba, E.G. and Lincoln, Y.S. (1981) *Effective Evaluation*, Jossey Bass, San Fransisco, USA.

Holsti, O.R. (1969) *Content Analysis for the Social Sciences and the Humanities*, Addison–Wesley, Mass., USA.

McIntyre, N. (1987), 'Self-concept Change as a Result of an Extended Outdoor Education Residential Experience', *Proceedings of the Fifth National Outdoor Education Conference*, 11–15 January, Woodman Point, Perth.

McRae, K. (1987) 'Giving Outdoor Education a Greater Environmental Orientation', *Proceedings of the Fifth National Outdoor Education Conference*, 11–15 January, Woodman Point, Perth.

Nowack, P.F. (1984) 'Direct Evaluation: A Management Tool for Program Justification, Evolution and Modification', *Journal of Environmental Education* 15 (4).

O'Brien, M. (1987) 'Reaching the Unreachable', *Proceedings of the Fifth National Outdoor Education Conference*, 11–15 January, Woodman Point, Perth.

Oppenheim, A.N. (1979) *Questionnaire Design and Attitude Measurement*, Heinemann Educational Books, London.

Richards, G.E. (1987) 'Outdoor Education in Australia in Relation to the Norman Conquest, a Greek Olive Grove and the External Perspective', *Proceedings of the Fifth National Outdoor Education Conference*, 11–15 January, Woodman Point, Perth.

Scriven, M. (1966) *The Methodology of Evaluation*, AERA Monograph Series in Curriculum Evaluation, No. 1, Rand McNally, Chicago, USA.

Simpson, R.P. (1983) 'Wilderness Experience — How Can We Assess its Value', *Report to the Third National Conference in Outdoor Education*, Maroon, Queensland.

Smith, M.L., Gabriel, R. and Anderson, R.D. (1973) *Final Report: Project to Design an Evaluation of Outward Bound Boulder*, Bureau of Educational Field Services, University of Colorado, USA.

Stake, R.E. (1975) *Evaluating the Arts in Education: A Responsive Approach*, Merrill, Columbus, Ohio, USA.

Staley, F.A. (1980) 'Research, Evaluation and Measurement in Outdoor Education', *The Communicator* V (III).

Tuckerman, B.W. (1978), *Conducting Educational Research*, Harcourt, Brace Jovanovich, New York, USA.

Webb, J.W., Campbell, D.T., Schwartz, R.D. and Sechrest, L. (1973) *Unobtrusive Measures: Non-reactive Research in the Social Sciences*, Rand McNally, New York, USA.

14
Outdoor Education in the Australian States

1 Outdoor Education in Queensland

Norm McIntyre

There is no official published definition of outdoor education in Queensland and many different programmes have been given the label 'outdoor education'. However, most of these involve some combination of outdoor pursuits, field studies or environmental education and attempts to enhance the personal and social development of participants. Generally, the existence of outdoor education programmes in Queensland depends on such factors as the suitability of resources in the local area, the co-operation of the school Principal and administration and, above all, on the enthusiasm of the teacher.

Development of Outdoor Education

The present status of outdoor education in Queensland can be traced back to two major initiatives which occurred within the Education Department in the 1930s.

The first of these was the development of the Agricultural Project Club Branch which was initiated to encourage the introduction of new agricultural practices by involving primary school students in agricultural projects which used innovative and exemplary methods. With time this role diminished and in the 1950s and 60s, in sympathy with the mood of the times, the educational role of the branch became more concerned with nature-study and conservation. The branch has played, over the past two decades, an influential role in the development of environmental education throughout the state.

At about the same time, the Physical Education Branch was involved with the National Fitness Council in the School Camping Programme at Rockhampton, Toowoomba and at Tallebudgera on the Gold Coast. Subsequently, these sites were to become the basis of the residential centre network of the Queensland Recreation Council. The camps, based on the theme of Education for Social Living, were organised for students throughout Queensland. In the 1960s, permanent camps were developed on the coast in each of the regions and country children were brought to them by rail for a ten-day programme. The major purpose of these early camps was to facilitate the personal and social development of school students through the use of physical activities. This theme has persisted as a focus of the Physical Education Branch to the present.

Despite a brief reconciliation in 1976, when outdoor education was included in an environmental education policy published in the Education Office Gazette, the historical separation of the roles of these two branches of the Education Department, initiated in the 1930s has persisted.

The period 1974–77 saw significant growth in interest in the use of the outdoors in the education process. At this time, the term outdoor education first began to be used commonly in education circles, and a number of significant developments occurred which were to shape the future of outdoor education in the state.

In 1974, a Camp Development Committee was set up in the Physical Education Branch to examine such programmes as the Duke of Edinburgh Award Scheme and Outward Bound with a view to extending the school curriculum to encompass physically challenging activities in an educational framework. A significant outcome of this initiative for outdoor education was the development of a residential centre at Maroon in southeast Queensland. Maroon Outdoor Education Centre, as it is now called, is the major outdoor centre for secondary schools in the southern part of the state. Unlike the centre it initiated, the life-span of the Camp Development Committee was brief and it disbanded in 1978 after the Maroon centre was established. So the opportunity to extend the innovative planning and co-ordination which marked the initial development of this centre to other parts of the state was never realised. It was at this stage that outdoor education became part of physical education, and was incorporated into the syllabus of that subject. Given the training and interests of physical education teachers, it was probably inevitable that outdoor pursuits or adventure education should become the major focus of outdoor education.

At about the same time, a co-operative effort between the Agricultural Projects and Curriculum Branches of the state Education Department resulted in the development of a network of Field Study Centres. These catered mainly for primary school students and provided day and residential programmes in environmental education. Only a few of these centres were purpose-built, the majority being disused one-teacher schools, forestry barracks and old government buildings which were refurbished to provide basic facilities for students. In addition, most of the centres had permanent staff whose role was to provide on-site care and local expertise to visiting schools. Over the last 10 years, this network has extended from an initial 4 to a total of 10 centres dispersed throughout the state in a wide variety of natural and urban settings.

A third important contribution to the development of outdoor education in Queensland, the Commonwealth Schools Innovations Grants scheme, also occurred at about this time. This provided considerable impetus to the development of outdoor education within individual schools by providing 'seed money' for innovative projects, of which a large proportion involved outdoor-type programmes. Initiatives supported of these grants included the Arcadia Project (see Chapter 13), numerous grants for the purchase of outdoor equipment, and for the development of outdoor study areas within school grounds. Despite the fact that most of these projects have now ceased to exist, the grants served to provide much-needed recognition and encouragement to individuals and groups, many of whom have subsequently acted as foci for continued developments in outdoor education.

Another major project funded by the Schools' Commission was an Environmental Advisory team which was set up by the Education Department to survey the environment near each secondary school in the state. The outcome of this project was a total of 58 reports, each of which included an environmental inventory of the area, a series of activities and a summary of appropriate environmental strategies and techniques. These reports provided valuable references and formed the basis for the development of environmental education programmes in the schools concerned.

In 1977, the Graduate Diploma in Outdoor Education at Brisbane College of Advanced Education enrolled its first students. It was the first outdoor education programme in Australia to provide graduate training for teachers. In 1980, a part-time option was made available to facilitate access to the programme by serving Queensland teachers. This course was based on an holistic approach to outdoor education which gave equal emphasis to environmental, outdoor pursuits and personal development aspects of outdoor education. It was, therefore, at variance with the prevalent Departmental philosophy of outdoor education, and this led to some difficulty in its gaining recognition within the state system. These initial problems have now been overcome, and the course is now the major source of qualified graduates for both the state and independent school systems.

At the same time as these developments at the tertiary level and within the Department were taking place, outdoor education programmes blossomed in individual schools in the state and private systems. Whereas private schools leaned towards the development of outdoor centres, state schools opted for school-based programmes which made use of local resources as well as Departmental centres and other venues.

The growing enthusiasm for outdoor education among teachers prompted the formation of the Outdoor Educators' Association of Queensland in 1979. This aimed to further the cause of outdoor education within the state by providing a forum for the exchange of ideas and formulation of policy. Additionally, it sought to address the more practical goals of facilitating training and interaction with other state associations. In 1981, the Association hosted the Third National Outdoor Education Conference at Maroon Outdoor Education Centre and brought Colin Mortlock, a leading exponent of adventure education and author of a number of books on the topic, from Britain.

These influences individually and in combination have determined the present status of outdoor education, on a local, regional and state-wide basis, by facilitating teacher development and programme evolution through the provision of access to relevant training, funds, expertise, facilities and the formation of a professional body to advocate the cause of outdoor education at a state and national level.

State Education Department Outdoor Centres

The Queensland Education Department administers two types of outdoor centres: the Field Study Centre network and the Maroon Outdoor Education Centre.

The Field Study Centre Network

These centres are administered by the Agricultural Projects Club Branch through its central office in Brisbane. The centres provide residential and day facilities in a variety of locations throughout the state, encompassing a diversity of natural and cultural environments. The programmes of the centres specialise in environmental education and are designed principally for primary schools. Teaching resources such as work-sheets, audio-visual aids and library materials as well as staff with local specialist knowledge are available at most centres. Residential camps are normally of three days' duration and may involve students in living under canvas. Marine study programmes, including visits to the Great Barrier Reef, are run at Boyne Island near Gladstone. Inter-tidal and mangrove studies and trawler trips on Moreton Bay are a focus for the Jacob's Well Centre to the south of Brisbane. Rain-forest ecology, back-packing, camping and environmental awareness are typically included in the programme at the Paluma Centre, in the ranges to the north of Townsville. Urban geography, town planning and history are featured at the Urban Field Study Centre in the heart of Brisbane. A heritage programme has been developed in co-operation with the Queensland National Parks and Wild-life Service at the former penal colony on St Helena Island. The reconstruction of a pioneer timber-getters settlement at Pullenvale, near Brisbane, has encouraged the incorporation of art and drama in environmental studies through experiences that recreate the life-style of these early settlers. These few examples serve to illustrate the diversity of programmes and the variety of experiences available to teachers and their students at these centres.

The Maroon Outdoor Education Centre

This is the only centre of its type run by the Education Department in Queensland. It is situated on the shores of Maroon Dam, a man-made impoundmant in south-east Queensland close to the rugged Border Ranges. Established in the period 1974–77 in buildings formerly used by dam construction crews, it has accommodation for up to 120 students. Because of the high student capacity, it is used almost exclusively by secondary schools, many of which have a preference for year group camps.

The centre offers general courses of an integrated nature involving aspects of outdoor pursuits, personal and group development and environ-mental education. School-specific courses, planned by teachers from the client school in co-operation with staff at Maroon, are becoming more common as awareness of the resources available at the centre increases. In addition, specialist programmes in adventure activities and field studies for older students are offered and the centre is increasingly being involved in courses for students identified as being at risk within the school system.

The provision of the Maroon facility with its specialist equipment and staff has been an important catalyst in the development of outdoor education in Queensland. However, it is the only centre of its kind in the state and, for this reason, it is incapable of adequately servicing the increasing demand for its specialist facilities. In turn, the lack of appropriately qualified teachers in the schools and the concentration of specialist staff and facilities at Maroon have combined to encourage a demand for the centre to provide adventure-type programmes to the detriment of its broader role in the provision of integrated outdoor education experiences.

Outdoor Education in Schools

For a variety of reasons, including the limited distribution and restricted availability of departmental centres, most state schools have developed a roving concept of outdoor education. This involves the use of resources in and around the school for day-to-day programmes, combined with periodic weekend or longer trips to more distant venues such as state forests, national parks and Departmental and other residential centres.

By contrast, most of the larger independent schools have developed their own outdoor centres as annexes to the school. In this case, the majority of the school's outdoor education programmes are based at the centre. Although some of these schools run trips for their seniors to other venues in Queensland and inter-state, most tend rather to involve these students in a leadership role in their final years. The centres usually have one or two residential staff who are responsible for programme design and for the integration of the centre experience with the school curriculum, in co-operation with school staff. Students are normally involved in a five-day experience each year throughout their school life, and a sequential developmental programme characterised by increasing skills and level of challenge with increasing age, is the norm at such centres. In some instances, this base programme is supplemented by special camps in geography, history and the natural sciences run by specialist teachers to provide the field component of the school curriculum in that area. Most of the centres incorporate a broad definition of outdoor education in their stated aims, including environmental studies. While this latter area is generally addressed in some parts of the programme, it is largely peripheral to the main thrust, which is personal and group development through challenging adventure experiences. It is evident that many of these owe much to the philosophy of Outward Bound and gurus of more recent vintage such as Karl Rhonke.

Structural difficulties such as subject specialisation, and school administrators who are unsympathetic to timetable disruption, often work against a significant commitment to outdoor education in many secondary schools. By contrast, the relatively simpler structure of the primary school facilitates the integrated approach to learning provided by outdoor education. For this reason, many primary schools have introduced outdoor programmes which are fully integrated into the school curriculum. Such programmes frequently make use of the local area such as school grounds, nearby creeks, parks and industries, all of which may be within walking distance of the school. The intensive use of the local area is a reflection of the age of the students and the need to keep transport costs to a minimum. A relatively high level of participation has been facilitated by the provision of the Field Study Centre network which has provided an appropriate venue for day visits or overnight stays for older students.

Sequential development of knowledge and skills is a feature of these programmes, starting with nature walks and other activities in the school grounds, progressing to day visits to nearby areas and Field Study Centres and culminating in extended camps to more distant venues. Fundraising activities to provide transport costs and equipment; parent evenings involving talks, films and displays about childrens' camps; bush dances and family outdoor weekends; are all methods which have been used to foster parent support and co-operation for school outdoor education.

Teacher Preparation in Outdoor Education

At the moment the majority of outdoor education programmes are being conducted by teachers with a lot of enthusiasm but little experience or training. Safety and emergency procedures are often overlooked, and opportunities to make the best use of the outdoor environment are missed.

This statement summarises the state of teacher preparation in outdoor education as perceived by the Outdoor Educators' Association of Queensland and suggests an inadequate level of preparation of teachers in this area of education. However, opportunities for both formal and informal training in outdoor education are increasing and it is hoped that, as more new graduates with appropriate training enter the workforce, and as a greater number of in-service teachers take advantage of study leave and short-term courses, the situation will improve.

A graduate qualification in outdoor education has been available at Brisbane CAE since 1977. The Graduate Diploma in Outdoor Education is now offered as a full-time one-year course only, which makes access to it difficult for serving teachers. Graduates find employment in key areas including the various Departmental and independent outdoor centres and with organisations such as Childrens' Services and Outward Bound. However, the course produces only 10–15 graduates a year, not all of whom are teachers. This small number, combined with the limitations of access to serving teachers, means that insufficient graduates are available to meet the needs of schools for trained staff.

The Physical Education Departments in the various teacher education institutions throughout the state offer elective programmes in outdoor education. Most of these have a strong emphasis on outdoor recreational activities such as canoeing, bushwalking, camping etc. and, with few exceptions, place little importance on an holistic approach to outdoor experiences. In addition, as these programmes are electives and are really only available to physical education students, they do not meet the need for appropriate training for the primary school teacher or other discipline specialists in the secondary schools. If outdoor education is to realise its full potential within the school system, both pre-service and in-service opportunities need to be extended within the institutions and access to such courses needs to be facilitated by a more liberal attitude to study leave and financial support by employing authorities.

Departmental centres such as Maroon and the Field Study Network also fulfil an important role in the further education of teachers by providing short training programmes, appropriate classroom media and print resources and incidental training through participation in activities at the various centres. This role, which many within the department perceive as the primary purpose of the centres, contributes substantially to the development of the necessary confidence and expertise in teachers, to enable them to implement independent school-based outdoor education.

Canoeing in Western Australia

Some directors have appointed Camping Officers to co-ordinate outdoor programmes and facilitate teacher development within the particular region under their jurisdiction. Notable among these is the Peninsula region in north Queensland, where such officers have taken on the role of advisory teachers in outdoor education. They have produced a newsletter, conducted workshops in a variety of topics and co-ordinated outdoor experiences for schools in co-operation with Outward Bound.

In recognition of the need for staff training, a few state high schools have recently obtained funds from the Department to run workshops in elements of the particular school's outdoor programme. By extending the pool of suitably qualified individuals, this allocation of resources and time to the development of staff expertise enables a more equitable distribution of the heavy commitment required by such programmes and may also insulate the programme against its premature demise if key staff are transferred.

The Outdoor Educators' Association, as well as running numerous workshops and producing a quarterly journal, has also played an important in-service role by subsidising visits of various overseas specialists such as Karl Rhonke, Colin Mortlock and Steve Van Matre.

Conclusion

Outdoor education in Queensland is characterised by a lack of focus. This is not unique to Queensland and relates to the diffuse nature of outdoor education: it is many things to many people. For this reason it is likely to remain unco-ordinated and, to a large extent, unrecognised and, therefore, will continue to be vulnerable to political expediency and funding cuts both at the school and organisational level.

Experience in other states of Australia and overseas, particularly in New Zealand and Britain, indicates that state education systems can provide the necessary organisational focus for the growth of outdoor education. However, in Queensland, a more integrated view of outdoor education would be required than is currently reflected in the present Departmental structure, which separates environmental and outdoor (adventure) education. Some rationalisation and integration of functions at the Departmental level could be affected by initiating appropriate staffing and programming policies in the various outdoor centres and by examining the role of outdoor/environmental education in the total school curriculum. Such initiatives would have the potential to provide an appropriate focus for the development of outdoor education and, in the process, would address more effectively the broader needs of the total school community.

Recent developments indicate that some measure of rationalisation is going on, with the initiation of joint projects between the Physical Education and Agricultural Projects Branches, the supply of outdoor recreational equipment to selected Field Study Centres, and the employment of secondary school teachers at others. In addition, the establishment of camp schools similar to Maroon Outdoor Education Centre are being considered in each of the regions. Finally, in the curriculum area, a specialist outdoor education committee has been set up to develop a policy document on outdoor education, to include a definition, a description of the character and extent of participation and to make recommendations on future directions.

2 Outdoor Education in New South Wales

Bruce Hayllar

Outdoor education, as defined by this book, has a short yet vital history in New South Wales. It is a chronicle of daring initiative, changed horizons and pious hopes for the future.

The term outdoor education did not appear in curriculum documents of the New South Wales Department of Education until quite recently. So, in reporting the history of outdoor education, attention must be focused on other areas of the curriculum where the educational foundations of outdoor education, as we conceive it, are apparent. In general terms, the concepts and contexts of outdoor education are most evident within the evolution of the environmental education and physical education curricula. Indeed, it is the dynamic relationship between these two which has largely shaped the history of outdoor education in this state.

Up until the early 1950s, conducting studies of the natural environment within field settings was largely unknown as a form of teaching practice. In secondary education, the teaching of science did involve the study of discrete elements within the natural world, but this was largely a static, classroom-based activity. At the primary school level, it was the exceptional teacher who undertook these studies at all. However, while there was generally little formal teaching of the natural sciences, there were 'traditional' observances like those of Wattle or Arbor Days. Press reports document the importance of these occasions for some schools. For example, in 1942, the Minister for Education, Mr Clive Evatt, urged children of the Epping Primary School to 'never chop down a tree unnecessarily as they were of great usefulness to man'.

In this early period, the teaching of physical education in schools was also limited. In the late 1930's, however, there were the beginnings of a movement to redress this. Voluntary associations and professional groups such as the Boy Scouts, the YWCA, the YMCA, the Australian Council for Youth, the Parks and Playgrounds Movement and the Town Planning Association, were all involved. An umbrella organisation, the Recreation and Leadership Movement, was particularly outspoken. Dr C.E.W. Bean, the noted Australian historian and Vice-President of the Recreation and Leadership Movement, consistently argued through both private correspondence with the Minister for Education, Mr Drummond, and Letters to the Editor, that the establishment of a state-wide physical education policy for schools and the general community, was a necessity. These groups were particularly strident in their opinions that action needed to be taken concerning the fitness of youth. Their views were undoubtedly influenced by the growing spectre of European fascism. In a letter to the *Sydney Morning Herald* in August 1937, Bean noted:

> Post-war experience, in particular the perilous rivalries of Europe, is forcing the democratic peoples to devise means of developing and increasing numbers of 'whole Men and whole Women' active enough in body and mind and imagination to maintain the democracies in vigorous competition with states of other ideals.

Bean sought a form of physical education that was a balance between regimentation and the need for independent self-directed exercise. The rigid gymnasia of Europe were anathema to his vision. It was clear that he was impressed by the ideals of Lord Baden-Powell, who argued that fresh air and outdoor exercise were more appropriate to *British* traditions of democracy!

Due in large measure to his efforts and those of the Physical Education Advisory Committee of New South Wales, a Director of Physical Education was appointed in 1938. The appointee, Mr Gordon Young, set out to develop a modern physical education programme for the schools of the state. As part of this process, Young sought to promote the principle of school camping by establishing facilities which would enable large numbers of children to have this experience as part of the school curriculum. This became a reality when, in 1939, land was set aside for the establishment of a residential camping centre. In a speech to the Physical Education Advisory Committee, the chairman reported:

> For some time I have been anxious to secure a permanent camping site for the use of the various activities presented in physical education. We have introduced an annual summer camp for teachers which has proved most popular and I have no doubt it will become a permanent factor in our school calendar. Our camping activities should not stop at teachers, however, and we should provide for fresh air camps to which underprivileged and under-nourished children from the congested areas of the city might be sent to give them an opportunity of obtaining physical education under ideal conditions . . .

After considerable search, an area of land of approximately 400 acres has been discovered at Patonga on the Hawkesbury River. This area is at present reserved for public camping purposes but has not been developed in any way . . . the area is ideal for camping purposes as it is on the water with facilities for boating and swimming.

With this proclamation, the first permanent site for outdoor education in Australia was established. The first campers, a group of high school girls, attended for a week in December 1940. According to Wearing (1983) the development of Broken Bay meant that the New South Wales Department of Education was the first school system in the world to establish organised camping, an experiment keenly observed by other nations, particularly the United States. In 1941, the newly-established National Fitness Council

Recording

allocated additional funds to the state Education Department to conduct and develop a camping programme. Thus the Broken Bay National Fitness Camp became a reality and the tradition of sending primary school children off to 'the fitness camp' became part of the educational folklore of New South Wales. For many children then, as it is today, this was their first introduction to outdoor education.

Although the first camping programmes, had physical education as their philosophical foundation, as implemented they reflected a much broader interpretation of their role. Field studies (plant studies, rock studies, animal studies and bushcraft) entered the first camping programmes due to the interests of staff rather than as part of a planned educational initiative. The practices adopted were a deliberate attempt to get away from ideas of nature-study which, to that time, implied observation and labelling (Webb 1988). Once established at this first site, the notion of field studies spread to the other National Fitness Camps as they were developed. The second, Point Wolstoncroft, on Lake Macquarie near Newcastle, was opened in 1942 and, by 1955, 9 camps were in operation with a variety of programmes ranging in length from 3 to 15 days. By 1988, the New South Wales system of Sport and Recreation Centres consisted of 12 residential and 5 under-canvas camping sites.

While National Fitness Centres continued to develop, there was also a discernible change in attitudes towards interpretation and understanding of the natural environment in school-based studies. Natural Science was beginning to appear in Department of Education curriculum documents with clearly-defined guidelines and programmes of study. At this stage, in the mid-1960s and early 1970s, Natural Science was directed toward plant and animal studies and issues relating to their preservation. The Natural Science Curriculum (1965 Revision: 47), for example, states that:

> The course is concerned with two broad aspects of conservation, the preservation of our Wild-life Heritage and the principles and practices of the conservation of resources . . . Care and concern for all living creatures which do no harm to man, pride in our national wild-life, opportunity to know the local bushland and scenic areas and to appreciate and enjoy scenic beauty in its many forms, once developed, will evoke an habitual response towards the environment.

There was also recognition in this document of the value of experiences away from the school environment as aids in the understanding of scientific concepts. Thus, it was stated (p. 44) that:

> every opportunity for a lesson or part of a lesson to be taken outdoors ought to be exploited, but training must be given to enable the children to make good use of this valuable experience. The ideal situation prevails when the teacher has been over the ground beforehand, has full knowledge of things likely to be seen and has clearly indicated planned objectives before setting out . . . An excursion is only valuable when children return with relevant facts, observations, comparisons and questions.

The above notwithstanding, there was still a marked emphasis on collection and observation *within* the classroom setting. However, the idea of education in the outdoors was at least underway at the school level. Outdoor education could now be more than the one-off experience offered by the 'fitness camps'.

Parallel to this gradual movement towards Natural Science in the outdoors was the promotion of Field Studies Centres along the lines of those being developed in Britain. In 1964, Mr Allan Strom, who was at the time Chief Guardian of Fauna within the Fauna Protection Panel, proposed that two centres be established. Although funds were granted, the dissolution of the Fauna Protection Panel and its replacement by the National Parks and Wildlife Service resulted in a hiatus for Field Studies, and it was not until 1973 that two centres emerged: Muogamarra (near Cowan, to the north of Sydney) and Wirrimbirra (near Bargo, to the south). These centres were field extensions of the classroom Natural Science Curriculum. Emphasis was given to curriculum needs in specific subject areas, the bush setting was the norm and programmes paid little attention to issues and problem-solving (Webb 1988: 15).

Thus, the objectives of outdoor education were being developed at three levels: the continuation of the National Fitness Camps, development of Field Studies Centres and a move, albeit hesitantly, towards the use of outdoor settings for broader curriculum purposes.

Interestingly, the development of Field Studies Centres in New South Wales, paralleled a gradual change in the programmes offered in the National Fitness Camps (now Sport and Recreation Centres). The latter half of the 1970s was a period in which there was a growing awareness in the Australian community that decreasing working hours, greater disposable income and longer annual leave entitlements meant that Australians had increasing periods of leisure time. As part of the response to this phenomenon, a greater degree of interest was shown by the government in leisure-related issues. (The formation of the NSW Sport and Recreation Service and, later, the Department of Sport and Recreation, were practical outcomes of this interest.) As a consequence, the orientation of the Sport and Recreation Centres began a subtle shift away from outdoor education in its broadest sense to a more narrowly-defined notion of outdoor physical recreation: i.e., leisure education. Therefore, the environmental aspects, which gave these centres a more holistic base, declined in importance. However, these aspects, were being increasingly addressed by Field Studies Centres, which were operating both day and residential programmes.

The late 1970s and early 1980s also saw the emergence of school tent camping as a more widely-used approach to outdoor teaching. This was a period in which there was growing public awareness of the natural environment both as a venue for particular types of leisure activity and as a place worthy of preservation for its special qualities. These changes in public perception and awareness were coupled with a period of funding growth, particularly through disadvantaged schools programmes and grants for educational innovation. Increased funding provided schools with the opportunity to: travel further afield; purchase equipment; and provide in-service training for teachers. Thus schools now had options for outdoor education experiences outside the traditional sources.

To some extent, the ideas of the 1970s and 1980s have continued and the latest policy documents, particularly in the physical education area, point to a continuation of these trends. It seems likely that there will continue to be a separation of the disciplines of physical and environmental education and, consequently, limited opportunity for the development of generic outdoor education curricula. For example, the current physical education policy conceives outdoor pursuits as an element of school sport, and very much a junior partner to 'traditional' sports. Activities such as bushwalking and orienteering are only permitted to be taught for 1 term each year over a 4-term year. 'Activities should only form part of the school sport programmes where the conditions and facilities available in the local community warrant some minor inclusion' (Sport Policy Document 1986: 6).

The new environmental education policy, to be released in 1989, offers some hope for an integrated approach to outdoor education. It emphasises that environmental education should take place in a variety of learning environments and through a range of teaching practices and methods. The extent to which this will lead to the realisation of the broad objectives of outdoor education remains to be seen.

In the non-government sector, there has been growth in the development of residential outdoor education centres specifically geared toward adventure-type activities. While Knox Grammar was the first school (in 1974) to have a co-ordinated outdoor education program, its lead has been followed by many others. It is generally agreed that involvement by private schools in outdoor education will continue to expand.

New South Wales has been involved in outdoor education in Australia from the beginning. Its checquered career has largely been the result of disciplinary differences, as each discipline sought to establish territory for itself within the outdoor setting. While outdoor education is alive and well in New South Wales in a diverse range of practices, it is still in the philosophical backwaters as a co-ordinated, holistic form of educational practice.

References

Wearing, S. (1983) 'Outdoor Recreation and Environmental Awareness', Bachelor of Town Planning Thesis, University of New South Wales.

Webb, J. (1988) *A Survey of Environmental Education Centres in New South Wales*, Kuring-gai College of Advanced Education, Sydney.

Curriculum for Primary Schools (1965) *Natural Science, Health and Physical Education*, Department of Education, Sydney.

Department of Education, (1986) *Sport*, Policy Document, Sydney.

State Council of Physical Fitness (1939) Minutes of Inaugural Meeting, November.

Northern District Times (1942) 'Arbor Day Celebrations', August.

Sydney Morning Herald (1937) 'Letter to the Editor', August.

Acknowledgement

Reference was made to the private journals of Dr C.E.W. Bean. Thanks are due to the NSW Department of Sport, Recreation and Racing, for access to this material.

3 Outdoor Education in Victoria

Vanessa Reynolds

Early Developments

Any history of outdoor education in Victoria begins long before it came to be called by that name, and long before school camps and excursions were regarded as part of a school's usual activities. We can trace outdoor education from its foundations in the enthusiasms and vision of individuals to its much wider acceptance today as a valid educational experience which should be offered to all students.

Outdoor education began as outdoor adventure activities and the conduct of regular education in outdoor settings. Bushwalking as a recreation was established by the 1880s in Victoria, and the Federation of Victorian Walking Clubs was formed in 1934. Students at Geelong College in the late 1940s participated in summer expeditions to the south-west of Tasmania, and elsewhere. They found routes on to Federation Peak and one party was the first to reach the top. Geelong Grammar School established its Timbertop annexe in 1952. The extension of adventurous activities into schools gradually followed.

Bushwalking

The expansion of secondary education in the late 1950s and 1960s was an important factor in this extension, as more teenagers stayed on longer at school. Some teachers in secondary schools had personal experience and skills in outdoor activities, often gained through membership of Scouts, Guides, youth organisations and university mountaineering clubs. They offered adventure activities to students as extra-curricular activities, as year-level camps and in end-of-year programmes. In late 1972, students from Footscray Technical School bushwalked through the Cradle Mountain–Lake St Clair National Park in Tasmania. Sadly, one student died, and the adequacy of preparation, equipment and leadership was questioned. The incident lead directly to the formation of the School Camps Branch, which was given the responsibility of ensuring the safety of secondary school groups undertaking outdoor adventure activities and school camps. It strengthened the role of the existing School Camps Committee. Primary school camps and excursions remained the responsibility of District Inspectors.

The School Camps Branch became a vital component in the transformation of outdoor activities and camps into outdoor education. In-service education was an effective tool in improving the skills and safe practices of teachers leading camps and activities. Safety guidelines were established and published as *Safety in Outdoor Adventure Activities*, in 1975 and were enforced through rigorous checking by officers of the School Camps Branch. Publications often accompanied in-service activities, and were widely available to all teachers.

The School Camps Branch maintained close contact with the Bushwalking and Mountaincraft Training Advisory Board (BMTAB), which was established in 1968 to run training courses in bushwalking and mountaincraft leadership and skills. Close contact was also established or maintained with other bodies responsible for training and certification in outdoor activities. Community organisations such as the Victorian Board of Canoe Education, the Australian Ski Federation and the Australian Yachting Federation offered skill and leadership courses leading to certificates which were recognised in the guidelines for the different activities.

Such certificates were not a mandatory requirement before teachers could undertake such activities with students, but they were regarded as equivalent to various levels of skill and periods of experience. Many of the in-service activities offered by the School Camps Branch were run in conjunction with the appropriate community body, or by School Camps Branch personnel who were qualified to the level required to be able to test participants for various certificates. Many of these courses were run in school time, with teacher-release common for attendance.

Period of Expansion

Clearly, the 1970s under the impetus of School Camps Branch was a period of expansion for outdoor education in Victoria. Factors other than those mentioned previously contributed to this growth. It was a dynamic period in education. The Schools Commission poured money into schools for innovative programmes as well as to redress disadvantage. Around the

Canoeing

world, educators were questioning the roles, values and traditions of education and challenging schools to offer more relevant and attractive curricula. Alternative schools, both public and private, tried to address some of these issues in radical ways, while ordinary schools offered alternatives within conventional arrangements. Schools took responsibility for curricula as central guidelines were relaxed or abandoned. These factors all contributed to a dramatic growth in outdoor activities being conducted by schools, to schools developing their own camps and to the purchasing of camping and outdoor equipment which helped encourage continuity of programmes and activities.

Some of the issues that arose during this period remain as issues today, with various attempts at resolution by a variety of groups in the interim. The safety of students remains a key issue. Checking procedures are still problematic. Schools continue to find it difficult to adhere to recommended staff-student ratios. Staff training, including the obtaining of certification, is still being undertaken by teachers in their own time as they are not able to obtain time-release for professional development. Curriculum development also remains an issue: schools are still developing their own curricula without the benefit of any published curriculum guidelines, and with little acknowledgement of outdoor education as a legitimate curriculum area. In the 1970s, many outdoor educators saw participation in adventure programmes as a means of redressing social disadvantage and injustice. Disadvantage and injustice has not been eliminated and the issue continues to be important.

Belt-tightening

The boom period of the 1970s gave way to a belt-tightening period in both education and outdoor activities in the 1980s. There have been significant changes in the Victorian Education Ministry which have had a direct bearing on the operation and development of outdoor education in Victoria. These include regionalisation; the investing of responsibility for safety with school councils; the demise of the School Camps Branch; changes to central curriculum structures and the place of outdoor education in these structures; and the new Victorian Certificate of Education (VCE) for Years 11 and 12. Changes in outdoor education, in general, have included the formation of the Victorian Outdoor Education Association (VOEA); the development of tertiary courses in outdoor education; increasing numbers of commercial operators in outdoor activities; and developments in other outdoor activities leading to the formation of the Outdoor Recreation Centre and the Camping Association of Victoria.

Many of these events occurred in a very short time and had an impact on one other. In December 1981, the inaugural meeting of the VOEA was conducted. The Association began strongly, with a proposal for a curriculum project to be conducted by the Education Department. This proposal was eventually successful but not until after the Outdoor Education Section, which had become the School Camps Branch in 1983, had been disbanded because of changes to central branches and the regionalisation of the Education Department. The curriculum project, which many people had been advocating for some time, became the responsibility of one person who had to work without the support of the group of experts which had been built up in the Outdoor Education Section. It began as a three-year project designed to produce a curriculum document guiding outdoor education in schools from a sound educational base.

Meanwhile, teachers in schools continued to teach outdoor education and run outdoor activities in a regionalised Education Ministry. In early 1983, responsibility for approving excursions, camps and activities which involved adventure activities or overnight stays devolved to school councils in all schools, secondary and primary. Other excursions remained the Principal's responsibility. Regional officers had to be notified of, and check, all camps and adventure activities. Generally, the regions took their responsibilities seriously, and appointed officers with some experience in outdoor activities to the tasks. These, however, did not have the expertise of the disbanded Outdoor Education Section staff, and they were unable to maintain close and regular contact with each other. Additionally, the officers were frequently distracted by other responsibilities and, consequently, their involvement in outdoor education became limited to the checking of safety procedures. Little time was available to advise teachers about their programmes. There were very few in-service activities in outdoor education in this period because few people were available to conduct them. Some teachers in schools took the initiative and conducted courses but as most in-service funding was controlled by regional officers, obtaining funds was often a time-consuming and difficult task. Without easy telephone access to outside experts, many teachers felt isolated and abandoned.

At the same time, the VOEA was consolidating its strong beginnings. It conducted working parties to investigate a range of issues, including the perennial question of accreditation and certification, the 'tagging' of outdoor education positions in schools, and matters relating to the career structure and promotion possibilities of outdoor educators. The VOEA also conducted annual conferences which helped to fill the gap in in-service activities. The Professional Development section of the Ministry also gave some support to outdoor education in-service activities.

The Ministry of Education, in its 1983 restructure, reduced the number of curriculum committees and rationalised the curriculum into ten areas. A curriculum centre was established for each area in the restructured Curriculum Branch. Outdoor education was placed in the Personal Development Centre along with an assortment of subjects: Health Education, Home Economics, Physical Education, Textiles, and Traffic Safety. The group of outdoor educators who believed that outdoor education existed primarily for students' personal development found this a satisfactory arrangement. Those who believed that the main purpose of outdoor education was to introduce students to outdoor adventure activities were not so pleased. The debate still rages about the role of outdoor education and whether adventure is a means to an end or an end in itself. The pendulum at the moment is definitely swinging towards the 'means to an end' argument. Indeed, there are many people who argue that personal development and a sense of adventure could be achieved through outdoor activities which are more passive and less threatening than physically-demanding and stressful adventure pursuits.

In the restructured Curriculum Branch, it was proposed that Victoria should have curriculum guidelines in all ten areas to help schools. A Curriculum Frameworks Project was established to develop the guidelines — an enormous task. Unfortunately for outdoor education, this project overtook the original outdoor education curriculum project and eventually replaced it. At the time of writing (February 1989), the Personal Development Framework still has not been published, although we have been promised that it is at the printers and due for release very soon. It is the last framework to be released and teachers have already been copying parts of drafts and selectively using them to develop their courses.

Currently, there is no outdoor education position in central branches of the Ministry. Some regions have specifically designated outdoor education positions. More commonly, outdoor education has been joined with another subject area, such as physical education. The issue of safety checking for outdoor activities remains vexed, especially in the three larger metropolitan regions. Fortunately, most of the country regions have been able to retain the staff who used to do this job and the advisory structures which assist outdoor education teachers. The three very large metropolitan regions have really had to start again in all aspects, however. Checking in at least one of the three regions is done by administrative personnel with no previous experience or expertise in the area, and the self-help group that used to exist did not meet or receive any regional support in 1988.

Hopeful Signs

In early 1988, the report of the Ministerial Review of Outdoor Education Activities was finished and, in May, it was submitted to the Minister for Education. The review commenced in July 1986 following a number of incidents involving school groups in the outdoors. The chairman of the Review (1988: ix) noted that:

> Collectively, these incidents had created concern about the adequacy of the Ministry's guidelines and procedures for dealing with outdoor education activities . . . The position of this Review is that the level of incident is too high . . . [and] we would attribute the cause of this underlying problem to the breakdown of excursion advice procedures and in-service training opportunities since 1982 . . . In its recommendations the Review proposes the support, training and resources needed to make a devolved system work, and keep the level of incident as low as possible at minimum cost.

The Review committee, which was widely representative of the Ministry, parents and teachers and the VOEA, made a great effort to consider the issues thoroughly. It is unfortunate that the report has not yet been sent to the new Minister. All outdoor education teachers still hope that its recommendations will be accepted and that appropriate regional support and advice will be implemented.

Outdoor Education in Years 11 and 12

One current curriculum change which has given outdoor education teachers a chance to get together, share ideas and feel that they are contributing to the development of outdoor education in Victoria is the development of the VCE and the consequent reshaping of outdoor education for Years 11 and 12. After years of discussion and planning, outdoor education became a Victorian Institute of Secondary Education (VISE) accredited Group 2, Year 12 subject from 1983. This was regarded by teachers as a breakthrough in the recognition of outdoor education as a legitimate subject. The number of students undertaking the course has remained low, but steady. Data from the SCOPE project (Students' Choice of Occupations and Paths in Education 1988: 15) reveals that in 1986, 1.2 per cent of Year 12 students, 400 in total, studied outdoor education. Male students predominated in outdoor education in all except independent schools at this level. Technical schools had the highest rate of participation for both males and females.

A number of other outdoor education courses have received accreditation from VISE, now the Victorian Curriculum and Assessment Board (VCAB). The most notable of these is the T12 (Technical Year 12) course in environmental and outdoor education at Boronia Technical School. Others have included a Schools Tertiary Entrance Certificate outdoor education course at North Geelong High School. In 1986, 7.5 per cent of T12 students were undertaking outdoor education courses. These courses build all the other subjects being studied (e.g. mathematics, science, English) around the core subject of outdoor education. An interesting feature of the Boronia Technical School course is the number of mature-age students it attracts, including 9 out of the 13 enrolled in 1988. One of the many difficulties it faces is the staff-intensive nature of the course, which affects the overall staffing ratio of the school as well as the personal life of the teachers involved. This effect on the outdoor education teacher's personal life is a common concern, and frequently a cause of teachers moving out of the subject. Time in lieu for overnight activities, and the working conditions of outdoor education teachers in general, remains an unresolved issue today.

The current plan is to include outdoor education in a field of study called Human Development in which students will investigate factors which influence the way people live, including the physical, hereditary, ecological, social and cultural. It is intended that students will come to understand that these influences shape human development, i.e., the development of individuals. Thus, personal development is seen as an outcome of education, not the content. The VCE takes 2 years of study to complete, and students are required to undertake 24 units of study and to pass 16 units. A unit takes half a year, 1 semester, to complete. Outdoor education has currently received provisional accreditation for 4 units. Units 3 and 4 are designed to be taken as a sequence, and there are no prerequisites for Units 1, 2 and 3. The VCAB has seconded a writer to develop the course and it intends bringing outdoor education teachers together in workshops to develop more detailed material within the course guidelines. One such workshop has been held already. Outdoor Education Units 1 and 2 will be introduced in 1991, and Units 3 and 4 in 1992. The number of units, the order in which they will be introduced and the time of the year they will be offered will be decided by each school. All other Year 12 courses will disappear. However, at the moment they are individually registered each year, so that the T12 course at Boronia Technical School continues on an annual basis.

Other School-Based Outdoor Education Programmes

This description of outdoor education in Victoria so far has looked mainly at the organisational and bureaucratic aspects of outdoor education. I have tried to indicate how issues have arisen or remain current, but I have not described outdoor education at the school level in the state. The diversity of what happens in schools under the name of outdoor education makes such description very difficult.

Excursions/Camping

In primary schools, most schools offer a camping and excursion programme. Many of these include camping-under-canvas at some stage, but they are mostly designed to be one part of an experiential programme which includes tours and study camps, rather than part of a sequential outdoor education programme. Primary schools have always been good at integrating their programmes, however, so such activities usually relate well to classroom work and other subjects. Secondary schools generally still offer some sort of camping and tours programme, although increasing costs associated with these programmes have had an impact on the frequency of the activities. As in primary schools, activities are often held only once a year for each year level. Fully-integrated camp programmes are not common.

School-owned Camps

Many secondary and private schools, and some primary schools operate their own camps including Glen Waverley High School, Carwartha High School, St Kevin's College, Caulfield Grammar School and Ivanhoe Grammar School. These camps have specialist staff either resident at the camp or attending the camp with every group. The specialist staff are responsible for the programme and the class teacher, who usually attends with the class, also participates and supervises. The benefits of such a programme which offers continuity, specialist staff and perhaps a more diverse and exciting programme, are clear, but the cost is often unacceptably high. In government schools, staffing ratios have become increasingly tight. In private schools, there are the direct and obvious costs of employing specialist staff.

Mobile Programmes

Another category of outdoor education programme which is similar to the camp-based programme involves schools employing specialist staff to run programmes which go to different locations to conduct a sequential, planned and coherent outdoor education programme. For example, De La Salle College, each Year 4 to 10 class participates as a group in a compulsory programme conducted by 3 full-time staff. One variation of this type of activity involves what could be described as mega-camps, where all students in one or more year levels are away from school at one time, often at one site. Students either choose a number of activities from the range offered or rotate through the total programme over a week to 10–day period. The programme at St Paul's, Woodleigh, is notable because the outdoor activities are run as part of a whole school elective programme and their mega-camps include the full range of students from Years 7–10.

Outdoor Education as an Elective

Finally, outdoor education is offered in many schools as an elective subject. It is a common option at senior levels above Year 9, with 4,200 students, 6.1 per cent of all Year 10, choosing outdoor education in 1986. This compares favourably with enrolments in other subjects, e.g., economics (4.2 per cent), legal studies (7.8 per cent), automotive practices (6.4 per cent) and Italian (5.8 per cent) at Year 10 level. When a student in Victoria chooses outdoor education as an elective at the Year 10 or Year 11 level, what will she or he do? Programmes vary considerably depending on the personal interests and expertise of the teachers; the equipment the school owns or has access to; the geographic location of the school; the accessibility of suitable venues and on the previous experience and skills of the students. While the curriculum basis for some elective courses is questionable, many are thoughtfully developed, well-balanced and based on sound educational principles.

Ministry of Education Camps

Victoria also has three camps or residential centres run by the Ministry of Education: Somers, Bogong and Rubicon. The camps are staffed by teachers who have, or develop expertise in a range of outdoor activities. The camps are available to all government schools, but demand exceeds supply and places at Bogong and Rubicon are balloted from applications. All camps operate similarly to those already described; class teachers accompany groups and work alongside specialist staff. Somers camp operated for two years from 1947 at Queenscliff before being moved to the current location at Westernport Bay on the southern Mornington Peninsula in 1959. The camp offers 10-day residential programmes for upper level primary students and 160 students attend each camp. They aim primarily to develop social skills. All activities, including camp duties, are geared to this. There is also an emphasis on environmental activities, including studies based on the beach environment. Outdoor pursuit activities offered include aquatics, bushcraft and high and low ropes courses. Bogong School Camp was established in 1971 in the State Electricity Commission village of Bogong in the Kiewa valley 15 kilometres from Mt Beauty on the road to Falls Creek ski resort. Rubicon School Camp was established in 1978 on the Goulburn Valley Highway between Alexandra and Eildon. Both these camps cater for secondary students in sub-alpine environments. Both offer several different types of camp targeted particularly at Year 9 and Year 10 levels. There are 8-day and 10-day general camps which offer students a wide range of activities and usually an overnight activity such as bushwalking away from the base camp. Both camps offer skiing in winter and special Year 12 outdoor education camps for VCE students during the year. All activities bring together students from two or more schools and Rubicon has been conducting camps which integrate disabled and able students. This is significant now that the Victorian Ministry of Education has a policy of integrating disabled students into regular schools wherever possible. The problem confronting outdoor education in the coming years is whether *all* students will have access to outdoor education programmes. Rubicon has also been taking secondary students for work experience, and both camps take tertiary students for field placements. This raises the need for practical experience for students undertaking tertiary studies in outdoor education, and the difficulties involved in ensuring a quality experience for these student without burdening the providers.

Field Placements for Tertiary Students

Field placements for tertiary students may become more of a problem as tertiary courses in outdoor education expand. Currently, Chisholm Institute of Technology offers a graduate diploma at its Frankston campus, and Bendigo College of Advanced Education offers a graduate diploma and an undergraduate Arts degree in outdoor education. It seems likely that more graduate courses will develop, although the Higher Education Contribution Scheme may affect this, as scholarships and study leave are not easy to obtain. Graduate courses are usually undertaken by practising teachers so field placements are less difficult because they are usually in a position to apply their learning in their own schools. It becomes more of a problem with full-time undergraduate courses, but expansion in this area seems slower.

TAFE Courses

One area that looks likely to expand soon is the area of TAFE courses for people working in the field. This relates particularly to the increasing numbers of commercial organisations which offer their services to schools and other groups and to those which offer programmes in 'adventure tourism'. A working party in Victoria is currently considering the need for industry-based training and accreditation to be offered in conjunction with TAFE courses. Such developments, which seem likely to occur, will certainly have an impact on outdoor education in Victoria.

Outdoor Education Issues: A Summary

It is important to try to draw together some of the issues in outdoor education that have been mentioned in passing and to consider their implications for the future of outdoor education in Victoria and Australia. The issues fall into four general categories: safety issues, curriculum issues, staff issues and social justice issues. In very general terms, within each of these, the following areas still need to be addressed:

Safety issues
Guidelines and ratios

Staff expertise

Safety checking and
  responsibility
Legal issues
Regional support

Curriculum issues
Lack of curriculum information and
  guidelines
The place of outdoor education in
  schools
Student outcomes, intended and
  unintended
Staff knowledge and understanding
Need for central and regional support

Staff issues
Skill training
Leadership training
Curriculum knowledge
Study leave
Working conditions
Career structure

Social justice issues
Access to outdoor education for:
  the poor
  the disabled
  girls and women
  migrant groups
  disadvantaged groups

Conclusion

Most of these specific points are not new. Many of them have been addressed in various ways in the past. Some of the issues appear to be close to resolution. Others may never be resolved. New issues will arise. Solutions which appeared to be satisfactory at one point may not be appropriate in new and changed circumstances. Whatever arises, it is imperative that outdoor educators remain optimistic. I believe that outdoor education in Victoria is moving forward well, gaining wide acceptance, consolidating a sound educational base. It is too easy to be despondent and claim that we are no better off than we were 15, or even 5 years ago. We *are* better off. If we consider the general categories of issues, I believe we can claim to have progressed in all 4 areas, and that we will continue to make progress. If the price of freedom is eternal vigilance, then vigilance has to be the watchword for outdoor education. We need to be constantly vigilant for the safety of the students in our care, a paramount concern. We need to be vigilant for their personal well-being and to ensure that the curriculum matches their capabilities. We need to be vigilant for our own welfare so that we do not burn ourselves out. And finally, we need to be vigilant for society's health, so that social justice is a natural part of all we do.

4   Outdoor Education in Tasmania

Graeme Cooksey and Malcolm Wells

Introduction

Tasmania's topography and ready access to a wide range of environmental opportunities provide children with the foundations for participation in excellent outdoor educational experiences. In Tasmania, the term outdoor education refers both to field studies and adventure activities. Most schools run quite extensive outdoor education programmes as an integral part of the curriculum, as a means of curriculum enrichment, of enhancing awareness of the environment and of personal development through challenging adventure activities outdoors.

Although outdoor education programmes have existed in Tasmanian schools for decades, a landmark was established during the early 1970s with a residential conference at Poatina of teachers and administrators who had an interest in the outdoors. As a consequence of this gathering, the Committee on Outdoor Education Experiences (COEE) was formed by the Director-General of Education. This group provides the Education Department with policy and planning advice for all aspects of Outdoor Education.

Aims of Outdoor Education Programmes

A comprehensive survey of all schools in the state, conducted in 1988, identified the major aims of outdoor education programmes. These are listed and discussed briefly below together with some typical comments:

—The development in students of personal qualities such as self-confidence, self-esteem, independence, self-discipline, leadership and self-discovery and skills such as decision-making and problem-solving. This aim was the most frequently mentioned by all sectors:

'What is unique, special and powerful is that many of the activities have a strong powerful challenge . . . they build personal and inter-personal skills and a level of close relationship.'
'We aim to develop the individual's ability to plan and organise him/herself.'

—The acquisition of certain social learnings such as co-operative be-haviour, the sharing and accepting of responsibilities, trust, group decision-making and adaptability, which are particularly important to harmonious communal living and other shared experiences. This aim was again a very high priority for all sectors. The development of a belief in the trustworthiness or reliability of a person (comradeship, teamship) or thing is an important aspect of this aim, particularly in relation to adventure activities, and especially to those taken in the secondary and senior secondary sectors:

'We use outdoor education to develop in children an appreciation of self and others . . . to "weld" staff and students by establishing

relationships not possible in the usual school situation.'
'The provision of opportunities for students to be co-operative, make social adjustments, develop individuality and self-reliance, develop loyalties and live by the rule of social behaviour is fundamental to these programmes.'

—The recognition and appreciation of students (by both teachers and other students) from different backgrounds with personalities and abilities to be developed as fully as possible. This particular aim, probably the most basic to education, is seen as particularly relevant to outdoor education and was often alluded to in either the personal or social development aims. Included in this aim is the development of a sense of group identity and cohesion.

'Our Year 7 camps are held early in the first term . . . (and are held on) a "get to know you" basis with peer groups.'

—The understanding and appreciation of and respect for the natural environment by students.

'We have an outdoor laboratory where children can learn about aspects of the natural environment which cannot be learnt in the classroom.'
'The aim is to provide experiences likely to cultivate life-long interest in and appreciation for the outdoors.'

—The broadening of students' knowledge and understanding of less familiar environments through the provision of first-hand experiences, e.g., a city environment in the case of country children.

'Our students come from the inner city and a day excursion . . . enables them to experience grass, trees, farm animals . . . things not available to them in our asphalt playgrounds.'

—To reinforce, enrich and supplement classroom learning and also to bring a sense of relevance to this learning. The opportunities for language enrichment through participation in outdoor education was specifically mentioned. The development of functional and life skills was a particularly important aim in special schools.

'We show how classroom learning is applied to real-life situations.'
'Our aim is to take the classroom outside and to take the outdoors inside.'
'The real classroom is outside.'
'Opportunities for experiential learning leading to understanding and the clarification of abstractions.'
'To provide practical experience in the areas of money-handling, shopping, mobility, language, safety, social behaviour, self-help skills, leisure pursuits, work experience and community service' (special school)

—The development of an interest and skills in various leisure pursuits which can provide enjoyment and relaxation throughout life. This particularly applies to some of the adventure activities: e.g., bush-walking or canoeing. This was an important aim for the programmes offered at the secondary and senior secondary levels. Included in this aim at all levels was the acquisition of some outdoor living skills.

'We aim to give positive exposure to a range of leisure activities.'

—Some secondary schools extended this and other aims to include preparing students for future decisions about further education, employment and leisure and developing an awareness of education as a life-long process.

—Promotion of physical fitness and good health through exercise, nutrition, etc. The planning and preparation of nutritious menus for camp programmes was often an important aspect, particularly in cases where children's knowledge of this is limited.

'We aim to develop their physical fitness and improve their health through enjoyment in wholesome leisure activities designed to overcome the drabness of modern living.'

The priority order of the first three aims, i.e., personal development, social interaction and love and understanding of the natural environment, was the same for both the primary and secondary sectors. The high schools mentioned the 'educational' aim less frequently than the primary schools and the development of an interest and skills in leisure activities more frequently.

The unlinked kindergartens aimed to better integrate the developmental process in the child: i.e., social, emotional, physical and cognitive, through outdoor education experiences.

The Relationship between Outdoor Education and the Total Curriculum and between Field Studies and Adventure Activities

Primary outdoor education activities are almost totally integrated within the curriculum. In general, primary schools consider it an approach to, or a setting for, education. This applies particularly to field studies, while approximately 80 per cent of adventure activities are integrated.

A different and more diverse setting for outdoor education applies in the secondary and senior secondary sectors. Here a variety of approaches apply. Approximately 50 per cent of high schools and colleges offer outdoor education as a subject in its own right, often by means of short courses. Others see outdoor education as a support to other subject areas. It is also integrated across a range of subjects, particularly in camping programmes.

Unlike primary schools, where the greatest emphasis is on field studies and a fully integrated approach, secondary schools have extended their programmes to include a focus on adventure activities that tend not to be

Abseiling

integrated with other school activities. A great deal of out of school time is utilised for these.

Colleges offer subject-based outdoor education activities, a subject known as Expedition Skills, and electives provided within recreational programmes.

Camping programmes, which apply to all levels of education other than kindergarten and the early infant years, are viewed by schools as providing an ideal setting in which to integrate field studies and adventure activities and to achieve their aims in outdoor education. The majority of schools in Tasmania have camping programmes, ranging from extensive to modest. In many cases programmes commence with preparatory classes by means of a 'sleep-in'.

Aiding

In general, then:

— field study excursions and exploration and use of the playground area and local parks are an integral part of kindergarten outdoor education programmes

— in primary schools, the greatest emphasis is placed on field studies to achieve the aims of outdoor education; about one-third of these studies occur as part of camping/residential experiences

— high schools place about equal emphasis on adventure activities and field studies, and various camping programmes are frequently used for this purpose

— field studies and camping/residential experiences are equally important and are vital aspects of the outdoor education programmes of special schools

— the emphasis in secondary colleges is increasingly on adventure activities, and the encouragement of enjoyable and challenge leisure pursuits. There is an emerging focus on the provision of experiences which may lead to an interest and preliminary training in various areas of future employment which have a component of outdoor work or have special needs such as a good understanding of shared decision-making and the ability to relate well with many people, e.g., ranger, forestry worker, field geologist.

Field Study and Outdoor Centres

A number of specialist centres have been developed by the Education Department to cover a range of outdoor education opportunities. In general, the major aim of each is the promotion of teacher expertise which is achieved through exemplar programmes or support to teachers conducting programmes at the centre. The Department of Sport and Recreation manages another 6 residential camps which are used by schools, although only 1 has teaching staff.

Molesworth

Located in the southern region, Molesworth is a day-visit centre specialising in the field study aspects of outdoor education. The centre caters largely for K–6 groups. Field studies and environmental problem-solving programmes are its main emphasis.

Marine Studies Centre

Situated in the Southern Region, this purpose-built day-visit centre caters for children K–12. The Centre has its own 16-metre research vessel that is used by secondary groups as well as an array of touch tanks, aquariums and a large viewing pond.

Hagley Farm and Environment Centre

A residential and day-visit centre in the northern region, Hagley is an operational farm that provides students with the opportunity to experience rural life as well as offering a wide range of field study opportunities. Programmes cater for K–10 students, although the majority are of primary age.

Waddamana Field Study Centre

Located close to the geographic centre of the state in the remains of a Hydro-Electricity commission township, this centre is managed by the Department of Sport and Recreation, has an Education Department resource teacher and offers residential programmes in a remote highland location. The majority of user groups are from the primary sector and, therefore, the programmes are oriented towards field studies.

Sprent Environment Centre

A residential and day visit centre in the north-west region, Sprent provides programmes and opportunities for field and rural studies to, mainly, primary groups.

Port Arthur Education Centre

This facility has been established to provide teachers with access to interpretational material, and assistance in planning and conducting visits to the historic site. The development of a broader range of historical resources is being initiated from the centre.

Storey's Creek Centre

Located in an abandoned mining town in the northern region, this centre was established by a high school. However, staffing assistance is provided by the Education Department to enable full-time use to occur. The centre provides residential accommodation and is located in an area that lends itself to field studies as well as a wide range of adventure activities.

Mt Cameron Centre

This is a purpose-built centre in the north-east of the state that was established by a local high school. Residential programmes of field studies and adventure pursuits can be conducted here. Some assistance is provided by the Education Department to enable the viability of the centre to be retained.

Maria Island Education Centre

This unique and isolated National Park is extensively used by school groups and the appointment of a part-time resource teacher has provided a major boost to visiting teachers. Residential and day-visit programmes are conducted for children from Grades 5–12.

Outdoor Pursuits

At this stage, Tasmania does not have a purpose-built adventure pursuits centre. However, this situation will be redressed when a facility is constructed at the Lake Barrington International Rowing Course by the Department of Sport and Recreation. This will cater for the broad spectrum of community adventure pursuits training. The centre will be uniquely located, less than thirty minutes drive from world-class canoeing, bushwalking, caving and climbing areas.

Other Government Centres

Since the 1940s, the government camps in Tasmania have provided low-cost residential bases for outdoor education experiences, generally through programmes conducted by both primary and high schools. Most of these were managed by the National Fitness Council, later the Division of Recreation (which was part of the Education Department), but are now run by the Tasmanian Department of Sport and Recreation.

During the 1970s, outdoor education operations and policy received considerable attention from the Education Department during which time the Department acquired both the ex-Hydro-Electricity Commission village at Waddamana for use as a Field Study Centre, and the ex-Legacy Club Camp at Coningham.

In 1987–88, 10,960 school children stayed at the camps. The majority of these were attending school camp programmes. Although all these camps have full-time managers, only Waddamana had a teacher, the others relying on visiting staff.

Coningham Camp

The camp is situated on the coast overlooking a sandy beach and bay and has a common boundary with the Lands Department Sheppards Hill State Recreation Area.

The location and environment are ideal for outdoor recreation activities and provide an excellent topographical transect for field study purposes from sea to 185 metres.

Esperance Camp

Programmes at Esperance Camp utilise the natural features of bush, sea and coast and the mountains, caves and white-water rivers, all within one hour's drive of the camp.

Port Sorell Camps

Camp Banksia

This has beach frontage, and the extensive grounds, both developed and bush. The nearby Rubicon River and Asbestos Range all provide a varied outdoor environment, which is well utilised for outdoor education experiences.

Sport Camp

Although identified as a facility suitable for sports training, the camp provides a most appropriate base for outdoor education programmes as it shares the same environment and nearness to a national park and river as Camp Banksia.

Wirksworth Sports Training Centre

Situated in the Hobart suburb of Bellerive, the centre has provided visiting country school children with a Hobart-based visitation/education programme since the late 1940s. The Department of Sport and Recreation plan to develop the centre as a sports training facility with emphasis on adult, community and sports organisation usage.

Several secondary schools and most of the larger private schools own some form of residential camp. The Forestry Commission also has an environmental centre in the north-west, which is extensively used by schools.

Community Outdoor Education Programmes

A variety of outdoor education experiences are offered to the Tasmanian community. These include environmental and skill development programmes conducted by Adult Education, the Department of Sport and Recreation, and summer programmes offered in national parks by the Lands, National Parks and Wildlife Department. A number of community environmental groups also conduct regular programmes, and there are commercial outdoor tour operators active in the state.

Teacher Training

Some specialist training is available through the School of Environmental Studies at the University of Tasmania.

Leadership Training

The Tasmanian Department of Sport and Recreation's Bush and Mountaincraft Board has been a integral part in the development of outdoor education in the state. Originally set up under the Education Department, it has sought to increase involvement in safe, sensitive and enjoyable bushwalking through a broad range of community education courses. Through this broad spectrum, both traditional school-based programmes and the wider community benefit considerably.

Underlining the Mountaincraft Board's programme is the leadership course. Participants joining it are already highly skilled in most aspects of bushwalking and are learning how to manage different groups more effectively in varying terrains, climates and conditions. This approach enhances the interpersonal and group dynamics process that is essential for sensitive leadership within an overall framework of safe bush and mountain practices.

The board conducts a number of skills courses for the general public. These encourage participants in the leadership course to gain up-to-the-minute skills and to practise disseminating this information to a wider audience. It also ensures that a high base standard of material is available for the general public and reputable commercial operators. The result is a more informed and safety conscious public.

Since the course began in 1980, over 150 people from all aspects of community life have participated in the course, with about half having been school teachers. As part of the requirements of those under training, candidates have to lead at least 10 overnight trips each year.

The average length of time that each persons stays with the leadership award is 4 years. About 36,000 people days have been spent in the Tasmanian bush under the guidance of a safe and sensitive leadership student.

Future of Outdoor Education in Tasmania

In comparison with the rapid growth of outdoor education programmes in the 1970s, there is now a more stable base and greater long-term commitment on the part of schools. A result of the earlier development was that some schools which set up extensive programmes around their own residential centres found the ongoing maintenance costs too high. This has been paralleled by increasing pressure on public sector funding and the withdrawal of some curriculum development support.

It is likely that the government will in the future apply its resources to fewer, but better staffed and equipped centres. These will provide models of excellence in particular fields of outdoor education and this should ensure a slower but more manageable growth in the full range of outdoor education programmes. The establishment of a subject in outdoor education in Years 9 and 10, the continual growth of Expedition Skills and the development of further opportunities in Years 11 and 12, will provide students with greater opportunities to be involved in outdoor education.

These developments, coupled with the development of a quality outdoor pursuits centre and expansion of the community and commercial centres should see Tasmania re-establish itself as a leader in the field of outdoor education in the 1990s.

5   Outdoor Education in South Australia

Robert Hogan and Elizabeth Liebing

Introduction

A detailed history of outdoor education in South Australia and a description of its current status would take much more space than this report permits. It is, then, a selected history, concentrating on developments which have influenced outdoor education within schools. Only brief reference will be made to administrative developments, and to other significant school outdoor education resources, such as the Arbury Park Outdoor School, the residential centre servicing all schools in the state.

The Early Days

It is impossible to say exactly when outdoor education commenced in South Australia, but there is no doubt it preceded the adoption of the term itself. From the early days of schooling in the state there were individual teachers who conducted excursions to outdoor areas, either for learning or for a break from classroom routine.

While the earliest recorded school camping experiences in the state occurred in the early 1950s, the number of schools involved in school camping or regular excursions grew only slowly through the 1960s. Those that were conducted were mostly seen as extra-curricular, and more often than not were optional weekend or vacation activities. Schools were oriented towards what is now recognised as a somewhat narrow academic curriculum. The dramatic increase in the number of approved school camps, from 15 in 1962 to 735 in 1972 (Education Department of South Australia Records), and of excursions was a consequence of a number of changes which began to occur in schools during the late 1960s and 1970s, with moves toward greater school and teacher autonomy, and the broadening of curricula.

The 'Freedom and Authority Memorandum' issued in 1970 by the then Director-General, Mr A.W. Jones, gave to schools:

> the widest liberty to vary courses, to alter the timetable, to decide the organisation of the school and government within the school, to experiment with teaching methods, assessment of student achievement and in extra-curricular activities.

This memorandum was followed, in 1971, by the *Karmel Report* (Education Department of South Australia, 1971) which paved the way for the establishment of comprehensive high schools and a further broadening of school curricula.

Three aspects of educational thinking during this time created the environment within which interest in outdoor education was to grow. Teachers were becoming increasingly concerned that schools should play a role in social development. Interest in the whole development of the child led teachers to look for ways in which students would develop such attributes as self-confidence, independence, and the ability to work co-operatively with others. Secondly, teachers were becoming concerned about the appropriateness of conventional teaching methods. The mood of the early 1970s was for relevance in the selection of learning activities and, as far as possible, for students to learn from first-hand experience and through practical activities.

The third aspect was the increasing influence of the environment and conservation movement and the growing awareness of the many threats to the environment created by our urbanised and industrial society. Conservation became an important social issue of this period. While not necessarily clearly articulated, many teachers felt that children were becoming increasingly remote from their living world. The mood amongst some teachers at this time was that urban children needed greater exposure to natural and rural environments in order to develop positive attitudes towards their conservation, and to understand the many inter-related aspects of the total environment.

In the light of such thinking, and the mood for change of the early 1970s, school camps and excursions began to be recognised as 'legitimate' aspects of the school curricula. While much of the enthusiasm and momentum came from within schools, two groups within the Education Department were important catalysts to this movement.

The Physical Education Branch in 1970 appointed an adviser to be directly responsible for school camping. This clearly gave greater impetus to the camping movement as such a person played an important role not only in advising teachers already planning camps, but in promoting school camps among those who were only vaguely interested. School camps were promoted by the Physical Education Branch as not only valuable recreation activities, but also important vehicles for social development.

At the same time as the Physical Education Branch was promoting camping, key figures in the field of science, particularly senior school biology, were conducting their own campaign to encourage teachers out of schools. In 1972, the first Biology Consultant was appointed, with the brief of 'improving the standard of biology teaching in South Australia' (Smith 1976). The incumbent, with the support of the then Inspector of Secondary Science, saw the 'relatively untried methodology of using the outdoors' as a key aspect of this. From 1972–76, a major in-service emphasis was in the area of 'field studies'. As the Biology Consultant and the Physical Education Branch camping adviser (a new appointee in 1972) became aware of each other's work, they began planning co-operative programmes. From this development the notion of the integrated camp was born. It was advocated then that, in addition to camps being recreational and social experiences, they also become 'educational' by incorporating topics emanating from the classroom setting. There is little doubt that the adoption of the term outdoor education occurred in this changing perception of school camps. No longer were they seen as extra-curricular recreation or social activities, but as involving aspects of the regular academic curriculum. While initially often differentiated as 'study camps', adoption of the label outdoor education was soon widespread and probably contributed to legitimising such activities as aspects of school curricula.

This collaboration or joint effort on the part of teachers from the physical education and field studies areas (particularly biological sciences) was to continue throughout the development of outdoor education in

South Australia. Outdoor education was, from this point, seen to foster curriculum integration rather than being just the province of one traditional curriculum area. In particular, outdoor education was seen as encompassing the areas of field studies, leisure education and social development. While debate as to a definition of outdoor education and to its fundamental purpose raged between the various groups involved, and even trickles along today, this served to strengthen the co-operative endeavour in schools, rather than fragment it.

A Period of Rapid Growth

The climate was now right for rapid growth in outdoor education activities. The 'fuel' to launch this emerging educational phenomenon came in the form of a massive injection of Commonwealth money, through the introduction of Schools Commission Grants Schemes. Schools tapped both the Disadvantaged Schools and Innovations Grants Schemes to establish outdoor education programmes. From late 1973 through to 1975, $211,000 in grants were awarded to South Australian school outdoor education programmes (Outdoor Education Report 1975) through the Innovations Grant Scheme alone. In addition, over $250,000 was contributed towards the development of the Arbury Park Outdoor School, the first major move by the Department itself. The exact amount of money allocated through the Disadvantaged Schools Scheme, including teacher salaries and student subsidies was not reported to the Outdoor Education Committee but is said to have exceeded $500,000 in the same period. Through the Schools Commission Priority Education Programme, there have always been some supporting funds for outdoor education, and still are today.

Schools used these funds to provide a diverse range of resources, including: camping and outdoor recreation equipment (tents, ruck-sacks, canoes, cooking gear, parkas and sleeping bags), buses, purchase and development of residential camp-sites, and outdoor learning areas within the school (aviaries, fauna enclosures and so on). Commonwealth funds were also used in the area of teacher salaries, allowing extra staff to be appointed to schools for one to two year terms, often with the sole responsibility of conducting the outdoor education programme.

Hooper (1978), in a survey of 26 secondary schools (including 3 private schools), reported considerable differences in actual practice from school to school, although most programmes came under the umbrella title of outdoor education. The range included field study camps for each class at different year levels; introduction of bushcraft and camping skills courses as a 'subject' for all students within a year level, involving regularly scheduled lessons followed by 2–3 day bushwalks or lightweight camps; adventure activities camps for various year levels; and the development of one-day study excursions using a particular location or field study centre. While in some schools the programme was a blend of several different aspects, in others it was seen more precisely as only one.

A similar variety of programmes was developing in primary schools, although not with the bushcraft and lightweight camping components. It is important to note that developments of outdoor education programmes were not confined to those schools able to secure a Commonwealth grant of some kind. These were definitely the most active schools and often set the trend others chose to follow but, in many schools, programmes were developed within the constraints of their own resources. In general these were more modest attempts, but this did not necessarily make them less effective.

The diversity of such developments was seen as a desirable expression of school-based curriculum development but, in line with the philosophy of the 'Freedom and Authority Memorandum', there was also concern that development was occurring in an *ad hoc* fashion. In part, this was concern at the apparent monopolisation of resources by some schools (particularly closed country school camp-sites) and the apparent wastage of funds, as well as concern about the safety of students being exposed to a range of potentially hazardous activities and environments, in the hands of teachers not necessarily trained or experienced in this new teaching role. There was also the question of Departmental support for outdoor education. Schools were placing increasing pressure on the Department for various forms of support, including assistance with development and maintenance of camp-sites, additional teaching staff and reimbursement of some teacher costs. To add to this seemingly *ad hoc* development, different groups within the Departmental structure itself were making decisions regarding aspects of outdoor education, in a clearly unco-ordinated manner.

In response to concerns expressed from within the Education Department and by the Schools Commission, worried that the bulk of submissions for funds were in the area of outdoor education and yet the state had no structures to support their initiatives, the Department set up an inquiry into outdoor education and its development in schools. It presented its final report in November 1977, recommending wide support for further outdoor education development. The status of both committees within the department, their wide terms of reference and the substance of the reports made, clearly indicated to schools that the Department viewed development of outdoor education in schools as a worthwhile curriculum initiative. Indeed, the committee, in its final report, stated its: 'underlying belief that outdoor education programmes should be an integral aspect of schooling, to be included in every child's formal education' (Outdoor Education Committee 1977: 1).

It is worth noting that it was the schools who led from the start in this initiative. The Department, in establishing an inquiry, was responding to activity in schools and attempting to both support their needs and rationalise a great many unco-ordinated and somewhat inefficient efforts. The school initiatives carried the Department along and the presentation of the report meant official blessing and some support.

A critical need identified in the report was the development of a co-ordinated developmental plan for the in-service education of teachers. In general it was felt that many teachers, although keen to be involved, 'lacked specific expertise and skill in outdoor education leadership'. Very few teachers had any formal pre-service training in outdoor education, and opportunities to attend in-service courses had until 1975 been limited.

Responsibility for this programme fell to the Outdoor Education Advisory Team which was established in 1977 to provide an advisory support service to schools. This group, initially five seconded teachers, initiated a comprehensive in-service programme for teachers on a

Grass Skiing

statewide basis. Included were training programmes for inexperienced teachers, and a series of co-ordinators' conferences, designed to bring key teachers from various schools together to exchange information on the development of programmes. These conferences were of considerable importance in bringing greater clarification of the purposes of outdoor education in schools and understanding of appropriate patterns of organisation and programme conduct. In addition, this group prepared resources and provided an advisory service for schools and individual teachers. The task was 'not to get teachers outdoors, but to help them use the outdoor environment effectively' (Hogan 1980). While their work clearly promoted outdoor education in those schools not already committed, the greatest effect was in fostering a climate of self-reflection, oriented towards programme consolidation.

Reduction in Support

Since 1982, in the wake of economic recession, changes in government and a general tightening of the situation regarding funding and the staffing of schools, a reduction in outdoor education activity has been apparent.

The Education Department itself has progressively reduced the number of advisory teachers to the point where, in 1988, the one remaining position was abolished. Within schools, a reduced allocation of time for teachers to be involved in outdoor education and reduced provision of resources to support excursion and camping programmes has meant that only schools with committed staff have maintained outdoor education as a school-wide curriculum area. This does not necessarily diminish the enthusiasm of individual teachers offering outdoor education as part of their class activity, but indicates that, in some schools, outdoor education was seen more as a desirable extra than the integral aspect of schooling described by the Outdoor Education Committee.

Positions of full-time or half-time Co-ordinators of Outdoor Education were often the first to be cut when staffing formulas became more rigid, leading to a reduction in the programme of many schools. While in some cases staff attempted to continue a programme as well as teach regular classes, in general enthusiasm waned under increased teaching pressure. In a few cases, there was no attempt to maintain the programme at all; the person assigned to the position was merely displaced. In addition, many schools found their equipment wearing out, no further grant funds available to replace it, and no provision made to do so from within school funds. A number of schools owning their own camp-sites and buses found them to be a financial millstone, or that they were no longer being used, and disposed of them. While increasing costs of some activities also led to programme modification and reduction, a 'back to the basics' philosophy led to moves in some quarters to fit outdoor education to the school organisation in a manner causing less 'disruption' to the regular curriculum. This, together, with a move to shorter camps and fewer excursions, led not only to a reduction in the amount of outdoor education in which students were involved, but to compromises in the quality of the experience.

Such changes do not seem to be unique to South Australia and can be seen as a part of a world-wide reaction to similar circumstances. In part, however, the failure of outdoor education to become an integral and lasting feature of a number of schools can be explained in the context of the factors which led to the failure of educational innovations generally. Brady (1976: 30) suggests that common reasons for the failure of educational innovations include:

—The lack of teacher understanding of the innovation
—the lack of teacher understanding of the new role demanded by the innovation
—the lack of teacher expertise in fulfilling the new role
—the lack of necessary resources
—the lack of necessary communication in the school (opportunity for feedback)
—school organisation which is incompatible with the innovation

Analysis of a movement which developed very rapidly, for which outside resources are so critical, and for which few teachers had received any professional preparation, supports Brady's argument very well. A detailed analysis of this aspect is, however, beyond the scope of this report.

Some Success Stories

Within South Australia there are, however, a number of schools where we do see outdoor education as a success story. A brief description of a selected few of these best illustrates the nature of outdoor education in the state and factors important in its development in schools.

Overall, outdoor education is best supported within the independent school sector. A number of independent schools, notably Pembroke School, Prince Alfred College, Pulteney Grammar, St Peters College, Scotch College and Westminster School, employ teachers with specific responsibility for the co-ordination and leadership of outdoor education. In the main, these teachers conduct adventure programmes, with personal development being a key aim. The students involved are generally from the lower to middle secondary school years. Prince Alfred College is perhaps the exception and, at its Scotts Creek Field Centre, activities are based around Steve Van Matre's Sunship Earth and Earth Keepers programmes. Resources provided in the form of camp-sites, vehicles and programme equipment appear very adequate, particularly as judged by teachers from the public school sector.

Most primary school outdoor education programmes in South Australia are based around camping activities. They have been developed through the interest of a key teacher, and in some cases are a result of special funding grants. In some of these situations, a more broadly-based programme of activities has developed to include studies related to students gaining knowledge and understanding of how particular outdoor environments function.

In recent times, the influence of Van Matre has made a strong impact on many primary programmes. Students have come into contact with Sunship Earth, Earth Caretakers and Earth Keepers through facilities such as Para Wirra Field Study Centre, Scott Creek Field Study centre and Parndana Outdoor Education Centre. These activities add quite a different dimension to the simple camping programme.

Special teaching appointments in outdoor education at the primary level are few and far between. Where teachers do have a designated role in teaching and co-ordinating outdoor education, the beliefs and influence of the school principal can be seen as a key factor.

Madison Park is an example of one primary school that has developed a comprehensive programme. The school owns its own camp-site and has had a specialist teacher working in the school to develop and co-ordinate the programme. The initial programme was based around developing outdoor living skills, with students using the school grounds and their camp-site. The key teacher met with each year level and, over a period of time, 3 units of work were developed, covering 10 skill areas ranging from fire safety, first aid and map and compass to environmental care and care of equipment. These skills were sequentially arranged through the year levels.

After the Outdoor Living programme became established, activities were broadened to include experiences that would help children learn about natural environments. School grounds and camp-sites were also used as the programme developed a real 'living and learning in the outdoors' flavour.

A significant factor in the success of Madison Park was an administration that was committed to the value of outdoor education as an offering in the school curriculum. This permitted the role of a specialist teacher to continue, someone who performed such crucial functions as staff in-service and resource development. Having the 'luxury' of a specialist provided opportunities for the programme to grow and move into other areas. Skills of outdoor recreation became a new focus, as aquatic activities were introduced. These skills were then used to discover and learn about new (to the students) outdoor environments.

The programme described operated successfully at Madison Park for six years. At present, staff are adapting to a changed school focus, and the loss of the specialist teacher's position, brought about since the appointment of a new Principal.

In the state secondary school system, outdoor education is most typically manifested in the form of class or year group camps, again with one or all of curriculum enhancement, leisure education and social development objectives. These are generally organised and led by teachers who do this in addition to a conventional teaching load. In a number of schools outdoor skills courses, generally based around bushwalking or canoeing 'expeditions' of 2 to 5 days, exist as one aspect of physical education or more general elective programmes. In 1986, the state Senior Secondary Assessment Board approved a Year 12 course in outdoor education which integrated the learning of outdoor skills and the development of environmental awareness. In 1988, 8 schools offered the subject.

An Exemplary Model: Marion High School

The best developed outdoor education programme in the public school system is generally acknowledged as being that of Marion High School. Marion owns its own camp-site near Cape Jervois, 100 km from Adelaide, its own bus, and has accumulated a pool of camping and outdoor recreation equipment. Most significantly it has a team of some 7 outdoor education teachers, all of whom teach other subjects, but have varying proportions of their teaching load designated for outdoor education. On this basis, the equivalent to 2 full-time outdoor education teaching positions is seen as part of the staffing complement of the school taken from within their normal formula allocation. As a result of this, class sizes and teaching loads of the entire staff are slightly higher than they would be if they did not have such a programme, but this is considered an acceptable price to pay.

The programme at Marion is based around General Study Camps, an adventure/bushcraft elective programme and an extensive excursion programme, encouraged as an aspect of all subjects. Students attend a study camp of from 3 to 4 day's duration, in their class groups, at Years 8, 10 and 11 (15–30 students) and subject groupings in Year 9 (30–80 students). The programme for these camps is drawn from relevant classroom work and methodologies which seek to enhance appreciation and valuing of the outdoor environment. These camps also have a strong social education element. All camps are attended by the class teacher and assisted by people from the outdoor education team, or other teachers associated with that class and committed to the outdoor education philosophy.

The adventure/bushcraft element commences in Year 9, with a compulsory unit of one double lesson per term, culminating in an overnight bushwalk in the Adelaide hills. In Year 10, and then again Year 11 and 12 elective programmes, adventure electives centring around bushwalking, canoeing, rock-climbing, skiing and sailing are offered. These are term units of 4 to 6 lessons per week culminating in at least 1 expedition varying from 4 to 7 days. Approximately 100 students per year are involved in the Year 10–12 adventure programme. All courses are taught by the outdoor education team, sometimes assisted by those keen to be involved on an 'apprentice' basis.

A significant feature of the Marion programme is that it is seen as an integral aspect of the school. Total staff support is apparent, to the extent that almost all staff are involved in the general study camps. The ethos of the school supports outdoor education. Disruption to regular lessons when some or all students are absent on camps or excursions is accepted. A system of student accountability places the onus on students to chase up subject teachers to ensure they catch up on missed classroom work.

Adapting to the Changed Environment

While a general pessimism about the future of outdoor education in schools in South Australia is apparent, there are those, including ourselves, who see this more as a process of adaptation to a changing environment. There is no doubt that schools will continue to experience difficulty in obtaining the necessary resources to conduct outdoor education programmes and that the days of structural support from the Education Department are over. This is a situation similar to other states and overseas countries and is not, of course, limited to outdoor education. Most curriculum areas, in South Australia at least, now receive far less support in terms of advisory teacher assistance, access to in-service training programmes, and release of teachers from normal duties to carry out curriculum tasks.

There will always be, however, a hard core of teachers committed to the philosophies of outdoor education and keen to provide meaningful learning experiences for its students. In South Australia, a number of these have formed the Outdoor Educators Association of South Australia and see this as maintaining a self-help support network for teachers. In two metropolitan Adelaide locations, funding from the Schools Commission Priority Projects Scheme and Area Education Offices has allowed cluster groups of primary schools to share an outdoor resource teacher to further develop and support outdoor education in these schools. In two country locations, a resource teacher supports teachers conducting excursions to Kangaroo Island and the lower Flinders Ranges respectively. The Arbury Park Outdoor School continues to attract school bookings and to expand its range of programme offerings, particularly in the area of nature conservation. Here, teachers from visiting schools work with professional staff appointed to Arbury Park and are exposed to ideas which can be taken back to their own schools. The Graduate Diploma of Outdoor Education at the SACAE Salisbury Campus continues to attract students, most of whom are practising teachers. Such developments are reasons for optimism.

A most significant feature of outdoor education in South Australia is, and always has been, the emphasis on school-based programming. With the exception of Arbury Park, which opened in 1976, there has never been the development of outdoor education centres there has in most other Australian states. While centres generally do provide a concentrated pool of skilled staff to facilitate good programming, such experiences are often isolated from mainstream school life and lack the continuity and developmental approach which characterises good school-based programmes. The South Australia experience shows the lack of resources can lead to significant problems in attempting to develop such a programme, but that when a school does give the allocation of resources sufficient priority and has a pool of committed and professional staff, outdoor education can indeed become an integral aspect of schooling.

References

Brady, L. (1980) *Curriculum Development in Australia*, Prentice-Hall, Melbourne.

Karmel, P. (1971) *Education in South Australia*, Report of the Committee of Enquiry in South Australia, Department of Education, Adelaide.

Hogan, R.A. (1980) 'Helping Teachers to Use the Outdoor Environment Effectively', *Proceedings of the First National Conference*, Australian Association for Environmental Education.

Hooper, W.S. (1978) 'Outdoor Education in the Secondary School Curriculum', Unpublished thesis, Diploma in Teaching, South Australian College of Advanced Education.

Outdoor Education Committee (1975) *Report to the Director-General of Education on Outdoor Education: Preliminary Report*, Department of Education, Adelaide.

Smith, J.H. (1976) *Report of the Consultant in Biology 1972–76*, Wattle Park Teachers' Centre, South Australia.

6   Outdoor Education in Western Australia

Lesley Pearse and Keith Cook

Introduction

There are a wide variety of programmes from all areas of the curriculum in Western Australian education which are described by the term outdoor education. The common factor in each of these is the method of learning: through direct experience in the natural environment.

This experiential process is encouraged throughout the Western Australian curriculum as a complementary and/or alternative way of learning. Many of the affective goals of education are in this way achieved. What is more, a valid framework for this method also provides a wide scope for the achievement of cognitive goals. When outdoor education is structured to a problem-solving approach and there is genuine educational *experience*, these outdoor activities can make a positive contribution to the general aim of education: to develop an intelligent rational human being.

The subject called outdoor education in the Western Australian curriculum is a part of this policy. It has its conceptual base in physical education and a major goal is to develop students' ability to manage the physical challenge of the natural environment.

The framework developed for experience-based education fits comfortably into the normal expedition format. It uses the facts and technical skills of expedition and the forces of nature as the foundation for developing objective judgement in the outdoors. This goal is intrinsic to the process which evolves from the stated objectives (*brief*) and criteria for assessment (*debrief*) so that objectives are tested and changed for a new level of challenge. The dynamic nature of the process is appropriate for the dynamic process of expedition which continually involves choices and decisions.

If the procedure follows a person-oriented scientific method of problem-solving, the expedition affords opportunities to develop the self-reliant decision-maker for our democratic society. The risk factor, the challenge of the unknown, inherent in the unpredictable nature of the natural environment, is an essential quality of outdoor education. It provides the infrastructure for the development of judgement and, consequently, self-responsibility because individual differences require individual judgement. Furthermore, self-knowledge and self-understanding rely on the ability for self-assessment and self-commitment. The challenge only becomes adventure when there is self-responsibility for success. Planning and preparation are major components for the successful adventure, but the unpredictable nature of the environment requires decisions in circumstances for which there is no specific precedent. The ability to make an objective judgement gives back to the individual the opportunity to be in control, to be in charge and to take care of him or herself, the group and the environment. This is fundamental to the development of the autonomous person and the main task of outdoor education.

The Beginning of Outdoor Education in Western Australia

Experience-based education method was encouraged by the introduction of Camp Schools in 1946. National Fitness camps at Point Peron (near Perth) and Albany were used by isolated schools and from 1956 there was an annual camp held for ninety students who were flown over 2,000 km south (from north-west schools) for 3 weeks. The expansion of camping and outdoor activities led to the appointment of a Camp Schools' Officer in 1966. It was a seconded position for a physical education teacher, as were the positions of Camp Directors.

Adventure Camps, held during the summer vacation, were introduced in 1967 for boys and girls from every school in Western Australia who had completed Year 9. Students were introduced to the technical skills of outdoor pursuits and the planning and preparation for canoeing and sailing expeditions. These were the forerunner of the outdoor education courses now offered in high schools for Years 9–12 (aged 14–17 years).

The Education Department (now the Ministry of Education) gradually acquired other camps: a forest camp in Pemberton, the Point Peron camp on Cockburn Sound and, by 1976, an ocean-front camp at Bluff Point in Geraldton.

In recognition of the growth of outdoor education in schools and the changing nature of Camp Schools, the position of Outdoor Education Officer was formalised in 1970, incorporating the role of Camp Schools Officer.

Outdoor Education advisory staff were employed to give programme assistance and teacher development services to schools. With the support of the Australian Schools Commission, in 1975 an Outdoor Education Centre was established on a bushland promontory of the Swan River at Point Walter. Staff assistance, curriculum guidance and equipment were given to schools. It was from here that research into the use of expeditions in education resulted in pilot programmes for schools. Expedition Skills Courses were set up for outdoor leaders and resources and texts were reviewed including Wilderness Education material from the state of Washington, in the United States. Books and visual aids were imported and in-service courses were introduced.

The Sailing Centre at Crawley was an outcome of the Adventure Camps and it was established at the Mounts Bay Sailing Club in 1976. It used GP14 sailing dinghies and sailboards for courses of 10 weeks. It has 2 permanent staff who also conduct 1–week intensive programmes for country schools.

By 1986 there were 8 Camp Schools, including those strategically located at Kalgoorlie, Bridgetown, Carnarvon, Dampier and Broome. Adequate facilities are within reasonable reach of all the centres of population.

The Camp Schools cater mainly for primary schools. Secondary schools now run their own Adventure Camps or, more precisely, Outdoor Expeditions. Pemberton, for example, has developed into a state centre for forest expedition activities and Bridgetown offers canoeing and cycling-based expeditions. Between 1967–76, a 3-masted 17-metre schooner was loaned to Adventure Camps each summer. In 1977, a project involving the

Figure 14.1   Camp Schools, 1986

purchase of this ocean-going vessel was accepted by the Schools Commission. They provided, under the special innovation programme, a grant sufficient for the Education Department to purchase and refit the schooner and it operated out of all major ports along the Western Australian coastline, from Esperance to Port Hedland, throughout the school year. The demand for places far exceeded the capacity of the vessel.

A Youth Sailing Foundation was established in 1984 with the objective of replacing the schooner with a larger sailing vessel. The 28m *Evening Star* was purchased in 1985, and is a most appropriate sailing vessel for the 14–17 year age group (Years 8–12) and their school outdoor education programmes.

In 1983, the Royal Australian Navy vacated their Leeuwin boatshed which was located over the Swan River, just downstream from Point Walter. The value of such a facility for outdoor education was conveyed to the State Minister for Education. His efforts, through the Premier of Western Australia to the Commonwealth government, were successful in obtaining the boat-shed for educational purposes, in 1984. The outdoor centre at Point Walter was incorporated into the Expedition Boat-shed. Gunter-rigged cutters form the nucleus of an extensive range of innovative resources used to help students learn to manage the outdoor challenge. Instruments for reading pressure, tides, wind, direction and so on; charts and maps; ropes and shackles, carabiners and pulleys; and all appropriate equipment for outdoor adventure are housed in this unique boatshed. The debriefing areas, the jetties, boat ramp, marine tank and the display boards of current adventure topics and maritime information, all serve to create a challenging atmosphere.

Outdoor Education became a Board of Secondary Education Achievement Certificate option for Years 9 and 10 after 1970. It had no precise definition, but was recognised as an alternative way of learning for school students. An Interim Overview was distributed to schools as a developmental sequence for understanding the relationship of the human being with the natural environment.

The Ministry of Education was re-organised during 1987 and, in December of that year, the Physical Education Branch was amalgamated with other subject branches, into the Curriculum Directorate. Camp Schools, the Expedition Boat-shed, *Evening Star* and the Sailing Centre continue, however, to be supervised by the Outdoor Education Officer, who is now attached to the Sports Services section of Curriculum Services Branch.

Current Practice

The objective of outdoor education in Western Australia is to develop students' abilities to manage the physical challenge in the natural environment. This must involve a study of the effects of the outdoor environment on the human being, on group behaviour, and the effect of the human being on the ecological balance.

The specific focus in these areas have been arranged in a developmental sequence in Figure 14.2. The sequence identifies the appropriate tasks for the school Years 1–12 and should achieve the general objectives:

Primary
—to recognise the individual nature of each person for the self-management of well-being
—to understand oneself as an element of a larger group identity
—to demonstrate ecological consciousness

Lower
Secondary
—to perceive group management as a dynamic process involving choices of behaviour
—to manage the objective factors of accident and environmental hazard
—to plan a personal adventure

Upper
Secondary
—to explore the wilderness environment
—to lead an expedition

The learning experiences can be integrated with any school field activity and, in primary schools in particular, they are seen as part of a general policy on outdoor education. They can be structured for residential camps, excursions and general group projects.

The subject of outdoor education is designed in accredited units from Year 8. However, from the earliest years in primary school it is an integrated programme for the acquisition of knowledge, skills and attitudes, to enable the student to make good choices in, and for, the natural environment.

Figure 14.2   Developmental Sequence in Outdoor Education (Years 1-12)

```
                                                    12 Outdoor
                                                       Leadership


        Wilderness Education                          11 Wilderness
                                                         Activities


                                                    10 Expedition Activities


                                                     9 Outdoor Emergency Response


                                                     8 Planning and Democracy


        Residential                                  7 Ecological Awareness
        Camping


                                                     6 Social Relationships


                                                     5 Finding the Way


        Self-management          4 Nutrition and Cooking


                                 3 Shelter and Protection


                              2 Hygiene and Safety


                           1 Personal Comfort
```

Expedition has been identified as the appropriate framework which provides both the content and the experiential process. The content has been specified in Figure 14.3.

The range of experience that students encounter in outdoor education will reflect a balance in the goals:

Management of— self
               — others
               — eco-system

The idea of management implies decision-making, which is based on principles perceived in the presentation of facts and the practice of skills:

—facts and skills of looking after the self out-of-doors: for example, equipment, nutrition, navigation pursuits
—facts and skills of looking after others: for example, group productivity, leadership, first aid, rescue
—facts and skills of looking after the eco-system, for example, ecology, minimum impact.

Teachers have been provided with curriculum assistance and in-service resources in the form of week-long vacation courses using bushwalking, canoeing and sailing as expedition pursuits for experiential education.

Figure 14.3 Outdoor Education Content (Years 1–12)

(1) Personal Comfort

    Comfort zone
    Planning ahead
    Essentials
    Responsibilities (Self-care)

(2) Hygiene and Safety

    Characteristics of natural
      environment
    Energy and pollution
    Injury

(3) Shelter and Protection

    Heat flow
    Insulation
    Temperature control
    Equipment and shelters

(4) Nutrition and Cooking

    Food selection
    Food planning
    Cooking
    Sanitation

(5) Finding the Way

    The Map
    The Compass
    The Route
    The Log

(6) Social Relationships

    Self-responsibility
    Group co-operation
    Conservation
    Camp organisation

(7) Ecological Awareness

    Home, Habitat, Community
    Producers, Consumers, Decomposers
    Adaptation
    Living together

(8) Planning and Democracy

    Planning for camp
    Democratic organisation
    Decision-making
    Group responsibilities

(9) Outdoor Emergency Response

    Fitness for outsiders
    First aid kit for remote areas
    Rope-handling
    Life-saving

(10) Expedition Work

    Acclimatisation
    Mobility skills
    Map and compass
    Communications and records

(11) Wilderness Activities

    Living in a natural environment
    Adventure pursuits
    Navigation
    Survival awareness

(12) Outdoor Leadership

    Wilderness
    Planning and route-finding
    Leadership
    Search and rescue

These Expedition Skills Courses have been used by teachers from all areas of the curriculum and from primary to tertiary years.

Sailing

The outdoor education network of the Ministry of Education, which includes the eight Camp Schools, the Expedition Boatshed, the Sailing Centre and the brigantine *Evening Star*, is the major resource used by teachers and students in the vast number and variety of programmes presented in Western Australian schools. The Expedition Boatshed has been conscientiously designed to help teachers develop their own outdoor programmes and adapt them to the specific area of the curriculum. The main function of the boatshed is to enable schools to use to advantage the vast marine environment of Western Australia. Those sections of the education system using this and the other valuable assets of the network include:

—primary and secondary schools
—special schools for the disabled
—post-graduate course at the Western Australia College of Advanced Education
— undergraduate elective units at the University of Western Australia

Undergraduate students from the Department of Human Movement and Recreation Studies, University of Western Australia, have since 1981 participated in outdoor education courses as an elective in their third year of study for the Bachelor of Physical Education degree. Students continuing on to the Diploma of Education participate in a compulsory outdoor education course. These courses are designed in conjunction with Ministry of Education outdoor education staff and use Ministry facilities.

The boatshed acts as a base for the expedition sailing programme on the *Evening Star*, the replica of the nineteenth-century trading vessel that provides a unique social environment for twenty-four students and school staff on a week-long off-shore expedition. Under the watchful eye of the permanent crew they recognise their individual roles and responsibilities in the efficient running of the sailing ship. A scientific expedition to the Abrolhos Islands or marine studies in the Monte Bello or Dampier Islands can be the highlight of a Year 11 programme.

A Year 9 Unit

The following example of a Year 9 unit indicates the nature of the current guidelines which will determine the future of outdoor education in schools.

Outdoor Education 3.2

Unit Description
This unit is designed to develop a growing sense of competence in dealing with the natural environment, with an emphasis on safety. The method uses an experiential process to develop self-responsibility. The student will gain an understanding of emergency response through emphasis on survival techniques.

Unit Objectives
At the completion of this unit the students will be able to:

—demonstrate the use of ropes and associated equipment in solving problems in the natural environment
—demonstrate adaptation of life-saving techniques in diverse circumstances

Specific Objectives
—identify the properties of ropes and associated equipment
—recognise vocabulary and terminology for communication in ropework
—build a rope ladder with splices and hitch techniques
—haul a weight up and lower a weight down an embankment
—transfer an object across a hazard or imaginary river
—make a shelter with knots and hitches
—demonstrate emergency communications
—construct a stretcher and carry out evacuation procedures
—improvise direction-finding by day and night
—apply the principles of conservation of energy
—demonstrate survival floats and swims
—explain the natural forces of buoyancy in water
—perform life-saving resuscitation and tows

Literacy Objective
—participate in learning activities which encourage discussion and research for reaching generalisations and require a record of activities

Assessment

Self-appraisal is an essential factor in the achievement of outdoor education goals. This is implemented by the use of descriptors for four grades D to A. Each descriptor should be expanded to define the specific understandings which will be evident and observable during the students' performance.

Future Perspectives

The Expedition Boatshed, the *Evening Star*, the Sailing Centre and the eight regional Camp Schools now form a network of curriculum service to the schools, and are developing a computerised system of communication and resources.

Outdoor education staff currently preside over the Curriculum Committee convened by the Secondary Education Authority for the subject outdoor education, for Years 11 and 12 (aged 16–17 years). These courses have been accredited along with those for Years 8–10 (aged 13–15 years), but require alterations for the new unified curriculum. For instance, Years 8–10 are now referred to as Stages 1–6 in the accredited lower secondary, with one stage being a 20 week unit of 40 hours. All secondary school units are now accredited and, as current guidelines are distributed to schools, there should be more uniformity (not conformity).

The initial Expedition Skills Courses set up for the teachers will now be complementary to an Expedition Leadership Course which will be established this year by an Advisory Board convened by the state government. It will be a resource for teachers to learn through an appropriate experiential process.

The position paper of the Board states that:

> Expedition participants must be prepared to become safe people, to accept and practise self-responsibility for sound objective judgement . . . Without an effective leader the experiential learning process (directly represented by the expedition process) cannot function efficiently.

A graduate diploma of outdoor pursuits was offered from the Claremont Campus of WACAE for the first time in 1986. The first group of graduates from the course completed their study in 1987. Liaison with the Ministry of Education has seen the course recognised as one to allow teachers to gain four-year status but at present staff are not able to utilise this award for promotion. This course may eventually transfer into the education section of the Western Australia College of Advanced Education which would better serve the needs of teachers who require experience in developing and adapting curricula on a conceptually sound educational foundation.

15
Outdoor Education in Other Countries

1 Outdoor Education in Canada

Joan Thompson and Chuck Hopkins

Introduction

In order to grasp the nature and extent of outdoor education in Canada, one must first appreciate the incredible size and diversity of the country. It stretches 3,000 km from the Pacific to the Atlantic Ocean and almost the same distance from the border of the United States to the Arctic Ocean. The majority of its 22 million people live close to the southern border, predominantly in the large urban centres of Ontario and Quebec. If the country is huge in area, it has a relatively small population and is blessed with the greatest diversity of natural resources of any country in the world.

Outdoor education in Canada, therefore, encompasses several broad categories: (1) Adventure education (or outdoor pursuits) which capitalises on the rich natural beauty of the land and attempts to bring students into contact with the oceans, spectacular rivers, mountains, lakes, snow and ice of the country; (2) environmental education, which attempts to increase an awareness of the diverse environments of Canada and of the need to manage resources and protect them wisely; and (3) field studies which teach those parts of the curriculum which are best taught outdoors, for example, in the areas of art, history, and geography.

Provincial Policy

Politically, Canada consists of ten provinces and two territories. Education is a provincial responsibility and, therefore, the treatment of outdoor education across the nation is as diverse as the country itself.

To begin with, no provincial department of education recognises outdoor education as a subject area or entity on its own though the term is mentioned often in many official documents. All provinces officially recognise the term environmental education and most have policies or philosophies regarding it. The trend across the country at the elementary level appears to be the integration of environmental education into existing curricula rather than the development of discrete courses, and the use of outdoor education as a teaching medium or methodology.

What most education departments refer to as environmental education really has components of all three areas defined in the introduction. Outdoor pursuits are generally part of the physical education curricula, especially at the secondary level. The provinces of Ontario and Alberta suggest that teachers should look for opportunities for an inter-disciplinary approach to environmental education in the areas of language arts, mathematics, science, social studies and art. This is what is referred to as the field studies component of outdoor education in the introduction.

Environmental education meaning awareness and care of the environment, is more global in nature, transcending subject boundaries. According to Saskatchewan Department of Education, 'The key words in environmental programmes are "awareness" and "attitude" while key words in implementation have been "co-ordination" and "integration".'

At the secondary level, there are more environmental education courses than any other science courses. Most provinces have components of environmental education incorporated into sciences and social studies curricula while some, such as Alberta and Ontario, suggest that teachers should look for opportunities for an inter-disciplinary approach to environmental education in language arts, mathematics, science, social studies and art.

Historical Perspective

Historically, nature-study has been taught by many teachers in the past and forays into the great outdoors to study the environment were taken for granted even in the early one-room schools scattered throughout the countryside of the new nation. Every child in the first half of this century had leaf collections and was expected to know the birds of his area. In the past thirty or so years, however, a greater emphasis has been placed on outdoor education as the public and educators respond to increasing environmental problems.

In Southern Ontario, for example, a devastating hurricane in the 1950s which resulted in massive damage due to flooding, led to the realisation that a watershed style of conservation planning was a priority. As a result, the Metropolitan Toronto Region Conservation Authority was established, with part of its mandate to educate the public.

A man with considerable vision, Bob Dennis, was instrumental in starting the first school board-owned outdoor education centre, Toronto Island School, in 1960. It was followed closely by the opening of Albion Hills Field Centre, run by the Metro Toronto and Region Conservation Authority. Many other outdoor education centres sprang up across the country in answer to the increasing need for such education. These will be dealt with in greater detail later.

Many other provinces responded to concerns for the state of the local environments by creating Departments of the Environment which, in turn, led to inter-governmental committees to develop complementary education programmes. At the same time, many private industries and non-profit groups were developing educational packages and programmes. For example, the Forestry Association in British Columbia operated an outdoor education centre. Several power utilities companies have produced teacher resources including a travelling drama productions dealing with energy conservation. A number of naturalist clubs have produced resource kits for students on such topics as wetlands and endangered species.

Three large-scale projects which involve the fostering of awareness and attitudes towards the environment are Project Wild, Project Learning Tree and SEEDS (Society, Environment and Energy Developments Studies). The unique feature of such programmes is that they are joint ventures of business, industry and education, developed by teachers at arms-length from sponsors. All of these packages include well-developed materials and outdoor activities for teachers and their classes. It is difficult to present topics which attempt to influence attitudes and behaviour without some controversy. Some critics claim that these programmes present a biased viewpoint and also that very serious environmental issues are reduced to simplistic games. Nevertheless, at least five provinces actively endorse these projects for their schools.

Another recent phenomenon which is having a profound effect on the school system is the increase of multicultural diversity in Canadian society. Conflicting cultural values as they relate to the environment must be faced. Education of children can lead to education of parents and grand-parents. Some social agencies and community school programmes have begun to involve parents and grand-parents in outdoor sessions and overnight experiences.

Current Outdoor Education Practices

In order to be most effective and to have the greatest educational impact, the environment must be experienced first-hand. Much of what is called environmental education is, unfortunately, taught indoors. Outdoor experiences for students in Canada range from first investigations in the schoolyard, to studies of local parks and communities, to visits to outdoor day centres, to residential field centres and extended trips. For example, in the Northwest Territories there are programmes where students spend extended periods surviving off the land in an effort to retain native skills. Numerous students across the land re-enact native methods of travel through canoe trips and excursions on snowshoes. History is studied by following the routes of early explorers, by canoe or overland. In Ontario at Ste Marie among the Hurons, a seventeenth century Jesuit mission, students may live in restored buildings reliving the hard winter conditions of those early missionaries. They cook and heat with fire and learn the trades of the time by candlelight. In most provinces, as in Manitoba, school camping and wilderness tripping are important. The same is true in Northern Ontario where school-based Outers Clubs are popular.

Day centres operate across the country, some owned by Boards of Education, some privately owned and some by groups such as conservation authorities. In New Brunswick, one such centre is the Huntsman Marine Laboratory. A staff member travels across the province presenting workshops to students who, in turn, may visit the centre for a closer look at marine biology. The Kortright Centre for Conservation north of Toronto has practical displays and demonstrations of conservation topics for the general public as well as school groups.

Urban studies programmes in cities like Toronto, Hamilton, Waterloo and Vancouver introduce students to environmental issues and community studies in an urban setting. The Toronto Board of Education has a large Urban Studies Centre offering a variety of programmes and resources for its teachers and students.

The value of a residential outdoor education experience for children is recognised in all provinces. Facilities range from leased camps where students and teachers plan and cook their own meals in addition to the programme; to extensive complexes such as the newly opened Mono Cliffs Outdoor Education Centre north of Toronto, which doubles as a professional development site for teachers.

The commitment of the six Metropolitan Toronto school boards to outdoor education is evident in that they all now own their own residential centres to which all children have free access. The value of bringing city children, especially the high proportion who are recent immigrants, into direct contact with the natural environment cannot be underestimated. The future of the country and indeed the world depends on environmentally aware and informed citizens.

Unique Programme Approaches

Across the country from the Strathcona Centre in British Columbia to Father Brennan Outdoor Environmental Centre in Newfoundland, the programmes and facilities are varied and unique. Programmes offered typically reflect the special skills of the staff or the unique local resources. Often, too, the programme reflects the particular mandate of the governing body. In addition to full and varied curriculum offerings, centres have one or two distinguishing peculiarities. For example:

—Strathcona Centre, on the Pacific coast, in British Colombia, offers sea kayaking
—Fort Whyte Nature Centre near Winnipeg and Mont Ste Hilaire near Montreal are located in International Biosphere Reserves
—The MacSkimming Centre near Ottawa has a farm operation and apiary
—Sheldon Centre for Outdoor Education near Toronto capitalises in its local pioneer history and has a small hands-on museum
—Boyne River Natural Science School, owned by the Toronto Board, has rock-climbing and a working sawmill
—In Quebec, where two separate school systems exist, French and English-speaking, some schools lease small resorts (Ecoles de Neige) where students study academic subjects for half the day during their stay and spend the other half skiing
—North Vancouver Outdoor School has a large on-site salmon hatchery
—Camp Kandalore, in northern Ontario, is one of several camps that places an emphasis on water sports. Adjacent to it is the Kanawa Canoe Museum.

The programme emphasis of residential centres can vary from adventure to environmental to social to values oriented, but is usually a combination of all of these.

Some programmes also exist for special populations such a Project DARE in northern Ontario which was developed to give troubled youths an intense groups living, high adventure experience in order to foster feelings of self-worth. Similar programmes exist in other provinces.

Skiing in Canada

Teacher Education and Support

Most teacher training institutions include at least a small component of outdoor or environmental education in their programmes. Some, however, are better known for specific programmes. At Simon Fraser University in British Columbia, for example, teachers are trained to use local community resources. Queen's University in Kingston offers a special undergraduate diploma in experiential education. Lakehead University at Thunder Bay offers special outdoor education programmes to undergraduates. Nipissing University in North Bay prepares teachers to work with indigenous students in outdoor skills. The Nova Scotia Teachers' College gives environmental education courses to student teachers at a residential field centre. Many colleges and universities such as Memorial University in Newfoundland produce environmental materials and resources for teachers.

At the graduate level, York University, Queen's and Brock in Ontario all offer course towards Masters degrees in Education with an environmental focus. In the province of Alberta, the University of Alberta, at Edmonton, Calgary and Lethbridge have transferable post-graduate courses in the field to facilitate teacher in-service.

Outdoor and Environmental Education Associations

Active outdoor or environmental education associations of teachers exist in most provinces. They range in membership from 300 to 700 members each, drawn from all levels of education, camps, government agencies and conservation authorities. Several, including those in British Columbia, Alberta, Manitoba and Ontario, have regular newsletters and hold conferences and workshops. Two multi-national conferences (Man-Environment Impact) were held in 1976 and 1982. These drew over 4,000 participants. As yet, there is no national organisation, although the North American Association of Environmental Education includes over 600 members from both Canada and the United States.

Studying

Problems Faced in Outdoor Education in Canada Today

As could be expected in a country where the small population is spread over such a large area, communication is a major problem. Teachers tend to operate in isolated pockets even within provinces and have little opportunity for dialogue and the exchange of ideas. In provinces with active professional organisations, conferences and newsletters help. In Ontario, the government subsidises travel of teachers from remote areas to larger centres for professional development in outdoor education. This greatly facilitates provincial outdoor organisation. Because no national organisation exists, neither does a national communication mechanism. Through the Man and the Biosphere Information and Training Network (MAB-NET), a working group on Environmental Information and Teaching has sprung up with representatives across the country. They are now connected electronically via telecommunication and it is hoped that, through this group, the inter-provincial sharing of environmental information will increase, perhaps even leading in the future to the production of a national journal of environmental education.

Recognition of outdoor education as a valuable, indeed necessary part of education, is still a problem in many parts of the country. The British Columbia Department of Education is concerned with how to evaluate outdoor education effectively. There is a need for more research to provide concrete evidence of the value of such education. The body of research in the field is growing in Canada and more concrete evidence of its value, as an educational tool, is expected.

Future Trends

Canada is changing at an accelerating rate. Technological advances, increasing pollution of air, soil and water are all putting additional pressure on governments, business, industry and education. Environmental education has moved through phases of first creating awareness and increasing knowledge about the world around us to try to control, manage or manipulate the environment. At a time when there is a call for 'back to basics' in education, there can be nothing more basic than the survival of our planet. The forces of nature are too strong to bow to man's manipulation. We must learn to live with constant change and teach our young people the skills to adapt to change which is inevitable.

Summer camps, long a Canadian tradition, have contributed to increased independence and confidence in young people and a level of skill in outdoor pursuits which carries over into adult life. Many such camps are now open year-round as outdoor centres for the use of school groups and other organisations, and some are beginning to devote time to seniors through the Elderhostel movement.

Organisations such as the Federation of Ontario Naturalists and Outward Bound are expanding their clientele to include trips and courses for groups such as senior citizens, indigenous people, the handicapped and women.

People in Canada, especially in urban areas, appear willing to travel further and further to experience a little 'wilderness' and adventure in their leisure time. Hence the increased interest in boating, snow-mobiling, white-water rafting, hot-air ballooning and even dog sledding. Conflicts inevitably develop between recreational user groups and recreationists and those who traditionally have earned their livelihood from the land through lumbering, mining, trapping and so on. As technology advances and the world becomes an increasingly impersonal place, people will look more and more to the natural environment to improve the quality of their own inner environments. Experiences in the natural world will play an increasingly valuable role in the lives of adults and senior citizens as the population ages.

Over the past several years, there has been a proliferation of environmental sub-groups: experiential educators, adventure educators, earth educators and so on. It is important, though we all have our own special areas of interest, not to become too fragmented. It is imperative that we remember what we are all about—for our children and for the future. Outdoor education has an important role to play in preparing people of all ages for the changing world and in helping promote a commitment to protecting the environment from the often destructive impact of humankind.

2 Outdoor Education in Britain

Chris Loynes

Origins

The use of the outdoors for education began in Britain because two men felt it was the right thing to do. They were concerned about the moral fibre of young men and saw the outdoor challenge as part of an approach to education that would address the need to develop them physically, socially, morally and spiritually. The modern equivalent is called development training and it is perhaps appropriate that the current popularity of this approach is so well founded in the roots of the concept. The two men were Baden-Powell and Kurt Hahn.

Baden-Powell recognised the positive benefits of the outdoor life while fighting the Boer War. Adventure, challenge, a common purpose, comradeship and living together were all recognised as important at this stage. On return to England, Baden-Powell experimented with simple camps operating a troop structure with programmes which involved a residential experience, group work, and new and adventurous activities which sought to promote self-reliance. This was quickly followed by the Guide movement for girls. Often the initiative for the formation of a troop came from the boys, who then sought a leader. Baden-Powell also set standards for leadership, being first and foremost interested in the development of young people, understanding their needs, leading by example, delegating responsibility, and using a discovery method of learning. If 'backwoodsmanship' set a bad example in environmental ethics it was through ignorance rather than design. The modern Scout and Guide movements, the largest voluntary youth movement in the world, are still founded on these essentials. The expedition and the outdoors are still major and central parts of their curriculum.

The expedition was also a central part of Hahn's early thinking, as part of the personal development programme at Gourdonston School where he was Head. The forerunners of what was to become the Duke of Edinburgh's Award Scheme, also inspired and initiated by Hahn, incorporated an expedition. The scheme and its aims bear a striking resemblance to those developed by the Scout movement, and the two now work closely together. However, it was with Outward Bound that Hahn made his biggest impact and this is really the birthplace of outdoor education. Starting in 1941 with the first school at Aberdovey on the Welsh coast, Outward Bound developed month-long adventure programmes incorporating adventure and group activities, expeditions and community work. Challenge, self-reliance and leadership were key ingredients. The aim was character building and the setting wild country. The schools were not elitist, recruiting participants from factories and Borstals as well as schools. The approach did not emphasise athletic achievement but rather tenacity of pursuit and the education of the whole person. Courses for girls began in 1951. Six schools were founded in Britain, of which five remain. There are now many more world-wide.

The Birth of Outdoor Education

In 1950, Derbyshire Local Education Authority founded Whitehall Open Country Pursuits Centre and began a trend of activity in the outdoors that acquired the title outdoor pursuits. The increasing number of schools, youth clubs and colleges that became involved during the 1960s initially used land-based activities. Participation was mostly outside school time and voluntary in nature. Participants were mostly of average intelligence, fit, motivated and obedient, and the expectations leaders had of them influenced the kind of experience offered. The aim of such programmes was largely proficiency and self-sufficiency, very different from the personal development aims of Outward Bound and the Scout movement. The focus was on the activity rather than the participant. With an emphasis on skill development, teaching styles were directive and inflexible. Early and justifiable concerns about safety tended to reinforce this approach as the best way to ensure the necessary ability for safe performance.

Field Studies

The Field Studies Council runs a number of centres in Britain. In developing courses for students taking higher school and university subjects related to the environment, the council devised an approach which was quickly adopted by schools. Attendance at a field studies course is currently the commonest means by which students gain residential experience, and participation is frequently required by the examining boards' syllabuses.

Increasingly, project work and excursions are made in the local environment. The approach shifted from the use of the field as an outdoor classroom to using it as a laboratory, applying a discovery method of learning. Recent work takes an issues-based approach. The learning model involved can be summarised as head, heart and hands, i.e., from knowledge and understanding to empathy and action. One Devon school prepares a centre spread on community issues for the local newspaper researched and written by the students. The primary school curriculum lends itself to work based around outdoor visits. Here are to be found some of the best examples of curriculum enrichment with the outdoor experience being integrated into every aspect of the schools' work. Additionally, basic concepts of global and local ecology are being introduced and environmental awareness is practised rather than preached.

Development and Change

Over the last fifteen years, the three strands of personal development, outdoor pursuits and field studies have seen many developments and much change.

More young people are involved in a wider range of activities, some of which, like board-sailing and mountain-biking, are very recent innovations. Many activities have developed offshoots which bear little resemblance to the pure forms from which they sprang. For example, abseiling is often provided as an activity in its own right, completely divorced from climbing.

Improvements in the range and standard of equipment now available also permit groups to operate at higher levels of achievement without lowering safety standards. A good example is the change from canvas to glass fibre and now plastic and aluminium canoes.

The Ambleside Area Adventure Association, a voluntary community group in the English Lakes District, has a strong canoeing club working with all ages (in Britain canoeing is a generic term for the sport; this association uses kayaks). In competition the club has trained junior national and world champions and has several members competing in the premier British slalom division. Expeditions include a 100-mile, 4-day trip on the Wye, a Welsh river with several rapids, undertaken independent of adults by 12-year-olds; and a sea tour off the Scottish coast with a group whose ages range from 13 to 40. Quality coaching and committed members made this possible, but so did modern materials and designs without which the progress made with young members would have been impossible, the risks faced on the Wye and the sea unacceptable, and the competition achievements unattainable.

The settings in which activities take place have also diversified. For logistical and financial reasons it is often easier to bring the activity to the client than it is to take the client to the activity in its natural surroundings. Increasingly, adventure activities can be found in the wasteland aftermath of urban renewal, and canals and small reservoirs are being used for water-based sports. The ultimate extension of this has been the creation of artificial environments such as dry ski slopes and climbing walls. Perhaps the leading example is the Ackers Trust within a mile of the centre of Birmingham on an old waste tip, where a canal and a railway cross. Nearby are the derelict buildings of the old BSA works. The area is characterised by old residential housing. It is a poor district with a wide variety of ethnic groups represented. The BSA social club was taken over as a community centre, and the derelict land set aside as a nature reserve and park. The contours of the rubbish heap have been used as the base for a motor bike scramble course and road training facility. A trim trail quickly sprouted followed by a ski slope on the biggest mound of rubbish and a climbing tower was built in the centre of the park. There are plans for an indoor equestrian centre in an adjacent empty factory. The canal has been dredged (there are more miles of canals in Birmingham than in Venice) and two narrow boats and a fleet of canoes are available. There is open access to the local community as well as educational and recreational groups. The site managers provide supervision where necessary but prefer to train group leaders in the skills needed to run their own sessions.

With the raising of the school leaving age in 1974, the experiential approach of outdoor education has increasingly found a home as part of the school timetable as a more relevant way of learning for low-achieving pupils. The recently-introduced programmes of personal and social education in many schools also often use outdoor education, further increasing the use of the local environment as the arena for outdoor education.

Cumbria Local Education Authority was the first to issue a policy statement on outdoor education. It begins:

Outdoor education is widely accepted as the term to describe all learning, social development and the acquisition of skill associated with living and journeying in the outdoors. In addition to physical endeavour, it embraces environmental and ecological understanding. Outdoor education is not a subject but an integrated approach to learning, to decision-making and the solution of problems. Apart from opportunities for personal fulfilment and development of leisure interests, Outdoor education stimulates the development of self-reliance, self-discipline, judgement, responsibility, relationships and the capacity for sustained practical endeavour.

The Authority owns and staffs three residential centres and has mounted an in-service training programme for teachers to acquire the necessary skills and concepts. They state:

> Outdoor Education embraces three interlinked areas of experiential learning, through outdoor pursuits, outdoor studies and the residential element.

A curriculum model incorporates these 3 strands from ages 4 to 19 and advisory teachers have been appointed to promote and resource its implementation.

Experiential Learning

Few would disagree that outdoor education and experiences in a residential setting have a unique part to play in extending opportunities for young people to develop, learn and grow, because of the range of opportunities available for experienced-based learning. This approach to education and training relies almost totally upon the participants being completely involved in their learning and taking a genuine responsibility. They are invited to think, share ideas, make decisions and exercise independence in the carrying out of activities. However, educationalists assumed that learning automatically occurred as a result of experience-based activities; that, when participants are subjected to a range of exciting and challenging activities, attitudes are automatically moulded or re-shaped. There is little evidence to support this assumption and the realisation of this has seen one of the more recent major developments in approach.

If activities are to affect personal and social development and have full impact and more relevance, then there must be opportunities for preparation, evaluation and reflection. This has led to a change in the approach of many leaders, who have adopted a facilitative approach, a long way from conventional styles of imparting, instructing and directing. In particular, it requires sensitivity to draw out the personal learning as a result of an activity or experience. One trainer put it: 'I sit them down at the end of each activity and tell them what they did wrong!': this is the old approach. The changed process has become known as reviewing.

The Brathay Hall Trust, founded in 1946, was the first residential centre to develop this approach and is now widely regarded as a centre of excellence. They were responsible for coining the term development training and have applied it to activities such as work experience as well as the outdoors, which they regard as only one, albeit a potent one, of the tools available. Development Training is based on the learning model 'do, review, apply' illustrated in Figure 15.1. After an experience, people in the learning group articulate their reactions while reviewing how they worked together, drawing conclusions and applying these to real life situations. The tutor facilitates this process by helping the group to structure their thinking and to confront the issues that arise.

Figure 15.1 Reviewing as Part of the Experiential Learning Process

To illustrate this method, imagine a group of school children on the early stages of a residential course aimed at exploring group co-operation and individual capability. The tutor decides to use the low ropes course and, after a practice run, ties the group together with a long rope and asks them to see how far they can get as a group. During the task, problems arise in managing the rope; also, the fit people at the front have not made allowances for the more timid near the back. In review, the tutor asks the group to model where they were at a particular point of tension and helps each person to explain how they felt about the task and the group at that point. In discussion, the group decides they need to set up a buddy system, listen to each other, speak up more when help is needed, respect individual strengths and support weaknesses. This activity might be followed by a mountain walk or a climbing session where the group can apply this experience to a new task. Later, they will consider how to apply his new understanding to work situations into which they are going. The Brathay Hall Trust have found this approach particularly useful in management and leadership training, therapeutic work and for personal development at times of transition such as school to work.

Residentials and Expeditions

Residential experience as an aid to learning is not a new idea. In 1963, the *Newsom Report* confirmed the conviction of many teachers that a wide range of activities developed in a residential context provided an abundance of opportunities to enhance and extend learning. Out of it emerged an almost unique environment to promote social and personal development and to bring teachers and young people into closer contact. In the last twenty years, the increasing use of residential centres by schools, youth clubs and colleges testifies to the rapid demand for such provision. Significantly, most of the major curriculum initiatives currently being developed stress the potential value of a period of residential experience. Many education authorities have their own centres, often in distant wild country locations. Some schools use other facilities as a base for running their own programmes.

A recent trend has been the acquisition of simple accommodation by individual schools, often quite close to home for maximum accessibility. The Peers' School in Oxford is an example. The simple hut, with its own wind-generated power and water supplies and two fields from any road, is within half-an-hour of the school. The rural setting and the simple life-style and teaching style are deliberately in contrast with the school environment. Groups can use the centre on a part-day or residential basis and it is built into the curriculum in many ways including field studies, personal and social education, outdoor pursuits and class tutorial work. In such a setting it is easy to have a different kind of relationship with pupils.

It has also become common to recognise that pupils who are involved in the design of their own experience will learn a great deal more from it due to their investment in the outcome. A Bradford school uses a series of day and multi-day journeys designed, organised and carried out by pupils as the centre of a curriculum for low achieving pupils. Their literacy, numeracy, practical skills and life skills are all focused on the task of carrying out the residential programme. This is achieved on a minute budget and at a site which is no more than a day or two's cycle ride from the school. The danger has become that the rest of the school's pupils would like the same approach! In Dudley, one school has done just that and each pupil carries out a residential in each year of their school career, with increasing amounts of responsibility. However, right from the start, each student chooses the activities, the location and member of staff who will help them. It is apparent that the most effective residential programmes are carefully structured to meet predetermined aims and the learning experiences integrated with the curriculum. The use of the residential has also expanded across the age range with many effective examples from the primary sector.

Yet another popular approach incorporating many of the above factors is the expedition. The Young Explorers Trust, the umbrella body of youth expeditions in Britain, annually advises and supports some 40 trips and is aware of some 40 others. This is the tip of an iceberg as it only includes overseas trips. There will be many more within the country. Destinations range right round the world with recent venues in Nepal, Peru and China as well as the Arctic, the desert and rain forest. Projects range from adventure and field work to community service. The recent trip to Nepal by St Xaviers School from Essex, five years in the planning, combined with a Nepalese school to climb in the local mountains. All the equipment is home made and that which was used by the Nepalese students was left with them along with the equipment to make more and the training to do it. This was an excellent example of both cultures learning about and from each other for, in return, the Essex students received some Gurkha-style survival training from the Nepalese.

Diversity

Traditionally, most user groups have operated within the structures of local education authorities. However, recent developments have encouraged other groups to use the outdoors for their own, equally valid, purposes. Social services, recreation programmes, the Manpower Services Commission and community groups are all part of this growth.

Opportunities to gain proficiency in the skills of an activity are no longer confined to remote and inaccessible outdoor centres but can increasingly be found in the community as part of the recreation department or youth service provision. The Sobell Sports Centre in the centre of London was the first such centre to include outdoor activities in its programme. In addition to the centre facilities of ski-slope and climbing wall, a programme of activities such as street orienteering and canoeing was established in the neighbourhood and trips away arranged for the clients. This became a busy focus involving many in the outdoors for the first time.

Fringe groups only marginally related to mainstream education are becoming increasingly involved in exploiting the potential of the residential. Where a residential experience is recommended as part of a course, as is the case with the Youth Training Scheme for unemployed 16-to-18-year-olds, it is often associated with some use of the outdoors as a medium to develop personal effectiveness. IBM run such a scheme over 2 years during which the trainees attend three 5-day residentials. The first aim to develop the participants' confidence and their ability to work together. The second explores taking responsibility for standards and making things happen. The last is a chance to reflect on their own abilities and aptitudes and put them into practice. The supervisors of the trainees also attend a residential to experience what the trainees have gone through first-hand and acquire facilitating skills to help them transfer the learning to the workplace.

The social service and the probation service have been exploring the value of outdoor and residential programmes for restoring self-esteem and developing positive attitudes in young offenders and children-at-risk. This is meeting with increasing success, especially when it is linked with continued opportunity for participation back in the community. The Drake Fellowship, which arose from the successful Operation Drake, forerunner of Operation Raleigh, operate teams of staff in the inner cities of a dozen towns. Their task is to identify disadvantaged young people from all backgrounds and to use outdoor programmes to give them a new direction and perspective. After a standard, two-week programme there are opportunities for several exciting extension projects and drop-in facilities in the urban centre. Some undertake community work, and a great deal of advice and counselling is given. Many of the staff are in fact ex-students of the programme. Although the scheme has the advantage of accessibility and street credibility in the towns in which they work, they also face the burden of the seemingly insurmountably adverse circumstances of inner cities and their crushing effect on people. The fellowship is often the only positive opportunity for many.

There are many new programmes with therapeutic goals intended for the mentally and physically handicapped to extend themselves, work towards independence and to mix with able-bodied people. The Calvert Trust in the Lake District aims to give disabled people as equal access as possible to adventure activities by adapting equipment and appropriate supervision. There is a strong feeling that disabled people have as much right to the benefits of risk-taking and challenge as everyone else. They often display qualities of determination and courage others cannot manage and the delight is always apparent.

Outdoor activities are no longer just the preserve of the young. A number of schemes aim at increasing participation among the unemployed and the retired. The male-dominated approach to challenge and adventure is also in the early days of being reassessed and 'feminine values' are being introduced, with girls' participation a priority. Outward Bound Eskdale ran the first all-women's course, with participants exploring their attitudes and their capabilities. The Water Activities Centre, run by Manchester Youth Service, has also addressed female participation by various strategies including all-girls' sessions, changes in teaching style and content, and positive discrimination doubling girls' participation in the centre over five years.

The most recent trend is the increasing interest being shown by urban community and play groups, initially in local environments, but moving further afield as confidence and experience grows. All this demonstrates a greatly expanding range of users with diverse aims and approaches.

Relevance

The impact of diversity has brought about what are perhaps the most important developments in outdoor education to date. There have been fundamental changes in philosophy. The natural environment and its activities have come to be regarded by many no longer as simply a subject to be taught. The outdoors is seen as a medium and the concern is to use it as a vehicle to provide situations for learning with the aim of developing self, social and environmental awareness. The emphasis is moving from learning about a subject or an activity to the process of learning itself. The early thinking of Baden-Powell and Hahn is undergoing a reappraisal and, with updated values, is being found to be increasingly appropriate as an approach to learning for a modern world.

3 Outdoor Education in West Germany

Oswald H. Goering

Introduction

The natural environment has always been important to the people of Germany. The climate is pleasant and the landscape is inviting. The landscape, with its intermingling of fields, forests and picturesque villages beckons one to partake of its beauty by wandering through it. As one travels in Germany, one cannot help but be impressed with the large numbers of people out strolling or hiking through its fields and woods. There has developed among the German people a deep appreciation for the outdoors and great support for conservation of the natural environment.

It seems only natural that schools should include outdoor and community activities in their educational programmes. In fact, throughout modern German history, schools have made extensive use of outdoor and community resources as an integral part of the educational process. It is common to see teachers with their children on the sidewalks of cities, observing some historically significant building or monument, or wandering in the woods or mountains. Some of these activities in outdoor settings may, for brief periods of time, focus on some specific subject matter. Or they may last for several weeks, and take place in a resident outdoor education centre.

Teachers are encouraged by the state education offices as well as by the general public to include outdoor activities as part of their classroom work. Historic buildings, churches, monuments and museums, accessible fields and forests and a supportive public do much to support and encourage teachers to include outdoor experiences in their educational programmes.

The German School System

The public schools of Germany are independently administered by each of the states forming the Federal Republic. This means that school codes, requirements and methods vary from state to state. Teachers certified in one state may not meet the certification requirements of another.

The foundation of the educational system is the Volksschule (primary or people's school) where the educational process begins for all children. All children attend the Volksschule for a minimum of four years. Then those desiring to enter the Gymnasium (high or university preparation school) take an examination. If they pass they will enter the Gymnasium the following year. There are other routes to the Gymnasium, such as taking an examination after the sixth year of primary school. Once there, they will continue their studies to Grade 13 before taking the final examinations while, if passed, grant them entrance into university.

The school system provides a variety of other educational opportunities. A child may stay in the Volksschule until Grade 8 or 9 and enter a trade school to learn a specific vocation. Instead of going into a Gymnasium which places a great deal of emphasis on the classical languages, pupils can now select schools focusing on modern languages or on the sciences.

The educational system in Germany has undergone radical changes since World War II. The formal classroom, where a child did not speak until spoken to, is now much more relaxed, with students working in 'committees'. The schools established for American dependants after the War served as models, and American teaching methods were soon copied by the German teachers.

The daily school schedule begins with classes at eight in the morning, and children remain in school until 1–1.30 pm. At about 10 am there is a break, during which the children will eat a sandwich. Children carry all their books to and from school, as class time is used primarily for lecture and discussion, and they have heavy homework assignments. Physical education is a part of the school programme although athletics is conducted by sports clubs rather than being part of school.

History of German Outdoor Education

Activities conducted outside the classrooms in German schools can be put into three categories which will be discussed later in detail. These are the Wandertag (school hikes), Unterichtsgange (field trips), Schullandheim Aufenhalt (resident outdoor education) and extended field trips to other cities. The state school codes encourage teachers to have their classes participate in each of these activities. If the outdoors has always played an important role in the German Education system, little was written about it before World War 1. School journeys which permitted teachers to take their classes as excursions lasting as long as a week to study natural history and geography first-hand were started in the province of Saxony at the end of the nineteenth century.

Another important precursor was the beginning of the Wandervogel (Birds of Passage) movement, in 1901. Karl Fischer, a senior student in a secondary school in Berlin, started to organise groups of students and other youths for hikes into the countryside to 'discover nature in adventurous and spartan travels'. Although this movement lasted only until the beginning of World War 1, its influence was considerable, resulting in the establishment of the Youth Hostel and Resident Outdoor Education Programmes.

Richard Schirrmann was a young elementary school teacher in Altena in Westphalia at the beginning of the century who regularly took his classes on school journeys. Some of these lasted as long as 8 days and covered as much as 300 kilometres, mostly on foot. One of the problems that he encountered was that of overnight accommodation. On one of these journeys, in 1909, he passed an empty school building in a village and the idea came to him that almost every village had a school building with some empty rooms that could be made available to teachers and youth groups. From this idea evolved the youth hostel movement. Today, there are over 600 youth hostels in West Germany, many of which were especially designed for school use, providing day rooms as well as room and board. In 1986, in the state of Bavaria alone, there were 108 Youth Hostels with over 12,000 beds and a total of 1,560,000 over-nights. School classes accounted for 55.5 per cent of this total. Many of these hostel facilities are located in scenic and/or historical places, ranging from restored buildings and castles to modern buildings.

During World War 1, children were taken out of the large German industrial cities into rural villages to help with agricultural work and get away from bombing. This rural experience was later recognised by parents and school authorities as being both healthy and educationally valuable. Independently, schools acquired or built homes in the country to which their teachers were encouraged to take their classes for 2–4 week periods.

By 1925, there were over 100 of these residential outdoor education centres. It was decided at a national education convention in Berlin in that year to form a national organisation called Verbandes Deutscher Schullandheime (Association of German School Country Homes). Further national conventions were held in Hamburg in 1928, in Dresden in 1930 and in Hanover in 1933. After this period of rapid growth, by 1939, there were over 400 of these resident outdoor education centres in Germany.

The War years were difficult times for the centres. When the Nazis came to power, control of them was taken out of the hands of the schools and placed into those of the Hitler Youth. Later on in the war they served a variety of purposes, being used, for instance, as hospitals and refugee centres.

After the War there was renewed interest in the programme. Once again there was rapid growth. In 1949, there were 116 centres in West Germany, but the number grew to 360 in the 1960s. In 1986 at the National Outdoor Education Convention in Hamburg, the current number of resident centres was reported as being 348. The drop in the numbers in the last few years is attributed to the drop in the number of children in school due to smaller modern families. The outdoor education association, located in Hamburg, publishes a quarterly journal, *Das Schllandheim*.

Outdoor Education Programmes

Outdoor experiences are today an integral part of educational programmes in both primary and secondary schools. Since the classes are self-contained in the Volksschule, it is easier to arrange for field trips than it is in secondary schools, where educational programmes are departmentalised. Some secondary schools schedule field trips for the entire school on the same day so as not to interrupt the school programme. The home room teacher plans the experience for their own students.

All teachers are encouraged to include Unterichtsgange (educational field trips) in their classroom activities. These may be to an arboretum to study plants, a zoo to study animals, a natural area to study wild-life inter-relationships, or to a rock quarry to study rock formations or fossils. They may be as short a period as a half-hour or as long as a full day, depending on the distance to be travelled and the nature of the experience. The central purpose of this type of field trip is to study a specific topic or to clarify a concept.

School hikes (Schulwanderung) differ from educational field trips. Their objectives are more general and focus on the development of an appreciation and understanding of the natural environment, the establishment of better student-teacher and student-student relationships, and the provision of a change of pace for students from the normal school schedule. The school hike programme begins with Grade 5 and the

Bavarian school code suggests that a teacher take from 6 to 8 days a year for activities of this nature. The duration of a school hike is usually a day, but may extend over a number.

In the primary school, where there are self-contained classrooms, teachers may schedule activities at their pleasure and where it best fits their schedules. In secondary schools, where programmes are departmentalised, scheduling becomes more difficult. In some of these schools, all classes in the same grade will go on a school hike on the same day. In some cases the entire school will go on specified days, and a visitor may find the entire school empty. In the primary school, it is not uncommon for some classrooms to be empty as teachers and their pupils participate in out-of-class activities.

A typical school hike will begin at eight in the morning, with the children meeting at the school where they take a bus or a train out of the city. Reduced prices for bus and train tickets make student travel relatively inexpensive. The atmosphere is relaxed, as there is no set subject matter to be learned. Conversation is focused on what is relevant, whether geological land formations or interpersonal relationships. Lunch is usually taken along by the students and a rest stop is made at a place where drinks are available. School hikes are eagerly looked forward to by the children because they are enjoyable and a pleasant change from daily school routine.

The school code for the state of Bavaria says that teachers should take their pupils into a country home (Schullandheim Aufenhalt) for not less than 2 weeks and not more than 4, per year. This kind of encouragement helps to promote such outdoor education programmes, for teachers know that they have the support of the school authorities as well as parents and the community.

The country school homes vary. Some of the outdoor education centres are owned by a school district. The City of Munich, for example, owns four such facilities, which are available to any teacher in the system. More frequently, however, the centres are owned by the school or its parent-teacher organisation. In this case, the parents and the children feel a link with the facilities, and participate in events held there throughout the year. They also participate in work projects such as remodelling, general cleaning or repairs.

Many of the older centres are homes which were acquired though a gift; they may formerly have been the great house of a village or a farm-house. Some of the newer buildings have been specifically designed and built. In almost all, sleeping accommodation is provided for 4–8 children per room. Usually there is a day room which serves as both a multi-purpose room and a classroom. In some cases, the day room is also used as a dining room, but separate eating facilities are preferred. Most of the homes can accommodate 2 classes at once, with each having its own dining room and sleeping quarters.

Each of the homes has resident caretakers, usually a man and his wife. The man will do the maintenance work and the wife will be in charge of the kitchen. In larger homes, there may be an additional cook for bigger groups. Seldom do the resident personnel take part in the educational programme of the children, and nor do they supervise the children at night.

The organisation of the schedule and the educational programme lies with the teacher, usually helped by a person of the opposite sex, who may be student-teacher or a parent. These two are not only responsible for the educational and recreational programme, but also for the supervision of the children 24 hours a day, for the duration of the session, including supervision at mealtime and seeing that the children get to bed.

Historically, the primary purpose of resident outdoor education programmes was to provide children with an experience that would improve both their physical and mental health: city children got good meals, fresh air and exercise. Also important was the relaxed schedule, in contrast to the formal, rigorous classroom one and demanding school assignments. It was also felt that a stay in a rural home would give city children an appreciation of rural life-styles.

Subject matter is not forgotten in modern resident programmes, and children do take their school books along to the outdoor education centres. Teachers feel that even a week away from courses such as languages and maths, would be detrimental. In all the centres that this writer visited, the teachers held regular morning classes while the afternoons were more relaxed, taking in activities such as hiking and field trips. Classes, too, are more relaxed than in schools, and attempts are made to make them relative to the environment of the home. Foreign language evenings or meals are held and vocabulary related to things found in the outdoors emphasised. In all cases, the activities of the week reflected the teacher's interests and skills. If the teacher, for example, is interested in music, then there is singing and/or playing of musical instruments. If the teacher is a naturalist, then the children spend more time outdoors studying the natural environment.

Social learning is emphasised and one of the reasons for the longer period of time spent in homes today is so that there will be enough time for such learning to take place. Teachers were in agreement that 5-day trips were too short, being largely wasted in nervous energy. In a 5-day experience, children are never faced with the fact that they have to develop their own code of living and also get some sleep in order to be able to enjoy the rest of the session. All agreed that real progress in social learning is made during a second week at a centre.

Outdoor Pursuits/Adventure Education

The teaching of outdoor skills in adventure/high risk activities in Germany has traditionally been the responsibility of private schools and clubs. Public schools have included little of these activities in their resident or day outdoor education programmes. Some schools have included activities such as orienteering, hiking, skiing, and outdoor living skills (living in tents and some water sports) but usually do not include higher-risk types of activities.

Shortly after World War II, having founded the Outward Bound programme in England, Kurt Hahn came back to Germany to found the private boarding school in Salem, which is based on participation in adventure/high risk activities. This school has achieved international fame for its programmes.

Before it was set up, there were 4 other centres which focused on short-term (4-week) experiences featuring Outward Bound-type activities. Two of these focused on water activities and were located on the shores of the North Sea in Schleswig-Holstein. These centres are no longer in operation, but 2 more centres have been established in the Bavarian Alps, at Berchtesgaden and Baad, concentrating on mountain experiences including rock-climbing and survival experiences. These experiences last 2 weeks.

Teacher Education

Historically, Volksschule teachers received their education in the Padegosche Hockschule (Teacher Training College), separate from universities. Gymnasium teachers went through the regular university programme, majoring in their chosen field of specialisation. They then served a two-year internship in schools, during which time they gained practical experience and attended teaching-related seminars conducted by university personnel. Today, universities have absorbed the responsibility of educating primary school teachers. The teacher education system now resembles the system of the United States and Australia.

In the state of Bavaria, for example, secondary interns spend one week at an outdoor education seminar, usually in a youth hostel, at the beginning of their second year. Primary school teachers attend similar seminars during the school year. In 1986, the Bavarian State School Administration sponsored 33 of these outdoor teacher education seminars with a total of 702 student teachers as participants. The focus of these was on the preparation of teachers for all kinds of outdoor activities, including educational field trips, school hikes, and residential outdoor education.

These centres have at times used residential school facilities as a place for their short-term programmes but not as a part of the school programme. In the private section, there are a number of clubs that a person can join that focus on adventure activities, but these are not school-related.

4 Outdoor Education in New Zealand

(1) General Overview

Colin Abbott

In 1971, having sailed out of Melbourne some 5 months before, I arrived along with 3 other people in Auckland, New Zealand, on board a small ketch. Our plans to sail around the world were beginning to feel a little ambitious, so we decided to settle instead for a 5-month Pacific trip, terminating in Auckland. As it turned out the mountains, rivers and national parks of this beautiful country were to keep a hold on me for the next 15 years, before I returned to Australia to live. My involvement in the outdoors in general and in outdoor education in particular were the major reason for staying.

Because of New Zealand's small size and its amazingly diverse natural terrain, there is a wide variety of accessible opportunities for outdoor recreation. As a result of its geography and decentralisation, New Zealanders feel closer to the outdoors than Australians, and generally either the coast or the mountains, or both, are within easy reach.

Inevitably, too, outdoor education feels much more a natural part of education. More Headmasters believe in it, more teachers are keen to run trips, and there are fewer problems in getting schoolchildren to bring along a sleeping bag and the other outdoor gear that is needed to run a trip or camp with a minimum of fuss.

Outdoor education in New Zealand is not just outdoor pursuits. In fact, the country has adopted the term Education Outside the Classroom (EOTC) to ensure that the diversity of opportunities beyond school walls are all given credibility in the development of a curriculum. An EOTC trip can be anything from a factory visit to a bird watching trip, from a geography excursion to a rock-climbing excursion or even a mountaineering expedition.

The cultural traditions of the Maoris are also much more a part of the New Zealand way of life than our Aboriginal culture is here in Australia. They are integrated into outdoor education experiences. The Maoris' strong links with the land, their bush survival techniques, their awareness of edible plants and animals, and their folklore are all valuable in developing an environmental and physical ethic for use in the New Zealand outdoors. This process is not only relevant to outdoor education, but also very affirming of Maori children in schools and of the multi-cultural society as a whole.

Another key factor in the development of outdoor education in New Zealand has been the 'no fault' Accident Compensation Scheme. While it was not apparent to me that this led to any reduced level of responsibility among outdoor leaders, it did remove that paranoia that is evident in North America, and is growing in Australia, of potential litigation following possible outdoor accidents.

The outdoors has always played a part in New Zealand education. References to its use in an education context have been noted in documents over a century old. A more recent push began with the School of Physical Education in Otago in the 1940s and 50s, due primarily to the influence of Professor P.A. Smithells, who believed that outdoor education could 'more effectively achieve more educational goals than any other subject'.

In the 1960s and 70s, a number of residential outdoor education centres sprang up, many of them employing resident teachers. Some were funded jointly by a consortium of local schools or in conjunction with a 'trust' body. Gradually, this trend became part of Education Department policies and more tangible support followed. Outdoor education seemed to have come of age when, in 1982, a national conference was held that attracted some 320 participants.

The practices of outdoor education in New Zealand are not very different from those in Australia.

For many schoolchildren, outdoor education begins in the primary school. For the lucky ones, it will continue in a structured and progressive way right throughout primary, intermediate and secondary school. Generally, it will be an integrated programme involving outdoor pursuits and environmental education, with a varying emphasis on personal development opportunities. Some schools in New Zealand own and operate their own camp-sites, while others use either private or Education Department sites, or commercially-operated camps or those independently run by non-profit 'charitable' trusts.

Because of the greater affinity with the outdoors and its more significant place in the lives of New Zealanders, outdoor education has become more solidly entrenched in the New Zealand school system. Not that it doesn't have to fight for funds as Australian outdoor education does. It does, however, seem more acceptable to society at large, and has attracted support in a variety of different ways.

Through continuous series of seminars and workshops, a number of background and working documents for practising teachers and their Principals has been developed. A basic *Policy Statement on Education Outside the Classroom* sets out not only basic policy and aims, but also ideas on programme development, safety and supervision and environmental responsibility. In addition, an outline of advisory sources and supporting agencies is included.

While some of the aims are very similar to those that would be used in Australia and elsewhere, they are interesting in their diversity and breadth:

—To enrich the curriculum by including enjoyable learning experiences outside the classroom relevant to the differing needs of students
—To further opportunities for personal and social development through activities outside the classroom
—To help students to appreciate the inter-relationships within the environment and between people and their environments
—To develop an understanding of the environmental values of differing ethnic and cultural groups and their attitude to land use
—To build up experience and competence in skills for movement with safety and confidence in urban, rural and wilderness settings
—To provide opportunities for adventure and challenge
—To develop with students an appreciation of aesthetic and recreational values

—To enhance the self-esteem of students by developing those strengths and abilities not evident in the classroom
—To provide opportunities for student participation in community and environmental processes
—To provide further opportunities for the community to participate in the education of young people

Another key document, which has been well received in schools is the *Principal's Guide to EOTC*. This not only covers the Principal's responsibilities, and some of the above issues, but also deals with teacher training, leadership and safety guidelines for many of the commonly-run adventure activities.

Another recent development is the Risk Management Training Scheme. This involves a number of training and assessment courses in which participants are given in understanding of key issues in minimising risks in running EOTC programmes. Its completion may be credited towards a Diploma of Teaching or may attract a service increment.

Support for EOTC at national level involves one full-time advisory position as well as regular supporting publications and documentation. In some rural areas a Rural Education Activities Program (REAP) has been set up. Some of these programmes have chosen to employ Co-ordinators of Education Outside the Classroom. One significant development has been the log-book, which includes the logging of outdoor experiences and the self-assessment of personal competence, i.e., teachers are encouraged to take some personal responsibility for their own competence and training. There is Departmental support for various forms of teacher training, both pre and in-service. Limited funding is also available for some of the incidental expenses involved in running school programmes.

There are, in addition, a wide range of community organisations that can provide support for EOTC. Such bodies as the Royal New Zealand Forest and Bird Society, the Mountain Safety Council, the Water Safety Council, the New Zealand Yachting Federation and the Federated Mountain Clubs (to name just a few) are constantly called on to enhance school programmes.

Within these broad frameworks, each school is encouraged to develop its own philosophy and programme. In fact, outdoor education in New Zealand has developed a diversity of activities and facilities. At a primary level, these include a range of camps and camp-sites, many with environmental interpretation facilities and low-key outdoor activities. Typically at this level, activities include walks, initiative games, structured awareness activities and perhaps some basic canoeing. At intermediate level, there are more activities offered, including longer, sometimes overnight, walks, and low-key adventure activities, with more emphasis being put on the children taking some responsibility for themselves. Camps used will probably be in more demanding terrain and may also have available a ropes course.

The types of activities offered at secondary level are more diverse still. They vary from extended base camp experiences to longer walking trips and activities such as rock-climbing, sailing and canoeing. Environmental activities at this level, too, may be quite sophisticated and often curriculum-related, including areas such as geography, mathematics, social

Cycling

studies and science. Many secondary schools use a camp as a way of developing school leadership skills in the top forms.

The facilities offered for outdoor education, especially for secondary level, are quite exciting in their diversity. The *Spirit of Adventure* sail training vessel and, more recently, its sister ship the *Spirit of New Zealand*, offer sail training experiences to a substantial number of young New Zealanders every year. These vessels are based in Auckland and take around 30 young people each trip for 10-day intensive experiences in co-operation, personal awareness and sailing skills.

The Outdoor Pursuits Centre, on the edge of the Tongariro National Park in the centre of the North Island, offers courses to secondary school groups, not only in general mountain activities, but also offers skills training courses in most outdoor activities to school groups, teachers and the general public. It is the most extensive operation of its kind in either Australia or New Zealand.

The Marine Education Centre offers children in the Auckland area a taste of a range of aquatic activities and studies. While it focuses on sailing, it also offers a base for other one-day activities within easy reach of a major population centre.

Outdoor education for other special groups in society, especially, for the disabled and the youth-at-risk, has also developed a strong focus in New Zealand. As in Australia, skiing and riding for the disabled have moved ahead quite strongly. There have also been moves to integrate special groups into general school outdoor education programmes and to design outdoor education facilities with the needs of these groups in mind.

The youth at risk group has benefited from the development of special extended wilderness courses in several centres throughout the country.

These have been officially supported by several government Departments and other major agencies. For instance, probation officers use a range of wilderness experiences offered either by themselves or by outdoor centres as part of the probation/rehabilitation process.

The training of teachers in outdoor education has become very well-established as part of the teacher education system, both in primary and secondary colleges. In some colleges, outdoor education is available as a major subject and, in most of them, teacher trainees get at least a basic introduction to the concepts of Education Outside the Classroom.

In addition to pre-service opportunities, in-service training programmes are often run in schools by nominated skilled teachers and these provide a limited but valuable adjunct to other forms of training.

The use of the outdoors in education, then, has come a long way in New Zealand. It has not only developed a clear philosophical basis, but is also becoming much more widely accepted as a valid educational medium. It has managed to separate itself from the physical education sector of teaching which, in the early days, was where many New Zealanders saw its proper educational place. Today, it has very strong links with environmental and social education, but has also established itself as a valuable approach to education in its own right.

What the future holds will depend very strongly on available finance and the continuing input of its many energetic enthusiasts. I believe the future will also be shaped by such influences as debates on national and international environmental issues, the rapid growth of adventure tourism and the pressing need for our children to have a broad education that gives them the initiative and adaptability to live in a rapidly changing world.

Tramping

(2) Another Perspective

Ian Street

In terms of scenic beauty and diversity of recreational resources, New Zealand is probably one of the most well endowed countries in the world. So it is not surprisingly that use of the outdoor environment is at a high level from a wide range of users, including commercial tourist operations, environmental awareness programmes, management training courses, school curricula, personal development courses and so on.

From each of these fields a number of organisations have been selected as being more or less representative of their genre. Descriptions are designed to be brief cameos of a broader field.

The Hillary Commission for Recreation and Sport

This is an independent, statutory body whose aims are to make sport and recreation accessible and appealing to all New Zealanders. Access to profits from the Lotto lotteries enables the Commission to have a strong base for its discretionary distribution of funds to sporting and recreational bodies throughout the country. Its intentions are:

—to reduce the amount of bureaucratic complexity facing sporting and recreational bodies, so that practitioners exert more control over matters relevant to them
—to establish the place of recreation and sport within the education system
—to emphasise the community and social values of recreation and sport
—to encourage professional thinking in management
—to develop sports science and medicine resources
—to recognise sport and recreation as useful resources in dealing with wider social issues.

The Commission addresses matters of fair play, racism, sexism, physical disablement, non-participation, etc., in an attempt to provide equality of opportunity for everybody (Hillary Commission 1986).

Outdoor Education for Personal Development

The *Cobham Outward Bound School* has been operating at Anakiwa in the Marlborough Sounds of the South Island since 1962. The 'standard' courses offer physical and social challenges in the outdoors to people aged from 18 to 23 years and are designed to enable participants to take a different perspective of their own lives. The 24–day course is organised on a 'scheme' basis, where a scheme is a 3–day expedition which concentrates on such activities as tramping (bushwalking), kayaking on white-water rivers and sailing on the waterways of the Queen Charlotte Sound. Students render service to the community with such activities as helping with geriatric or intellectually disabled patients in nearby towns, clearing public walking tracks for the Maritime Parks Board, collecting litter and so on. They also have a 'solo' scheme where the students are left alone in the bush for 3 days of contemplation.

This Kurt Hahn-inspired course operates on the theoretical basis that young people experiencing success in what they perceive to be challenging tasks will have their self-esteem raised, and that this change in perception is of benefit in their development from adolescence to adulthood. The effectiveness of the courses has been evaluated for some years by a consultant psychologist (Mitchell and Mitchell 1988).

Outward Bound also offers courses specifically designed for people over 30 years old, for school teachers, for the physically and intellectually disabled, for management training, and so on.

Outdoor Education for Youth at Risk

There are more than 30 programs (associated as Te Rangitahi Wilderness) running in different population centres in New Zealand. They are all designed to reduce the anti-social behaviour patterns adopted by adolescents disadvantaged by broken homes, failure at school, etc. In the current economic climate, there is a very high rate of unemployment, especially in the unskilled labour market, which is disproportionately represented by Maori and Pacific Island groups. Rural cities in the North Island (such as Gisborne, Rotorua, Hamilton and Whangarei) have high percentages of these ethnic groups and, consequently, have become centres of social unrest, with large numbers of troubled adolescents.

Northland Wilderness Experience was established in Whangarei (with funding grants from the Department of Social Welfare and the Presbyterian Support Services) to operate as a research body into the 'alienated' and 'at risk' behaviour syndromes, as well as acting as a therapeutic intervention programme for clients. Most of the participants have adopted alternative behaviours (such as alcohol and solvent abuse) to those held as socially acceptable, as their experience with 'normal' behaviours have been unsuccessful (i.e., they have failed at school, etc.). The initial course is a 10-day tramping and kayaking expedition in the rugged coastal regions of Northland, during which the instructors encourage the use of basic communication skills, the expression of feelings, and physical mastery of the immediate situation by participants.

After the initial course, most participants undertake a 'follow-up' programme which can last for up to a year-and-a-half and consists of further contact with the NWE staff for about one day per week. Activities can include more outdoor pursuits such as swimming or rock-climbing or kayaking, but a large proportion of the participants prefer simply to use the buildings as a 'drop-in' centre where they can talk to those instructors with whom they have developed sound relationships. This follow-up programme is also designed to demonstrate an understanding of what is required of individuals if they are to become viable units in the workforce.

From its very earliest days, the NWE programme has been evaluated by a consultant clinical psychologist, who has maintained current qualititative and quantitative files on all its aspects programme and is able to advise the staff of the relative effectiveness of various intervention methods they have employed. This action research has both enabled the direction of the courses to be modified over short time-spans and indicated that the rehabilitation rate, in terms of long-term employment and decreased reoffending, is vastly more cost-effective than imprisonment (O'Brien 1987, 1988).

Outdoor Education, Secondary Schools

There are many different approaches taken to the provision of outdoor education for school students. As a result of considerable discussion, the Department of Education has laid down guidelines for teachers taking classes outside the classroom (Education Department 1988). There is a reasonable degree of homogeneity in such areas as staff/student ratios, but actual offerings vary enormously:

(1)   *St Paul's Collegiate, Hamilton* runs an outdoor education centre at Tihoi in the volcanic plateau areas of the central North Island. The whole of their Form 4 (Year 9 equivalent) spend 6 months at the centre, doing normal classroom-type schoolwork, embedded in an outdoor programme which involves a considerable amount of time in a wilderness environment.

(2)   *State Schools* have access to programmes operated by the Education Department at outdoor centres in many different parts of the country. Schools send whole classes to the centres for a one-week outdoor programme which is seen largely as an adjunct to the school curriculum. Exceptions to this occur in instances where senior classes may attend the centres for environmental education or biology field trips, as an integral part of their academic course.

(3)   *Avondale College, Auckland* is a state secondary school which runs its own outdoor centre, near National Park. Students from all levels of the school attend the centre for about a week per year, taking part in a graduated series of programmes which provide new challenges for students at each year level. Many parents choose Avondale College for the education of their children because of the strength of their outdoor programme.

(4)   *St Cuthbert's College, Auckland* is a private girls' school whose orientation has traditionally been towards academic achievement. For some years it has run week-long outdoor programmes for the Form 4 (Year 9 equivalent) girls but, more recently, it has run a year-long internally-assessed outdoor education course as an academic subject for the sixth form certificate (Year 11 equivalent).

Skills Acquisition Centres

A number of organisations exist in New Zealand to cater for the market. People wanting to learn a specific skill in the outdoors can acquire a high degree of the physical expertise in activities such as rock-climbing, kayaking, sailing, scuba diving, wind-surfing, hang-gliding, skiing, and so on, by attending courses at a number of different centres.

Alpine Guides Ltd is a well-known mountaineering instruction and guiding operation based in the Mount Cook area. It enjoys a reputation for high quality courses and draws its clientele from many parts of the world. The Southern Alps provide high alpine peaks, spectacular scenery, a network of sound mountain huts and a long climbing season, as well as some excellent areas for glacier skiing.

Penny Whiting's Sailing School, Auckland is another New Zealand institution. It teaches the finer points of practical sailing, racing and cruising on the magnificent waterways of the Hauraki Gulf Maritime Park, near Auckland. The school caters for all standards of sailor, from novice to advanced, and runs courses of different lengths to suit the needs of practically all potential clients.

Management Training

Matataki Lodge, Pauanui, Coromandel is a modern centre located on a magnificent site close to river, beach and bush. The staff use the outdoors as a medium for educating clients in aspects of management such as lateral thinking, group processes, team-building, communication skills and so on. Their clientele range widely, but generally come from the middle to upper echelons of larger companies in the North Island, though their nationwide and international reputation is growing.

Commercial Tour Operators

Mount Cook Line is a major tourist organisation which not only runs an air-line, a coach line and a large fleet of rental motor-homes, but also offers package trips into the outdoors for glacier skiing, jet-boating and similar types of adventure recreation. Their target market is primarily the foreign tourist trade from Japan, Australia and the United States, with the emphasis of their operation being on travel, accommodation and sight-seeing in the more scenically interesting areas of the country.

References

Education Department (1987) *Guidelines for Education Outside the Class-room*, Wellington.
Education Department (1987) *Safety and Supervision Guidelines for Outdoor Pursuit Activities in Further Education and Training*, Wellington.
Hillary Commission (1986) *Statement of Intent*, Wellington.
Mitchell, M.J. and Mitchell, H.A. (1988) *A Study of Aspects of Self-Concept over a Two-Year Period: Possible Effects of an Intervening Outward Bound Course*, Nelson.
O'Brien, M. (1987) *Reaching the Unreachable: Why Wilderness Programs Work as a Treatment Strategy for 'at risk' and 'alienated' Youth*, Proceedings of the 5th National Outdoor Education Conference, Perth, Western Australia.
O'Brien, M. (n.d.) *Reaching the Unreachable: A Brief Report on Findings on the Therapeutic Impact of the Northland Wilderness Experience Program on the Youth of Northland, NZ*, Northland Wilderness Experience, Whangarei.